St. Louis Community College

Forest Park
Florissant Valley
Meramec

Instructional Resources
St. Louis, Missouri

GAYLORD

MINORITIES IN HIGHER EDUCATION

MINORITIES IN HIGHER EDUCATION

Edited by
Manuel J. Justiz
Reginald Wilson
and
Lars G. Björk

AMERICAN COUNCIL
ON EDUCATION
Series on Higher Education
ORYX PRESS
1994

The rare Arabian Oryx is believed to have inspired the myth of the unicorn. This desert antelope became virtually extinct in the early 1960s. At that time several groups of international conservationists arranged to have 9 animals sent to the Phoenix Zoo to be the nucleus of a captive breeding herd. Today the Oryx population is over 800 and nearly 400 have been returned to reserves in the Middle East.

© 1994 by American Council on Education and The Oryx Press
Published by The Oryx Press
4041 North Central at Indian School Road
Phoenix, Arizona 85012-3397

Published simultaneously in Canada

Printed and Bound in the United States of America

♾ The paper used in this publication meets the minimum requirements of American National Standard for Information Science—Permanence of Paper for Printed Library Materials, ANSI Z39.48, 1984.

Library of Congress Cataloging-in-Publication Data

Minorities in higher education / [edited] by Manuel J. Justiz,
    Reginald Wilson, and Lars G. Björk.
        (American Council on Education/Oryx series on higher education)
        Includes bibliographical references and index.
        ISBN 0-89774-817-4
        1. Minorities—Education (Higher)—United States. 2. Minority college students—United States. I. Justiz, Manuel J. II. Wilson, Reginald, 1929– . III. Björk, Lars G. IV. Series.
    LC3731.M5575   1994
378.1'9829'073—dc20   94-11397
                                                                   CIP

CONTENTS

• • • • • • • • •

CONTRIBUTORS

• • • • • • • • • •

EDITOR PROFILES

Manuel J. Justiz is dean of the College of Education at The University of Texas at Austin, where he holds the A.M. Aikin Regents Chair in Education Leadership. From 1982 to 1985 he directed the National Institute of Education in Washington, DC, under former Secretary of Education Terrel Bell. Dr. Justiz has published extensively on topics relating to minorities in education, partnerships between education and business, and higher education policy.

Reginald Wilson is senior scholar at the American Council on Education, Washington, DC. He originally joined the council as its director of the Office of Minority Concerns. Before that, Wilson was president of Wayne County Community College, Detroit. He has co-authored and edited writings on the issues of the urban community, civil liberties, and racial equality in higher education. Wilson serves on the editorial board of *The American Journal of Education* and *The Urban Review*. He received the Anthony Wayne Award and the Distinguished Service Medal from the city of Detroit.

Lars G. Björk is an associate professor in the Department of Educational Leadership, Technology and Research, where he coordinates the Doctoral Degree Program, at Georgia Southern University in Savannah. Björk has served as a member of advisory and coordinating committees and task forces in the United States Department of Education. The author of numerous scholarly works on organizational change, leadership, and educational policy, he has presented his research at international and national conferences. Currently he is serving as a Consulting Editor for *People and Education: The Human Side of Schools*.

CONTRIBUTOR PROFILES

Alexander W. Astin is professor of Higher Education and director of the Higher Education Research Institute at University of California, Los Angeles. He is author of *What Matters in College? Four Critical Years Revisited* (Jossey-Bass, 1993), *Assessment for Excellence: The Philosophy and Practice of Assessment and Evaluation in Higher Education* (Macmillan/Oryx, 1991), and other books and articles in the field of higher education. He is the recipient of 10 honorary degrees and numerous other awards from national educational associations. His main interest is in how students are affected by their college experiences and in improving and reforming American undergraduate education.

Alison R. Bernstein is the director of the Education and Culture Program at the Ford Foundation in New York City. She is the author of *American Indians and World War II: Towards a New Era In Indian Affairs* and *The Impersonal Campus* (with Virginia B. Smith). She has published numerous articles on community college transfer issues, access for women and minorities into higher education, and the impact of women's studies. She holds a Ph.D. in History from Columbia University and is a former associate dean of faculty at Princeton University.

Don M. Blandin is the director of the Business-Higher Education Forum of the American Council on Education. The forum is a membership organization of 100 selected chief executives of major American corporations, colleges and universities. Since joining the forum in 1981, Mr. Blandin has helped the forum address such critical issues as international economic competitiveness, education and training, R&D partnerships, science and technology, global interdependence, health care, and the environment and the economy.

Shirley Vining Brown is a senior research scientist in the Division of Education Policy Research at Educational Testing Service. The focus of her research has been on talent flow issues in the higher education pipeline and, more recently, on race and sex equity issues in higher education. She has written numerous policy reports on minorities including, *Increasing Minority Faculty: An Elusive Goal*, and serves as a consultant on educational issues for various programs and institutions in higher education.

Patrick M. Callan is executive director of The California Higher Education Policy Center. The Center is an independent, nonpartisan nonprofit organization that conducts and sponsors policy studies and stimulates public discussion and debate on the future of California higher education. Callan has previously served as vice president of the Education Commission of the States and as executive officer of higher educator boards and commissions in the states of California, Montana, and Washington. He has written and consulted extensively on educational policy.

Mark W. Clark is assistant vice president for academic affairs and dean of graduate and summer programs at Adams State College (in Colorado). He has worked both on college/university campuses and in educational associations. Mark received his Ph.D. in Education at Stanford University. He has written and presented numerous works in the fields of education, sport, and career mobility. He is currently working on a book that focuses on the African American experience in baseball.

Alfredo G. de los Santos Jr., is vice chancellor for Educational Development at the Maricopa Community Colleges. He is coauthor of *Building Bridges: Using State Policy to Foster and Sustain Collaboration* and is author of numerous articles on minorities in higher education and community college issues. He has served on the board of directors of major associations and currently serves on the board of trustees of the Tomas Rivera Center at Claremont University, American College Testing, the Partnership for Service-Learning, and the Carnegie Foundation for the Advancement of Teaching.

Richard Durán is associate professor in the Graduate School of Education, University of California, Santa Barbara. He has published numerous articles concerning literacy and academic skills acquisition of Latino students and on prediction of Latino student's college performance. He is currently conducting research on use of cooperative learning methods with Latino students and on innovative assessment techniques for Latino students.

Judith S. Eaton currently serves as president of the Council for Aid to Education in New York City. Prior to her appointment at the council, she was a vice president at the American Council on Education in Washington, DC. Dr. Eaton earned a Ph.D. in education from Wayne State University (Michigan) and holds three honorary degrees. She has produced many articles for educational publications and has edited several books including *Colleges of Choice: The Enabling Impact of the Community College* (1988). Her most recent book, *Strengthening Collegiate Education in Community Colleges*, was published in March 1994.

Hector Garza was named director of the Office of Minorities in Higher Education at the American Council on Education on July 1993. Prior to this appointment, he served as the associate graduate dean for Academic Program Development and Review at Eastern Michigan University. Mr. Garza is a doctoral degree candidate at the University of Michigan. The degree will be conferred on December, 1994. Mr. Garza has published on topics relating to minorities in higher education and has made numerous presentations to professional groups and associations. He has been a consultant for numerous colleges and universities, professional associations, and foundations.

Arthur M. Hauptman has been an independent public policy consultant since 1981. He has written extensively on issues of student financial aid, college costs, and higher education finance more generally. He is author of *The College Tuition Spiral*, a 1990 report to the College Board and the American Council on Education, and *The Tuition Dilemma*, a 1990 publication of the Brookings Institution. He previously served on the staff of the U.S. House of Representatives Budget Committee and the U.S. Senate Committee on Labor and Human Resources.

Marilyn C. Kameen is the associate dean for teacher education and student affairs in the College of Education at The University of Texas at Austin. From 1974 to 1990, Dr. Kameen was at the University of South Carolina, where she served as director of the Office of Accreditation, director of the Office of Field Experiences, and coordinator of the Higher Education Administration Program in the Department of Educational Leadership and Policies. She has published on topics relating to college student development, minorities in education, effective college teaching, and comprehensive assessment programs in higher education.

Clara Sue Kidwell is currently assistant director for Cultural Resources at the National Museum of the American Indian, the Smithsonian Institution. She is on leave from the University of California at Berkeley where she is associate professor of Native American Studies. She has published on the history of the Choctaw Indians in Mississippi, on the roles and status of American Indian women, and on systems of knowledge in the New World. She has written a forthcoming book on Choctaws and missionaries in Mississippi 1818-1918 that will be published by the University of Oklahoma press.

Sara E. Meléndez is president of Independent Sector in Washington, DC. Most recently, she was president of the Center for Applied Linguistics in Washington, DC. Dr. Meléndez has taught in undergraduate and graduate programs, directed teacher training programs, and written and spoken extensively around the country on multicultural education, bilingual education, English as a Second Language, diversity, and equity for people of color and women. Her publications include a book on bilingual education published by

Teachers College Press, chapters in *Leaders for a New Era*, and *Educating the Majority: Women Challenge Tradition in Higher Education*, both published by Macmillan; and articles in various publications. Dr. Meléndez has been actively involved in numerous professional organizations and as a member of boards and committees. A product of the New York City public schools, Dr. Meléndez received her B.A. in English from Brooklyn College, and a doctorate in education from Harvard University.

Frank Newman is president of the Education Commission of the States, a national organization created in 1965 by the states as an interstate compact to help state leaders formulate public policy in education. Dr. Newman was the president of the University of Rhode Island from 1975 to 1983 and then a president fellow at the Carnegie Foundation for the Advancement of Teaching. He became president of ECS in 1985. He is the author of a number of books on higher education, most recently *Choosing Quality: Reducing Conflict Between the State and the University* and *Higher Education and the American Resurgence*.

Amaury Nora received his Ed.D. in higher education from the University of Houston in 1985. His research focuses on college persistence, the role of college on diverse student populations across different types of institutions, the development of financial aid models which integrate economic theories and college persistence theories, and theory building and testing. His inquires have not only contributed to traditional lines of research on college persistence but have opened research on women and minorities in community colleges. Nora is on the Editorial Board of *The Journal of Higher Education, Research in Higher Education* and *The Review of Higher Education*. Nora was the recipient of the Association for the Study of Higher Education "1991 Early Career Scholar Award."

N. Joyce Payne is director of the Office for the Advancement of Public Black Colleges (OAPBC) and director of Minority and Human Resources Programs of the National Association of State Universities and Land-Grant Colleges in cooperation with the American Association of State College and Universities. She is responsible for congressional and federal relations for 35 historically Black public universities and for the Commission on Human Resources and Social Change. She has published "Hidden Messages in the Pursuit of Equality" in *Academe*, "The Role of Black Colleges in an Expanding Economy" in *Educational Record*, and "Black Women in Urban Schools" in *Men, Women and the Consequences of Power* among many other articles.

Laura I. Rendón is associate research professor in the Division of Educational Leadership and Policy Studies at Arizona State University, where her teaching and research focuses on educational partnerships, higher education, community colleges and cultural diversity in education. Dr. Rendón is affiliated with the ASU Hispanic Research Center and is the author of numerous articles. She is associate editor of the *Journal of Women and Minorities in Science and Engineering* and serves on the editorial boards of *The Community College Review*, *The Journal of Planning for Higher Education*, *The Teaching and Learning Forum* and *the Journal of the Freshman Year Experience*. She is currently a member of the National Board of Directors of the American Association for Higher Education, The National Advisory Board of the Woodrow Wilson Fellowship Foundation, and the Technical Advisory Board of the Quality Education for Minorities Network. Dr. Rendón earned a Ph.D. in higher education from the University of Michigan.

Paul E. Resta is a professor of Instructional Technology in the Curriculum and Instruction Department and director of the Learning Technology Center at the University of Texas at Austin. Dr. Resta has published numerous articles on educational technology and research and frequently serves as a keynote speaker at national and international educational technology conferences. He has served as president of the *International Council for Computers in Education* and as founding co-president of the *International Society for Technology in Education*. The founder of the Educational Native American Network (ENAN), a network that serves students, teachers and administrators in schools in 28 states, Dr. Resta is the recipient of numerous awards for his contributions to higher education.

Antonio Rigual is professor of Spanish and director of the Office of Sponsored Programs at Our Lady of the Lake University (OLLU) in San Antonio, TX. Following a 15-year teaching and administrative career at OLLU, Dr. Rigual led the efforts to establish the Hispanic Association of Colleges and Universities in 1986, and was HACU's founding president. Rigual guided the association as it became the national voice for Hispanic-serving institutions of higher education. In 1991, he returned to his faculty position at OLLU. Dr. Rigual also is the president of Rigual and Associates, Inc., a Hispanic-focused consulting firm specializing in education, workforce diversity and fund raising.

Patricia Smith is budget examiner for student aid in the U.S. Office of Management and Budget. In this position, she is the primary analyst responsible for reviewing the budgetary implications of federal student loan programs and proposals. Previous to assuming this position in 1993, she was director of Legislative Analysis for the American Council on Education.

Bob H. Suzuki is the president of California State Polytechnic University at Pomona and professor of engineering and education at that institution. He is the author of many articles on Asian Americans and education and a specialist in the fields of multicultural and international education. He has also been active for more than two decades in the areas of civil and human rights and in 1976 was the first recipient of the National Education Association's Human Rights Award for Leadership in Asian and Pacific Island Affairs.

PREFACE

•••••••••

With the rapid transformation of American society in recent years, now is an appropriate time to look at what impact these changes will have on higher education and what new policy considerations will be required. The demographic changes are compelling. Of all immigrants to the United States in the last decade, 43 percent were Asian and 40 percent were Hispanic. People of color comprise nearly one-quarter of the American population today and are expected to be one-third by the year 2000.

Yet people of color are not taking their places in colleges and universities as rapidly as expected, and the barriers preventing them from doing so are formidable. The American Council on Education (ACE) became sufficiently concerned about this situation that it convened a commission of distinguished Americans, chaired by former presidents Jimmy Carter and Gerald Ford, to discuss the problem. This culminated in the publication of a report, "One-Third of a Nation" (1988), which was widely distributed, and led to the minority initiative of ACE dedicated to this issue of national importance. Now that six years have passed since that publication, it is time to do an in-depth assessment of the status of minorities in higher education. That is the reason for this book.

In books dealing with higher education and public policy, the significance of the work is often associated with both the immediacy and magnitude of the issue addressed. That is clearly the case with this book. During the last two decades, American society has struggled to adopt to intensified international economic competition, economic decline, and the dramatic transformation in the social fabric of the nation. This in turn has increased demands on our institutions of education to produce more technologically skilled and socially competent citizens, and our educational institutions have often been found wanting in meeting these demands. Numerous national commissions and reports, as a consequence, have indicted our educational institutions for failing our nation's youth and contributing to the declining economy and ruptures in the social fabric. Whether fair or not, this criticism has been responsible for shedding a very searching light on our institutions of education.

One result of this searching light was the increasing awareness of how our educational institutions have failed our minority communities. Given their growing size and increasing importance to the viability of the American economy, the education of American minority communities becomes inextricably tied to the health of the economy of the entire United States. Morality thus becomes pragmatic. The development of human capital therefore becomes a necessity for the survival of the nation.

The development of the potential of the minority community is fraught with many difficulties and problems. First, is the necessity of facing the harsh reality of our past and removing the barriers of racism and discrimination we have (sometimes legally) placed in the path of certain groups. Second, is compensating for the disadvantages and inferior education they have endured. Third, is getting them into our higher education institutions while respecting the rights of others to enter as well. Fourth, is seeing that they obtain graduate degrees and also secure their place in the faculty. And finally, fifth and most important, is seeing that the education they receive reflects the richness of all the experiences of everyone on this planet.

Addressing these concerns is enormously difficult and has extraordinary implications for societal transformation. But some changes have already begun, and other challenges are being struggled with and debated on our nation's campuses. That is what this book is about: a report card, if you will, on the country's successes and failures in achieving educational equity for our minority citizens in the recent past and, in some cases, predictions and suggestions for the future.

Reginald Wilson
Manuel Justiz
Lars Björk

INTRODUCTION

· · · · · · · · ·

Juliet V. Garcia

As you read the research studies in this book, you perhaps will have a similar reaction to that of my own. At first it was one of great interest to discover how much our efforts had helped change the picture of higher education in the United States. After all, we've been working diligently, devising new strategies and innovations; we've bent backward trying so desperately to make a difference.

But then, as I continued reading through the articles, I began to worry and feel a tremendous sense of frustration. Where were the fruits of our labors? After all the dust of the 1980s settled, had we done nothing more than rearrange the chairs around a larger table, with only a few new faces present?

Finally, recovering from my dismay, I discovered new energy. Energy that comes from the sense of urgency described in these pages. An urgency to admit our failures, applaud our successes, and renegotiate the terms of our commitment to providing access and success for those minorities too long disenfranchised from our systems of higher education.

This, then, is a call for strong and involved leadership. The kind of leadership that presidents and chancellors must provide. In only the rarest of cases, can such profound change as required by these findings and suggested by these authors occur without the strength and moral initiative of a president. In fact, I would propose that it is the absence of presidential leadership that has produced such marginal gains in some areas and such intolerable backsliding in others.

Presidents must not seek to avoid the ethical dilemmas related to issues of higher education for minorities. Instead, what rightly is assigned to them, to us, is the call to light the path.

To help light the path, the 19 articles in this book discuss a broad range of issues relating to minorities in higher education. From university presidents to college deans and professors, the authors of these chapters bring a wealth of experience and talent to the challenges facing our nation.

In the first chapter, Manuel Justiz gives an overview of the profound demographic and technological changes that are impacting the nation's culture, government, economy, and education systems. It provides a foundation for examining the current circumstances of minority cohorts and discussing their participation in the social, economic, and political life of the nation into the twenty-first century. Recommendations for removing the obstacles to minority access, representation, and success not only formulate a clear and inexorable challenge to the nation's institutions of higher education to renew their commitment to increasing minority opportunities, but also frame the work of the other contributing authors.

In the next chapter, Don Blandin notes that although a significant percentage of minority citizens have improved their social and economic standing during the last several decades, the number who remain outside of the mainstream of American life is a problem of numbing magnitude. His focus on the relationship between the national economy and the need to use the untapped reservoir of minority talent to sustain economic activity and prosperity is uncommonly insightful. His human capital development perspective frames his analysis of minority problems, progress, and issues. His findings lend special urgency to the public debate on minority policy.

In chapter three, Alexander Astin provides an authoritative review of the issues associated with student testing and assessment as they relate to expanding equity and excellence in colleges and universities. He notes that the continuing reliance of institutions on reputational and resource conceptions of excellence make it difficult for disadvantaged or minority students to gain access to higher education opportunities. He presents a thoughtful case for developing different devices for college admissions that enhance minority enrollments, and he challenges traditional arguments that lowered admission standards will erode academic standards. Astin's talent development view, which focuses on excellence in terms of what institutions do for students once they are admitted, is consistent with the notion of social responsibility of public institutions.

Next, Paul Resta discusses the rapid changes that are unfolding in the use of computers in colleges and universities. His examination of the potential for integrating computer technologies and electronically accessed information resources into the teaching and learning process is insightful. His discussion, however, also examines the implication of present inequities in minority precollegiate experiences that add a technological dimension to existing fiscal, cultural, and educational deficits. The effective use of information technology tools and resources is viewed as a means through which institutions of higher education may achieve greater minority representation. Resta presents a number of strategies and recommendations for removing these deficits.

Arthur Hauptman and Patricia Smith examine high school graduation rates, college enrollments by institutional type, and student retention and completion rates. The data indicate that, despite the continued growth in the nation's minority population, little progress has been made in increasing minority student participation in colleges and universities. Although expressions of concern have led to calls for generally expanding student aid and related programs, the authors describe and assess the prospects for success of a number of strategies. In an age of scarce resources, it appears that the greatest amount of leverage for increasing minority student enrollments and completion rates may be gained from strategies that deliver the greatest amount of aid to each minority student.

Increasing and targeting student financial aid has been a dominant theme in the national debate on how to expand minority attainment of doctorate degrees. Sara Meléndez examines the effectiveness of financial aid programs enacted during the 1960s on minority student enrollments and doctorate completion rates. The positive impact of these policies stands in sharp contrast to the consequences of modifying the requirements for eligibility for student financial aid during the late 1970s and the reduction in federal support for graduate education during the 1980s. These policy changes had a disproportionate impact on students of color and reversed earlier gains. These policies, in the context of rising inflation and the increasing cost of higher education, had a negative impact on low-income minority student enrollments and doctoral completion rates. With the labor market demanding higher levels of education and skills, the consequences of "race blind" federal policies may have an even more severe impact on these cohorts in the future. The author calls for building a shared conviction in support of these explicit policies.

Making college an attractive choice for minority students presents a significant challenge facing American higher education. Laura Rendón and Amaury Nora examine the high level of minority enrollment in two-year colleges. The transfer functions of these institutions serve as the principal entry point to senior institutions and play a pivotal role in minority students seeking baccalaureate, professional, and graduate degrees. Because nearly half of all minority students who complete baccalaureate degrees transfer from a community college, reported transfer declines in recent years raise serious questions as to whether students are provided adequate counseling, sufficient preparation, and reasonable opportunities to undertake studies in community colleges that will transfer to senior institutions. The authors note that if these institutions want to regain their legitimacy as viable members of the nation's higher education system, they must work vigorously to restore the vitality of the transfer function.

Alison Bernstein and Judith Eaton examine several programs funded by the Ford Foundation that effectively deal with the issues of institutional decentralization and student transfer. While decentralization and institutional autonomy are sources of pride for the American system of higher education, there is cause for concern that these characteristics may also be detrimental to minority students. Examining the structural characteristics of the nation's higher education system both illuminates the impediments to minority progress and potential solutions. Observations of the Ford programs confirmed the negative effect of decentralization on students, particularly minority students, but found that these obstacles may be overcome. The characteristics of effective transfer programs include an emphasis on cross-institutional faculty cooperation in building academic programs; ensure comparable quality in course content, scope, and rigor; involve public and private senior institutions; span state boundaries; and have a substantial institutional commitment to the transfer function. The authors conclude that if institutions of higher education wish to preserve decentralization and autonomy and serve low-income and minority students, they must sanction the portability of the academic experience.

Richard Durán addresses a major policy issue by focusing his discussion on the performance of Hispanic students on standardized tests and their educational attainment, their rapidly increasing representation in the nation's population, and the vitality of the American economy. The author argues that underserved Hispanic and other minority students will require more radical educational reforms than have been proposed in the education reports released during the past decade. He identifies two priorities for enhancing Hispanic student achievement in public schools and strengthening the education pipeline to higher education. His recommendations focus on expanding the number of Hispanic teachers in the workforce, increasing the cultural sensitivity of nonminority teachers, intensifying exposure to effective pedagogies and intervention strategies for at-risk students, and drawing upon the student's family and community as opportunities for enhancing classroom learning. His recommendations go beyond limited exposure as part of preservice teacher preparations that produce superficial results to extended staff development and mentorship programs.

Alfredo de los Santos Jr. and Anthony Rigual, present a definitive longitudinal (1975-1991) review of the condition of the nation's Hispanic population with regard to a number of crucial indicators of parity and participation including population, income level, high school graduation, college enrollment rates, trends in degrees earned as well as their representation as faculty and administrators in institutions of higher educaiton. The data, effectively displayed in a series of figures, puts the issue of Hispanic access and participation in American higher education in bold relief. His longitudinal perspective underscores the need to address the limitations that have emerged from historically defining the issue of underrepresentation only in terms of student access. He argues that in order to make substantive progress a more comprehensive approach must be launched that incorporates retention strategies and a focus on graduation. Accomplishing these tasks, Hispanics will need to build community, "hacer pueblo," through mutual commitment, cooperation, involvement, and accountability. In his view, accountability is essential to assess whether the Hispanic community, public policy makers, and institutional leaders have met their commitment to initiate corrective solutions.

Next, Reginald Wilson provides a review of the participation of African Americans in higher education, first in historically black colleges and universities (HBCUs) and in the years following the GI bill in 1945 and the 1964 Civil Rights Act. Federal education initiatives directed toward increasing minority representation on college campuses led to a dramatic increase in African American students attending college during the 1960s, however, the growth was predominantly in two-year institutions located in the North and West. While these institutions expanded educational access, weak academic curricula and low transfer rates inhibited baccalaureate degree attainment. Wilson notes that the decline in college enrollments of African American students during the 1980s was exacerbated by restrictive federal policies under the Reagan/Bush administrations. During the 1990s the decline was arrested and enrollments began to rise. Under the Clinton administration, policies favorable to increasing minority opportunities in higher education may reinforce this positive trend. The author also examines the need to improve elementary and secondary education in large urban school systems where minority students are enrolled in overwhelming numbers. Improving the quality of schools and enhancing student outcomes will require a comprehensive approach involving the collaborative efforts of parents, teachers, administrators, and support staff committed to academic performance.

For the past decade, references to emerging global interrelationships and the profound influence these changes will have on the way Americans will live, work, and educate the nation's youth have dominated discussions concerning educational reform and the role of institutions of higher education. N. Joyce Payne examines the profound impact these social, economic, and political changes will have on the future of historically black colleges and universities. While these institutions have been resilient in the face of adversity and have a rich history of ameliorating uneven educational access and opportunities, they are facing unrelenting challenges. The author presents a compelling argument for the need to strengthen these institutions as a means of strengthening the nation's ability to compete in a global arena in the twenty-first century.

Clara Sue Kidwell surveys the history of Native American participation in American higher education and its emerging role in the development of Native American communities. The author discusses the factors that contribute to low test scores and defines the issue of low participation rates in higher education in terms of the "dominant" society rather than in terms of the prevailing values of Native American communities. She stresses that unlike American society, Native American communities may not regard students who opt out of college before completing a baccalaureate degree as failures if they return to their tribes and play productive roles. The development of the American Indian Higher Education Consortium reflects the desire of Native American communities to control their own educational institutions to meet their immediate needs. Although the mainstream of American higher education has been used by the United States government as a means of forced acculturation and loss of identity, Native American people have persisted and have found ways to use education as a means of bridging the gap between themselves and American society.

In the past, the relatively low level of interest in Asian American issues in higher education may have resulted from their small numbers in the population or from the widespread perception that this extraordinarily successful "model minority" had few, if any, problems. Bob Suzuki notes that being recognized as the fastest growing minority cohort in the population forced examination of the needs of Asian Americans. As a result, many learned that the "model minority" stereotype was overly simplistic and naive and contributed to perceptions that may have constrained attempts to identify their needs and solve their problems. His categorical examination of preparation, access issues, academic development and achievement, curricular and instructional issues, socio-psychological environment, hiring and promotion issues, and returns on higher education raises questions that are subsequently answered through a concise review of research literature. His findings contradict the widely held perception that Asian Americans are a model minority and illuminate the urgency for institutions of higher education to address the real needs of these groups objectively and fairly to ensure equitable and effective treatment.

Manuel Justiz and Marilyn Kameen note that the release of the report *Involvement in Learning* in 1984 was a significant part of one of the most intensive examinations of quality in American education during the past decade. This report contributed to escalating concern by state policy makers that colleges and universities become more accountable for student outcomes. Colleges of education were challenged to assume a leadership role in increasing the academic rigor of elementary and secondary schools through improving preservice teacher education programs while increasing the number of minority teachers joining the workforce. While assessment in higher education may be viewed as an obstacle to the preparation of minority teachers, it may also serve as a valuable mechanism for expanding access while strengthening academic standards. The coauthors suggest that these goals may be accomplished without negatively impacting minority students if colleges of education design thorough teacher assessment procedures that are combined with comprehensive learning assistance programs.

Mark Clark and Hector Garza assess the current status of minorities in graduate education by reviewing data on enrollments and degree attainment. They also examine how the impact of student and institutional characteristics contributed to the lack of progress during the past decade. The coauthors propose that without the personal commitment and leadership by graduate deans this trend may not be reversed. The centrality of the graduate dean's role in the academic community provides excellent opportunities to interact, observe, and articulate a specific vision of the graduate enterprise that includes a minority presence in graduate education. Their discussion of the contextual factors that may impede minority progress provides a foundation for examining intervention models that have proven successful in enhancing the enrollment and degree attainment of minority students.

Although considerable progress was made during the 1960s and 1970s in increasing the number of minority faculty, these gains have tapered off. Shirley Vining Brown provides an authoritative discussion of the shortage of minority faculty as well as the benefits derived from faculty diversity that have been central to this debate for more than a decade. The role of faculty members, college and university administrators, and policy makers are discussed in advancing the diversification process. She presents a number of public policy options directed toward increasing the number of minority graduate students earning doctorate degrees and increasing the number of minority faculty hired during the coming decade. The task of revitalizing the academy is monumental and will require institutional commitment and a federal presence.

Patrick Callan notes that as the nature of the federal role diminished during the 1980s, states assumed the mantle of leadership and formulated public policy initiatives in response to increasing international competition, technological advances, and demographic changes. Numerous national commission and task force reports identified widespread deficiencies in schools, colleges, and universities, and educational reform became the centerpiece of state-level policy agendas. The author notes that states have the leadership and policy tools to set goals, provide resources, and assess outcomes for minority progress comparable to their proportional representation in the population. His categorical analysis of state student aid policies; minority retention, achievement, and graduation rates; school-university collaboration initiatives; and institutional missions presents a comprehensive strategy for achieving these outcomes. These goals, grounded in moral and economic urgency, present a powerful agenda for leadership at the national, state, and institutional levels.

Frank Newman presents compelling evidence that opportunities in higher education and the professional life of the nation are not yet equally open to all, and they must be open to talent if the economic, cultural, and political life of the nation is to prosper. The author assumes that full participation of minorities in every aspect of American life cannot fail to become an urgent priority of the nation. He brings an optimistic sense of the possibility to the national debate. First, he recognizes that inequities are rooted in the deep structures of society and only a shared resolve of states, colleges and universities, families, students, and the federal government may generate solutions. Second, he draws upon the lessons of recent history of federal involvement in minority affairs to illustrate that whenever the American people have acted in concert on matters of profound conviction they have proved a potent force in ensuring equal educational opportunity. The principles that underlie Frank Newman's suggestions for an emerging federal role that helps foster the aspirations of minority participation in higher education capture the need for subtlety and nuance rather than relying on the force of law and monetary enticement. A sustained federal role must match a sustained institutional commitment not only to understand the minority issues from the perspective of those who experience college and university life but also work toward making that college experience feasible, desirable, and comfortable.

In total, this book makes an important contribution to the national debate on how to expand minority participation in higher education and in the social, economic, and political life of the nation. The collected talent that has been convened to address these complex issues is unmatched in the field of higher education, state, and federal policy. Observations, discussions, analyses, and recommendations on how to proceed in resolving these pressing national issues are both thought provoking and stimulating.

This book is intended for the use of state and federal policy makers who influence higher education and minority policy; individuals in philanthropic organizations who support innovative corrective strategies; heads of educational associations who are concerned with enhancing minority participation in colleges and universities; presidents, provosts, deans, and faculty in institutions of higher education who are committed to equal educational opportunity; and members of minority communities who work to shape policies that impact their lives. It is anticipated that this book will be of particular interest to individuals who conduct policy research and students who study policy implementation in seminars and courses in political science, public administration, and higher education in colleges and universities.

MINORITIES IN HIGHER EDUCATION

CHAPTER

Demographic Trends and the Challenges to American Higher Education

Manuel Justiz

P erhaps Bob Dylan said it best, "The times, they are a changing!" And we, as Americans, are also changing. We are changing in virtually every way there is to change—our age, our skin color, our family size, our educational needs, our work habits, our political inclinations, and our culture.

Four modern trends reflect these changing times: Our population has virtually stopped growing, we are older than we have ever been (Wilders, 1991), many of our major concerns are concentrated around population growth among specific populations, and now more than ever technological expansion is demanding a more highly educated workforce. Although these factors are irrevocably linked, each factor exerts different influences on our society and its component parts—culture, government, economics, and education. Demographers are quick to point out trends that confront our present situation, an American society in which the majority is White and Anglo-European in origin—while, in fact, what is occurring is that those longtime stable and predictable conclusions are being altered dramatically by the

The author wishes to acknowledge and thank Terri Matthews, doctoral student in the Higher Education Program at the University of South Carolina, Columbia, and Dr. Rosemary Gillett-Karam, Office of the Dean, College of Education, The University of Texas at Austin, and visiting associate professor, North Carolina State University, for their research assistance in this project.

enormous changes in the composition and growth of nonwhite groups in America.

POPULATION GROWTH

At the present time the population of the United States is 249.9 million (U.S. Bureau of the Census, 1991). This number is less than 10 percent higher than the 1980 census count of 226.5 million marking this period of growth as the second lowest in census history. During the depression the growth rate was at 7.3 percent as compared to the 18.5 percent growth rate of the 1950s. Projecting to the future, the U.S. Bureau of the Census suggests a 2 percent decrease every decade until the year 2030, at which time it predicts a minus figure growth decline. Although the overall birthrate is declining, an examination of the rate in comparison to cultural and racial groups demonstrates the greatest decline among Whites—Asians, Hispanics, African Americans, and Native Americans are not experiencing similar declining birthrates. Demographers' predictions about declining rates apply mainly to the majority population, which is White; these figures do not represent the so-called minority groups in America.

The term minority group is beginning to lose its meaning. Never a term that has had a positive connotation, the term is losing its applicability. Native Americans, African Americans, Asian Americans, and Hispanics together number 61 million, or 25 percent of the nation (*Western Interstate Commission,* 1991). And the growth rate for these groups is not declining—for example the growth rate for Hispanics was 18 times higher than the national growth rate in the 1980s. In just two decades, Hispanics will number 47 million and African Americans, 44 million; in other words, Hispanics will begin to outnumber African Americans for the first time (Hodgkinson, 1991). The fastest growing group in total numbers is the Hispanic population whose population will double in 30 years. In 20 years Asian immigrants and native populations will double in number—they will outnumber the Jews in America. And in 30 years, immigration will cause more population growth in the United States than natural births; presently this population is arriving mainly from Asia and Central and South America. Major American cities such as Los Angeles and San Antonio already have "majority minority" populations, populations of African Americans, Hispanics, Native Americans, and Asian Americans, who when combined outnumber the White population. In California, English will be the second language for the majority of the population by the end of the century. Projections for the mid twenty-first century are for these groups to become the majority population (Edsall and Edsall, 1991).

POPULATION AGE/FAMILY

While we have long been known as a "youthful" nation, the data demonstrate that we are getting older. Almost 47 percent of our population is now 35 or older, 27 percent is 18 to 34, and 26 percent is birth age to 17. Approximately two out of every three people are 25 years of age or older. By 2000, the median age will increase by three years to age 36, and this trend will continue through the twenty-first century when the median age is expected to be 40 and older. By the year 2000, more than half of all children will spend part of their lives in single-parent homes, and this will be either a single male or single female household. By 2010, married couples will no longer form the majority of households, and an increasing number of unmarried women will bear children.

More and more, the emerging data suggest population shifts that are dramatically altering present conditions: Although the birthrate is declining, it is declining for certain groups but increasing for others; although we are getting older, our youthful population is increasingly drawn from non-White groups; and although we must learn to compete in a global market, our workforce is less and less educated for increasingly technological occupations. That these emerging, greater-populated groups reflect problems in our society—these are the problems of underrepresentation in business, politics, and education—is a reality that must be addressed.

THE PROBLEMS OF EMERGING, DOMINANT AMERICAN POPULATIONS

An important issue around the culture of diversity is to raise the question of what is the characterization of "minority groups" in America? All of the attributes of this population cause reflection and alarm—this characterization includes high levels of poverty, unemployment, medical needs and infant mortality, lower life expectancies, and lower educational attainment. It also demonstrates more single-parent families and teenage pregnancies. And finally, it is characterized by its segregated communities, inner urbanization, inadequate housing, and high levels of crime. These are, according to Auletta (1982), the attributes of an underclass in American society. To others, these are the characteristics of the undeserving poor (Edsall and Edsall, 1991). More and more, the tone of the American voice, whether the politicians, the conservatives, or the press and media, is one of alarm over the growing distinction and division in America around the concept of class. Affirmative action, introduced to remedy past discrimination and underrepresentation of certain cultural and racial groups in America, is now the subject of heated debate and efforts to expose "reverse" discrimination. Attempts to include multiculturalism in American education is being seen as "politically correct" and particularist. But we cannot ignore the realities and concerns around the issues of great population shifts in American society, and the need to address these issues for a healthy future.

What are these problems? They begin with income and job disparities. Between 1973 and 1986 income levels for African American males decreased by 50 percent (Commission on Minority Participation, 1988). By 2000, most new jobs will require more than a secondary education. At the same time, less-educated, low-income workers will be unable to send their children to college. The 1988 Statistical Abstract of the U. S. reported that 31 percent of African Americans and 27 percent of Hispanics had incomes below the poverty level—nearly three times the level for Whites across the board. The unemployment rate is 4.6 percent for Whites, 12.2 percent for African Americans, and 9.3 percent for Hispanics (although in south Texas this figure is at 30 percent; U. S. Bureau of Labor Statistics, cited in *Commission on Minority Participation*, 1988).

In 1986 African American life expectancy at birth was 71.4 years, while for Whites it was 74.4 years (Statistical Abstract of the United States, 1988). In 1985, the African American infant mortality rate rose nationally for the first time in 20 years (*Children's Legal Defense Fund*, 1988), and the immunization status of non-White infants has worsened substantially in recent years (Johnson, 1987). While as a nation we are hopeful that work and education can alter these grim realities, the present picture of work and education, at all levels, is itself deleterious.

MINORITIES AND THE WORKFORCE

The future of the workforce also seems daunting. Of the additions to the present workforce, about 15 percent are White males, while 60 percent are female, and 25 percent are non-White. Demographic trends indicate that the economy will be dependent on the contributions of "minority" workers and women, who will comprise 50 percent of the workforce. Although demographers expect a 1.2 percent per year annual workforce growth from between now and the year 2000 (which is considerably slower than the previous decade's 2 percent annual growth rate), they are also predicting that one-fifth of the labor force will be 45 to 54 years old. In less than 10 years, one-third of the workforce will be members of minority groups, and in the same period, a majority of all new jobs will require a postsecondary education (Cappo, 1990). By 2020, two-thirds of American workers will be female or members of minority groups who have historically had less education and training and fewer advantages. As the growth of the American labor market slows, women, Hispanics, and African Americans show the strongest gains (Dreyfuss, 1990). The changing marketplace, expanding technologies, and global competition require that we have a more highly educated workforce. Jobs in the future will require more advanced math and science skills, and a more literate society. To meet this situation, America simply has to do a better job educating its people, and if demographic changes are driving our population shifts, we must pay critical attention to who will be attending our schools and to what we must do to educate these students to face emerging realities.

MINORITIES AND EDUCATION

Rendón (1989) reports that public school's face is changing. In the last 20 years White children's numbers fell 16 percent, while African Americans grew 5 percent and Hispanics, 103 percent. The American Council on Education (1989) predicts that by 2020, 39 percent of the school-age population will represent racial and ethnic minorities, and by 2060, this figure will increase to 60 percent. But future predictions of great changes as a nation only underscore the realities of the present. In all 25 of the nations largest schools, minority students comprise the majority population (*Carnegie Corporation Project*, 1990).

Chicago public schools provide a glimpse of the present status of "majority-minority" schools: five out of six students are members of racial and ethnic minorities. These students are attending segregated, inner-city schools characterized by overcrowding, inadequate counseling, increasing emphasis on vocational-technical education and less on collegiate and transfer programs of study, and a teaching faculty who rarely have advanced degrees (Orfield and Paul, 1987-88). Moreover, illiteracy, high dropout rates, and low graduation rates follow these populations. Approximately one of every five Hispanic and African American students who are sophomores will drop out of high school before graduation (Vining Brown, 1987).

While two-thirds of our population graduate from high school (last year this meant approximately 2.8 million students), the high school dropout rate has remained fairly constant for the last 25 years, hovering between 27-28 percent. Moreover, school statistics indicate that 43 percent of Hispanic students and 26 percent of African American students drop out of high school, and that those who do graduate are not prepared for higher education. The American Council on Education (1993) reports that since 1984 there has been no further improvement in the combined high school completion rate for African American men and women, due to stagnation in the rate for African American men.

The high school completion rates for Hispanics, aged 18 to 24, dropped from 62.8 percent in 1985 to 56 percent in 1989. Native Americans and Native Alaskans also complete high school at extremely low rates, around 56 percent. Southeast Asians and Filipino Americans have significantly lower rates of high school completion than Japanese and Chinese Americans. Most Asian groups, however, have higher educational levels than do native-born Americans (American Council on Education, 1991). By 1995, Whites will be a smaller proportion of the overall elementary/secondary population—from 71 percent to 66 percent; Asian American and Pacific Islander enrollments are increasing more rapidly than any other group in public schools (70 percent growth rate from 1985-86 to 1994-95); Hispanic enrollments are also rapidly increasing (more than 54 percent) while African American growth is at a slower rate, 13 percent (*Western Interstate Commission*, 1991).

While the nation is experiencing growth in public school attendance, the question of educational attainment remains critical: One out of five 18 year olds is functionally illiterate. This figure is higher than in any other industrialized nation. Conservative estimates place the number of adults who are unable to functionally read or write at about 20 million.

Our college-going rate is also in a holding pattern: It has remained nearly constant at 34 percent over the past 20 years (for Whites, the rate is 38.8 percent, for African Americans this rate is 30.8 percent, and for Hispanics the rate is 28.7 percent (*Chronicle of Higher Education*, 1992). The only major change in the rate has been an increasing female rate of going to college and a decreasing male rate (American Council on Education, 1991).

Enrollment of African Americans, Asian Americans, and Hispanics represent almost 20 percent of the total enrollment in higher education. This figure represents a 1988-90 growth increase of 10 percent of these groups attending college (*Chronicle of Higher Education* 1992). But male African American and Hispanic enrollment has declined considerably over the last decade. The primary reason for declining enrollment seems to be economic. These groups seek the workforce, the military, and short-term proprietary school training before they seek out higher education. Almost two-fifths of all African American students who attend colleges and universities rely on financial aid.

African Americans constitute 12.3 percent of the population but only 8.7 percent of college enrollment and 5.7 percent of college graduates. Hispanics, who account for 7.7 percent of the population, make up 4.9 percent of higher education enrollments and 2.7 percent of graduates (National Center for Educational Statistics, 1990). While Native Americans, Hispanics, and African Americans represented 14 percent of college and university enrollments in 1986, they received just 9 percent of all bachelor's degrees, 8 percent of all master's degrees, and 6 percent of all doctoral degrees. In 1990 Hispanics earned 698 doctorates, African Americans earned 828, Asian Americans, 617, and Native Americans, 73. And women earned 36.3 percent of all doctorates in 1990, up from 30.3 percent in 1980. (They earned more than half of the doctorates in fields other than science and engineering, and 27.7 percent of those in science and engineering.) But there is also a decline in the number of doctorates earned by U.S. citizens over the last 10 years, from 83.6 percent of all doctorates earned in 1980 to 72 percent in 1990. More than half of the engineering doctorates earned in American universities last year went to foreigners (National Center for Educational Statistics, 1990).

Community colleges have a higher proportion of their student body who are Hispanic, African American, and Native American than do senior institutions. And independent institutions enroll slightly more of these students than do state institutions, 17.7 percent compared to 17.5 percent. While 36 percent of all White students were enrolled in community colleges during the fall of 1988, 56 percent of all Hispanic, 54 percent of all Native American, and 42 percent of all African American students were enrolled in two-year institutions (Gillett-Karam, 1991). All three groups and Asian Americans show a significant growth period in the last decade; in some states the percentage of students enrolling in community colleges is significantly higher than the 46.7 percent national total. Hispanics remain concentrated in two-year institutions where their enrollment grew twice as fast as in four-year institutions. On the other hand, African Americans' enrollment in four-year institutions significantly outpaced their enrollment in two-year colleges, 6.7 percent to 1.3 percent (Astin, 1990).

By 1995, one out of every three students enrolled in higher education will be 30 or older (28 percent of all males, and 38 percent of all females). Higher education costs will rise, and so too will the number of jobs. Many young people will work before starting college, but they will probably start college anyway. Dual incomes and more flexible employers will allow a greater number of workers to attend college while holding part-time jobs. By 2000, women, who already total more than half of all college students, will comprise 56 percent of all college students, and almost half of the workforce. Between now and the year 2000, college classes will increasingly be made up of diverse groups, including Hispanics, African Americans, Native Americans, Asian Americans, immigrants, and foreigners—many of the students from these groups will be economically disadvantaged as a result of changing demographics and the growth of single-parent households.

We are aware that the number of individuals who are 18 to 24 years old will decline from 30 million in 1980 to 25 million by 2000. This represents a loss of 5 million of the college-going age cohort over a 20-year period. Some would suggest that this figure represents an institutional deficit at a time when colleges and universities must also face an educational deficit in the number of racial and ethnic minorities for whom a college or university education could make a difference. Not only does this deficit manifest itself in the number of students being served but also in the number of faculty represented. For example, excluding historically Black colleges and universities, African American scholars made up about 1 percent of the faculty at colleges and universities in the 1960s. Twenty-five years later, African Americans hold about 4 percent of the nation's professorate, and this number includes those at the HBCUs (historically Black colleges and universities), which is at 2 percent. Thus of the 3,200 predominantly White institutions of higher education only 2 percent of the faculty are African American: *This is an increase of 1 percent in 25 years.* Hispanic faculty constitute around 2 percent of the nation's professorate, and Native Americans less than 1 percent. These numbers are slightly higher in the community and junior colleges, but not by much. Judging by the past and projected counts for faculty, in the year 2000 there will be even a greater shortage of minority faculty. And although some of these data are affected by the same situation that women found themselves in—they suddenly had a choice of occupations and professions opened to them—not much is being done to study the decline of interest in the teaching profession, nor is much being done to encourage and strengthen the profession (Gillett-Karam, Roueche, and Roueche, 1991).

The rate of participation of racial and ethnic minorities in higher education over the last 25 years demonstrates social and political manifestations. During the late 1960s and the decade of the 1970s, minority enrollment increased dramatically, but by the 1980s the momentum that witnessed huge increases in college and university enrollment, attendance, and graduation began to diminish. All "minority" groups lost ground, but Hispanic and African American student populations decreased more than Asian American students. The American Council on Education, in their 1989 status report on minority education, explains that the college participation rate for low-income African American high school graduates between 18 and 24 years old has dropped significantly, from 39.8 percent in 1976 to 30.3 percent in 1988, and for Hispanics the rate fell from 50.4 percent to 35.3 percent over the same period (p. 5). Low-income Whites moreover experienced a 2 percent gain in college participation in that same period—between 1976 and 1988. Other serious considerations for minorities who attend college and university include high attrition rates in both community colleges and senior institutions, low transfer rates from community to senior college (Grant and Eiden, 1982; Richardson and Bender, 1987), poor entry-academic skills, and low performance scores on standardized admission and placement tests (consider the averages on SAT scores reported below).

Percentages Scoring Below 400 (**SAT**)	Verbal	Math
African Americans	73%	64%
Hispanics	59%	45%
Whites	31%	22%

Also included were limitations of the actual disciplines or fields of study both available to and chosen by minorities in undergraduate, graduate, and professional schools (Ramist and Arbeiter, 1986).

Blackwell (1988) reports that in 1976 Whites in graduate schools comprised 83.9 percent of that population, and in 1984 White students still held about eight out of ten slots in the nation's graduate schools. The small percentage of difference (83.9 percent to 80.5 percent) was attributable to the growth of Asian American and Hispanic enrollment in graduate school—African American graduate student representation fell 22.4 percent in those eight years, accounting for a loss of 15,000 students. Thus, there was a decline of nearly 40 percent in master's degrees awarded to African Americans and of 10 percent in those awarded to Hispanics. Ottinger (1987) reports that while graduate degrees earned by Asian Americans increased in this period, Whites earned 76 percent of all master's degrees, and 78 percent of all doctorates. Minorities are relatively absent in fields such as engineering, math, biology, and hard sciences. Hirschorn labels a "discouraging sign" the lack of growth of minority applicants to medical schools (1988). Blackwell (1988) and Brazziel (1987-88) report that over 50 percent of the doctorates earned by African Americans are in education, resulting in uneven distribution of African Americans in other academic fields.

With population growth slowing down, we raise an alarm—who will fill these new workforce positions that will require a college degree? Perhaps we will have to look to globalization, and outside the standard isolationism that we have always resorted to in U.S. history, to find answers. We have growing "ethnic markets" even at home—thus diversity has a level of urgency not found even in the affirmative action heyday.

THE ROLE MODEL DILEMMA

Many of the experts of American education are raising warnings around the rapid growth of minority populations in American schools and the declining numbers of minorities who are becoming teachers and role models for these populations. The Carnegie Forum (1986) predicted that the nation's schools would need about 50,000 new minority teachers just in 1994, while less than 12 percent of the nation's teachers are currently African American and

Hispanic. Rudner (1987) accurately predicted a decline of African American and Hispanic teachers to 5 percent in 1992. The National Alliance of Black School Educators reports the rate of increase for the African American and Hispanic school-age population between 1980 and 1984 was twice that of the rate of increase of African American and Hispanic teachers (Carter, 1988). That the data demonstrate a serious underrepresentation of African American and Hispanic teachers is evident—obviously the decline in the number of minority college students, their decline in declaring education majors, and the institutionalization of teacher competency tests suggest that African Americans and Hispanics as classroom teachers for the expanding minority populations in the schools are an "endangered species" (Irvine, 1988). And while African Americans and Hispanics are not well represented as part of the teaching community, they are virtually nonexistent as administrators of public schools. John Hope Franklin, long a voice for African Americans in this country suggests that if this trend continues, the need for minority teachers will most likely reach a point of desperation. Young minority students will be deprived of yet another role model they need, and the notorious "vicious cycle" will reappear. With students lacking positive role models, advocates, and mentors, they are less likely to do well in elementary and secondary schools, decreasing again their staying in school and being exposed to challenging educational programs (1988).

While the hue and cry may focus on the public school dilemma, the situation is not any better for African Americans and Hispanics as administrators and faculties of colleges and universities. The Commission on Minority Participation in Education and American Life (1988) reported that minorities held 10 percent of the faculty positions in American colleges and universities; and where compared to White faculty, they were and are concentrated in lower ranks and less likely to receive tenure. Harvey (1986) suggests two words describe the presence of African Americans in predominantly White colleges and universities—"small and nonexistent." In terms of numbers of college and university presidents who are African American (5 percent) and Hispanic (about 2 percent), these numbers are even more negligible. Of the 100 African American college presidents more than half head historically Black colleges and universities and similarly half of the Hispanic college presidents are community college presidents (Mooney, 1988).

POLITICS AND BUSINESS

The critical word for women and members of racial and ethnic groups in politics and business is underrepresentation (Gillett-Karam, 1989; Gillett-

Karam, Roueche, and Roueche, 1991). In both the political arena and in American businesses, the lack of leadership of these groups is both noticeable and symbolic. The percentage of managers who are women, although the number has increased in the last 10 years, is at about 27 percent, and the figure for members of racial and ethnic minorities is at about 10 percent. The rate for CEOs is negligible among both groups. In United States government, the only significant change in the status of minority groups has been in the growth of the number of African American mayors in the United States. At all other levels, representation of women and minorities is practically nonexistent. In the United States Senate, for example, there are now 7 women, 2 Asians and Pacific Islanders, and 1 Native American senators. Of the 435 members of the House of Representatives, 48 are women, 39 are African American, 19 are Hispanic, and 6 are Asians and Pacific Islanders. Of the 50 governors of the United States, 1 is a Pacific Islander and 4 are women. In a nation where half our population is women and almost a fourth of our population is African American, Native American, Hispanic, and Asian American, these numbers remain unrepresentative of our changing national face.

REMOVING THE BARRIERS TO SUCCESS AND FULL REPRESENTATION

Among the critical attributes of leadership, according to House and Mitchell Path-Goal Theory, is the provision of reducing the inevitable barriers toward goal achievement. Not only must leaders envision the goal or goals they and their followers need and want to attain, but they have the further obligation to help to eliminate obstacles that stand in the way of their consensual goals. Rather than dwell on responsibility for past discrimination, or on blame for injustice, integrative problem solving suggests common issues for discussion, evaluation, and eventual solution. Its emphasis is on issues, not people. This is precisely the kind of leadership that is being called for in American society, where demography is causing change more dramatically than government policy has ever done. We can readily see that globalization, the challenge of expanding technology and the need for a changing workforce and the evolution of the marketplace are forcing the issue of diversity and giving it a level of urgency that affirmative action never had.

More and more, at all levels of American society, we can see responses to the challenges that will affect our future. And more and more, our observations are informing us that single efforts by single individuals or institutions are failing at what is being understood as a national issue. The economy, business, government, and education are component parts of the common problem and are dependent on each other to accomplish goals and reduce the obstacles that stand in the way of progress and national growth. Turning to the issues of this discussion, we find we cannot single out American higher education to eliminate the barriers that prohibit minorities from participating fully in education, the professions, the sciences, politics, and business.

Rather, the call must be for coordinated action taken at every stage of the educational system, from early childhood programs to graduate and professional schools. And at the same time, educational programs must respond to economic, governmental, workforce, and societal challenges. While facing the national dilemmas, colleges and universities must take immediate action in their own environments. Improvements in policies, programs, and practices will place higher education institutions in a position where they will play key roles in fostering the changes necessary to give members of racial and ethnic minorities the educational tools necessary to prepare them for present and future leadership roles.

Several areas are seen as obstacles in the success of minorities in colleges and universities. These include institutional culture and climate (including curriculum, faculty-administrative hiring, selection, and advancement), assessment, financial aid, articulation and recruitment, and transfer. As Green (1989) and others suggest, "leadership from the top" must acknowledge these obstacles and provide an atmosphere to address and remove the barriers restricting representation of minorities in colleges and universities, and ultimately, in society. Present leaders face a difficult position, especially in a time when there is a definite backlash (Faludi, 1991) around the very issues that demonstrate historical disadvantages for racial and ethnic groups. Although the situation is difficult, it is not insurmountable; and more important, the consequences for not addressing the issues are more threatening than the present backlash. Thus, the place to begin is with campus culture (those sets of experiences and traditions that define the characteristics of a particular campus) and campus climate (the current responses toward culture on a campus). Nettles (1988) reported that 76 percent of all African American students in "predominantly White" colleges and universities have felt the effects of discrimination and alienation in those institutions. In the last few years, both students and faculty have reacted strongly to affirmative action, multiculturalism, and both entrance and hiring policies. Campus climates are in danger of continuing conflict and turmoil over issues of race and ethnicity.

Campus culture must be assessed and addressed by all constituent groups of the college or university and the community that surrounds the campus. Etzioni (1992) would suggest a sense of communitarianism here—that instead of being motivated by individual efforts and plans, a common group effort for problem resolution be employed, since the groups involved best know the problems and can work for resolutions to the difficulties at hand in a community. In most colleges and universities, the college culture as we know it today, with its restrictive and norm-based standards, precludes the inclusion of most minority groups who come to higher education institutions with educational deficits. And even in institutions without entrance requirements, community colleges, the transfer rate for minority students is low. Some would say the lack of minority faculty as role models, the lack of multicultural perspectives, the lack of a culture of diversity, the absence of a critical mass of minority students, a lack of academic support services, a lack of sufficient counseling services, a lack of mentor programs, and a lack of intervention programs demonstrate the "real" attitude of colleges and universities to their minority students. These factors contribute to the interpretation of students of a hostile environment and result in feelings of isolation, which in turn interfere with academic and personal achievement.

Culture and Climate

Hale (1991) suggests that there be an inventory of campus culture and environment and joint decision making around solutions to perceived problems and barriers to success for students, faculty, administrators, and the community. Of course, strong leaders must point the way to change where culture is monolithic and ethnocentric. Embedded language, customs, patterns, rituals, values, and artifacts must be examined for exclusionary emphases, and transcendence over the one like-minded way of doing things must occur (Green, 1989). An institutional climate that promotes multicultural experiences, encourages diversity, and promulgates pluralism is one that demonstrates that it is one that can change its values and its behavior. A supportive institutional climate is one that ensures that all students are involved in their education, feel a sense of belonging and enhanced self-esteem, and are encouraged to take advantage of the special experiences offered on the college or university campus. Institutions can provide their commitment to adopting a supportive institutional climate by emphasizing high standards of teaching and learning, by encouraging faculty to become role models and mentors for students, by creating an environment of peer support, by strengthening their counseling services, and by providing remedial education programs to ensure academic success.

Perhaps more than any other aspect of campus culture the institutionalization of the curriculum seems sacrosanct and untouchable. In the last 10 years, the hue and cry against a curriculum that includes "add-on" subjects, such as women's role in history or science or the African American experience, have come under critical examination by American scholars who are claiming an adulterated and particularist curriculum. For the most part, these scholars are opposed to a course of study that eliminates inquiry and examination and replaces it with dogma. But all scholars are justifiably opposed to this as an untenable teaching practice. As teachers and instructors and professors, faculty are in the business of helping students achieve their own understanding, but certainly this can be done by integrating our curriculum as well. A curriculum that pointedly ignores the contributions and the lifestyle of a significant part of its population does that population a huge disservice and eventually contributes to the "knowledge" that anything we know about that group is knowledge about a subculture or deviant, non-norm based action (Gilligan, 1982). We profit from and honor our students' accomplishments and future by integrating their history into American history.

Increasing the numbers of minority faculty and administrators is a critical aspect of changing institutional culture and climate. Values for the importance and effectiveness of minorities in faculty and leadership positions must become part of the culture of higher institutions. Engaging in the damaging and disparaging rhetoric of competencies of minorities in these positions is damaging and accounts for additional exclusionary beliefs and policies. Rather an enlightened hiring policy, excellent retention program, and a strong mentoring program should be put into place to alleviate what are already known difficulties—absence of role models, tokenism, and alienation (Gillett-Karam, Roueche, and Roueche, 1991). Increasing faculty and administrative positions among members of racial and ethnic minorities enhances the students' bonds with the institution; moreover, it demonstrates to nonminority students that minorities can serve in leadership roles, thus providing a basis for future acceptance and expectation. Therefore, an examination of campus culture must also include an evaluation of its hiring and recruitment policies.

Assessment

In the 1984 National Institute of Education report, *Involvement in Learning*, higher education responded to accusations of mediocrity by instituting new assessment programs as a tool to improve teaching and ensure accountability. But as a safeguard against lowering expectations among college students, assessment rigor can be a double-edged sword. It can diminish even further those populations in urgent need of higher education and training. While assessment provides an accountability factor for educational achievements, it also can refer to standardized exams used to determine access to higher educational institutions. This assessment technique, when used as a sole instrument of college entrance, has been and is a barrier to minority access to higher education. This, more than any of the barriers and obstacles to higher education that minorities face, is most linked to the idea that institutions of higher learning cannot resolve the dilemmas of education without holding accountable and acknowledging the responsibilities of other educational institutions, including elementary and secondary schools and community and junior colleges.

If assessment is used as a pigeonholing or gatekeeping devise, it is discriminatory; and rather than enhancing students' possibilities for success, it can actually prevent them from participating in college at all. Of course, no one advocates that standards of program quality be sacrificed. Attention must be paid to the unwanted and unfortunate side effect of assessment; what can be done, where, and at what cost should be questions that begin to uncover the problems minority students encounter with assessment as a gatekeeping entrance requirement. Possibly, one answer lies with the community college, with its open access and admissions concept, where students are provided with skill development and training before enrolling in their academic curriculum. Another alternative asks higher education institutions to develop comprehensive assessment programs that use testing as only one of multiple measures to provide an accurate profile of student performance. Colleges and universities should review and implement assessment programs for special minority populations, including diagnostic feedback, remediation, and counseling. Ongoing feedback throughout a student's college career, and indeed, throughout any course the student takes, is a must for student success. Academic standards, entrance and exit requirements, and transfer requirements should be clear and stated information for all students at all levels of their college experiences.

Financial Aid

The rising cost of a college education added to the reductions in federal and state support for student financial aid creates significant problems for all low-income students. Moreover, since we know that income levels for minority students are the lowest in the nation, we are aware of the restrictive nature of cost and higher education. Carter (1988) and others note with chagrin the alternatives of this obstacle, especially as applied to the least college-going populations, young Hispanic and African American males who opt for the military or trade schools as alternatives for the cost of higher education. As the current level of subsidized loans and grants decreases and the recession continues in the early 1990s, so do the reasons for further diminishing these subsidies. At times when the economy is troubled, governmental expenses for education diminish, and the local economy cannot make up for the decreased aid. Moreover, loans become more unattractive; studies demonstrate that low-income minority students are the least likely to borrow money to attend school (Henderson, 1987). The idea of further indebtedness to those already struggling for survival is unrealistic and unattractive.

Even when financial aid is available the procedure is so complicated that the process becomes a barrier for students who could most profit from the aid (Collison, 1988). Many students, especially first-generation college-going students, are discouraged from applying for financial aid when they are left alone to face complex forms (Astin, 1982). Institutions of higher learning therefore have an obligation to intervene and ensure cooperation with other agencies, schools, and federal and state programs to ensure that aid is available for needy students regardless of national financial exigency. Partnerships with the private business sector must be encouraged, and emphasis must be placed on special scholarships, grants, and low-interest loans that encourage students to seek higher education and college and university degrees. Simplification of applications must be addressed as a barrier restricting minority, low-income, and first-generation college students from loan application. Intrinsic in this goal is evaluating our attitudes and values around financial aid; since we are a nation that rewards the work ethic and denigrates "aid" and "welfare," we must face up to our distaste for aid in most forms, even financial aid to needy students for college education. Looking at financial aid as an investment in human capital offers a win-win situation to all. In the long run, a student who graduates and earns a degree will be a contributing member of society, both as a taxpayer and an active citizen. Moreover, we need to offer alternative situations for debt payment in addition to repaying debts with money—programs that demand community service, teaching apprenticeships, and internships can be designed and implemented as alternatives for debt repayment for college loans.

Articulation and Recruitment

Articulation is the process in which collaboration works best. Agreements are made between higher education institutions and high schools, community colleges, and other four-year institutions. Not only does the senior institution have the responsibility to "articulate" the academic requirements of their college or university to other learning institutions and students, but also they need to develop an understanding among in-feeding institutions and their students of what it takes to be successful at their institution. To some extent, the articulation concept is nothing more than the spelling out of requirements of higher education to primary-secondary school and community college students. But it is more than that, too. It is an introduction of the college option to students of all ages and as such it is a demystifying experience especially to potential first-generation and minority college-going students. Observances demonstrate to us that as a nation, we tend to "overlook" the potential of these students as college-going students and inadvertently track them into vocational programs (Brint and Karabel, 1989). Moreover, frequently a lack of informed counseling fails to recognize that these groups more than others lack a home environment that can emphasize the rewards of a solid academic experience, or even recognize the requirements for successful college preparation in elementary and secondary school. In many cases, non-native English speakers are at a disadvantage, are mislabeled as learning deficit, and are therefore tracked as *special* education students.

Programs that improve articulation are aimed at providing year-long programs in math and science enrichment, special courses in career exploration, summer institutes in various disciplines, collaborative internships in local business and industry, and homework centers. Each of these programs is aimed at increasing awareness among students that they can succeed in college, and that there is support to do so. In many cases articulation agreements are influenced by local and state programs that create strategies and plans to increase awareness and participation among all levels of society. In this regard, articulation is essential to improving access for minority students and ensuring the retention and transfer of minority students throughout the educational pipeline.

Institutions, therefore, must also work together to develop systematic recruitment programs that have a particular emphasis on attracting minorities to facilitate the flow of minority students through the education pipeline—at the two-year, four-year, graduate, and professional levels. Recruitment must be seen as a part of the articulation process. By strengthening the efforts to attract academically prepared minority students, we are soliciting those students to become an integral and regular part of our institutions of higher learning. When we develop and implement special programs that identify and support minority students who have or can attain academic potential (in an environment that has too long overlooked and inadequately nourished that potential, talent, and ambition), we are recruiting these students. And finally, by expanding our informational and promotional efforts with college fairs, career days, and special brochures and catalogs focusing on opportunities for minority students, we are recruiting. Such efforts are being made now by innovative leaders who understand the urgency and importance of linking articulation and recruitment and who understand that collaboration must occur between elementary and secondary school and college and university faculty with regard to course expectation and content, materials and text, and transfer requirements.

Transfer

Obviously articulation and recruitment are elements of the transfer function, but this concept also requires additional information primarily because the largest numbers of racial and ethnic minorities attend community and junior colleges, colleges in which the dominant population is Hispanic, and historically Black institutions. In other words, transfer to higher educational institutions from community colleges and transfer to graduate and professional schools is clearly indispensable to the success of minority students and their futures. Richardson and Bender (1987) and Cohen and Brawer (1989) point out there is a critical need to foster minority achievement through the transfer function and to address the immediate obstacles and barriers preventing transfer at the present time. Data would indicate that, especially for minorities, the number of students who successfully transfer are low and are, in fact, actually decreasing since the mid-1980s. The transfer function underscores the need for greater articulation and recruitment programs from senior institutions, but it also asks institutions to become more introspective of their own policies and programs and to address the problems that prevent their students from transferring with success and obtaining degrees.

RENEWING COMMITMENTS AND OPPORTUNITIES

At various periods in our history, we have, as Americans, recommited ourselves to goals that strengthen our nation and our populace. We must recommit ourselves to goals that strengthen us as a nation and a people. Now more than ever, as demography drives change and provides a new face of the American people, our response must reflect the challenges posed by a changing demographic reality: We are a nation where there is no single majority population or dominant culture, we are rather a nation of many peoples and many cultures that collectively contribute to a diversity which constitutes the strength of our nation. Thomas Jefferson saw that the enabling element of a culture of diversity was education, and it is education in America that provides men and women with the quotient for equality. The heart of America believes education is an inalienable right for all its population and an essential ingredient for democracy. The American system allows citizens the opportunity to improve the quality of their life. But in examining a system that is severely underrepresented from its now majority population, it is obvious that women and members of racial and ethnic minorities, including African Americans, Hispanics, Asian Americans, and Native Americans, are being denied opportunity. The lack of leadership roles in all sectors of our society is a result, in part, of the inability of the nation's higher and professional educational institutions to succeed in recruiting, retaining, and graduating minority members to fill such positions. And it is to our nation's educational institutions that we must look to redress these inequalities and this underrepresentation.

Auletta (1982) predicted the rise of a permanent underclass in America, stating the unthinkable—that, in fact, democracy is more fiction than it is fact. If he is proved right, it is because our educational institutions do not or will not face the realities of a changing demography and an overwhelming challenge to the system as it exists now. Higher education must lead the way in providing models for national reform and in providing greater opportunity for its great diversity of people. A renewed commitment is required to confront an uncertain future.

REFERENCES

American Council on Education. 1993. *Eleventh annual status report on minorities in higher education.* Washington, DC: ACE, Office of Minority Concerns.

American Council on Education. 1991. *Ninth annual status report on minorities in higher education.* Washington, DC: ACE, Office of Minority Concerns.

American Council on Education. 1989. *Eighth annual status report on minorities in higher education.* Washington, DC: ACE, Office of Minority Concerns.

Astin, A. W. 1990. *The Black undergraduate: Current status and trends in the characteristics of freshmen.* Higher Education Research Institute, Los Angeles, CA.

Astin, A. W. 1982. *Minorities in American higher education: Recent trends, current prospects, and recommendations.* San Francisco: Jossey-Bass.

Auletta, K. 1982. *The underclass.* New York: Random House.

Blackwell, J. 1988. Faculty issues: The impact on minorities. *The Review of Higher Education* 11 (4): 417-34.

Brazziel, W. 1987/1988. Black Americans find roadblocks at graduate school. *Educational Record* 68 (4): 69 (1), 108-15.

Brint, S., and J. Karabel. 1989. *The divided dream: Community colleges and the promise of educational opportunity in America, 1900-1985.* London: Oxford University Press.

Cappo, J. 1990. *Future scope: Success strategies for the 1990s and beyond.* Chicago, IL: Longman Financial Services.

Carnegie Corporation, Quality Education for Minorities Project. 1990. *Education that works: An action plan for the education of minorities.* New York.

Carnegie Forum on Education and the Economy. 1986. *A nation prepared: Teachers for the 21st century.* New York: Carnegie Forum Task Force on Teaching as a Profession.

Carter, D. 1988. Help wanted: Minority teachers. *Educational Record* 68 (4): 54.

Children's Legal Defense Fund. 1988. *A call for action to make our nation safe for children: A briefing book on the status of American children in 1988.* Washington, DC.

Cohen, A., and F. Brawer. 1989. *The community college.* San Francisco: Jossey-Bass.

Collison, M. 1988. Complex application form discourages many students from applying for federal financial aid. *Chronicle of Higher Education* (July 6): A19, A 30.

Commission on Minority Participation in Education and American Life. 1988. *One-third of a nation.* Washington, DC: American Council on Education.

Dreyfuss, J. 1990. Getting ready for the new workforce. *Fortune*, April 23, 167-81.

Edsall, T., and M. Edsall. 1991. *Chain reaction: The impact of race, rights, and taxes on American politics*. New York: W. W. Norton.

Etzioni, A., ed. 1992. *The responsive community*. Washington, DC: George Washington University.

Evangelauf, J. 1992. Minority groups enrollment at colleges rose 10% from 1988 to 1990, reaching record levels. *Chronicle of Higher Education* (January 22): A33, A37.

Faludi, S. 1991. *Backlash: The undeclared war against American women*. New York: Crown.

Franklin, J. 1988. The desperate need for Black teachers. *The Educational Digest* 53 (7): 14-15.

Gillett-Karam, R. 1989. Women in leadership roles and leadership concerns. In *Shared vision*, edited by J. Roueche, G. Baker, and R. Rose. Washington, DC: Community College Press.

Gillett-Karam, R., S. Roueche, and J. Roueche. 1991. *Underrepresentation and the question of diversity: Women and minorities in the community college*. Washington, DC: Community College Press.

Gilligan, C. 1982. *In a different voice*. Cambridge, MA: Harvard University Press.

Grant, W., and L. Eiden. 1982. *Digest of educational statistics 1982*. Washington, DC: National Center for Education Statistics.

Green, M. 1989. *Minorities on campus: A handbook for enhancing diversity*. Washington, DC: American Council on Education.

Hale, H. 1991. *Institutional effectiveness*. Ohio State University.

Harvey, W. 1986. Where are the Black faculty members? *Chronicle of Higher Education* 96 (January 22).

Henderson, C. 1987. How indebted are four-year college graduates? *Educational Record* 68 (13): 24-29.

Hirschorn, M. 1988. Medical school concerned over slow growth in minority enrollment. *Chronicle of Higher Education* 31: (June 16).

Hodgkinson, H. 1991. *Beyond the schools: How schools and communities must collaborate to solve the problems facing American youth*. Arlington, VA: American Association of School Administrators.

Irvine, J. 1988. An analysis of the problem of disappearing Black educators. *The Elementary School Journal* 88 (5): 503-15.

Johnson, K. 1987. *Who is watching our children's health? The immunization status of American children*. Washington, DC: Children's Legal Defense Fund.

Mooney, C. 1988. The college president. *Chronicle of Higher Education* 34 (29): 14-16.

National Center for Education Statistics. 1990. *The condition of education*. Washington, DC: Government Printing Office.

Nettles, M. 1988. *Toward Black undergraduate student equality in American higher education*. Westport, CT: Greenwood Press.

Orfield, G., and F. Paul. 1987/1988. Declines in minority access: A tale of five cities. *Educational Record* 68, no. 4: 69, no. 1: 56-62.

Ottinger, C. 1987. *1986-1987 fact book on higher education*. New York: ACE/Macmillan.

Ramist, L., and S. Arbeiter. 1986. *Profiles, college bound seniors, 1985*. New York: College Entrance Examination Board.

Rendon, L. 1989. The lie and the hope: Making higher education a reality for at-risk students. *AAHE Bulletin* 41, no. 10 (May): 4-7.

Richardson, R., and L. Bender. 1987. *Fostering minority access and achievement in higher education*. San Francisco: Jossey-Bass.

Rudner, L. 1987. *What's happening in teacher testing: An analysis of state teacher testing*. Washington, DC: U. S. Government Printing Office.

Statistical Abstract of the United States. 1988. Table 106, 70.

Study Group on the Conditions of Excellence in American Higher Education. 1984. *Involvement in learning: Realizing the potential of American higher education*. Washington, DC: U. S. Government Printing Office.

U. S. Bureau of the Census. 1991. Population trends and congressional apportionment. *1990 Census Profile* no. 1 (March).

Western Interstate Commission for Higher Education and The College Board. 1991. *The road to college: Educational progress by race and ethnicity*. Boulder, CO: WICHE.

Wilders, K. 1991. The demographics of diversity. Presented at Leadership 2000 Conference, Chicago, IL.

Vining Brown, S. 1987. *Minorities in the graduate education pipeline*. Princeton, NJ: Educational Testing Service, Minority Graduate Education Project.

CHAPTER

Three Realities: Minority Life in the United States—The Struggle for Economic Equity

Don M. Blandin

Editors' Note: *In June 1990, the Business-Higher Education Forum of the American Council on Education—a nonprofit organization of 90 chief executives of Fortune 500 corporations and leading colleges and universities—called for a new national commitment to bolster America's large and growing minority middle class and to help unskilled African American and Hispanic workers and the underclass.*

The central finding of that document, Three Realities: Minority Life in the United States, was that a significant percentage of minority citizens have improved their social and economic standing in recent decades, but large numbers still have far to go to move into the mainstream of American life.

The report was prepared by a task force of corporate and academic CEOs, co-chaired by Clifton R. Wharton, Jr., (at the time, chairman and chief executive officer, TIAA-CREF, later appointed deputy secretary of state by President Clinton in January 1993) and Steven Mason (president and chief operating officer, The Meade Corporation).

Don M. Blandin, director of the forum, adapted the forum's report for this chapter.

INTRODUCTION

Every 30 minutes about 250 new Americans arrive in this country. Nearly 220 are born here; 30 immigrate. The names are rich and strange, echoes from the far corners of the globe. The color of their skin varies. Some are wealthy; some are comfortable; too many are poor. All of them are, or aspire to become, Americans.

In that same 30 minutes, more than 160 young people in the United States make personal decisions that affect them for the rest of their lives. Their families, their communities, and the entire nation also live with the consequences. Nearly 50 drop out of school; 85 commit a violent crime against another human being; 27 teenage girls give birth, 16 of them out of wedlock.

And each succeeding half hour, another 160 young people repeat the same mistakes. By the end of each school year, 1 million students have dropped out of school; over 1.3 million young people have committed a violent crime; and 478,000 adolescents have given birth.

Each of these young people is also an American, and a disproportionate number of them are members of minority groups. Most of them are not immigrants.

This chapter is about minority progress and minority problems in the United States. It surveys a broad and complex field and touches on controversial matters. It has two fundamental goals. The first is to address ways to bring African Americans and Hispanics more fully into our nation's economic and educational mainstream.

For decades, huge reservoirs of human capital represented by the nation's African American and Hispanic citizens have gone largely untapped while the United States's economy was weakened by the material costs of their economic and political disenfranchisement. Despite the successes of the civil rights movement of the 1960s, our society continues to lose generations of urban minority youngsters, deeply alienated from, and disaffected by, the larger social, economic, and political culture. Sustaining economic activity and prosperity in the United States in the twenty-first century will require the talent of every one of us. Now a new factor lends special urgency to this task.

The new factor is demographic change. Because of immigration and differential fertility rates, African Americans and Hispanics are becoming an ever-larger part of the American population. At the same time, the population as a whole is aging, the growth of the workforce is slowing, and the twin burdens of greater productivity and supporting an aging population will fall mostly on younger workers. About one-third of these new workers will be members of minority groups, traditionally the least well prepared for productive participation in the nation's economic life.

The second goal is to help clarify the terms of the public debate about minority policy and progress in this nation. The current discussion rarely reflects the complicated reality of minority life in the United States. Most of that discussion, in both academic and popular journals, appears predicated on the assumption that all minorities are poor, and much of it concentrates on the severe problems faced by a substantial segment of African Americans— problems so acute that they threaten not only the welfare of these families but the functioning of the American economy and society.

The great contribution of this discussion is that it has kept the problems of minorities before the American people. Its great failure has been to slight the solid achievements of many members of minority groups. At the same time, the significant contributions of public and private actions to reverse discrimination have been overlooked.

But the progress is there. It exists on the record. It can be found in the data and in homes and communities across the country. It belies growing disillusionment about whether the pace of minority progress in the United States can be accelerated. Preoccupation with problems alone threatens to reinforce the stereotypical thinking that lies at the heart of racial distrust.

This chapter is concerned with "all minorities." It relies, in the main, on data that describe the condition of African Americans and Hispanics because these are generally the only useful data available.

Discussions of the problems minorities face at the national level are strewn with numbers of a magnitude that numbs both mind and soul: X million unemployed, Y million in poverty, Z million illegitimate, addicted, abused, and abandoned. So conceived, the problems appear insuperable, the solutions feeble.

Great human problems can be described statistically and the forces for their resolution set in motion at the national level. But the resolution works itself out slowly and steadily at ground level. The nation does not have a great deal of time to solve the problems identified here. The 1992 riot in Los Angeles following the trial of Rodney King adds a disturbing urgency to the words of the Business-Higher Education Forum in 1990, "Unless we have made substantial progress by the turn of the century, the difficulties identified in this [report] may be beyond our collective ability to overcome." We cannot, in other words, afford to waste another 30 minutes.

THREE REALITIES

The civil rights revolution in the United States has been difficult, emotional, and often traumatic. The task ahead—to make it work—may be even harder.

By the time today's high school graduate retires, at least 3 Americans of every 10 will be a minority. The national heritage of pluralism makes that prospect a cause for celebration. However, the fact that many members of most minority groups have not entered fully into that heritage casts a shadow over what should be cause for rejoicing.

But where the nation's leaders should have made common cause to make that heritage real for all, they have often ignored their obligation, settling for finger pointing and blame. Some, oblivious to the power of history and economic forces, have pointed to dependency and welfare abuse as the root of the problem. They have blamed the victim. Others alleged racism at every criticism or setback, no matter how well grounded the criticism or temporary the setback. They have evaded responsibility. Neither blame nor evasion can substitute for thoughtful public policy and energetic private leadership.

The dynamics shaping the lives of minorities in America are best understood in the context of access to employment and to education. When the people of the United States have united in determination to provide opportunities to minority citizens, African Americans and Hispanics have prospered. Minorities denied these opportunities, or unable to take advantage of them, remain mired in poverty.

This chapter makes three major points:

- It is self-evident that, in general, the U.S. economy and educational system are not working as well for minority Americans as they are for members of the majority.
- Nevertheless, generalities are a poor guide to the complexities of minority life in the United States. The system has worked better than its critics concede, but not nearly as well as its admirers believe.
- The system must now work even more effectively if Americans of all racial and ethnic backgrounds are to grow and prosper in the twenty-first century.

In General

As measured by virtually all statistical measures of income, opportunity, education, access to health care, and personal security, it is clear that the *typical* minority American does not begin to enjoy anything close to parity with the life experiences of the average White American. The general picture is deeply disturbing.

But useful though statistical averages are, they conceal as much as they reveal. Just as understanding the average daily temperature in the continental United States would not prepare the visitor for August heat or January frost, so, too, understanding the average situation for members of minority groups does not illuminate the remarkable diversity of minority life in this country. To oversimplify, that diversity amounts to three separate realities for minority Americans.

The first reality is that a significant number of minority group members— African American and Hispanic—are **succeeding** in the American society, economy, and culture.

The second is more troublesome. It involves, overwhelmingly, working minority Americans who are **on the margins** of making it in American life. Despite their best efforts, they have trouble keeping pace with rising demands of the workplace because of limited educational opportunities, low levels of literacy, and the lack of marketable skills. They are falling behind, and almost no one is paying any attention.

The third reality confounds America's idea of itself. An **underclass**, almost entirely African American and Hispanic, now exists in the United States. Although most readily apparent in the nation's cities, it extends, as well, into isolated rural areas with large numbers of people, majority and minority, living in poverty. Keeping hope alive becomes hard: Dreams for one's children and aspirations for a better life slowly give way to hopelessness and disillusionment.

Making It

No fair-minded student of history will deny the role of the United States in enlarging human freedom and equality. That progress can be found in minority communities as well.

African American Progress. Despite the difficulties of incomplete and inadequate data, and the frustrating variation in terms and their definition among different scholars, it is clear that the African American middle class experienced a remarkable expansion during the latter half of the twentieth century. Whether the definition is a straightforward one based on weekly wages or a more complex delineation based on occupations, the African American middle class appears to have increased tenfold since 1910, with most of the growth coming in the last generation. One analyst associated with the pre-eminent African American think tank in the United States, the Joint Center for Political Studies, believes the African American middle class may exceed 50 percent of the African American population by the turn of the twenty-first century. (See Figure 2-1.)

Since 1940, the incomes of working African American men—whatever their age, education, or socioeconomic status—have risen relative to comparable incomes for working Whites. Average weekly wages for African Ameri-

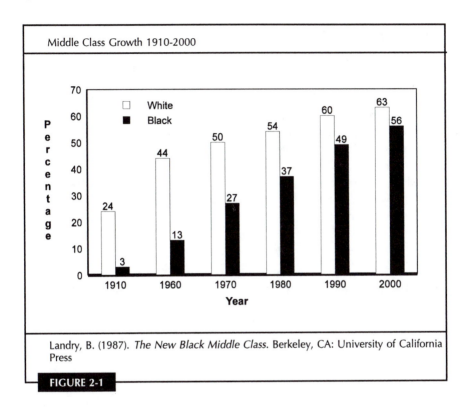

Landry, B. (1987). *The New Black Middle Class.* Berkeley, CA: University of California Press

FIGURE 2-1

can men, compared to the wages of white men, rose steadily from 42 percent to 72 percent between 1940 and 1980. A RAND/UCLA analysis attributed most of this growth to improvements in education programs and educational attainment for young African American men.

The successes are not just statistical artifacts. They are real in human terms as well: Nearly half of all African Americans (44 percent) own their homes according to the Bureau of the Census. One and a half million African Americans work as managers, business executives, and professionals; the number of African American elected officials increased sixfold in the last 20 years, to a total of nearly 7,000, including over 300 Black mayors.

Hispanic Progress. The Bureau of the Census reports that 18 million Hispanics lived in the United States in 1986. Nearly two-thirds were of Mexican origin; the next largest group, Puerto Ricans, made up 13 percent of the Hispanic population.

Data on the progress of Hispanics are not nearly as complete nor as encouraging. The deficiencies in the data are perhaps best illustrated by the fact that it was not until 1970 that the Bureau of the Census began to identify Spanish-speaking peoples as a distinct ethnic group in the United States. The discouragement can be seen in the fact that the proportion of Hispanic families enjoying incomes of $35,000 or higher (in constant 1987 dollars) grew only from one-fifth in 1972 to one-quarter in 1987. Indeed, between 1979 and 1983, progress in Hispanic income moved in reverse.

Nevertheless, there is clearly a core of reasonably well-established Hispanic households in the United States: About one in five Hispanic families always earns $35,000 or more annually, a proportion rising quickly to one in four when the economy is growing; Hispanic elected officials reached a new record of over 3,700 elected officials in 1989; and 40 percent of Hispanics live in their own homes.

At the Margin

There is a second reality. Despite progress, many working minority individuals and families are struggling. They live in poverty or close to its edge, yet opportunity and advancement remain within sight. They are the working poor—too undereducated and underskilled for the modern workforce—and the marginally employed, subsisting on minimum wage jobs and drifting in and out of work. The unskilled African American working class is thought to have represented 25 percent of all African American workers in the 1980s, compared to 17 percent of all White workers. About 23 percent of all Hispanic families in the United States have incomes below $10,000, about twice the rate for all races.

Life for poorly skilled working people whatever their ethnic group can be very difficult. But it is an especially harsh taskmaster for poorly skilled African Americans and Hispanics. These citizens are the forgotten victims of economic upheaval in the United States. They are vulnerable to every change in the economic landscape: automation and foreign competition, changes in immigration policy, or plant relocation.

The education and employment status of young minority adults who are members of the working poor is cause for particular concern. Hispanic unemployment is about 20 percent higher than that of Whites; African American males are twice as likely to be unemployed as Whites. At the same time, analyses of the educational attainment of 17 year olds indicate that the average proficiency of African American and Hispanic students approximates the attainment of White 13 year olds.

These findings have ominous implications in light of the changes in the workplace that we can already predict with some confidence. Low-skill jobs are expected to decline throughout the 1990s, and jobs requiring much higher levels of skill and education are expected to increase. Indeed, as any number of analyses from government agencies and think tanks illustrate, the process of replacing the low-skill jobs associated with manual labor with more high-skill employment, requiring technical proficiency, is already well underway in the United States.

The Underclass

But a third reality needs to be taken up. In disentangling the complex reality of minority life in the United States, particular attention needs to be paid to what has been called "the underclass" because the persistence of severe minority poverty remains this society's most disturbing domestic challenge.[*]

Some heroic individuals are able to escape this reality. But for most, no amount of personal effort makes much difference. These individuals are overwhelmingly young, and they are fighting for their lives. The enemy is not a foreign foe, but the legions of despair: poverty, racial discrimination, illiteracy, family breakdown, unemployment, welfare dependency, crime, drug abuse, and teenage pregnancy.

The underclass is largely, but not exclusively, an urban phenomenon. The core of the problem, however, is found in about 30 cities, each with a population of 100,000 or more. These cities are as diverse as New York, Los Angeles, Cincinnati, and Charlotte. A member of the underclass is likely to be in the second to fourth generation of poverty, to be functionally illiterate and an early school dropout, and to have been raised in a household headed by a woman. He or she is likely to have been born out of wedlock, to be unemployed, and to be unemployable.

Today the crisis for inner-city African American and Hispanic youth is acute. Born into settings of formidable disadvantage, the majority of them are coming of age at a time when urban poverty has acquired an even more desperate hopelessness: An entire class has developed for which even the most basic levels of self-support and economic mobility may be passing beyond reach.

The institution that could serve as a base for renewal—the two-parent family—is in trouble in the inner city. The African American two-parent family in urban America virtually disintegrated between 1940 and 1980. In that time, the percentage of African American families headed by women more than doubled, so that by 1984, 43 percent of all African American

---

[*] The term "underclass" has entered common usage as a description of the problems of the inner-city poor. Many object to the term as derogatory, conjuring up an image of new untouchables requiring little attention from the larger society. Although sympathetic to these concerns, the forum uses the term because it has entered the popular vocabulary and captures so precisely the alienation of a group divorced from the mainstream of American life.

families were headed by women and 52 percent of African American children under the age of 18 were being raised by a single parent. In the inner city, these proportions are much higher.

These figures are of more than sociological interest. As the National Research Council noted in a major 1989 study of the status of African Americans, "It is no exaggeration to say that the two most numerically important components of the Black class structure have become a lower class dominated by female-headed families and a middle class largely composed of two-parent families." Fifteen percent of African Americans from *intact* families were poor in 1980, according to the Bureau of the Census. But 30 percent of African Americans in *all* families were poor, representing the overpowering weight of the large number of single-parent households.

Young African American Men.   No element of minority life is more significant, more puzzling, or more in need of attention than what has happened to young men in the inner city. They are in danger of becoming marginal citizens in their own communities. Young African American males are less likely than their sisters to graduate from high school, to hold school office, or to enroll in college. They are much less likely to hold a job, and if they do find one, it pays less and is unlikely to provide enough income to support a family.

Different Lenses

The data in this analysis make a strong case for looking at different elements of the minority population through different lenses. These groups face different futures. For those making it, the future is promising, but not assured. For those at the margins, there is every reason to believe the future also holds promise if society applies imagination and resources to the transition through which they are living. But for the truly disadvantaged, the nation must understand that the solutions that will, in fact, help those at the margin offer little hope for the underclass. The concentration of poverty that is the defining characteristic of this third reality, its youth, and the collapse of the family in one generation are unprecedented in their scope and speed. The response must be unprecedented as well.

COMMON ELEMENTS

Cutting across these three realities are a number of common elements that affect minorities, no matter how successful, in distinctive ways.

Racism

There can be no doubt that in the traditions of the United States racism has left a broad, deep, and corrosive stain on the American body politic. Americans living today can recall a time when mob violence, beatings, even the lynching of African American citizens were thought unexceptional, if regrettable, aspects of American life. Unfortunately, that history has not entirely ended. As the 1980s drew to a close, racial attacks in northern cities and even on prestigious campuses were reported.

When African Americans raise the specter of racism, therefore, they stand on very solid ground. That specter reflects a genuine reality in the life of the nation that plays itself out in business, in higher education, in athletics, in entertainment, and in civil liberties. Racism persists as a major barrier to minority advancement.

Poor Educational Attainment

Virtually every analysis documents the high correlation between educational attainment and moving into the economic mainstream. Yet, nearly 28 percent of Hispanic youth and over 15 percent of African American youth between the ages of 16 and 24 reported in 1985 that they had dropped out of high school.

Secondary Schools. It is encouraging that the percentage of minority students completing high school has increased significantly since 1976. But, detailed analyses show that the high school preparation of urban minority youngsters remains disappointing. One consequence is that the academic achievement of minority 17 year olds who persist in school lags, on average, far behind that of their majority peers.

Higher Education. In 1960, only about 100,000 African American students were enrolled in college. In each year of the 1980s, the number of African American students enrolled in college has exceeded one million.

But progress has stalled. The enrollment gains of the 1960s and 1970s were lost in the 1980s at the very time that the lifetime value of a college degree was skyrocketing. The most troubling sign is the 10-year decline in the proportion of minority high school graduates continuing their education. Since 1980 White participation has increased while the participation of minorities continued to decline. Today, African American participation rates do not match the levels of 1975.

Moreover, minority students are disproportionately enrolled in traditionally minority institutions or in community colleges. About one-quarter of African American enrollment is found in approximately 100 historically

Black colleges and universities, and almost 47 percent of the minorities enrolled in college in the 1980s were enrolled in community colleges, compared to about 36 percent of Whites.

As disappointing as these findings are, they represent positively benign news compared to the situation in graduate schools and on college and university faculties. Minority participation in graduate education is disastrously low. American universities award more doctorates to foreign students than to minority Americans. According to a 1993 report from the National Research Council, Hispanics earned only 2.9 percent of all doctorates awarded by U.S. universities in 1991; the corresponding figure for African Americans was 3.8 percent, a decline from 4.2 percent in 1976. African Americans in 1991 received, in all fields, only 1,082 doctorates, with more than 60 percent of the degrees awarded in the social sciences and education. A sampling by significant fields indicates how few African Americans are receiving graduate training at the most advanced level: African Americans in 1991 earned only 55 doctorates in engineering, 22 in business administration, 22 in chemistry, 11 in mathematics, 9 in physics and astronomy, and 8 in computer science. The figures for Hispanics, 657 doctorates earned overall, are equally distressing.

The Stranglehold of the Inner City

African Americans and Hispanics in the United States are, overwhelmingly, urban people. In 1980, long before the recent surge of Mexican immigration to California and Texas, two-thirds of all these immigrants lived in five states; over half were concentrated in five metropolitan areas. African Americans are even more heavily concentrated in our cities. About 85 percent of African Americans live in metropolitan areas. Seventeen cities had African American populations of 50 percent or more, and in 28 cities, the African American population exceeded 100,000.

It is hard to remember, but American cities were once the economic launching pad of the ethnic poor. But, beginning in the 1960s, according to Nicholas Lehman in a provocative set of articles in The Atlantic in 1986, middle-class African Americans began leaving the cities in droves. Taking advantage of new guarantees of civil rights, the abolition of discriminatory housing covenants, and expanded access to jobs and higher education, African Americans with aspirations for a better life—as lawyers, doctors, professors, teachers, and business owners—headed for the suburbs. Wage earners were often not far behind.

Bereft of the cohesion, leadership, and strength provided by these African American families, poorer and more marginal inner-city residents began to succumb to the pressures of modern urban life.

Gene I. Maeroff of the Carnegie Foundation for the Advancement of Teaching warns of a nation heading toward "American-style apartheid" with a growing underclass "not remotely connected to the rest of society, utterly unprepared to participate in any meaningful way." He speaks of a new generation growing up in American cities in which prison, drug addiction, weapons, and teenage pregnancy are the "new rites of passage" for youth.

Participation in the Nation's Economic Life

The powerful appeal of the civil rights movement was essential to removing the barriers to minority rights in the political and civil world. That appeal to the nation's conscience has also had some success in opening up the possibilities of economic equity. In particular, affirmative action efforts, required by the government of corporate contractors, have opened up new possibilities for economic independence and upward mobility.

In a sense, however, the nation appears to have reached the point of diminishing returns with the strategies employed so far and further progress requires fresh approaches.

Affirmative Action. The most detailed analyses of the effects of affirmative action on employment patterns and on wages indicate phenomenal success in the public sector and mixed results in the private sector. Nevertheless, this analysis needs to be understood in the context of two other dynamics in the life of American enterprise. First, the major affirmative action effort is directed at that sector of American business experiencing employment decline. In recent years, major employers in manufacturing, high technology, and services—giants such as General Motors, IBM, Eastman-Kodak, Apple Computers, and American Airlines—have announced massive corporate restructurings, often involving the elimination of thousands of jobs.

Small firms, on the other hand, are "the great American jobs machine." Firms with fewer than 100 employees—and in particular those with 20 or fewer—are creating most of the new jobs in the United States. Affirmative action does not reach most of them.

Second, entrepreneurial development in African American and Hispanic communities—as represented by the proportion of their small business ownership and the vigor of these enterprises—lags far behind the national average.

The aspiration to business ownership—to be "one's own boss"—is deeply embedded in the American ethic. It is embedded, as well, in the hopes and dreams of minorities, but it has been almost entirely frustrated. When the Fourth Atlanta University Conference on "The Negro in Business" met in 1898, over 1,900 African American businessmen participated. They hoped to develop a new African American capitalism, grounded in thrift and enter-prise, and doing double duty as a source of minority employment and of products and services for the minority community. Two years later, Booker T. Washington founded the National Business League to promote that goal.

But thrift and individual enterprise were weak reeds on which to rely in the year 1900. They flew in the face of a perverse racism that encouraged private enterprise to pursue African American consumers for some goods, while denying them essential personal services. The nature of African American businesses, in consequence, was dictated by the nature of the discrimination endured by the African American population. African American business owners cut hair, provided meals, cleaned and pressed clothes, and buried the dead.

The opportunity for minority business ownership in the United States may be better today than at any time since the turn of the century. The racial climate has clearly changed. The economic climate favors the small business owner and the entrepreneur, adept at sensing consumer needs and adapting to changing markets. The purchasing power of a growing African American middle class—already the target of sophisticated advertising campaigns by large corporations—promises a market for African American entrepreneurs not previously available.

Failure of Convention

Conventional approaches—whether generous or hardnosed—have little meaning arrayed against the forces described above. Attempts to engineer social improvement—either through transfer payments or strategies founded in education and training—have been pitifully inadequate in concept and resources. They have failed totally to account for the degree to which the least favored have fallen victim to the past, are profoundly alienated in the present, and have little hope for the future. The deficiencies of these ap-proaches become all the more apparent as the market for unskilled and semiskilled workers shrinks, income for all families stagnates, and the truly disadvantaged find themselves at an even greater loss.

RECOMMENDATIONS

If the United States is to move forward in bringing to bear the resources that will meet the needs of minority *people*, in the face of the powerful *forces* described above, the American people must focus the power of their *institutions* on these problems. Three institutions appear particularly important:

government, higher education, and the private sector, i.e., corporate America and the small business sector.

Public Policy

Federal, state, and local governments have carried much of the burden of devising and implementing solutions to the problems of minorities. Many of those solutions have worked; many, regrettably, have failed or been over-whelmed by events. The problems of minorities in a free society are the problems of all of us; they will, of necessity, remain matters of public policy.

Several areas appear to be ripe for new thinking.

Employment.   The purchasing power of public employment and training programs need to be restored to their 1980 budget levels.

Despite the staggering impact of economic change on the unskilled, federal outlays for state and local government support of employment and training efforts were cut by 40 percent in 1980 and never recovered. If adjusted for inflation, the drop-off is even more dramatic.

Despite budget pressures, a sustained effort to supplement these programs is essential to the nation's economic future. The country has a choice: It can pay now to prevent social problems or it can pay later to pick up the pieces. (See Figure 2-2.)

In particular, full teenage employment by the year 2000 is an important goal. Teenage unemployment, combined with the labor shortages projected for unskilled and low-skilled fields, appears to present a rare case of a problem tailor-made to become a solution. Calling for "full teenage employment" by the turn of the century, is far from a utopian goal. Major labor shortages are projected nationwide from the 1990s forward—shortages that encompass both highly skilled and relatively low-skilled positions. For these latter jobs, teenagers are eminently suited, both because they are less likely to be the sole source of family support and because they usually seek neither lifetime nor even long-term employment.

Public Assistance.   The nation needs a complete reexamination and rede-sign of public assistance programs.

It seems clear that the welfare apparatus as it currently operates is failing our society and the citizens who depend on it for the bare necessities of life. Policy thinking about public welfare needs new thinking, based on different premises, to open up fresh possibilities and move the problem in a more productive direction.

"Public assistance programs" include the entire array of benefits—public housing, cash assistance, student financial assistance, Medicaid and ancillary

Paying Now Versus Paying Later	
Preventing a problem costs society—	Picking up the pieces after the problem occurs costs society—
■ $1,100 to provide a teenager with a summer job	■ $20,000 a year to incarcerate lawbreakers
■ $2,500 to provide Head Start or day care for the child of a working mother	■ $7,300 to provide AFDC, food stamps, and heating assistance for a mother of two who cannot work because of her child-care responsibilities
■ $600 to provide a year of compensatory education	■ $2,400 to have a child repeat a grade
■ $600 to provide comprehensive prenatal care for an expectant mother	■ An average of $12,000 under Medicaid for intensive postnatal care and delivery for an unemployed teenage mother
■ $68 to provide family planning services to a teenage girl	■ $3,000 under Medicaid to provide prenatal care and delivery for an unemployed teenage mother
■ $654 million to provide literacy training and vocational experience to 40,000 trainees through the Job Corps	■ $8.6 billion to provide AFDC benefits to more than 3 million AFDC families

Source: Adapted from a Children's Defense Fund Analysis

FIGURE 2-2

nutritional programs for women and infants, food stamps, job training—that require means tests of participants.

It would be difficult, starting from scratch, to conceive of a more jerry-built system than the one now in place. Current efforts operate through several layers of government and institutions, with different actors and agencies responsible for different aspects of the problem at each level. Each program carries its own eligibility requirements and remarkably complicated application procedures. Frequently, additional benefits require welfare eligibility, acting as a clear disincentive for work.

We conclude that there is something fundamentally wrong with a "system" that discourages work and education and encourages family impoverishment before providing assistance. We believe a complete rethinking of the premises on which the entire effort rests can reduce inequity, help preserve the integrity of the family, create new options for education and employment, and break open the dynamic of "welfare dependency."

Out-of-Wedlock Births. We need a nationwide effort by states and municipalities to deal with out-of-wedlock births. The crucial historical role of the family in providing minority youth with a secure and stable environment underscores the destructive impact of out-of-wedlock birthrates.

The effort should incorporate preventing teenage pregnancy, postponing second births, keeping teenagers in school, helping them stay on grade level, and ensuring that young fathers take greater responsibility for their children.

Without a massive and focused effort to create new approaches to this problem, the prospects for advancement for those near the margin or in the underclass diminish perceptibly. Out-of-wedlock infants close off and shut down educational and employment options for many young women; they also burden the strained support mechanisms for housing, health, nutrition, and public assistance. Reduction in these rates is of fundamental importance.

As difficult as this issue is, some encouraging models exist. The Children's Defense Fund and the Albuquerque, New Mexico, school district, for example, offer noteworthy examples of programs that reduce the incidence of out-of-wedlock births, and a number of health education programs emphasize the obligations and rewards of paternity.

It appears of special importance that, in cases where the father is willing to help support the child, local eligibility criteria for education, employment, and public assistance should reward, not punish, the father's decision. If the father is unwilling to meet his obligations, states should vigorously enforce 1984 and 1988 federal legislation requiring child support.

Public Education. It is time to stop pretending that the piecemeal educational strategies of the 1960s are adequate to the problems of the 1990s. They are not enough. We must pour every effort into the one strategy that has proven, time and time again, that it works to change lives: education.

If our schools are to be able to attack the problems we have identified and students are to redeem their promise, three new efforts are essential:

- Full funding of Head Start.
- Full funding of Chapter 1 of the Elementary and Secondary Education Act.
- A special effort to direct funds to school districts with large proportions of low-income youngsters for remedial programs at the secondary school level.

Higher Education. Providing students with information about financial assistance for college in the 12th grade is to provide it at the 12th hour. It is patently inadequate for minority youngsters who may start thinking about dropping out of school in grade 7, 8, or earlier.

The "I Have a Dream" concept of New York philanthropist Eugene Lang is promising. This approach, operating in some 20 cities with over 100 sponsors, guarantees tuition costs for minority low-income youngsters in selected 6th grade classes. The great drawback of this approach is its arbitrariness: Youngsters in distress should not have to depend on the serendipity of private benefactors.

There is no reason why federal and state student aid efforts could not adopt the same strategy, to the great benefit of raising the sights of needy youngsters. Using free lunch counts, needy families can readily be identified by local school districts and informed of the amounts and kind of aid their children can expect to receive when they graduate from high school.

Finally, financial aid for low-income minority students should rely more heavily initially on grants, as opposed to loans. Students from many poor families, concerned about large loan burdens, and anxious—like all students—about their ability to survive in college, never consider college attendance as a serious possibility. But with two successful years behind them, and the newly realistic prospect of graduation and employment ahead of them, loans lose much of their intimidation.

The grants for which they are eligible over the course of four years should be applied to the first two, and the loans for which they are eligible applied later.

Colleges And Universities

The policy recommendations above—particularly those regarding elementary and secondary education and student assistance—can 1) help raise minority graduation rates from secondary school, and 2) halt the erosion in undergraduate participation rates of minority students.

That is the essential base that must be secured. But it is just the beginning. Our society must aim at nothing less than bringing the minority undergraduate population up to the level of the minority youth presence in the general population.

At a minimum, colleges and universities must continue what they are now doing but do more of it and do it better. In addition, new strategies can boost the proportion of minorities at the undergraduate and graduate levels and increase minority representation on the faculty. These include

- Institutionally sponsored "prep year" or "transition year" programs to improve the skills of minority students suffering from deficiencies in their secondary school preparation.

- Rigorous efforts to recruit transfer students from community colleges in which many minority students are now enrolled.
- University-sponsored, community-based tutorial and mentor programs that draw on the resources of corporations, professional associations, and civic service clubs.
- Annually setting specific and reasonable goals for departmental progress in recruiting minority graduate students and faculty members.

Articulation Agreements. Articulation agreements between many community colleges and four-year institutions serve more to demonstrate institutional cooperation than they add to the ease of student transfer. As they stand, too many minority students lack the incentive or the encouragement to look beyond an associate degree to baccalaureate status. Some "2+2" transfer arrangements appear to be working reasonably well and should be duplicated across the country, by both public and private institutions, to significantly improve minority retention and graduation.

Campus Environment. Institutions of higher learning should also move swiftly to make colleges and universities more hospitable environments for minority students. Above all, they must stamp out what appears to be an emerging strain of bigotry threatening to infect some campuses. Trustees and administrators must make it clear that race-baiting and prejudice will not be tolerated and that offenders will be held to account.

The curriculum needs attention as well. The "Euro-centered" curriculum in the arts, humanities, and social sciences—as typified by requirements that all undergraduates complete such courses as "Western Civilization"—should be broadened to permit undergraduates to study and learn from the cultures of the rest of the world.

Finally, all students need the opportunity to examine race relations, racism, and its history in the United States. Consciousness of race has been such a defining characteristic of the United States that all our youth need to understand its costs to our society throughout our history.

Academic Purchasing. Each of the nation's 3,400 colleges and universities is a substantial business presence in its own area. Indeed, in some communities, universities, colleges, and community colleges are major employers. As such, universities have many opportunities in nonacademic hiring and routine purchasing to advance minority economic well-being.

It really is time for academic institutions to consider minority-owned firms in purchasing. Colleges and universities should also cooperate with the Department of Labor's local Private Industry Councils (PICs) to provide job training and placement for disadvantaged minority youth.

Corporations

Here as elsewhere, the long-range needs and interests of our nation's minority citizens are fundamentally the same as the needs of the society at large. Corporations that fail to recognize and make use of the leadership potential of African Americans and Hispanics will be increasingly at risk in a society where one-third of consumers and workers will soon be non-White, and where better than half of all new workers will be African American or Hispanic.

Corporate Employment Practices. There is a clear need not only for attention to hiring people at entry-level positions, but also for continued and expanded affirmative corporate efforts to recruit minorities for middle- and upper-management positions, as well as for positions on corporate boards.

The increasingly larger minority role in our nation's workforce must be reflected across the board in our corporations. Nowhere is there a greater potential for constructive contributions to minority progress than in the executive suites and boardrooms of the nation's private corporations.

Even in companies with outstanding records for entry-level and middle-management positions, African Americans and Hispanics are dramatically underrepresented in the ranks of top administrators and directors. To suggest willful discrimination would be too harsh. Access to positions of the highest influence is limited, by definition, for all. Moreover, corporations seeking able African American leaders face a similar obstacle to that experienced by campuses looking for African American faculty—i.e., a severely restricted pool of candidates with training and experience in high-demand fields.

What is needed are both company-specific and industrywide efforts to involve more African Americans and Hispanics meaningfully across the entire spectrum of corporate professional opportunities. In this regard, adding affirmative action criteria to annual executive performance reviews is one of the most concrete manifestations of corporate commitment to a multicultural workforce from top to bottom.

Concentrated support for affirmative action, special attention to graduates of historically black colleges and universities, examinations of the corporate workplace environment, and special attention to employees' day care needs can go a long way to building the kind of representative workforce today's corporation needs.

Community and Small Business Development. The lack of stable, viable economic institutions in inner cities has been a continuous feature of the problems in many minority communities. Rebuilding these institutions is an indispensable first step along a new, rising path, and corporations can play a significant role in the rebuilding effort by:

- creating partnerships with local banks and community development groups to bring business back to the inner city;
- depositing a small percentage of corporate assets in the banks that form the cornerstone of these ventures, for availability as mortgage and business loans; and
- investing for profit directly in the venture capital efforts of community development efforts.

Only a very small amount of the capital controlled by major corporations—a fraction of 1 percent—can exert an enormous force for good in supporting these community-based organizations. It would also be a good idea for federal and state lending agencies and private pension funds to invest a percentage of their own trust funds and loan portfolios in community development networks.

Technical Assistance and Contracting. Minority small businesses, like every small business, need assistance with developing business plans, securing capital, identifying markets, and managing cash flow. The private sector is an unparalleled and virtually untapped source of counsel for new ventures on these matters.

At the same time, "outsourcing" from corporations, routine purchasing, and contract work for industry-affiliated groups represent a major market for many small firms. Corporations and industry groups should encourage direct contracting with qualified minority suppliers and subcontracting on the part of prime contractors.

Franchising represents a similarly ignored opportunity. Franchises represent a major portion of the small firm economy and the most significant distribution network for many corporations selling office products, durable goods and equipment, clothing, fast food, and convenience items. A franchise from a large corporation represents a major investment by the entrepreneur, an attractive opportunity for building personal wealth, and a significant source of employment in local communities.

It appears that very few franchises are minority owned. Data in this area are particularly unreliable, but a 1986 survey by the Department of Commerce indicates that of more than 2,000 corporations with franchises, over 1,500 reported no minority-owned franchisees. The same survey indicates that only about 4 percent of all of the franchises in the United States are owned by Americans who are African American, Asian American, Native American, or Hispanic.

It is not too much to expect that corporations relying on franchises to distribute their products should develop a plan for increasing minority ownership, a plan including 1) targets for minority ownership, 2) intensive training of potential owners, and 3) liberalized financing and capitalization.

FROM THE MANY, ONE

As the United States embarks on its third century, diversity remains its greatest strength. Although the record of our achievement in bringing today's minorities into the mainstream is uneven, it appears clear that, for a growing number, the American dream is being realized. For those making it, people in the majority need do little more than keep the educational door of opportunity open, create a society in which minority contributions are genuinely valued, and call prejudice what it is when it rears its head.

Among those who live closer to the margin, the problems are less tractable. For these people, there is cause for greater concern. But meeting the needs of this group still lies well within the realm of this society's competence, and just as importantly, its confidence.

The growing phenomenon of the underclass remains a genuine threat to our diversity and our unity: Americans face the possibility that the chasm of alienation with one group may be unbridgeable. This truly devastating possibility comes powerfully home among the young in our inner cities. The combined forces of poverty, racial isolation, and the host of other problems assaulting inner-city neighborhoods *may* be too strong to overcome.

But the United States must *choose* not to believe that. This society cannot afford to entertain the consequences of hopelessness. This nation cannot turn its back on the underclass and hope to remain itself. Unless we work to rebuild the part of America that daily becomes more of an island in our midst—and to reclaim the lives of those who live there—*e pluribus unum* will stand not as a vision of whom we might be, but as a reminder of how far short we have fallen from what we had hoped to become.

REFERENCES

Birch, D. 1981. Who creates jobs? *The Public Interest* (Fall).

Commission on Minority Participation in American Life. May 1988. *One-third of a nation*. Washington, DC: American Council on Education.

Cottingham, C. 1989. Gender shifts in Black communities. *Dissent* (Fall).

Edelman, M.W. 1987. *Families in peril*. Cambridge, MA.: Harvard University Press.

Ford Foundation Project on Social Welfare and the American Future. May 1989. *The common good: Social welfare and the American future*. New York: Ford Foundation.

Hill, P.T. 1988. The demographic future for business and education. Paper presented to the Task Force on Human Capital, Business-Higher Education Forum, February.

Hilts, P.J. 1989. Growing gap in life expectancies in Black and Whites is emerging. *New York Times.* October 9.

The Thomas Rivera Center. 1989. *Hispanic Texas: A sourcebook for policymaking.* Claremont, CA.

Jaynes, G.D., and R.M. Williams, Jr., eds. 1989. *A common destiny: Blacks and American society.* Washington, DC: National Academy Press.

Kostecka, A. 1989. *Franchising in the economy, 1986–1988.* Washington, DC: Government Printing Office.

Landry, B. 1987. *The new Black middle class.* Berkeley, CA: University of California Press.

Lehman, N. 1986. Origins of the under class. *Atlantic,* July/August.

Matusow, B. 1989. Alone together. *Washingtonian,* November.

McCarthy, K.F., and R. Burciaga Valdez. 1986. *Current and future effects of Mexican immigration in California.* Santa Monica, CA: The RAND Corporation.

The middle class. 1988. *Business Week,* March 14.

Mooney, C.J. 1989. Affirmative-action goals, coupled with tiny number of minority, Ph.D.'s set off faculty recruiting frenzy. *The Chronicle of Higher Education* (August).

Morin, R., and D. Balz. 1989. Shifting racial climate. *Washington Post.* October 25.

Morris, M.D., director of research, Joint Center for Political Studies. 1989. Interview. *Washington Post.* November 29.

National Research Council. 1993. *Summary report 1991: Doctorate recipients from United States universities.* Washington, DC: National Academy Press.

National Research Council. 1986. *Doctorate recipients from U.S. universities: Survey reports, 1986.* Washington, DC.

National Center on Education and the Economy. 1989. *To secure our future: The federal role in education.* Rochester, NY: National Center on Education and the Economy.

Rauch, J. 1989. Kids as capital. *Atlantic,* August.

Sawhill, I.V. 1989. The underclass: An overview. *The Public Interest* no. 96 (Summer).

Smith, J.P., and F.R. Welch. February 1986. *Closing the gap: Forty years of economic progress for Blacks.* Santa Monica, CA: The RAND Corporation.

Smith, J.P., and M.P. Ward. 1984. *Women's wages and work in the twentieth century.* Santa Monica, CA: The RAND Corporation.

U.S. Bureau of the Census. 1989. *Projections of the population of the United States by age, sex, and race: 1988–2080.* Washington, DC: U.S. Government Printing Office.

U.S. Bureau of the Census. 1988. *Statistical abstract of the United States, 1989.* 108th ed. Washington, DC: U.S. Government Printing Office.

U.S. Bureau of the Census. 1986. *We, the Black Americans.* Washington, DC: Department of Commerce.

Wilson, W.J. 1987. *The truly disadvantaged: The inner city, the underclass, and public policy.* Chicago: University of Chicago Press.

Zinsmeister, K. Black demographics. *Public Opinion* January/February.

CHAPTER

Educational Equity and the Problem of Assessment

Alexander W. Astin

Among proponents of "equal access" and "expanding opportunities" in higher education, there are few issues that generate as much heat as testing and assessment. The basis for much of the resistance to the use of assessment in higher education is easy to understand, given the following facts: 1) African Americans, Hispanics, and poor students are substantially underrepresented in American higher education, especially in the more select or elite institutions; 2) American higher education institutions rely heavily on two measures—the high school grade point average and scores on standardized college admission tests—to select their students; and 3) African Americans, Hispanics, and poor students tend to receive lower high school GPAs and lower test scores than other groups. Clearly, the continuing reliance on such measures by college and university admission offices will make it very difficult for any educationally disadvantaged or underrepresented group to attain equal or proportionate access to higher education opportunities.

The use of grades and test scores for admission to higher education has serious equity implications beyond the competitive disadvantage that it creates for certain groups in the college admissions process. Since the lower schools tend to imitate higher education in their choice and use of assessment

Adapted from chapter 10 in *Assessment for Excellence: The Philosophy and Practice of Assessment and Evaluation in Higher Education.* (Oryx, forthcoming).

technology, there is a heavy reliance on school grades and standardized tests all the way down to the primary schools. Given the normative nature of such measures—students are basically being compared with each other—students who perform below "the norm" are receiving powerful negative messages about their performance and capabilities. At best, they are being told that they are not working hard enough; at worst, they are being told that they lack the capacity to succeed in academic work. A young person who regularly receives such messages year after year is not likely to come to view academic work in a positive way and is not likely to aspire to higher education. Why continue the punishment? In other words, it seems reasonable to assume that the use of normative measures such as school grades and standardized test scores causes many students to opt out of education altogether, long before they reach an age where they might consider applying to college.

Even among students who will finish school and apply to college, the school's reliance on school grades and standardized test scores has a major impact on *where* any student chooses to send applications (Astin, Christian and Henson, 1975). A great deal of college and university "selectivity" is, in fact, *self*-selection. Very few students with mediocre grades or test scores apply to highly selective institutions. While some high-scoring students do apply to nonselective institutions, most of them apply instead to the more selective institutions. As a matter of fact, the self-selection by student applicants is so extreme that most of the highly selective institutions could admit students at random from their applicant pools and end up with an entering class that differs only very slightly, in terms of high school grades and test scores, from those admitted through the usual applicant screening process (Astin, 1971).

In short, colleges' and universities' continuing reliance on high school grades and test scores in the admissions process poses a serious obstacle to the attainment of greater educational equity for disadvantaged groups, not only because of the handicap that it poses in the admissions process, but also because of the profound effects that it has on students' decision making at the precollegiate level.

"EXCELLENCE" AND EQUITY

In earlier writings (Astin, 1982, 1985), I have argued that the principal driving force behind the use of grades and test scores in the admissions process is adherence to the resources and reputational views of excellence. "Excellence" in American higher education has traditionally been equated either with an institution's academic reputation or with its resources as measured by money, faculty, research productivity, or highly able students. Students with high grades or high scores on standardized college admissions tests are seen as a valuable "resource" (and, by implication, lower-scoring students as a liability), and having a select (high-scoring) student body enhances an institution's reputation because it is regarded as a sign of "excellence." The educational folklore that has evolved out of this process consists primarily of a hierarchy or pecking order of institutions with the most selective ("highest quality") institutions at the top and the least selective ("lowest quality") ones at the bottom. That students, parents, teachers, and counselors are well aware of this folklore is reflected in the considerable amount of self-selection that takes place among high school students before they ever apply to college.

For several years now I have been arguing that the resources and reputational views should be replaced by a "talent development" conception, whereby an institution's excellence is judged in terms of how effectively it is able to educate the students who enroll. Under a talent development view, an "excellent" institution is one that is able to develop its students' talents to the fullest extent.

Some observers have likened the American institutional hierarchy to a kind of de facto tracking system. Indeed, defenders of public systems of higher education such as California's, where institutions are segregated on the basis of selectivity as a matter of public policy, would have us believe that there is some kind of *educational* (e.g., talent development) rationale involved: a special type of college for each student based on the level of that student's preparation. But the fact is that California's and every other state's educational hierarchy differs in important respects from a true tracking system. For example, institutions at *every* level of the hierarchy seek the best-prepared students they can find, and many institutions use their own scholarship resources to lure such students. In a true tracking system, the best-prepared students would be admitted *only* to the top track, the middle students only to the middle track, and the weakest students only to the bottom track. In California and most other states, however, the best-prepared students are allowed to enter *any* public institution, while the middle-scoring students are allowed to enter all except the most selective universities. Only the poorest-prepared student is limited to a single choice of institutional type.

Despite its hierarchical nature and its strong inclination to favor the best-prepared students, American higher education has made substantial efforts to mitigate the handicaps posed by selective admissions and reliance on norm-referenced tests and grades. First we have "special" admissions or "affirmative action" admissions, wherein an institution accepts African American or Hispanic applicants whose grades and test scores fall below the minimum levels required to admit other students. Practically all selective institutions practice some form of special admissions, and many invest substantial resources in actively recruiting minority students. Beyond this, most institutions have some form of remedial or "developmental" educational programs for specially admitted students, which provide special tutoring and counseling to help students raise their performance levels to those of regularly admitted students. Nevertheless, judging from the continuing underrepresentation of African Americans and Hispanics at both the admissions and graduation levels (Astin, 1982), these special admissions and educational programs have not been able to achieve anything approaching proportional representation of Hispanics and African Americans among college students and college graduates.

OPPORTUNITY FOR WHAT?

One of the problems that one frequently encounters in discussions of "equal access" and " equal opportunity" is a great deal of fuzziness about the meaning of the term "opportunity." Opportunity for what? Opportunity to do what?

Perhaps the best way to approach this issue is from the student's perspective. What sorts of benefits can a student derive by attending a postsecondary institution? I see three major types of benefits (Astin, 1985): *educational* benefits, *fringe* benefits, and *existential* benefits. Educational benefits have to do with the changes in the student—in intellectual capacity and skills, values, attitudes, interests, mental health, and so forth—that can be attributed to the college experience. Educational benefits, of course, relate directly to the talent development model: to what extent are students able to develop their talents as a result of being exposed to particular educational programs?

From the student's perspective, the "fringe benefits" of college include those postcollege outcomes that are related to the institutional credential that the student receives, rather than the student's personal attributes. This situation has been called the "sheepskin effect" by some educators. Having a degree from a particular institution can confer certain social and occupational advantages that have nothing necessarily to do with the graduate's personal characteristics or qualifications.

The last category of benefit, "existential benefits," refers to the quality of the undergraduate experience itself, independent of any talent development (educational benefits) or sheepskin effect (fringe benefits). Existential benefits have to do with the student's subjective satisfaction derived from the learning process, peer contacts, interactions with faculty, extracurricular and academic experiences, recreational activities, and so on. Such experiences may, of course, lead to educational benefits, but the existential aspects of attending college are important in and of themselves.

DEFINING "EQUITY"

Some policy makers prefer to define educational equity in terms of the access concept. These observers would be content to believe that educational equity will be attained when *overall* enrollments in postsecondary education reach proportionate or near-proportionate representation for ethnic minorities, poor students, and other underrepresented groups. Indeed, measured by this standard, the United States, of all the countries in the world, has achieved the greatest degree of equity. If "opportunities" in American higher education were indeed equal, such a gross measure of equity might be acceptable. However, given the great disparities in educational resources and reputations that are associated with the institutional hierarchy, any definition of "equity" or "equality of access" must also take into consideration the quality of the opportunity offered. In other words, guaranteeing that opportunities are available for all does not ensure equity unless the opportunities themselves are comparable.

To provide some rough indication as to the great discrepancies among institutions in the United States, let us consider two extreme groups of institutions: the most selective (those whose entering freshmen average 1,300 or above on the SAT) and the least selective (those whose entering freshmen average below 775 on the SAT). Computed on a per student basis, for every dollar invested in "educational and general" expenditures in the least selective institution, the most selective institutions invest *three* dollars. The most selective institutions pay their faculty 60 percent more than do the least selective institutions (Astin, 1985). And more than 90 percent of the freshmen entering the most selective institutions live in residential facilities, compared to fewer than half the students entering the least selective institutions. Furthermore, there is considerable evidence (e.g., Henson, 1980) that graduates of selective institutions enjoy a great many fringe benefits not available to students at the least selective institutions. Among the several such benefits would be access to the best job opportunities and to the top graduate and professional schools, and increased lifetime earnings (Solmon, 1975). Finally, there are certain educational benefits to consider: longitudinal research suggests that a student starting out at a selective institution has a much better chance of completing a degree program than a *comparable* student (in terms of academic preparation and family background) who starts at a nonselective institution (Dey and Astin, 1989).

After thinking, researching, and writing about these issues for 20 years, it has become clear to me that the issue of "equity versus excellence" is really more a matter of *how we define excellence*. If we accept the reputational or resource approach to excellence, there is clearly a conflict with the goal of equity: there are only so many resources to go around and there are only so many institutions with great reputations, so if we allocate more resources to the educationally unprepared or admit more of these students to the prestigious institutions, we end up spending less on the best-prepared students and admitting fewer of them to prestigious institutions. In other words, under the reputational and resource approaches, we are playing a zero-sum game when it comes to excellence: there is only so much of it to go around and if we want to distribute more of it in the direction of the underprepared students we must dilute the "excellence" of education provided to the best-prepared students. In short, when it comes to affirmative action and the expansion of educational opportunities to disadvantaged students, it is the reputational and resource views, more than anything else, that pose the greatest obstacles.

The conflict has still other dimensions. From the perspective of an individual institution, admitting more underprepared students forces us to admit fewer of the best-prepared students, thereby diluting the "quality" of our institution ("quality" in this context being defined in terms of the level of preparation of the students who attend). Conversely, if we decide to become more "excellent" by raising our admission standards, we must necessarily deprive more of the less-prepared students of a place in our institution. Clearly, under this definition of excellence there is an inherent conflict between excellence and equity.

This zero-sum game also serves to foster a great deal of wasteful competition among institutions. If my institution succeeds in becoming more "excellent" by recruiting away some of your faculty stars or National Merit scholars, then your excellence is proportionally reduced. And the resources invested in this competition are lost from the system with no gain in overall "excellence."

A talent development approach to excellence creates a very different scenario. From this perspective, our excellence depends less on who we admit and more on what we *do* for the students once they are admitted. In other words, our excellence is measured in terms of how effectively we *develop* the educational talents of our students, rather than in terms of the mere level of developed talent they exhibit when they enter. While it is possible to create a competitive pecking order of institutions using the talent development approach (e.g., which institutions' students show the greatest change, learning, and development?), there is nothing *inherently* competitive or normative about talent development. That is, if my institution manages to be highly successful in developing the talents of our students, this fact in no way constrains or limits what any other institution can do. As a matter of fact, under a talent development approach institutions can learn from each other's successes and failures in the talent development enterprise, thereby enhancing the talent development (human capital development) that occurs in the system as a whole.

My advocacy of the talent development perspective toward excellence is by no means intended to suggest that there are not powerful forces supporting the resource and reputational approaches. College administrators are heavily rewarded for acquiring resources and enhancing their institutions' reputations. Regardless of where institutions stand in the pecking order, most of them want to move up, so administrators put a very high premium on enhancement of reputation and resources. At the same time, virtually every constituency of the institution—students, faculty, administrators, trustees, alumni, members of the local community—support the institution's drive for greater resources and reputation. Being associated with a prestigious institution makes each of us feel more important; it gratifies our egos. Clearly, for those who are interested in embracing a talent development conception of excellence and enhancing and expanding educational opportunities, it is an uphill struggle.

To me the most potent conceptual tool for expanding educational opportunities and achieving a greater degree of educational equity is the talent development approach. This is especially true in the case of our public institutions, since they are presumably committed to "serving the public." Clearly, the most appropriate public service that can be performed by such institutions is education. Since the explicit charter of the public institution is thus to serve society by educating its citizens, a public institution does not exist primarily to enhance its own resources and reputation or, to put it in the vernacular, merely to become as rich and as famous as it can. Indeed, public institutions exist primarily to confer educational (and possibly fringe and existential) benefits on large segments of the population.

What is particularly interesting about these issues is that many of the contemporary spokespersons for higher education have lately been arguing the "human capital" viewpoint as a basis for greater public support and funding. America's "competitiveness," they argue, depends upon educating all of our citizens to the greatest extent possible, not only to maximize the number of high-achieving scientists, inventors, and leaders, but also to minimize the number of lower-performing people who often represent a drain on the society's resources. The "human capital" argument, in other words, applies across the entire spectrum of ability and achievement. Such a view meshes very nicely, it seems to me, with the talent development approach. In both instances, we strive to maximize educational benefits.

ASSESSMENT AND "ACADEMIC STANDARDS"

While I believe there is considerable evidence supporting the idea that the primary justification for the use of high school grades and standardized test scores in college admissions is to support the reputational and resource conceptions of excellence, many college faculty will argue that the fundamental reason for selective admissions is to establish and maintain "academic standards." But what, exactly, is meant by the term "academic standards"? I see at least two different meanings that can be extracted from this phrase. First, academic standards can be interpreted as referring to the level of performance the student must demonstrate in order to be awarded particular grades or to earn the bachelor's degree. When the term is used in this sense, the resistance to lowering admissions standards to accommodate more underprepared students is actually a concern that final (exit) performance standards will also be lowered. Those who make such an argument forget that changed admissions standards do not lead inevitably to changed performance standards, simply because performance standards can be maintained independently of admissions standards.

The lack of a necessary relationship between admissions standards and exit performance standards can perhaps best be understood with an analogy from the field of medicine. In much the same way that education seeks to develop the student's talent to a high level, the exit performance standard for all forms of medical treatment is a sound and healthy patient. If a patient is admitted to a hospital for, say, a hernia repair, the exit "standard" is basically no different than it would be for a patient who has to undergo a more difficult and complex procedure such as the removal of a tumor from the lung. In both cases, the goal is the same: a sound and healthy patient. It *is* understood, however, that more environmental resources will need to be invested in the patient with the tumor: longer and more complex surgery, more intensive surgical care, a longer stay in the hospital, and possibly postoperative treatment with radiation or chemotherapy. At the same time, it is recognized that the *probability* of "success" (reaching exit standards of soundness and health) is higher for the hernia patient, since the surgical risks are less and the prognosis better (e.g., much less chance of malignancy).

In short, if a hospital admits a patient who is more seriously ill than the typical patient at the hospital, the hospital does not automatically set lower performance standards for that patient: It is hoped that all patients will eventually get over their illnesses and be healthy, productive citizens when they leave the hospital. It is true that the extremely ill patient may require a greater investment of resources to reach the hoped-for performance standards for discharge, and it is true that the probability of reaching those standards might be somewhat less than would be the case for an average patient, but the hospital does not automatically alter its performance standards simply because the patient has a poor prognosis at entry.

This medical analogy underscores one important reality about expanding educational opportunities. If an institution or a system of institutions wants to maintain exit performance standards *and* to enroll a greater proportion of underprepared students (students who, at college entry, have lower high school GPAs and lower standardized test scores than the average student), one or more of the following changes must occur: The underprepared students must be given more *time* to reach performance standards; a greater share of institutional resources must be deployed to deal effectively with the underprepared students; or the institution's dropout and failure rates must increase. In short, lowering admissions standards does not necessarily require any alteration in performance standards at the exit point.

In higher education our thinking about performance "standards" tends to be much more simplistic. Rather than attempting to achieve common performance standards by differential treatment, we try to "maintain standards" through selective admissions. This practice is basically no different in principle from trying to achieve performance standards in a medical setting by refusing to admit the sickest patients. Indeed, in American higher education we have developed a set of elite institutions that are so selective in their inputs that high performance standards are almost guaranteed, even if the institution contributes little to the students' educational development. Moreover, these same institutions have the best facilities and the most resources. To replicate such institutions in the medical field would be almost absurd: We would have an elite group of hospitals or clinics that would have the finest and most advanced equipment and facilities and the best-qualified and highest-paid staff but that would admit only people with common colds. All other perspective patients would be excluded in order to maintain the highest possible performance standards at exit.

A second meaning of the "maintaining academic standards" argument expresses a concern for the talent development process itself. The argument goes as follows: If larger numbers of underprepared students are admitted to an institution, that institution's academic program will become less demanding and will therefore lose some of its potency in developing student talent. This argument implies that, in attempting to gear its program to greater numbers of underprepared students, the institution will slight its better-prepared students, giving them a watered-down education that will lead to less talent development among the better-prepared students. It should be emphasized that this argument revolves around a problem that all institutions face, regardless of their admissions policies: How to deal effectively with students who come to college differing significantly in their levels of academic preparation. Even the most selective institutions face this difficulty, particularly when it comes to specific academic skills such as writing ability. Indeed, here is one place where good assessment can and has been used to enhance the talent development process: Good diagnostic assessment and appropriate guidance and course placement are among the techniques most commonly used to deal with differences in academic preparation. When such diagnostic assessment and differential placement is done thoroughly and thoughtfully, there is no reason why students at all levels of performance cannot be exposed to rigorous courses that challenge them to develop their talents.

THE "PREDICTION" ARGUMENT

When challenged about their reliance on high school grades and test scores in making admissions decisions, many faculty will respond that these assessment devices "predict grades in college." Many observers have argued, correctly I think, that grades leave much to be desired when it comes to their use as a college student performance measure. But even if we accept college grades as a valid performance measure, the prediction argument does not really hold up under scrutiny. Basically, the prediction argument asserts that students with high grades and high test scores should be favored in the admissions process because they are likely to "perform well" later on in college (i.e., get good grades). What this really means is that a high-scoring student is more likely than one with lower grades and test scores to do well on measures of academic performance (college grades, honors, retention, etc.). This argument is simply another way of saying that high school performance correlates with college performance. But does the argument really have anything to say about how much or how well the different students will actually *learn*? Does it say anything about how much talent development different students will eventually show? Unfortunately, it does not.

Consider the following scenario. Let's say that we were to admit all applicants regardless of their grades and test scores. But instead of educating them we put them in a deep freeze or in a state of suspended animation for a period of four years after which we revive them and give them a set of "final exams" in order to compute their college GPAs. As you might guess, those who had the best grades and the highest test scores at the point of entry will "perform better" on these final exams than those with lower grades and test scores, even though *no learning took place!* The point to be made here is a subtle but very important one: Just because past performance correlates with or "predicts" future performance does not mean that high performers in high school will learn more or develop their talents more in college than low

performers. In other words, *traditional selective admissions does not necessarily further the talent development mission of a college or university.*
Supporters of selective admissions might respond that my argument is flawed because a student's college GPA is indeed a valid indicator of how much a student has learned in college. On a purely anecdotal level, most of us who have taught in college have had personal experiences that refute such an argument. For example, we have all had students who were so bright and so well prepared at the beginning of a course that they could do well on the final examination without exerting much effort and without really learning very much. On the other hand, most of us know of students who showed great improvements (learned a lot) but whose final exam performances were mediocre because they came to us so ill prepared. But the evidence against the argument that "grades reflect learning" is not merely anecdotal. Harris (1970), for example, has shown that students who get mediocre grades in a course can be learning as much (as measured by score improvements in standardized tests given before and after the course) as students with the highest grades.
The evidence usually cited in defense of the prediction argument consists of moderate correlations of college grades with high school grades and admissions test scores. To see why "prediction" does not necessarily reflect "learning," one needs only to understand what a correlation really shows. Let's say we have three people who have obtained scores of 4, 5, 6, respectively, on a test given in the senior year of high school. Suppose they all gained two points during their four years of college so that, by the time they reached the senior year, they scored 6, 7, 8, respectively. The "prediction" of college performance from high school performance would yield a very high correlation (+1.0 in fact), even though all three students learned the same amount in college. Let's suppose, on the other hand, that the students learned absolutely nothing in college, so that their scores remained the same over the four years. The correlation would *still* be +1.0, even though the students learned absolutely nothing! Indeed, even if the students got dumber during college, with each score declining two points to 2, 3, and 4, respectively, the correlation would *still* be +1.0! In other words, the only requirement for high school performance to correlate with college performance is that the students' positions relative to each other show some consistency over time. Nothing in the correlation tells us how much learning has occurred or even whether there has been any learning at all.

EDUCATIONAL OPPORTUNITY AND THE DEVELOPMENT OF "HUMAN CAPITAL"

While some critics have tried to argue that the talent development approach compromises and threatens "academic standards," when we look at the educational system as a whole, *there is no better way to promote "academic standards" than to maximize talent development.* To see why this is so, imagine that we have 10 people to educate and that they come to us at the point of admissions with varying levels of developed talent. To simplify the argument, let's assume further that we can classify each person's level of developed talent on a scale from 1 to 10. Level 1 would represent illiteracy and level 10 would represent the intellectual talent level required for attaining a Ph.D. degree. Let's assume further that the "minimum standards" required for the bachelor's degree is 6. If we were working, say, in a large state university, a typically diverse group of 10 college freshmen might enter our college with the following levels of talent development: 2,2,3,3,3,4,4,4,4,5.(This last student, who has a score of 5, is almost functioning at the minimal level required for graduation.) Our first job as an educational institution, then, is to help as many of these students as possible to reach level 6. In essence, a talent development approach seeks to *add* as much as possible to each student's entering level of performance. Now if we are indeed able to "maximize talent development" among these 10 students, we accomplish at least three important goals:

1. We maximize the number of students who reach minimal performance standards (level 6).
2. We maximize the "margin of safety" by which students exceed this minimal level (that is the number of 7s, 8s, 9s, and 10s).
3. We minimize the number of students with borderline skills (that is levels 2 and 3).

This last accomplishment (# 3) is especially important, since we will seldom be successful in bringing all entering students up to performance standards. So even if some of our 10 students fail to reach level 6 and drop out of college without a degree, we have still made some contribution to their intellectual functioning and have thus added to their chances of eventually becoming productive members of society. In other words, a talent development approach is the surest way not only to "maintain academic standards" but also to maximize the amount of "human capital" available to the society.

The role of assessment changes dramatically under a talent development perspective. Rather than being used to promote institutional resources and reputation, assessment is used to place students in appropriate courses of study and to determine how much talent development is actually occurring by repeated assessments over time. These latter assessment activities would serve two functions: to document the amount and type of talent development that is occurring, and to provide, in combination with environmental information on the student's education experiences, a basis for learning more about which particular kinds of educational policies and practices are likely to facilitate talent development.

TALENT DEVELOPMENT AND PROFESSIONAL COMPETENCY

While maximizing talent development is the most effective way for higher education institutions and systems of such institutions to serve their students and the larger society, there are certain circumstances under which selection and placement may have to be based on other considerations. Perhaps the most obvious situations are those where we are trying to prepare students for entry into professions requiring very high levels of intellectual or technical competence: medicine, engineering, art, music, college teaching, and so on.

The talent development philosophy suggests that any student, given sufficient motivation and sufficient time and resources, could, in theory, reach any desired level of competence. From the perspective of the profession, however, there may be several negative consequences of admitting all applicants to certain types of programs. For example, the student with eighth-grade mathematical skills who enters a bachelor's program in engineering may well get discouraged and drop out, even if the program makes significant efforts at remediation. And even if such a student could manage eventually to finish the program, the resources needed to bring that student up to minimally acceptable performance standards might be more than the program could bear. Assuming that program resources are finite, programs that accepted all comers would end up producing fewer graduates. Finally, accepting all comers would almost certainly reduce the "margin of safety" by which graduates from the average program exceeded minimal performance standards. As a result, the overall quality of professional competence and performance in the field would decline.

This discussion suggests that there may be situations in which selective admissions should be based on considerations other than to maximize talent development. While such a view may well be reasonable and valid from the narrow perspective of a single program, institution, or profession, it seems less appropriate from the broader perspective of the entire educational system or the society at large. When we view such decision problems from a larger system's perspective, we must concern ourselves with the fate of *all* candidates, winners and rejects alike.

The real problem would seem to be *placement* of people in appropriate courses and programs within the total system. If a person with eighth-grade math skills wants to study engineering at the college level, there should be a means available to help develop that person's mathematical talent to the level where it would not cause a disproportionate drain on the resources of the engineering program. Furthermore, the person should be assured that, if the math remediation is successful, there could be a place available in the engineering program. This same set of principles—appropriate placement with assurances of future opportunity—should be applied to all persons at all talent levels and to all fields of academic and professional study. An educational system designed and operated according to such principles would not only provide educational opportunities for all, but would also encourage each person to view education in its proper light: as a place to develop one's talents rather than as a place that merely screens and sorts or that limits opportunity. And, if students were permitted to avail themselves of educational opportunities as long as they continued to develop their talents, the public would also be getting maximum "bang" for its educational "buck."

In short, when we view educational decisions—selection, placement, and the like—from a larger societal perspective, the goal of maximizing talent development makes more sense than any other educational philosophy, since there is no better means by which we can maximize the "human capital" available in the society.

EQUITY FROM SYSTEMS PERSPECTIVE

This discussion suggests that our *conceptualization* of the problem of equal access and equal opportunity would take on a very different character if educators were more willing to 1) look at the issues from a *systems* perspective rather than an institutional perspective and 2) see educational institutions as analogous to hospitals, clinics, or other organizations whose primary purpose is public service.

The systems perspective is an especially important viewpoint from which to examine issues of educational opportunity. By "systems" perspective I mean the overall interests of the state and the nation as far as the education of its citizenry is concerned.

The social significance of such policies depends on a number of factors, perhaps the most important being the *absolute* levels of competence or developed talent. Assume that we identified three points—A, B, and C—on such a talent continuum, ranging from the most ot the least developed talent. If point C represents borderline literacy (which is probably the case when it comes to high school graduates who do not attend college and even to many community college students), then how the policy affects such people may have serious long-term social and economic repercussions. Since persons functioning at the C level may not be able to avail themselves of decent-paying work, they may end up on the welfare rolls or, worse, pursue a life of crime. Note that the failure of the system to develop these individuals' talents creates problems associated not only with limited vocational and job skills, but also with those interpersonal and social skills that are very often learned in school and college and which become so important to effective community living and citizenship. In fact, judging from most college catalogs, the development of character and citizenship is clearly one of the major goals of a liberal education.

Thinking about educational objectives in these terms makes it possible to develop educational policies that are relevant to an entire population of citizens rather than to the more parochial interests of individual institutions. In earlier writings (Astin, 1973, 1985), I suggested that there are at least three different social policies which can be symbolized by the continuum just discussed. A policy that primarily favors the "A" students might be termed as "elitist," since it favors primarily those whose talents are already well developed. A policy that distributes educational resources equally across all levels (A, B, and C) of the developed talent continuum might be termed as "egalitarian," whereas a policy which disproportionately invests resources in the least well-educated citizens (the "C" students) might be termed as "remedial" or "social welfare." While American higher education clearly tends toward the elitist model, it combines certain elements of both the egalitarian and the remedial model. For example, an open admissions policy is clearly egalitarian, while having special services and programs for educationally disadvantaged students might be characterized as "remedial." The elitist character of the system, of course, is to be found primarily in the hierarchical arrangements of institutions, which is supported by selective admissions and which is characterized by a pattern of allocation of resources and opportunities that is skewed toward the elite institutions *within* public and private systems.

Educators and policy makers who are concerned with educational issues at the state and federal level need to address a number of critical issues that are suggested by a systems perspective.

WHAT ARE THE SOCIAL RESPONSIBILITIES OF PUBLIC SYSTEMS?

While the institutional hierarchy within the private sector of higher education developed more or less by historical accident, the hierarchies that exist within most of our state systems have been established as a matter of public policy. These systems, in turn, are sustained by a system of selective admissions that relies heavily on the students' high school grades and scores on standardized tests. In the typical state system, there are one or more "flagship" universities that occupy the top rungs in the hierarchy. The middle rungs of most public hierarchies are occupied by the state colleges and universities (many of them former teachers colleges), and the community colleges occupy the bottom rungs. The prototype of this model is the state of California, whose master plan formally recognizes these three levels. Most other states have emulated the California model with minor variations. As with the private hierarchies, the resources and opportunities are unequally distributed within the public hierarchies, with the greatest resources and opportunities concentrated in the flagship universities and the fewest resources and opportunities at the community college level (Hayden, 1986).

While it is well known that poor students and members of educationally disadvantaged minority groups are severely underrepresented in higher education as a whole, it is often not recognized that poor and minority students are not equally distributed across different types of institutions *within* most public systems. To achieve proportional representation, large numbers of minority and poor students would have to be moved from the community colleges to the state colleges and flagship universities, and some would probably also have to be moved from the state colleges into the flagship universities. Thus, to achieve proportional representation in the flagship universities, the number of African Americans attending these institutions would have to be more than doubled, the number of Hispanics would have to be increased by more than 80 percent, and the number of Native Americans would have to be increased by more than 60 percent (Astin, 1982). Note that "proportionate" in this context refers solely to the distribution of currently enrolled students *within* these public higher education systems. Given that all three of these groups are substantially underrepresented in higher education as a whole relative to their proportions in the population, the problem of equal access to higher education is far more serious than these substantial figures suggest.

A similar result occurs when we look at how low-income students are distributed among the public institutions (Astin, 1985b). If we define "low income" as including each student whose family's income falls in the lowest 20 percent for college students nationally, the number attending flagship universities would have to be more than doubled to achieve proportional representation in these institutions.

In an earlier study of the 65 flagship universities across the country (Astin, 1982a), 56 had significant underenrollments of African Americans, 48 had significant Hispanic underenrollments, and 46 had significant underenrollments of Native Americans. Moreover, the degree of underenrollment was greatest in those states with the largest minority populations. To attain proportionate representation of the underrepresented minorities in the flagship universities in New York, Texas, California, and most of the southern states, the numbers would have to be increased by between 200 and 600 percent!

The maldistribution of minorities and low-income students becomes even more pronounced if we look only at the 24 most selective flagship universities (that is, those whose entering freshmen score above 1,100 on the SAT composite test). While these institutions enroll 4.8 percent of all college students in the United States, they enroll only the following percentages of minorities: African Americans, 2.1; Hispanics, 2.5; and Native Americans, 2.3. It might be added that Asian Americans, who are slightly underrepresented in all public universities, are actually overrepresented by nearly 100 percent in the most selective public universities (these institutions enroll 9.3 percent of all Asian Americans compared to only 4.8 percent of all students).

The flagship universities and their supporters are willing to defend this state of affairs primarily because, in one way or another, they all support the resources and reputational views of excellence. But what of the public university's broader mandate? To what extent is the pursuit of institutional self-interest through resource acquisition and reputation enhancement compatible with the public university's mission of serving the public interest? Does not the "public interest" include the education of *all* the citizens and expansion of opportunities for minority and low-income students?

While it might be argued that the flagship universities are "not equipped" to educate underprepared students, most universities have explicitly acknowledged their responsibilities in this area by introducing special admissions programs, remedial and support services for underprepared students, and the like. Programs of this type are especially generous when it comes to academic assistance for specially admitted athletes. The real issue seems to be the *numbers* of such students that these universities are willing to take in. In this connection, it should be noted that several major research universities in the Midwest have a long-standing policy of open admissions. At the same time, virtually every state has acknowledged its commitment to expanding opportunities by providing all high school graduates with access to *some* type of public institution. This analysis indicates, however, that these "opportunities" tend to be confined to the community colleges and, to a lesser extent, the state colleges.

It seems clear that the flagship university's interest in expanding educational opportunities to disadvantaged groups directly conflicts with its quest for "excellence" in reputational and resource terms. Judging from the current distribution of low-income and minority students among our public institutions in most states, it appears that the quest for excellence has been given much higher priority than the issue of equal access. As a consequence, in most states low-income and minority students do not have equal access to the best educational opportunities.

Lest the reader be tempted to conclude that proportionate representation is a utopian ideal that would never receive much public support, the recent report from the Joint Legislative Committee that reviewed California's Master Plan for higher education has specifically established proportional representation of minorities and poor students as a specific goal for California for the year 2000 (California Legislature, 1989). This remarkable document challenges the University of California and the California State University systems not only to achieve proportional representation of disadvantaged minority groups by the year 2000, but also to reduce dropout rates for these groups to the level for White students. Whether or not the state of California will be able to achieve these objectives is debatable, but the fact that both houses of the state legislature are willing to commit the state to such a radical goal is remarkable in and of itself.

Let us return briefly to consider once more the role of assessment in promoting equal opportunity. Several years ago my colleagues and I obtained national college admissions test data from the College Entrance Examination Board and the American College Testing Program, which allowed us to determine just how the representation of minority and low-income students would be affected by changing the way in which high school grades, test scores, and other assessment information is used in the college admissions process. Following are some of the major findings of that simulation study:

- Both African Americans and Hispanics are put at a competitive disadvantage when high school grades and standardized admissions test scores are used in making admissions decisions. Test scores pose a greater handicap than high school grades do, especially for African Americans.
- The handicap resulting from the use of test scores and grades becomes greater as the selection ratio increases. A simple combination of test scores and grades produces an 80 percent underrepresentation of African Americans when the selection ratio is one and four, but only a 65 percent underrepresentation when the selection ratio is one in two.
- Much of the handicap posed by the use of test scores and grades can be mitigated by the use of a "disadvantagement index" based on the income and educational level of the student's parents. This index

gives special credit for students whose parents are poor and/or relatively uneducated.

- Underrepresented minorities benefit differentially from the use of a disadvantagement index, but such an index must be given substantial weight to overcome the handicap imposed by test scores and grades.
- Given the considerable handicap posed by standardized test scores, the use of a disadvantagement index benefits minority students more if it is combined with grades alone rather than with grades and test scores.

This last finding is of particular relevance since a number of studies have shown that standardized test scores contribute little to the prediction of academic performance once the student's high school grades are taken into account.

Besides modifications in the use of different assessment devices for college admissions, there are other avenues available to public universities that may wish to enhance their enrollments of minority and low-income students. One such alternative relates to the structure of public higher education systems. The California model, with its three-tiered system, is not necessarily the only or even the best model. States such as Pennsylvania and Kentucky, for example, have developed public university systems that, in effect, combine the community college model with the research university model by means of two-year branch campuses that offer the first two undergraduate years. A student attending one of these branch campuses is admitted to the university for upper-division work without having to go through the usual application and transfer paperwork. Another version of this alternative would be for universities to "adopt" existing community colleges and to standardize the lower-division transfer curricula. Although these alternative structures may degenerate into an implicit hierarchy (through comparisons of the branch campus with the main campus, for example), they appear to represent some advance over more rigidly stratified systems.

SUMMARY

The "conflict" between equity and excellence in American higher education is caused in part by our continuing reliance on the reputational and resource conceptions of excellence. Under these views, students with good grades and high test scores are highly sought after because they are seen as an important "resource" that enhances the institution's reputation; lower-scoring students, on the other hand, are shunned as a liability that detracts from institutional "excellence."

Under a talent development view, the performance level of *entering* students is of much less importance, since the institution's "excellence" would depend primarily on how effectively the institution was able to *develop* its students' talents.

The traditional argument that lowered admissions standards necessarily erode "academic standards" is challenged, as is the argument that test scores and high school grades should be used in admissions because they "predict" college grades.

Considering that public systems of higher education, in particular, are responsible for extending equal educational opportunities to all citizens of a state, the existence of hierarchical public systems supported by selective admissions based on test scores and grades is questionable. There is reason to believe that the "flagship" universities in most states could substantially increase their enrollments of underrepresented minorities without seriously compromising "academic standards."

REFERENCES

Astin, A. W. 1971. *Predicting academic performance in college*. New York: Free Press.

————., C. E. Christian, and J. W. Henson. 1975. *The impact of students' financial aid programs on students' choice*. Los Angeles: Higher Education Research Institute.

————. 1982. *Minorities in American higher education: Recent trends, current prospects, and recommendations*. San Francisco: Jossey-Bass.

————. 1985a. *Achieving educational excellence: A critical assessment of priorities and practices in higher education*. San Francisco: Jossey-Bass.

————. 1985b. Selectivity and equity in the public research university. In *The future of state universities: Issues in teaching, research, and service*, ed. L. W. Koepplin and D. Wilson. New Brunswick, NJ: Rutgers University Press.

California Legislature. Joint Committee for Review of the Master Plan for Higher Education. 1989. *California faces—California's future: Education for citizenship in a multicultural democracy/Joint Committee for Review of the Master Plan for Higher Education*. Sacramento, CA: Joint Publications Office.

Dey, E., and A. W. Astin. 1989. *Predicting college student retention: Comparative national data from the 1982 freshman class*. Los Angeles: Higher Education Research Institute.

Harris, J. 1970. Gain scores on the CLEP general examination and an overview of research. Paper presented at the Annual Meeting of the American Educational Research Association, Minneapolis, MN.

Hayden, T. 1986. *Beyond the master plan*. Sacramento, CA: Joint Publications Office.

Henson, J. W. 1980. Institutional excellence and student achievement: A study of college quality and its impact on education and career achievement. Ph.D. diss., University of California at Los Angeles.

Solomon, L. C. 1975. The definition of college quality and its impact on earning. *Explorations in Economic Research* (Fall), 537-87.

CHAPTER

Minorities and the New Information Technologies: Barriers and Opportunities

Paul Resta

INTRODUCTION

Students in today's technology-rich higher education environments are presented with unprecedented opportunities to use and integrate the new technology tools and electronically accessed information resources into their academic studies. Students now have access to sophisticated computer pods in which they may access state-of-the-art desktop publishing, database management, spreadsheet, multimedia, statistical analysis, systems modeling, and other types of software tools. Many have access to a wide range of university computation services such as electronic mail, online library catalogs, and reference materials. Using computer-mediated communications, they are able to ask questions of their instructors, access information resources, and work on projects with fellow students. In addition, many students have access to the computer-network leviathan Internet, with its hundreds of networks, databases, user groups, bulletin boards, information services, and library catalogs across the globe. These new information technology tools and resources are providing exciting and unprecedented opportunities for higher education students to enhance the quality of their academic studies and to collaborate with and compete with their peers in these new knowledge environments.

Regrettably, many minority students are entering higher education without the skills and experience necessary to immediately and effectively use the new information technology tools and resources. This lack of skills becomes yet another barrier (in addition to the fiscal, cultural, and educational barriers) minority students must confront in competing academically. This chapter discusses:

- the rapid changes that are taking place in the use of computers and related technologies in higher education institutions;
- the potential impact of present inequities in precollege access and use of computers experienced by minority students, particularly African American, Hispanic and Native American students; and
- strategies and recommendations to enhance the technology competence of minority students in institutions of higher education and public schools.

THE ACADEMIC IMPACT OF THE NEW INFORMATION AND COMMUNICATION TECHNOLOGIES IN HIGHER EDUCATION

During the past decade, there has been an explosive growth in the use of computers and related technologies in higher education. Most faculty in universities have computers in their offices, and the number of computer facilities that are available for student use continues to expand (Neff, 1987). Campuswide communication networks, which link the campus microcomputers together, provide increased access to shared computer systems and databases available both on and off campus. These "information-rich" university environments are beginning to radically change how faculty teach and how students learn.

As noted by Weissman (1987), today's users of academic computing technology come from nearly every discipline on campus. The greatest growth has come from those academic disciplines new to computing, such as the arts, humanities, education, history, and anthropology. The university faculty is discovering that traditional learning activities such as lectures, seminars, class projects, tests, library assignments, and personal assistance can be accomplished in very different ways with the new information technologies. The electronic university library is also coming. Electronic storage of text and graphics is more economical than storage of paper. Electronic books, serials, maps, and other documents will make it possible for faculty to develop customized textbooks and students to develop more current and comprehensive research papers.

A number of private universities now require all students to have computers. These are either supplied by the university or purchased by the student. In addition, a number of academic departments (e.g., computer science, engineering, and mathematics) in other universities may require students to also have their own personal computer. Most universities presently offer substantial discounts to students and faculty to purchase computers for personal use, and in recent years, we have seen a shift in the norms for student work in higher education. Handwritten and even typewriter-prepared papers are rapidly vanishing from the face of higher education. Increasingly, students are completing their papers using word processors, spelling checkers, and grammar/syntax checkers, and printing them out on university laser printers. Students with skills in using databases, spreadsheets, graphics and multimedia presentation tools, and desktop scanners, often have an advantage in compiling, organizing, and presenting information for their classes. In addition, students who have skills in using computer-based communications are able to access information resources and expertise from local, regional, national, and international databases and networks to enhance their research projects and papers. These are only a few examples of the ways today's higher education students are benefiting from the new information technologies. Other and far more powerful and sophisticated computer tools and applications are emerging in college campuses across the country.

It is clear that students who are experienced and comfortable in using computers are able to take full advantage of these new technologies in pursuing their academic studies. On the other hand, students entering college who are unfamiliar with these tools will find it increasingly difficult to compete with their peers. Based on results of the National Assessment of Educational Progress (NAEP) and other studies, it is clear that a disproportionate percentage of minority students entering higher education today are not equipped with the skills and knowledge to use the new information and communication technologies to enrich and support their academic studies. This problem stems in part from the inequities in access to and use of computers and related technologies in their precollege preparation. Unless the present trend is reversed, these students are in danger of becoming a new class of information-disadvantaged students.

RACE/ETHNICITY AND COMPUTER COMPETENCE

The differences in computer knowledge and skills between majority and minority culture students have been most clearly shown in the national study of computer competence conducted by Educational Testing Service (ETS). As part of the National Assessment of Educational Progress, ETS surveyed the nation's third-, seventh-, and eleventh-grade students for their knowledge and skill in using a computer. The study results showed that White students had a clear advantage over African American and Hispanic students at all three grade levels. The greatest performance differences, however, were found in the higher grades (Martinez and Mead, 1988).

COMPUTER EXPERIENCE AND COMPUTER COMPETENCE

As might be expected, the survey showed that computer experience is consistently associated with computer competence across all racial/ethnic groups. That is, the minority students who had experience with computers did consistently better than those who did not. For example, Hispanic eleventh-grade students who had completed a computer course had substantially higher scores than those who had not. Similarly, Hispanic students who had access to a computer at home had a higher mean score compared to those who did not.

The study points out that there are other potential contributors to computer competence associated with access to a computer in the home, particularly socioeconomic status, that may go well beyond whether or not a family owns a computer. Edwards (1989) indicates that the average income among purchasers of home computers is $35,000. The average income of African American families is $16,786 and the average income for Hispanic families is $19,027—both well below that of home computer owners. The important point, however, is that educational-computing instruction and home access to computers is related to student computer competence in all racial/ethnic groups. The NAEP study results confirm the observations of a number of educators that White students have a definite advantage over African American and Hispanic students in computer knowledge and skill at the high school level. They carry this advantage with them as they enter the increasingly computer-intensive university environments.

INEQUITIES IN PRECOLLEGE COMPUTER EDUCATION

What are some of the factors that may contribute to the lack of computer experience competence of African American and Hispanic students observed in the NAEP and other studies? Three factors identified by researchers indicate lack of access to computers, differential use of computers, and the lack of role models.

■ *Lack of Access to Computers*
  Despite the rapid infusion of computers into our nation's schools, there still remain major concerns about whether minorities have the same access to

and use of computers as experienced by White middle-class and upper-class students. A national survey of over 2,100 schools in the U.S. suggests that major inequalities in access to and use of computers still exist across racial and economic groups (Becker, 1986). The survey indicates that African American elementary school students were about three times as likely as White students to attend a school without computers. Cole and Griffin (1987) also indicate that more computers are being placed in the hands of middle- and upper-class children than in the hands of poor and minority students. This trend may not be reversed in the near future. As noted by Edwards and others (1988; Sutton, 1991), not only do schools with low percentages of poor and minority students have more computers than schools with higher percentages of poor and minority students, but they are also acquiring them at a faster rate.

- *Differential Use of Computers*
Although access to computers is necessary, it is not a sufficient condition to assure that minority students will develop the skills and knowledge to use computers to enhance their learning and productivity. Computers may be used as "cognitive enhancers" and personal productivity tools, or they can simply be used as "electronic drill sergeants," continuing and transferring the tedious tradition of workbooks to an electronic format. At present, poor and minority students are more likely to spend computer time on rote drill and practice learning and less likely to be asked or expected to make judgments, draw inferences, or engage in critical thinking or problem solving with computers (Educational Technology Center, 1985). The 1985 national survey, conducted by the Center for the Social Organization of Schools, indicates that low socioeconomic status (SES) students spend far more time on drill and practice activities than do high SES students.

Cole and Griffin (1987) also found that computers tend to be used more for rote drill and practice with poor children and for "cognitive enrichment" activities with middle- and upper-class students. They attribute the present situation in part to the long-held educational ideology that asserts that children must first learn the basics before proceeding to higher-order problems. Stanley Pogrow, a professor at the University of Arizona, and others have demonstrated that minority and low SES students can learn higher-order thinking skills using computers. There is also emerging evidence that students engaged in higher-level computer applications can increase their proficiency in the "basic skills." For example, in one study, students working with problem-solving and simulation software showed greater gains in reading comprehension than did students taking widely used computer-assisted drill and practice reading programs (Norton and Resta, 1987).

There is growing recognition that the type of computer use is important for minority and poor students in their development of computer competence (Sutton, 1991). Although drill and practice software may be appropriate for certain educational needs, it should not prohibit minority students from using computers as writing, problem-solving, and personal productivity tools. As noted by Watt (1982), failure to do so will only exacerbate the present situation in which "affluent students are thus learning to tell the computer what to do while less affluent students are learning to do what the computer tells them." In addition, more research is needed to determine minority student interactions with computers. For example, a study by Emihovich and Miller (1988) reported that low-income African American students outperformed middle-class, White students when learning Logo Software Programming Language. More intensive research is needed to determine the most effective ways of using computers to help support the cognitive growth and learning of minorities and all students.

■ *Lack of Role Models*

An additional barrier to increasing minority student computer competence is the lack of computer-using role models for the students. The NAEP survey revealed that, both in the seventh and eleventh grades, more than 90 percent of computer coordinators were white. African American and Hispanic computer coordinators were underrepresented compared to the percentage of African American and Hispanic population. The problem of underrepresentation was particularly acute for Hispanic coordinators who composed only 1 percent of the high school computer coordinators (Martinez and Mead, 1988). These findings are consistent with those of Becker (1986), who found that White students are far more likely to have a computer-using teacher in the classroom than minority students.

As noted by Sutton (1991), computer use during the 1980s did not bring education closer to equal education opportunity but rather maintained and exaggerated existing inequities in processes of computer learning. Poor and minority students had less access to computers in school and at home and were more likely to use computers for drill and practice than were middle-class and White students. In addition, teachers, while concerned about equity, held attitudes that hindered access. They believed that better-behaved students deserved computer time and that the primary benefit of computers for low-achieving students was for the use of drill and practice. All of these problems must be addressed and overcome to enable minority students to develop the computer competencies needed to effectively use the new technology resources available in our nation's universities and colleges.

ENHANCING MINORITY ACCESS AND USE OF COMPUTERS IN PRECOLLEGE EDUCATION

To remediate the lack of computer competence of many entering minority students, institutions of higher education must act immediately. In addition, our nation's public schools must make a major effort to increase minority access and appropriate use of computers. At present, computers and other technological resources are more readily available in affluent schools across the nation. Efforts must be made to assure that computer hardware and other technological resources are equitably distributed among all schools. In addition, funds must be made available to help cover the multiple costs associated with effective utilization of computers including software, teacher training, technical assistance, and administrative support. The following are some recommendations that may help reduce the growing disparity in computer competence between entering minority and majority culture college students.

State Initiatives in Addressing Educational Computing Needs of Minority Students

States must play a major role in funding and developing plans for the equitable acquisition and distribution of computer resources. A few states have initiated efforts and plans to provide more equitable distribution of computer resources to schools. The governor of New Hampshire led a successful effort to secure state funding to provide teachers with computers for their personal use in the classroom or at home. Texas has recently completed an ambitious plan to increase the number of computers in schools in both rural and urban areas by providing a special per-pupil technology allotment fee. They have also provided funding to help restructure the teacher preparation programs with technology. Other states are also including provisions for technology resources in their educational reform packages. States also need to provide leadership in establishing standards to assure that all students, including minorities, are able to develop computer competencies and higher-order thinking skills. In addition, states need to provide support to colleges of education to increase inservice training efforts and to assure that they have the equipment, facilities, and resources to adequately prepare future teachers to use the new information technologies.

Role of the Federal Government

Leadership is also needed at the national level, and additional efforts should be made to integrate the computer education needs into appropriate existing federal programs. Chapter 1 funding, for example, has been used for the purchase of computers, but federal and state regulations often limit their use as a learning tool for disadvantaged students. In addition, Chapter 1 programs continue to emphasize the need for basic skills development in reading, language arts, and mathematics, and most frequently computers have been used for drill and practice. Within the past few years, there are some hopeful signs that this trend is beginning to change. For example, several Chapter 1 programs are now beginning to use computers as writing tools for children. Recent efforts to integrate higher-order thinking skills into the computer use of minority and poor students should be encouraged and expanded [e.g., Project Micro (Edwards, 1988), the Higher Order Thinking Skills (HOTS) program, etc.]. As will be noted later, the federal government also needs to increase the financial assistance and support for low-income minority students entering college.

HIGHER EDUCATION ROLES AND RESPONSIBILITIES

Institutions of higher education must also recognize and develop strategies to assist minority and other students who enter college with deficits in computer competence. Some strategies that may be helpful in remediating this problem include

Providing Special Programs and Summer Camps for Minority Students

Colleges and universities should work collaboratively with public schools to develop programs designed to enhance the interest, knowledge, and skills of minority students in math and science and the use of computers as a learning tool. These efforts may include:

- Sponsoring, after school sessions and Saturday academies for minority students using college science, mathematics, and microcomputer laboratory facilities, as well as college faculty and students as instructors and tutors. In addition to instruction in science, mathematics, and technology, the programs should also emphasize the writing process, using the computer as a writing tool.
- Involving college faculty and students (particularly minority members) in providing supplementary instruction and tutoring to minority students to motivate them toward higher education.

Minority faculty and students in universities can be helpful in demonstrating the uses of computers in their research and academic work. This can be done through serving as guest lecturers in classes, providing interesting demonstrations of uses of computers in their field, serving as sponsors or resource persons for school computer clubs and after school or community computer programs. Through such efforts they will serve as role models for students while enhancing student computer skills and awareness of the importance of computer-related technologies in all academic disciplines and career fields.

Increasing College Counselor Awareness of Importance of Computer Competence of Minority Students

College counselors and advisors need to become aware of the lack of computer knowledge and skills of entering minority students and should make a particular effort to inquire about the general computer experience and background of the student. As appropriate, counselors should encourage minority students to take advantage of courses, workshops, or other training opportunities available on the campus.

Providing On-Campus Computer Training and Technical Assistance to College Entry Minority Students

The institutions of higher education should assure that training opportunities are readily available on-campus for minority students both during the day and evening hours. Student microcomputer laboratories should be staffed by personnel who are able to help train and assist minority students with limited computer backgrounds. In several universities I have visited, these laboratories are often staffed by student hackers who only talk in "techno-speak" that is often incomprehensible and frightening to the naive user. Whenever possible, minority staff should be hired to serve in these positions.

Special computer application courses should be developed and offered for academic credit. Such courses should be organized around student productivity applications such as word processing, graphics, spread sheets, databases, and telecommunications. The awarding of academic credit for such courses is clearly warranted based on the importance of computer competence to students not only in completing their academic studies but also in their postbaccalaureate careers.

Providing Student-Buy and Financial Assistance Programs to Enable Minority Students to Have Access to Their Own Personal Computer

At present, very few African American and Hispanic students have access to computers in their homes compared to White students. In addition, low SES minority college students typically do not have the financial resources to acquire their own personal computers in college. As noted in the recent report, *Education That Works: An Action Plan for the Education of Minorities*, issued by the Action Council on Minority Education (McBay, 1990), the level of financial assistance provided through the Pell Grants has not kept pace with increases in the costs of attending college during the past decade. Spending on the Supplemental Educational Opportunity Grant has fallen 14.7 percent in constant dollars and spending on the College Work-Study Program has fallen 28 percent in constant dollars from 1980 to 1988.

The college loan burdens of minority students are often greater than the total annual income of their families. This situation is not only shattering the dreams of many minority students across the country but renders "unthinkable" the possibility of these students having access to their own personal computer. To remediate this problem will require efforts on the part of the federal government and higher education. The federal government should increase the level of financial assistance provided to low-income minority students. In addition, as a special incentive for the use of computers by minority students, a provision should be considered for inclusion in the present federal regulations to "forgive" the cost of the purchase of the computer if the student completes her/his program of studies.

Many colleges and universities have established "student-buy" programs that enable students to purchase computers at substantial savings. These efforts should be expanded, and universities should work cooperatively with other institutions or state education agencies to assure that they negotiate the best possible prices for computer hardware and software that may be purchased by students and faculty. In addition, universities should explore with local financial institutions the possibility of long-term loans for student purchases of computer equipment.

Providing Inservice Training for Teachers in Schools Serving Minority Students

Our nation's colleges of education must play a stronger role in helping change the current situation in which schools serving minorities have fewer computer-using teachers than those serving White children (Becker, 1986). To alleviate this problem, colleges of education must expand further their inservice training efforts to enable teachers in schools with minority children to make more effective use of their technological resources. States should facilitate such efforts by providing funding incentives to colleges of education to expand their training and technical assistance services to schools, particularly those situated in rural, isolated areas.

Colleges of education also need to review and revamp their programs to assure that all students in the preservice program will be able to effectively use the new learning tools in their classrooms. In many instances, the present teacher education curriculum may need restructuring to integrate the new information technologies into all methods and content area courses. To do an effective job, colleges of education must have state-of-the-art equipment and adequate facilities to carry out these new programmatic directions. Unfortunately, college of education needs are typically assigned a lower priority by the university central administration than needs of other colleges. Consequently, at present, many colleges do not have the needed equipment and facilities to train teachers in the use of sophisticated classroom-networked computer systems, hypermedia, interactive computer-videodisk, and multimedia computer applications. The central administration must recognize the important role to be played by the college of education and assure that it has the resources necessary to prepare teachers to competently use the exciting array of new computer-based learning tools.

Recruiting Minority Students into Teacher Training Programs

To provide needed minority technology-using role models in the schools, more effective strategies must be developed for recruiting minorities into the teaching profession and particularly in the fields of mathematics, science, and technology education. Universities need to expand their efforts to recruit minorities into the teacher training programs. They must also provide support services for minority students on campus, including counseling and tutorial assistance, to help retain these students. States can help encourage the recruitment of minority students into the teaching profession by providing financial incentives to the institutions for recruiting and retaining minority students. Colleges of education must also make greater progress in integrating technology into all content and methods courses to assure that prospective minority and majority culture teachers are well prepared to use the current and future technologies in the classroom.

Using Electronic Networks as a Means of Outreach to Minority Students and Teachers

Across the country, there is growing interest and awareness in the use of electronic networking as a means of providing information and facilitating communication between educators, school districts, state agencies, and universities. Institutions of higher education, with their extensive information processing expertise and resources, can and should play a leadership role in the development and use of educational electronic networks to

- Provide greater access to college information resources training and technical assistance to teachers, counselors, and administrators.

Through the use of computer-based electronic networks, a number of bulletin boards and databases may be developed to provide useful information to teachers and other educators. Electronic networks can also be used to help support on-site inservice training and to provide follow-up assistance to teachers. A number of networks such as the Texas Education Network (TENET) are providing an electronic means of addressing the diverse training and information needs of teachers, counselors, and administrators in schools. These networks have proven particularly helpful to teachers who often feel professionally isolated even within large urban school districts. For example, science teachers in Texas are able to share science materials with others, discuss common problems, and access other national science information resources through the Internet. They are also able to take online courses, such as those currently offered by faculty at the University of Texas.

In New Mexico, school counselors use electronic bulletin boards and databases to assist students in making college selection decisions and to track their admissions status. Information on university academic programs, schedule of classes, admissions requirements, financial assistance, and campus phone directories have proven very useful to counselors and other school staff.

Electronic networks can be specifically developed to address the educational needs of minority students. One such network, the Educational Native American Network (ENAN) (funded by the Bureau of Indian Affairs and the U.S. Office of Education), provides teachers with access to a wide range of information, technical assistance, and training resources. Through the network, teachers are able to share information on effective practices, classroom ideas, and materials, access curriculum materials and resources related to Native American education (from universities, national laboratories, museums, etc.), and take online courses. The network also supports multiple classroom site instructional projects (Resta, 1989).

- Provide supplemental instruction, tutorial assistance and information resources to minority students, particularly to those in rural areas.

Educational telecommunications can be an effective means for providing a number of information and instructional support services to minority students in rural areas. For example, the University of New Mexico and the Southwestern Indian Polytechnic Institute have developed a unique project to explore how computer-based communications can be used to enrich the learning opportunities of Native American and Hispanic students in rural, isolated schools in New Mexico and Arizona (Resta, 1991). The project provides a number of online activities and projects for students to strengthen their mathematics, science, communication, and computer skills.

An example of such an activity is our current Deep Space Probe Simulation Project. Schools on the network participate as separate earth-tracking stations. Over a period of weeks each station receives a specific flow of digital information over the network (much as they would from a real space probe satellite as it passes near a planet). The students at each school determine the quality of the data and compile, integrate, and analyze their data with that of the other tracking stations to develop an accurate picture of the planet. Network-based projects such as these help stimulate minority student interest and competence in science, mathematics, and in the use of the computer as a communications and problem-solving tool.

An example of such an activity was the Deep Space Probe Simulation Project. Schools on the network participated as separate earth tracking stations. Over a period of weeks each station received a specific flow of digital information over the network (much as they would from a real space probe satellite as it passes near a planet). The students at each school determined the quality of the data and compiled, integrated, and analyzed their data with that of the other tracking stations to develop an accurate picture of the planet. Network-based projects such as these help stimulate minority student interest and competence in science, mathematics and in the use of the computer as a communications and problem-solving tool.

In addition to such activities, students had access over the network to university faculty, national laboratory scientists, and others who served as "electronic mentors" to students, responding to questions and assisting them on science fair and other research projects. The minority students participating in this project established both "online" and personal working relationships with college faculty and students. Such contacts raised the interest and aspirations of minority students for entering college while strengthening their knowledge of science and mathematics as well as their skills in writing and the use of the computer as a tool.

These are only some of the ways institutions of higher education can help address the educational needs of minority students while building their skills in using the computer as a problem-solving and communications tool. There are many other effective strategies that may be used such as those found effective in increasing the mathematics participation and performance of Hispanic students (Resta, 1985). Through such efforts, minority students can increase their computer competence, take greater advantage of the information resources within the university, enhance their own academic productivity, and ultimately reap the full benefits of our increasingly technological society.

REFERENCES

Becker, H. J. 1986. Equity in school computer use: National data and neglected considerations. Paper presented at the 1986 Annual Meeting of the American Educational Research Association, San Francisco.

Cole, M., and Griffin, P. 1987. *Contextual factors in education; improving science and mathematics education for minorities and women.* Madison, WI: Wisconsin Center for Education Research

Educational Technology Center 1985. *Computers, equity and urban schools.* Cambridge, MA: Harvard University Press.

Edwards, C. 1988. *Enhancing minority student educational opportunities through instructional computing: a report on Project MiCRO.* Paper presented at Council of Great City Schools National Technology Forum, San Diego.

Edwards, C. April 1990. *Assessing success in analytical thinking skills: PROJECT MiCRO and schools.* Paper presented at the Annual Meeting of the American Educational Association, Boston.

Emihovich, C., and G. E. Miller. 1988. Effects of logo and CAI on African American first graders' achievement, reflectivity and self-esteem. *The Elementary School Journal* 88: 473-487.

Lapointe, A. E., and M. E. Martinez. 1988. Aims, equity and access in computer education. *Phi Delta Kappan* (September): 59-61.

Martinez, M. E., and N. A. Mead. 1988. *Computer competence: the first national assessment.* Princeton, NJ: Educational Testing Service.

McBay, S. M. 1990. *Education that works: An action plan for the education of minorities.* Cambridge, MA: Action Council on Minority Education, Massachusetts Institute of Technology.

Neff, R. K. 1987. Computing in the university: implications of the new technologies. *Perspectives in Computing* 7, no.2: 14-22.

Norton, P., and V. Resta. 1986. Investigating the impact of computer instruction on elementary students' reading. *Educational Technology* 26, no.3 (March): 35-41.

Resta, P. E. 1985. Strengthening math education for Hispanics: New community college, public school and private sector partnerships . El Centro, CA: Border College Consortium. (Ford Foundation Report)

Resta, P. E. 1986. Equity of school access and use of computer technology by Hispanic students. Paper presented at Technology and the Education of Hispanics: The Promise and the Dilemma Conference held at The Tomas Rivera Center, Claremont Graduate School, June 20-21, Claremont, CA.

Resta, P. E., and B. Kurshan. 1988. Educational telecommunications: The good, bad and the ugly. Paper presented at the First International Conference on Telecommunications in Education: Learners and the Global Village, August, Jerusalem, Israel.

Resta, P. E. 1991. *1990-1991 Annual report: University of New Mexico Upward Bound Project.* Albuquerque, NM: Center for Technology and Education, The University of New Mexico.

Sutton, R. E. 1991. Equity and computers in schools: A decade of research. *Review of Educational Research 61, no.4*: 475-503.

Watt, D. 1982. Education for citizenship in a computer-based society. In *Computer literacy* edited by R. Seidel, R. Anderson, and B. Hunter, 59. New York: Academic Press, 1982.

Weissman, R. F. 1987. The two cultures of academic computing. *Perspectives in Computing* 7, no.2: 4-12.

CHAPTER 5

Financial Aid Strategies for Improving Minority Student Participation in Higher Education

Arthur Hauptman and Patricia Smith

In recent years, growing concerns have been expressed about the disturbing lack of progress in increasing minority student participation in higher education. These expressions of concern have led quite naturally to suggestions that student aid and related programs should be employed to help increase minority participation. But there are a number of different ways in which the federal, state, and institutional student aid programs could be altered to achieve this goal. Some changes would be much more beneficial in raising minority student participation rates than others. It is also the case that certain changes in the student aid programs could have a detrimental effect on the participation rates of certain groups of students.

In this chapter, we look at both the existing data on minority student participation and the financing strategies that might be used to increase minority participation. We begin by examining statistics that have led to the concerns about current patterns of minority participation in higher education. We believe that these statistics can be very useful in pointing to the relative efficacy of various financial aid strategies. Most of the remainder of the chapter describes and assesses the prospects for success of the various strategies that might be employed for addressing concerns about minority student participation. These strategies include developing programs for minority students only; maintaining low tuitions in public institutions; redressing the loan/grant imbalance through expansion of student grants; expanding participation through earlier awareness and notification of students of their aid eligibility; improving student retention and completion of degrees through the greater use of student support services programs and other efforts; and neutralizing the negative effects of borrowing through expanded loan repayment options for low-income borrowers. The chapter concludes with a consideration of how an increase of $1 billion in funding might be most effectively used to address the issue of minority participation.

THE STATISTICS ON MINORITY STUDENT PARTICIPATION

Concerns about minority student participation in higher education emerge from a variety of statistics which suggest that, despite the continued growth of minorities as a proportion of the overall population, their particiption in higher education has not similarly increased. The lack of increase in minorities in higher education can be seen in data relating to a number of aspects of the educational process, including high school graduation rates, overall enrollment numbers, college participation rates for various groups of students, the kinds of institutions in which minority and majority students enroll, and the rate of retention and the completion of degrees.

High School Graduation Rates

An obvious place to start an examination of college participation is the rate at which students of traditional college age—18 to 24 year olds—complete high school or receive an equivalent degree. This rate helps to define the size of the basic pool of college applicants. The high school graduation rate for 18- to 24-year-old White students has been over 80 percent since the early 1970s, according to Census Bureau statistics collected from the Current Population Survey. But for African Americans, the high school graduation rate has gradually increased, from 67 percent in 1972 to 75 percent in 1988. The rate for Hispanics has not changed substantially; it was 52 percent in 1972, and 55 percent in 1988 (U.S. Bureau of the Census).

These trends in high school graduation rates would seem to be cause for some optimism in that the proportion of African American students graduating from high school and, therefore, ready to go on to college appears to be increasing and the gap between White and African American students seems to be closing. But nagging doubts about high school graduation rates increasing in the face of continued reports of staggering high school dropout rates in most urban areas seems to be a legitimate cause for guarded optimism regarding the Current Population Survey figures on high school graduation. It may well be the case that the Census Bureau's methodology of asking how many people in the household are high school graduates does not yield valid results.

Head Count College Enrollments

According to data collected from institutions by the National Center for Educational Statistics (NCES), African Americans had the smallest percentage increase in head-count enrollment between 1978 and 1988 for any racial/ethnic group. (See Table 5-1 for enrollment figures in 1980 and 1990.) The number of White students grew almost as slowly. By contrast, the number of Asian American students increased the most, and the number of Hispanics also grew rapidly (NCES, Trends in Racial/Ethnic Enrollment in Higher Education: Fall 1978 through Fall 1988, June 1990).

TABLE 5-1

RACIAL/ETHNIC ENROLLMENT IN HIGHER EDUCATION (NUMBERS IN MILLIONS)

	1980	1990	Percent Change
Whites	9.833	10.723	9
African Americans	1.107	12.47	13
Hispanics	.472	.783	60
Native Americans	.084	.103	23
Asian Americans	.286	.573	100
Nonresident aliens	.305	.391	28
TOTAL	**12.087**	**13.820**	**14**

Source: Digest of Educational Statistics, 1993, U.S. Department of Education.

Participation Rates

While head count enrollments are obviously a significant indicator, they do not provide a full sense of the participation issue in that they do not indicate the size of the pool of potential college students, the goals and aspirations of these students, or their success at achieving these goals. The rate at which students of a particular age group participate in higher education can be used to examine some of these broader issues. Such a rate may be shown in a number of ways, and several measures of participation are discussed here in an attempt to provide a variety of perspectives on this important issue.

Current Population Survey (CPS) data.   Although the number of minorities enrolled in college has increased over the past decade, the proportion of minority high school graduates who attend college did not increase from the mid-1970s to the late 1980s. Then, between 1988 and 1990, the college participation rate of African Americans increased sharply.

There are two ways of measuring participation rates using CPS data, and each shows a decline or leveling in minority student participation since a peak in the mid-1970s. One participation measure is the proportion of recent high school graduates who currently are enrolled in college, as shown in Table 5-2.

TABLE 5-2

PERCENTAGE OF 18-24 YEAR OLD HIGH SCHOOL GRADUATES CURRENTLY ENROLLED IN COLLEGE

	Whites, %	African Americans, %	Hispanics, %
1972	32.3	27.1	25.8
1976	33.0	33.5	35.8
1980	31.8	27.6	29.8
1984	33.7	27.2	29.9
1988	38.1	28.1	30.9
1990	39.4	33.0	29.0

Source: Current Population Survey Table A-7, Series P-20, No. 443

Interestingly, the differences in participation rates between White and minority students do not hold up for older students. For 25- to 34-year-old high school graduates, the college participation rates for Whites, African Americans, and Hispanics are all approximately the same—about 8 percent of these older high school graduates currently enroll in college.

Another measure of participation is the proportion of recent high school graduates who are currently enrolled or have attended a year or more of college. As Table 5-3 indicates, for African Americans and Hispanics, this rate has not increased since 1976. The increase in White student participation rates between 1984 and 1988 appears to be in large part a function of an increase in the rate for White females.

TABLE 5-3

PERCENTAGE OF 18-24 YEAR OLD HIGH SCHOOL GRADUATES CURRENTLY ENROLLED OR WITH ONE OR MORE YEARS OF COLLEGE

	Whites, %	African Americans, %	Hispanics, %
1972	53.9	42.0	36.7
1976	53.5	50.4	48.9
1980	51.4	45.9	47.3
1984	53.8	45.2	46.0
1988	58.6	46.6	47.1
1990	60.1	48.0	44.7

Source: Current Population Survey Table A-7, Series P-20, no. 443

NCES data on the cumulative enrollment rates of the high school classes of 1972, 1980, and 1982 in postsecondary education. The CPS data on which these trends are based, however, are a snapshot at the time the survey is taken. In contrast, the NCES longitudinal surveys of various high school classes track uniform age cohorts of individual students over time. These longitudinal surveys also include information on enrollments in noncollegiate postsecondary programs, thus providing a broader glimpse of the postsecondary activities of high school graduates. (See Table 5-4.)

Results from these longitudinal surveys indicate that participation of students from recent high school classes in postsecondary education has increased, and that females accounted for most of the increase, as participation in postsecondary education of females from all racial groups has increased. The proportion of female high school graduates who had enrolled in some form of postsecondary education within four years of high school graduation increased from 58 percent among 1972 high school graduates to 68 percent in the class of 1982. In contrast, the participation rate for males remained essentially level; it was 61 percent for 1972 high school graduates and 63 percent for the class of 1982. (Eagle and Carroll, 1988.)

TABLE 5-4			
CUMULATIVE POSTSECONDARY EDUCATION ENROLLMENT RATES WITHIN 4 YEARS AFTER HIGH SCHOOL GRADUATION			
	Whites, %	African Americans, %	Hispanics, %
1972 CLASS	61	55	41
1980 CLASS	69	66	60
1982 CLASS	68	58	57
Source: Eagle and Carroll, p. 31			

The proportion of Whites, African Americans, and Hispanics who enrolled in postsecondary education for some period of time in the four years after high school graduation increased among 1980 high school graduates over the rate for 1972 graduates, and the gap narrowed between Whites, African Americans, and Hispanics. The cumulative enrollment rate for African Americans in the 1982 high school class declined, however, because of a decline in the rate for African American men; there was not a similar decline for White and Hispanic males. For African Americans, the enrollment rate for 1982 high school graduates was not significantly different than for 1972 graduates, as the increase in the rate for African American women and the decline for African American men resulted in no change in the African American rate between the 1972 and 1982 classes. Thus, the apparent lack of change for African Americans overall masks a decline in the rate for African American men. For Whites and Hispanics, the small decline in the participation rates between 1980 and 1982 was not statistically significant (Eagle and Carroll, 1988).

Comparing the high school classes of 1972 and 1982, Whites, African Americans, and Hispanics all made net gains, although the increase for African Americans was not statistically significant, and the 1982 enrollment rates of Whites were still much higher than those of African American and Hispanic students. Moreover, differences still exist in the B.A. aspirations of Whites, African Americans, and Hispanics, particularly between those of Whites and Hispanics.

As Table 5-5 indicates, White high school graduates in 1980 and 1982 were more likely to enter a four-year institution than African American or Hispanic students, and Hispanic students were more likely to enter a public two-year college than either Whites or African Americans. Table 5-5 also indicates that the proportion of African Americans and Hispanics who had B.A. aspirations dropped noticeably between 1980 and 1982, and the propor-

TABLE 5-5

B.A. ASPIRATIONS AND ENROLLMENT PATTERNS OF 1980 AND 1982 HIGH SCHOOL GRADUATES

	Whites , %	African Americans, %	Hispanics, %
Planned to obtain a BA			
Class of '80	46	48	38
Class of '82	43	38	29
Entered a public four-year institution			
Class of '80	33	29	22
Class of '82	31	23	17
Entered an independent four-year institution			
Class of '80	18	13	9
Class of '82	15	9	8
Entered a public two-year college			
Class of ' 80	25	21	33
Class of '82	23	18	26
Entered a proprietary two-year institution			
Class of '80	5	8	6
Class of '82	5	8	6

Source: Special tabulations of NCES longitudinal databases

tion who entered four-year colleges also declined, suggesting a widening in the disparity between White and minority participation in the 1980 and 1982 classes.

One plausible explanation for the changes in aspiration and enrollment patterns between 1980 and 1982 may be the dramatic cuts in federal student aid proposed by the Reagan administration during the early 1980s (American Council on Education, *Student Aid in the Reagan Administration*). Even though the Congress did not make the reductions recommended in the president's budget during that time, these recommendations were widely publicized, and many people outside Washington do not realize that the Congress does not necessarily enact funding levels proposed by the administration.

Collegiate Enrollment by Socioeconomic Status and Preparedness

The picture of enrollment patterns is quite different when one controls for socioeconomic status (SES) or preparedness. These patterns can be discerned through longitudinal surveys in which socioeconomic status is determined through several variables and preparedness for postsecondary education is measured by a standardized test given to all survey participants (Educational Testing Service, 1986). We realize the limitations of a standardized test to evaluate the complicated issue of students' preparedness for postsecondary education, but we believe that the preparedness rankings based on the test results provide a helpful framework in which to compare groups of students. Further analysis is needed regarding the impact of other factors such as high school coursework on participation and retention.

African Americans. Interestingly enough, it appears that African American aspirations and enrollment rates in four-year programs are not less than those of Whites for equivalent SES groups. And even though African American overall participation declined between 1980 and 1982, a higher proportion of African Americans from each SES quartile had B.A. aspirations than Whites, except for the highest SES students, where rates between African Americans and Whites were comparable. (See Table 5-6.) In addition, the same or a higher proportion of African Americans from each SES quartile entered public and independent four-year institutions by February 1986 as Whites. Similarly, if one controls for preparedness, African Americans in each quartile were as likely as or more likely than Whites to enter public and independent four-year institutions by February 1986 (drawn from NCES special tabulations: tab 1, tables 13, 14; tabs 2, 3, tables 1, 7, and 8; and tab 4, tables 3a, 3b). (See Table 5-7 and 5-8.)

| TABLE 5-6 |

PERCENT OF 1980 AND 1982 HIGH SCHOOL GRADUATES WHO PLANNED TO ATTAIN A BACHELOR'S DEGREE

	By SES Quartile			
	Total	Whites	African Americans	Hispanics
Quartiles				
Class of '80				
Total	46.0	45.9	48.0	37.6
Low	25.6	19.4	37.7	27.6
Mid-low	35.0	32.7	51.1	39.3
Mid-high	49.9	48.3	64.2	51.9
High	74.1	73.9	75.0	68.8
Class of '82				
Total	41.6	43.1	37.5	28.9
Low	18.8	14.0	28.1	18.6
Mid-low	28.1	26.7	35.6	25.1
Mid-high	46.0	45.5	53.4	40.7
High	69.2	69.9	68.4	54.6
	By Preparedness Quartile			
	Total	Whites	African Americans	Hispanics
Quartiles				
Class of '80				
Total	46.0	45.9	48.0	37.6
Low	18.7	12.3	32.5	17.9
Mid-low	33.7	29.3	58.6	42.6
Mid-high	51.2	48.1	82.4	64.3
High	79.6	79.3	87.8	76.7
Class of '82				
Total	41.6	43.1	37.5	28.9
Low	13.7	8.8	23.1	8.6
Mid-low	22.6	18.1	38.7	28.7
Mid-high	42.9	40.6	67.5	52.3
High	75.1	74.9	80.6	70.9

Source: unpublished NCES tabulations

Thus, it appears that, controlling for preparedness, the aspirations and enrollment rates of African Americans are as high as similar groups of Whites, yet overall African American participation rates are much lower than those of Whites. This apparent anomaly is the result of the fact that African Americans are much more likely to come from low SES circumstances—49 percent of the African Americans in the 1982 class were low SES compared

TABLE 5-7

PERCENT OF 1980 AND 1982 HIGH SCHOOL GRADUATES WHO ENTERED A PUBLIC FOUR-YEAR.
INSTITUTION BY FEBRARY 1986

	By SES Quartile			
	Total	Whites	African Americans	Hispanics
Quartiles				
Class of '80				
Total	31.4	32.5	28.6	22.0
Low	18.4	16.2	23.0	17.8
Mid-low	25.2	24.5	30.1	24.9
Mid-high	36.4	36.2	37.3	31.4
High	52.4	52.4	48.2	53.6
Class of '82				
Total	29.2	31.4	23.0	16.9
Low	12.8	11.4	16.6	10.1
Mid-low	20.5	20.6	20.9	16.0
Mid-high	33.1	33.4	35.3	24.3
High	48.3	49.1	45.4	32.4
	By Preparedness Quartile			
Quartile				
Class of '80				
Total	31.4	32.5	28.6	22.0
Low	11.5	9.4	16.8	8.5
Mid-low	25.3	23.0	40.4	27.1
Mid-high	39.8	38.2	54.5	45.0
High	57.7	57.5	60.8	67.4
Class of '82				
Total	29.2	31.4	23.0	16.9
Low	8.5	5.2	15.2	5.4
Mid-low	16.1	14.6	21.5	16.1
Mid-high	31.0	30.1	41.6	31.7
High	53.6	53.7	55.1	42.0

Source: Unpublished NCES tabulations

to 19 percent of the Whites—and the fact that high SES high school graduates aspire to a B.A. at a higher rate than low SES high school graduates—69 percent of 1982 high SES high school graduates aspired to a B.A. compared to 19 percent of low SES students (tab 3, table 1 and unpublished ACE tabulations from the 1980 HS&B).

Hispanics.   Equivalent SES groups of Hispanics from the 1980 high school class had B.A. aspirations and entry rates into public four-year institutions which were similar to those of Whites, but analysis of the experience of

TABLE 5-8

Percent Of 1980 And 1982 High School Graduates Who Entered An Independent Four-Year. Institution By February 1986

	Total	Whites	African Americans	Hispanics
By SES Quartile				
Quartile				
Class of '80				
Total	16.3	17.5	13.1	8.5
Low	7.3	6.7	9.3	6.9
Mid-low	12.7	12.5	15.9	10.3
Mid-high	16.0	16.3	16.6	14.8
High	30.4	31.1	25.6	16.0
Class of '82				
Total	13.4	14.8	9.0	7.9
Low	4.3	7.9	13.3	26.6
Mid-low	7.9	7.4	10.9	9.0
Mid-high	13.3	13.6	14.0	11.6
High	26.6	27.6	20.0	15.8
By Preparedness Quartile				
Quartile				
Class of '80				
Total	16.3	17.5	13.1	8.5
Low	3.9	2.6	7.0	4.1
Mid-low	9.8	9.0	15.5	9.0
Mid-high	17.8	17.6	22.6	17.5
High	32.7	32.9	39.5	25.8
Class of 82				
Total	13.4	14.8	9.0	7.9
Low	2.7	1.7	4.3	2.9
Mid-low	6.4	5.4	9.8	8.3
Mid-high	11.8	12.1	12.1	8.1
High	28.0	28.3	29.1	23.2

Source: Unpublished NCES tabulations

equivalent SES groups from the 1982 high school class suggests that differences between Whites and Hispanics have not been reduced to the extent that they have for Whites and African Americans.

Among members of the 1982 high school class, Hispanics from high SES groups had lower rates of B.A. aspirations and entry into public four-year institutions than similar White and African American groups. And at all SES levels, Hispanics were much more likely to enroll in public two-year colleges than African Americans or Whites.

Analysis of equivalent preparedness groups of 1982 high school graduates indicates that the B.A. aspirations of Hispanics are not significantly different from those of Whites; they are roughly the same or higher. The aspirations of the lowest and highest quartiles of Hispanic students are very similar to comparable groups of White students, and Hispanics in the middle quartiles of preparedness have significantly greater B.A. aspirations than Whites, though not as high as African Americans.

Entry rates of equivalent preparedness groups of Hispanics and Whites from the 1982 class into four-year institutions were also comparable, except that Hispanic high school graduates from the top quartile were slightly less likely than Whites to enter four-year institutions, and more likely to enter public two-year colleges. All preparedness quartiles of Hispanics enrolled at public two-year colleges at higher rates than Whites or African Americans, except for Hispanics from the lowest quartile.

In sum, for equivalent SES and preparedness groups, African Americans have similar aspirations and enrollment patterns as White students. Differences are still apparent between comparable SES groups of Whites and Hispanics, but comparing equivalent preparedness groups, Hispanics are very similar to Whites except for one major difference—their much higher tendency to enroll in public two-year institutions.

Concentration of Minority Students in Certain Types of Institutions

Another concern with current patterns of participation in higher education is that African American and Hispanic students tend to attend certain types of institutions disproportionately. For example, 37 percent of all college student enrollments are in two-year institutions, but 57 percent of all Hispanic students are enrolled in two-year institutions. Similarly, 20 percent of African American college students are enrolled in historically Black colleges and universities (NCES, *Digest of Education Statistics*, 1989, tables 189 and 177).

It is also the case that African American and Hispanic students are much more likely to enroll in short-term programs in proprietary trade schools than are White students. According to the National Postsecondary Student Aid Survey (NPSAS), 39 percent of the students in trade schools are either African American or Hispanic, again a much higher percentage than their representation in the population, or their proportion of college enrollments (NCES, 1988 *National Postsecondary Student Aid Study*). We suggest a possible cause for this pattern in the later discussion of federal student aid programs.

These statistics serve to remind us that a concentration of minority groups in certain types of institutions continues to occur in American postsecondary education, although it appears that the degree of segregation may have declined somewhat over time. The goal of full participation in higher education of minorities should include the objective of reducing or eliminating these disproportionate patterns of participation by type of institution.

Persistence and Completion of Degrees

Over time it has become increasingly apparent that improving participation in higher education must involve increasing the persistence as well as the enrollment of low-income and minority students. Improving the enrollment rates of disadvantaged and minority students without also increasing their persistence and degree completion should not be judged a successful strategy.

While recent national data on persistence patterns are limited, certain generalizations can be made. For example, the available data from NCES longitudinal surveys indicate that high SES students tend to persist at higher rates than low SES students. (See Tables 5-9 and 5-10.) Rates of persistence through two years and through four years for all SES levels were lower for the 1982 class of high school graduates than the 1972 class (Eagle and Carroll, 1988), but the rate remained consistently lower for low SES students than for higher SES students.

White students persist at a higher rate than African Americans and Hispanics, but the persistence rate for two years and four years were lower for all three ethnic/racial groups of the high school class of 1982 than 1972 class. (Eagle and Carroll, 1988). Some of this decline may be attributed to different aspirations among these high school classes. In support of this hypothesis, there was an increase in one- and two-year degrees between the 1972 and 1980 classes, but after four years, there was no comparable increase in attainment of these degrees by the 1982 class (Eagle and Carroll, 1988).

Persistence through four years is strongest for those students who enter a four-year institution on a full-time basis in the fall immediately after high school graduation (Carroll, 1989). Unlike the stable data from the cross-tabulations on aspirations and enrollment, the data on preparedness are uneven.

Even though African Americans from equivalent preparedness groups of the high school class of 1980 enrolled at four-year institutions at higher rates than Whites, the persistence rate for four years of those who enrolled full-time in the fall following high school graduation was significantly below the rate for White students in two out of four quartiles. Comparing equivalent preparedness groups did substantially eliminate differences in two quartiles, but further analysis is needed on the characteristics of the students in the remaining quartiles. Dennis Carroll of the NCES warns that the timing of the follow-up surveys can have pronounced impact on survey results on apparent

TABLE 5-9

PERCENT OF 1980 HIGH SCHOOL GRADUATES WHO PERSISTED FOUR YEARS

By SES Quartile

	Total	Whites	African Americans	Hispanics
Quartile				
Class of '80				
Total	54.3	55.6	43.5	42.3
Low	41.7	43.2	41.2	40.0
Mid-low	54.1	57.1	36.8	52.0
Mid-high	51.4	51.0	49.3	43.8
High	60.4	61.0	48.8	45.7

By Preparedness Quartile

	Total	Whites	African Americans	Hispanics
Quartile				
Class of '80				
Total	54.3	55.6	43.5	42.3
Low	39.3	45.1	35.8	31.1
Mid-low	42.1	41.8	44.6	32.1
Mid-high	51.8	51.4	49.9	51.1
High	62.2	63.0	38.1	63.5

Source: Unpublished NCES tabulations

TABLE 5-10

PERCENT OF 1980 HIGH SCHOOL GRADUATES WHO EARNED BA/BS DEGREES BY SPRING OF 1986*

By SES Quartile

	Total	Whites	African Americans	Hispanics
Quartiles				
Total	52.5	55.8	30.3	32.3
Low	36.6	43.5	28.1	32.6
Mid-low	41.2	43.9	25.2	39.2
Mid-high	49.2	50.7	36.0	31.8
High	60.8	62.1	43.6	30.1

By Preparedness Quartile

	Total	Whites	African Americans	Hispanics
Quartiles				
Total	52.5	55.8	30.3	32.3
Low	25.9	33.8	20.8	16.9
Mid-low	42.4	47.1	30.4	29.0
Mid-high	44.6	45.6	36.4	28.6
High	60.4	61.8	28.5	56.5

* Given entry into a four-year institution the fall following graduation
Source: Unpublished NCES tabulations

TABLE 5-11

PERCENT OF 1980 AND 1982 HIGH SCHOOL GRADUATES WHO ENTERED A PUBLIC 2-YEAR COLLEGE
BY FEBRUARY 1986

	By SES Quartile			
	Total	Whites	African Americans	Hispanics
Class of 1980				
Total	25.2	25.1	21.2	33.3
Low	20.4	18.7	19.6	27.4
Mid-low	25.5	24.9	20.6	41.0
Mid-high	28.3	27.8	23.9	41.0
High	26.5	25.7	29.9	41.0
Class of 1982				
Total	22.7	22.9	18.3	25.7
Low	15.4	14.1	14.3	18.8
Mid-low	22.4	22.0	22.3	26.8
Mid-high	28.7	28.8	23.5	30.5
High	23.7	23.2	19.1	42.8
	By Preparedness Quartile			
Class of 1980				
Total	25.2	25.1	21.2	33.3
Low	21.0	19.3	20.7	27.1
Mid-low	26.9	25.4	24.8	42.7
Mid-high	29.9	30.0	13.8	40.2
High	23.1	22.8	22.2	35.1

Source: Unpublished NCES tabulations

rates of persistence, and that some of the differences seen in the cross-tabulations may be methodological.

The overall four-year persistence rate for Hispanics from the 1980 high school class who entered a four-year institution full-time immediately after leaving high school was 42 percent. Comparing equivalent preparedness groups eliminated differences between Whites and Hispanics in the higher quartiles, but again further analysis is needed to explore the causes of the lower rates for students in lower-preparedness quartiles.

Evidence from the longitudinal databases also indicates that African Americans do not achieve the baccalaureate at the same rate as Whites. Among high school graduates in 1980, a lower proportion of African Americans than Whites had achieved the B.A. by February of 1986 at every preparedness level. For example, 62 percent of highly prepared White 1980 high school graduates had completed their B.A.'s by February 1986, compared to 29 percent for highly prepared African Americans (tab 1, table 6). (See Table 5-10.) Analysis of subsequent follow-up data is necessary to assess to what extent the difference between African American and White achievement narrowed in future years. Like African Americans, a smaller proportion of Hispanics who entered four-year institutions full-time immediately after high school graduation had completed a B.A. by February 1986 than Whites, even within comparable preparedness groups.

Further analysis is needed to determine whether the larger proportion of Hispanics with B.A. aspirations enrolling in public two-year colleges do transfer to four-year institutions. Attainment of a baccalaureate appears to take longer, and is less likely for those who begin their college program in two-year colleges. Almost half of the graduates of the high school class of 1980 who entered a public two-year institution aspired to a baccalaureate, but only about a quarter of that group had achieved that goal by 1986 (Ross and Hampton, et al.).

Another major indicator of baccalaureate completion is annual earned degrees, which includes the degrees of all students, not just recent high school graduates. These data do not, however, allow the disaggregation of the effects of persistence and attainment from the effects of enrollment. According to Education Department reports, between 1978/79 and 1986/87, there was an 5.9 percent decline in the total number of baccalaureate degrees awarded to African Americans, but African American head count enrollments increased by 2.7 percent. During this period of time, all other racial/ethnic groups experienced an increase in the number of degrees—Whites, Hispanics, Asian Americans, and Native Americans. The decline in African American male baccalaureates (2 percent) occurred during a time when African American male enrollment also declined, full-time and part-time in both four-year and two-year institutions, from 453,000 to 436,000, a decline of 6 percent.

Curiously, however, during that period baccalaureate degrees to African American women declined 4 percent, but the enrollment of African American women increased from 601,000 to 646,000, or 7 percent. That increase in the enrollment of African American women was predominantly among African American women enrolled part-time, particularly in public two-year colleges. The full-time enrollment of African American women in four-year institutions decreased slightly during that period—from 250,000 to 248,000.

In 1988 full-time enrollment of both African American male and female enrollments in four-year institutions rose above 1978 levels, but it will be several years before we realize any impact of these increases on baccalaureate production (NCES, Degrees Conferred in Institutions of Higher Education; NCES Trends in Racial/Ethnic Enrollment, 1978 through 1988; NCES,

Trends in Minority Enrollment, 1976-1986; Enrollment in Higher Education, 1978).

FINANCING STRATEGIES

The preceding review of the statistics on minority participation points to several policy objectives. First, the data make it clear that steps are needed to increase the enrollment of minorities across a broad spectrum of institutions. Second, it is critically important to increase the rate at which minority students complete their programs of study and receive their degrees. Therefore, strategies that meet these criteria of broadening access and improving retention should be pursued. Strategies that do not meet these criteria should be reexamined and revised or given lower priority.

In developing these strategies, however, the data also make it clear that low rates of participation appear to be very much a function of students' socioeconomic status and academic preparedness. Thus, efforts that seek to help students based on their low socioeconomic status or which are designed to improve the academic preparation of students should be given high priority in the effort to improve minority participation.

In this section, we examine six financial aid strategies that have been suggested for increasing the participation of low-income and minority students in higher education. These strategies are:

- creating or expanding aid programs designed for minority students only;
- maintaining low tuition policies at public institutions;
- increasing the amount of grant aid that disadvantaged students receive;
- providing students with earlier awareness of their aid eligibility;
- pursuing policies that increase student retention and persistence; and
- neutralizing the negative impact of borrowing.

Strategy: Expansion of Minority-Only Student Aid Programs

For a variety of reasons, the tendency in publicly supported student aid programs has been to provide money generally to all students who meet financial need and other eligibility criteria, and not to limit eligibility to groups of students based on their sex, ethnicity, or racial category. There have been some exceptions, however. For example, the Patricia Roberts Harris program (previously called GPOP) provides fellowships to needy students enrolled in graduate and professional school programs, with special concern for underrepresented ethnic/racial minority groups and for women.

The most obvious and direct strategy for helping minority students is to expand the number of, and funding for, programs that help only minority students. In a similar fashion, a portion of the aid available through certain programs might be limited, or earmarked, to minority groups of students. This kind of approach would likely be effective in that funds would be targeted on the intended group of students. It is also the case that targeted programs of this sort tend to provide higher levels of support services for the aided students than programs that are not targeted on minority groups of students. Therefore, it may be the case that minority-only programs would result in greater persistence of minority students, thereby meeting another of the objectives that we would like to achieve.

Despite the obvious benefits of this approach, however, there are several reasons why it would be a mistake to rely extensively on minority-only programs as the way to improve minority participation in higher education. One is that it is difficult to achieve adequate funding levels for programs that single out a particular group of students for assistance on the basis of their skin color or nationality and that exclude other students in similar financial circumstances. For that reason, it has been easier to achieve greater levels of funding for programs like the Pell Grant program since funds are awarded to disadvantaged students of all ethnic and racial groups.

In addition, if it is the case, as the data seem to suggest, that low rates of participation are tied as much or more to socioeconomic status and preparedness than to ethnic/racial affiliation per se, then well-funded programs for the disadvantaged would achieve the same goal but have broader public support than more limited-funded programs that are designated solely for minority groups of students.

Strategy: Maintaining Low Tuition Policies at Public Institutions

It is worth reminding ourselves that the principal strategy that has been relied upon in this country to ensure access to a college education has not been student aid. Instead, it has been the maintenance of relatively low tuitions at public institutions brought about through substantial financial support from state and local governments. The state and local funds used to maintain low tuitions remain by far the largest single source of financial support for American higher education.

It is generally conceded that these low tuition policies have been the major factor in why public institutions have historically enrolled higher proportions of minority students than private colleges and universities. In recent years, however, some evidence is emerging that suggests that low public tuitions may be having an opposite effect. Public institutions, especially flagship universities, are now enrolling higher proportions of middle- and upper-income students. One possible explanation for this trend is that as the gap between public and private sector tuitions have continued to increase, more middle-income students have been attracted to those high quality public institutions that charge a price that is a small fraction of the price of a private institution. To the extent that admissions decisions are not based on a family's financial ability to pay, middle- and upper-income students may be squeezing out lower-income applicants, who then either choose to go to other, less prestigious public four-year or two-year institutions, decide to attend local or regional private colleges and universities, or do not continue their education at that time.

It is also the case that low tuition policies, by and large, are not a very efficient way of targeting subsidies on lower-income students in that all students who attend a public institution benefit from the low tuition. Moreover, if the low tuition is not accompanied by grants that offset the costs of tuition and living expenses, then disadvantaged students find they have mounting out-of-pocket costs that can serve as a financial obstacle to their continued attendance.

Strategy: Increasing Grant Aid

One of the most discussed and distressing trends in higher education over the past decade has been the growing imbalance between grants and loans as a source of student financial aid. The most frequently discussed means for redressing this imbalance has been to increase funding for grants, which are the major way in which the federal government has sought to achieve the goal of equal opportunity. The federal government presently spends over $5 billion annually on grant assistance to students in the form of Pell Grants and other federal grant programs. When the issue of flagging minority participation is raised, a common response is to increase the amount of Pell Grants and other grants in the belief that these funds will flow to minority students. Is this perception accurate?

The Pell Grant program is certainly more targeted to low-income students than low tuitions. It also is the most targeted of the federal grant programs. Therefore, we might reasonably conclude that expanded funding for Pell Grants should have more of an impact on the enrollment decisions of low-income and minority youth than a similar increase in the amount of state funding for public institutions. But a contrary view would hold that low tuitions are more visible and understandable to disadvantaged students than is the promise of grant assistance. Under this view, low tuitions are a more effective stimulus than grant aid, even if the grant aid would do a better job of reducing the out-of-pocket costs to low-income students. On balance, however, we believe that grant aid can be a much more effective tool at increasing minority participation than low tuitions.

Whether an increase in grant funds results in more access for low-income and minority students, however, depends critically on how the increase in grant funding is spent. For example, if the additional funds were used primarily to expand the eligibility of the program for students above the median family income, such a policy would not increase the participation of low-income students who have little or nothing in the way of family resources. If, on the other hand, the new funds were used to increase the award received by the neediest students, then the increased grant funds could have the effect of increasing access for extremely disadvantaged students. But if the maximum award is increased and all eligible students receive increases in awards, the price can be very expensive—for example, it presently costs about $270 million to increase the Pell maximum award by $100.

In the past several years, the notion of "frontloading" grants in the first two undergraduate years has been frequently suggested as a way to increase grants and redress the grant/loan imbalance. The theory is that students, particularly those at risk, should be required to borrow less in their first two years so that they will feel more free to experiment with higher education. For those students who succeed, they would then need to borrow more in their last two years to fill the financing gap.

It seems reasonable to assume that a policy of frontloading would, in fact, have the effect of increasing the number of low-income and minority students who enroll in some form of postsecondary education. But this increase in enrollment would most likely not be broad based as frontloading formulas tend to provide a strong incentive for many students to enroll in shorter-term programs where they can maximize their grant eligibility. In addition, a frontloading policy would most likely create a strong disincentive for disadvantaged students to persist and complete their baccalaureate since their grants would decline as they continued in school. Thus, a frontloading policy could well achieve the goal of greater access at the very dear cost of lower rates of retention and degree completion. This concern should lead to modifications in frontloading proposals that do not contain strong disincentvies for persistence.

Strategy: Providing Earlier Notification and Assurance of Awards

In recent years, Eugene Lang stimulated a great deal of interest with his "I Have A Dream" approach of reaching disadvantaged students early in their high school years or before. Assuring junior high school students that their their college costs will be met appears to be a powerful incentive, at least if the early evidence from the Lang and similar experiments is any indication. It also apprears to be the case that the neighborhood center that Lang provided so that the students could gather together to meet with their peers and mentors is as important as the additional aid and the assurance that aid would be available. The tutoring, counseling, and other support that the students received was by all reports a critical component in the dramatic increase in high school completion and college participation rates achieved by Eugene Lang's class. Assured access efforts in Cleveland, Boston, and other cities, some of which date back at least two decades, further confirm the importance of early intervention in raising college participation rates.

Another critical aspect of the success of the "I Have a Dream" and similar approaches is the fact that students are notified in junior high school or early in their high school years that sufficient funds will be available to finance their college costs. This early awareness was an important component of the initial thinking behind the Pell Grant program when it was enacted as Basic Education Opportunity Grants. The notion in the early 1970s was that students and their families would know as early as the ninth grade about their eligibility for Basic Grants. But the reality of the program has never matched the promise as funding constraints, legislative requirements, and administrative inertia led instead to a program in which students typcially do not know until the summer before they matriculate how much aid they might receive.

The question that arises from the success of recent philanthropic efforts is whether they can be replicated by governments, either federal or state. One move in this direction would be to make Pell Grants into entitlements so that students would know with assurance how much aid they would receive early in the year in which they applied for aid. But there are at least two limitations to this approach. First, making Pell Grants into entitlements would not materially affect when during high school students could be sure that they would receive college financial aid. They would still have to wait until their senior year to apply for aid. Second, the political prospects for enacting a new entitlement program are very slim, especially in a time of high federal budget deficits. Thus, fighting for entitlement status may detract from other, more feasible legislative amendments.

Another possible modification to current programs that may hold promise is to allow students to apply for aid when they are in the ninth grade or even earlier during the junior high school years. Under such an approach, students from impoverished families would be assured of maximum student aid eligibility when they were ready to enroll in college. One way to do this would be to establish an account for students in junior high school, which could earn interest until the student reached college age. This amount would then be available to the student, net of any federal aid that the student would be eligible to receive.

Early identification of student aid recipients would not add much to current program costs for the following reasons: Students who did not go onto college would not be eligible for aid; thus, not all of the funds put aside would actually be used. In addition, to the extent that students' aid eligibility would be subtracted from what they receive from the account, the net costs to the government would be small.

This kind of early eligibility plan, however, would face opposition from those who worry that some students will be eligible for Pell Grants based on their seventh grade circumstances who would not be eligible if they had applied as high school seniors, because of changes in their family financial circumstances in the interim. This concern is certainly valid, although the additional costs would be relatively small. Those students who are extremely economically disadvantaged when they are in the ninth grade are highly likely still to be poor and eligible for aid when they reach college age. Thus, the number of student aid eligibles would not increase much under an early application plan; instead, the students who would be eligible for maximum awards would simply know with certainty much earlier about their eligibility for aid than is currently the case.

Another aspect of a successful early intervention strategy is to provide disadvantaged students with better information on their financial aid opportunities. Regrettably, in the current student aid structure the students who are most in need are too often the ones who receive the least reliable information on what aid is available. For the students in inner-city schools, college catalogs and guidebooks are frequently out of date, the budget for counseling is inadequate, the interaction between college and high school officials is minimal, and many parents are uninvolved. In such an environment, it is not surprising to find that students do not have aspirations that match their ability and potential.

But in those cities and schools where a substantial investment has been made in providing more and better counseling and information, and where the parents of students are emphatically brought into the process, college participation rates have improved. Efforts to spread this kind of community-based approach should be encouraged. In addition, the federal government through the Department of Education could make a major commitment through the provision of printed and video materials, including publicity such as television spots, to make parents, counselors, and potential students aware of the need to take a high school curriculum that will enable the students to enroll in and succeed in college, as well as basic data on the kinds and amounts of student aid funding from federal, state, and institutional sources. Moreover, this kind of strategy, in contrast to many of the others discussed here, can be accomplished at relatively little financial cost.

Strategy: Pursuing Policies That Encourage Persistence

One reality that has emerged over time is that the current system of financial aid is more geared to providing students with access to a college education than it is to providing them with a reasonable chance for completion of their degree. This situation is clearly not in the long-term interests of higher education or society in general. This realization leads to the critical need to identify ways in which students can be encouraged to stay in school once they start, and to complete their degrees.

One means for moving in the direction of greater persistence, especially among low-income and minority students, is to devote additional resources for support services such as tutoring and counseling. The data cited earlier in this chapter indicate that lack of preparedness is a principal obstacle to greater minority enrollment and retention; it is simply not enough to make sure that disadvantaged students can pay for their college education without also providing early encouragement to attend college and a supportive academic environment once they enroll. The previous strategy addressed the need to intervene early in the high school years and to provide sufficient information to students.

The available evidence also strongly suggests that adequate support services are especially important for improving the retention of students once they enroll. The federal government's TRIO programs are designed to identify promising, disadvantaged students (Talent Search), prepare them to do college level work (Upward Bound), provide information on academic and financial opportunities (Education Opportunity Centers), and provide tutoring and support services to students once they reach campus (Special Services). These programs have generally received good grades for their ability to expand the number of low-income and minority youth who go on to college and who complete their degrees.

The federal role in providing support services for at-risk youth is not, however, well defined either in statute or through program operation. Although the statute does not indicate that the TRIO programs are demonstration projects, funding levels are clearly inadequate to serve all those needing such services. Only about one in ten eligible students ever receives assistance.

In addition, the statute requires that the secretary give consideration to the prior experience of service delivery under the program for which the potential grantee is applying, thereby concentrating funding among existing grantees. As a result of this requirement, the federal government is providing de facto long-term operating support to a small core of programs. Under the current structure, it is unlikely that appropriations will increase sufficiently to provide a dramatic increase in the number of young people served.

One way to clarify the current situation would be gradually to convert the existing TRIO legislative authority into a demonstration program, limiting eligiblity of new grantees to a set number of years, after which the institutions and, in the case of Talent Search and Upward Bound, community groups would be expected to assume funding for the program operations.

Also, colleges might be required to provide a minimal level of support services for their federal aid recipients, at least the lowest-income students. There might also be a modification in the current provision, which requires that federally aided students make satisfactory academic progress. Instead, these students, particularly those with academic deficiencies or those with family incomes below 150 percent of poverty, should be assessed at the time they enter the postsecondary institution to identify their need for remediation, and instituions should be required to provide counseling and remedial services through their own funds.

To emphasize the importance of persistence, the federal government could provide funds to institutions on the basis of the number of federal aid recipients they enroll beyond the freshman year. This could be done through the distribution of some or all of the funds in the TRIO programs. One possibility might be to continue to fund existing TRIO projects through at current funding levels, but to distribute any new funding for TRIO on the basis of sophomore through senior federal aid recipients. Some or all of the federal campus-based student aid funds might also be distributed in this fashion. If there is a desire to encourage completion of degrees, bonuses might be paid to institutions based on the number of federal aid recipients who complete their degrees.

Another key aspect of improving retention in American higher education is to increase the number of students in two-year institutions who transfer into four-year institutions and receive a baccalaureate degree. Currently the rate of articulation between two- and four-year institutions is quite low—about one-quarter of students who enter two-year colleges transfer to a four-year institution—although a major reason for this low rate is that less than half of community college students enter with the purpose of attaining a baccalaureate (unpublished ACE tabulations from the HS&B survey of 1980 high school graduates). Nevertheless, it is clear that improving the rate of articulation is a desirable goal and would lead to a better record of retention in higher education.

One reason why rates of articulation are low may be that student aid programs to some extent encourage students to stay at home and to enroll in shorter-term programs. Pell Grants, which are by far the largest federal grant program and are more specifically targeted to low-income students than the other federal programs, are the primary source of support of students enrolled in public two-year institutions. In the academic year 1986-87, in public two-year institutions, 83 percent of federally aided students received a Pell award and 39 percent of these Pell Grant recipients received no other form of aid (Ross, Smith, and Hampton, 1992).

Since the Pell Grant award is only slightly sensitive to differences in costs of attendance, a Pell Grant by itself covers a substantially higher proportion of the costs faced by students living at home and attending low-tuition public two-year colleges than those attending four-year institutions living on college campuses or on their own in the community (Breneman and Nelson, 1981). Thus, there could be said to be a bias in federal student aid in favor of students who live at home and attend low-priced institutions. This bias in favor of students living at home is reduced when students choose to borrow under the Stafford Loan Program, but it still exists, given the current size of the Pell Grant maximum award and the lower Stafford borrowing limits that apply to students in the first two years of college.

Many students undoubtedly opt for shorter-term programs or live at home for reasons unrelated to cost and federal aid availability. The public policy concern is that the current inadequate grant funding makes these two options the only true guaranteed access alternatives to postsecondary education for many low-income students; these students can minimize their borrowing or avoid it altogether by following one or both of these paths. Many of these short-term programs are purely vocational and the credits are not transferable to four-year institutions. There appears to be an unfortunate unintended bias in the existing programs at their current funding levels which discourages low-income, high-risk students in enrolling and persisting in a baccalaureate program.

The goal should be to make student aid neutral regarding the type of program in which students enroll. It would be preferable if the structure of the student aid programs did not lead students to enroll in certain kinds of programs; instead, financial aid and support services should help students achieve the most appropriate program for them. Under the current system, low-income students who transfer to a four-year institution will have a smaller proportion of out-of-pocket expenses paid for by federal need-based aid because of the probability that they will have to move away from home and pay dormitory expenses or live in the community. Even if students have avoided borrowing during their first two years, they may have to borrow to pay the increased costs in the junior and senior years.

What is needed instead are incentives that encourage rather than discourage students to transfer and try to earn a four-year degree. One way to encourage transfer and improve articulation between two-year and four-year institutions would be to increase the amount of grant aid provided in the last two years of college in the Pell Grant and campus-based programs. This option, however, runs counter to the strong desire previously discussed to reduce indebtedness during a student's first two years of undergraduate study. Another possibility worth exploring is to provide incentives to four-year institutions to enroll students who are transferring from two-year institutions. Additional funds (bonuses) could be given to four-year institutions based on the number of financial aid recipients enrolled who have transferred from two-year institutions. This could be built into the system of revised funding formulas for campus-based aid or support services programs previously discussed.

Strategy: Neutralizing the Negative Impact of Borrowing

The concern of public and institutional policy makers should be to ensure that student financial assistance is a positive influence on encouraging needy students to enroll and persist in postsecondary education, to minimize any disincentives in the student aid programs toward achieving these goals, and to ensure that students are not penalized unfairly for participating in student aid programs to finance postsecondary education if their educational experience is not successful. In the absence of adequate increases in federal, state, and institutional grant support, needy high-risk students have increasingly turned to federal loans during the last decade. Under any reasonable scenario there will not be enough grant assistance available in the future to free these students totally from the need to borrow.

The trend toward increased reliance on borrowing has produced at least two serious problems. One is the well-publicized increase in defaults, and the other is an incentive for students to enroll in shorter-term programs to minimize borrowing. There is also a disincentive for students to enroll in institutions away from home because it would increase the costs of attendance and thus might well require greater borrowing.

Student loan defaults represent one of the most discouraging aspects of federal student financial aid. Despite periodic efforts to "clean up" the system, the federal costs for defaults now exceed $2 billion annually. Perhaps most distressing is the fact that all the existing studies indicate that minority students are more likely to default than White students.

Often lost among all the arguments about default rates and costs is the fact that much of the reason for defaults stems from borrowers' inability to repay, as measured by their incomes once they graduate or leave school, rather than their unwillingness to repay. Recent survey data indicate that almost half of Stafford loan defaulters have incomes after leaving school of less than $6,000, and three-quarters have incomes of less than $15,000. Defaulters are primarily those who enrolled in vocational programs or those who dropped out of college programs (NCES, Characteristics of Stafford Loan Recipients, 1988).

Borrowers with relatively large debts currently have the option of consolidating their loans and choosing from a set of repayment options that allow them to stretch out their repayments in line with their incomes. While these consolidation provisions have had limited effectiveness and are used by a relatively small number of borrowers, they at least do exist. But no such opportunity exists for lower-income borrowers with relatively small amounts of debt, many of them minorities, who are typically not eligible for consolidation.

The benefits of loan consolidation, however, could be extended to low-income borrowers through a program of "low-income insurance." Under such an approach, borrowers whose debt repayment exceeded a percentage of their income could apply for relief through graduated and extended repayment terms or possibly could pay a set percentage of their income until their obligation was met. After a period of time, any remaining obligation might be forgiven. The purpose of such a program would be to reduce the number of borrowers who unfairly have been labeled defaulters in the current sytem and instead give them a chance to repay at a pace they can afford.

Given the probability that there will be no major increase in grant funding which would reduce the need to borrow, the "low-income insurance" discussed above would give students greater confidence to attempt a baccalaureate program; enrolling in or transferring to four-institutions outside their immediate community need not constitute unreasonable financial risk.

The organizations that seem most ideally suited to providing low-income insurance are the state-appointed guarantee agencies in the Stafford Student Loan program. Many of these agencies already are involved in this kind of approach in that they seek to collect on loans that have already defaulted. What we are arguing for here is that instead of quickly labeling these borrowers as defaulters, the guaranty agencies should try to rehabilitate these loans before the default claim is made to the federal government.

To reduce the additional federal costs attached to extending repayment terms beyond the normal length of ten years, the guarantee agencies should purchase these loans from the lenders as quickly as possible. To pay for these purchases, the origination fee that is currently charged to Stafford loan borrowers should be changed into a default fee and used in part to pay for the purchase of these loans from the initial lenders. This low-income insurance could also be financed through the reserves that guarantee agencies have built up over time to pay for their share of default costs.

CHOOSING AMONG ALTERNATIVE FINANCING STRATEGIES

Now that we have identified six potential strategies for improving the enrollment and retention of low-income and minority students in higher education, the question that remains is which of these strategies offers the best opportunity for progress. To place such a discussion of potential strategies within a realistic budgetary context, we might impose the following assumption:

A reclusive billionaire has generously provided an additional one billion dollars with the stipulation that it be spent in a manner that would maximize the increased participation of low-income and minority students in higher education. How should this largesse be spent?

We have specified this assumption because without such a financial constraint, we will have a conversation without a conclusion. Each of the strategies discussed above would certainly have a beneficial effect on the enrollment of targeted groups of students. If financial resources were unlimited, we would employ each as much as we could in our quest to increase the participation of low-income and minority students. But resources in the real world are not unlimited, as we all know, and so we must make choices.

If the entire $1 billion in new funds were used for the maintenance of low tuitions at public institutions, those tuitions would be held down or reduced by an average of $100 per student, which is not likely to have a major impact on the decision of very many students. It is also worth noting that the $100 in lower tuitions would go to all students attending public institutions and would not be targeted to particular groups of students at those institutions.

Another obvious candidate for use of the $1 billion would be to increase the funding of the Pell Grant program, since that has been and remains the principal federal program for increasing access to higher education. The present rule of thumb is that every $100 increase in the maximum award requires roughly $270 million in additional funding. Thus, $1 billion in new funding would allow for a $400 increase in the maximum award. But how much effect would $400 in additional aid per student have? It certainly would induce some number of students to enroll, although that number is not likely to be very large. It would have less effect on the schools that students choose since Pell Grants are not very sensitive to cost differentials among institutions. And it would likely have little or no effect on the persistence of students once they enroll.

Each of the other strategies discussed here, however, would not reasonably entail the expenditure of an additional billion dollars. For example, a fellowship program designed to encourage minority students to enter designated fields of study might require $100 to $200 million annually to have a substantial impact. To encourage more minority students to enter doctoral programs would require no more than $50 to $100 million per year in additional funding. The TRIO programs could be provided with an additional billion dollars, but such an increase in funding should only occur after the program-funding formula is reexamined to ensure that a broader base of institutions are able to participate.

A progam of early eligibility for grant assistance would involve additional funding only to the extent that more disadvantaged students participated in higher education as a result of their being more aware that they were eligible for aid. A realistic estimate of additional aid in this instance might be $200 to $300 million. A program of low-income insurance might not entail any additional costs in that it could be financed through the fees that student borrowers already pay to the federal government or state guarantee agencies.

In conclusion, the leverage gained through these smaller approaches recommends that they be a prominent part of a package for spending additional funds. By contrast, devoting an additional $1 billion entirely to the more traditional strategies of maintaining low tuitions or increasing the funding for Pell Grants would not result in large increases in aid for each student aided. In an era of scarce resources, it seems reasonable to focus on those strategies likely to provide the greatest amount of aid per intended beneficiary.

REFERENCES

American Council on Education. *Student aid in the Reagan administration: FY81-FY89.* Washington, DC: ACE Division of Governmental Relations.

American Council on Education. Unpublished tabulations from the NCES 1980 and 1982 high school and beyond surveys. Washington, DC.

Breneman, D. W., and S. C. Nelson. 1981. *Financing community colleges, an economic perspective.* Washington, DC: Brookings Institution.

Carroll, D. January 1989. *College persistence and degree attainment for 1980 high school graduates: Hazards for transfers, stopouts, and part-timers.* Washington, DC: U.S. National Center for Educational Statistics.

Eagle, E., and D. Carroll. December 1988. *Postsecondary enrollment, persistence, and attainment for 1972, 1980, and 1982 high school graduates.* Washington, DC: U.S. National Center for Educational Statistics.

Educational Testing Service. September 1986. *Study of excellence in high school education: Longitudinal study 1980-82 final report.* Washington, DC: U.S. Department of Education Center for Statistics.

Ross, L., and D. Hampton. 1992. How the nontraditional student finances her education. In J. Eaton (Ed.) (1992). *Financing nontraditional students: A seminar report.* Washington, DC: American Council on Education.

U.S. Bureau of the Census. *School enrollment—social and economic characteristics of students: October 1988 and 1987.* Series P-20, No. 443. Washington, DC.

U.S. National Center for Educational Statistics. June 1990. *Characteristics of Stafford Loan recipients 1988.* Washington, DC.

U.S. National Center for Educational Statistics. *Degrees conferred in institutions of higher education, by race/ethnicity and sex: 1976-77 through 1986-87.* Washington, DC.

U.S. National Center for Educational Statistics. 1989. *Digest of education statistics 1989.* Washington, DC.

U.S. National Center for Educational Statistics. 1978. *Enrollment in higher education.* Washington, DC.

U.S. National Center for Educational Statistics. *Special unpublished tabulations from the 1980 and 1982 high school and beyond surveys.* Washington, DC.

———. December 1988. *Plans, participation, persistence, and baccalaureate degree attainment of 1980 and 1982 high school graduates, by ability.*

———. February 1989. *Plans, participation, persistence, and baccalaureate degree attainment of 1980 high school graduates, by socioeconomic status.*

———. February 1989. *Plans, participation, persistence, and baccalaureate degree attainment of 1982 high school graduates, by socioeconomic status.*

U.S. National Center for Educational Statistics. *Trends in minority enrollment in higher education, fall 1976-fall 1986.* Washington, DC.

U.S. National Center for Educational Statistics. June 1990. *Trends in racial/ethnic enrollment in higher education: Fall 1978 through fall 1988.* Washington, DC.

U.S. National Center for Educational Statistics. June 1988. *Undergraduate financing of postsecondary education, a report of the 1987 national postsecondary student aid study.* Washington, DC.

CHAPTER

• • • • • • • • •

Funding Doctoral Studies
for Minorities

Sara Meléndez

For more than three decades, a recurring theme in virtually every discussion of the impediments to minority doctoral attainment is that of the cost, and invariably, discussants will recommend increasing financial aid, especially fellowships and grants, for minority doctoral studies. In 1968, speaking at a conference of the Council of Graduate Schools, Samuel Nabrit recommended several strategies, including financial aid, for increasing African American doctorate holders.

By the mid seventies, evidence of the effectiveness of the financial aid programs enacted during the late sixties was clear. African American and Hispanic participation and graduation rates at all levels of higher education increased significantly. In 1976 African Americans received 1,213 doctorates, the highest number ever achieved in one year at that time (American Council on Educaiton, 1985). By 1978, 3.1 percent of African Americans over the age of 25 had enrolled in a graduate program, a significant increase from 1.3 percent in 1968 (U.S. Bureau of Census, 1980). Hispanic doctoral attainment has continued to increase, with slight fluctuations from year to year, from 412 in 1980 to 700 in 1990.

In 1978, the federal government modified the requirements for eligibility for financial aid, thereby allowing middle-income students to qualify. Perhaps not coincidentally, by 1983, it was clear that the growth in minority doctoral degrees awarded of the seventies had slowed and that neither African Americans nor Hispanics had achieved parity. In fact, for African Americans, the gains appeared to be reversing. In 1983, the National Commission on Student Financial Assistance recommended federal policy to "ensure support for talented graduate students" and to "increase the numbers of talented minority students in graduate education."

In 1986, a group of educators met in Washington, DC, to discuss the factors that contribute to the continuing underrepresentation of minorities in graduate education. Among their recommendations was that institutions work to reduce the heavy dependence of minority students on external funding sources (Adams, 1986). Kidwell (1986) recommended that Native American tribes provide scholarship support for graduate education, including a program of loan forgiveness for those returning to work on the reservation.

Federal funding for graduate education declined in the early eighties, and the declines appear to have had a disproportionate impact on African American, Hispanic, and Native American students, who were forced to depend more heavily on loans. The National Research Council (Coyle, 1986) reported that 45 percent of Hispanic, 45 percent of African American, and 42 percent of Native American students had taken out student loans, compared to the 36 percent of Whites and 33 percent of Asian Americans who relied on loans. Fifty-two percent of Puerto Ricans, whose family income is lower than any group but Native Americans, had to resort to loans.

In a study of 1,352 doctoral students in large public institutions, Nettles (1990) found that 46 percent of African American and 43 percent of Hispanic students still had unpaid loans for undergraduate education, compared to 36 percent of White students. Furthermore, Hispanics borrowed more than both African American and White students.

After almost three decades since the first major national efforts to increase access to higher education (including graduate education) for minority students, the groups with the lowest family and per capita income rely more heavily on loans to pay for their education while the more affluent White students receive a higher proportion of grants and assistantships and rely on fewer loans. And yet, race-specific financial aid programs are constantly under attack as reverse discrimination and unfair to White students.

Although many reasons are given for the low doctoral attainment of Hispanics and African Americans, given the continued disparity in funding available to them and the continued disparity in family income, it is understandable that in 1990 each group earned only 2 percent of the doctorates awarded. In "Meeting the National Need for Minority Scholars and Scholarship: Policies and Actions," a policy/action group meeting at the State University of New York at Stony Brook in 1988 recommended:

1. Reversing the recent policy of emphasizing loans over grants and financing entitlement programs to fully fund all eligible students
2. Providing forgiveness of loans for minority graduates entering academic careers
3. Creating one-year awards for dissertation support of students in the arts, humanities, and social sciences
4. Identifying early the potential recepients for federally funded fellowship programs and including summer research grants, apprenticeships, advanced research, and training opportunities in these programs
5. Increasing funding for the Patricia Roberts Harris Fellowship Program and funding each recipient at the same level as the National Science Foundation fellows
6. Mandating principal investigators on federal research grants to provide research opportunities for underrepresented minority graduate students

While funding for undergraduate education has an entitlement basis, which is sensitive to need, this is not true of funding for graduate education. Much of the financial assistance for graduate education is rendered through fellowships and research and teaching assistantships. Much of this type of aid is merit based, which often means reliance on standardized examination scores. Furthermore, assistantships often depend on faculty who have research grants to dole out to students. Minority students have traditionally not received a proportional share of such funds.

Despite nearly three decades of policies and programs to increase minority doctoral attainment, minorities continue to receive a lower percentage of assistantships than White and foreign students. Nettles (1990) reported that while 54 percent of the White students in his study received a teaching or research assistantship, only 38 percent of the African American students did. African American students received proportionately fewer tuition waivers than did White or Hispanic students. In this study, a higher percentage of Hispanic students received teaching or research assistantships, but this is not the case in national figures.

Another continuing and sensitive issue is that universities spend a significant portion of financial aid resources on non-U.S. born, temporary residents (international or foreign students). Coyle (1986) reported that 61 percent of foreign-born, temporary residents of Asian background received research assistantships, compared with 60 percent for permanent residents and 52 percent for Asian American citizens. The same pattern holds true for African American students receiving research assistantships: only 20 percent of African American U.S. citizens received aid, but 33 percent of permanent residents and 31 percent of temporary residents of African background received research assistantships. Similarly, in the category of "other Hispanics," 33 percent of U.S. citizens received research assistantships, compared with 43 and 40 percent, respectively, for permanent and temporary residents. In 1990, university resources supported 42 percent of all American doctoral students, but 69 percent of foreign students and only 25 percent of African American students.

Not only do minority citizens receive fewer assistantships than foreign students of color, but they also lag behind White citizens in assistantships. The National Research Council figures on 1984 doctorates show that African Americans, Hispanics, and Native Americans received a dispropotionately low share of research assistantships compared to White students. While 38 percent of White students received research assistantships, only 22 percent of African Americans, 26 percent of Hispanics (but 22 percent of Puerto Ricans), and 26 percent of Native Americans did. Asian Americans received the highest percentage of research assistantships, 52 percent. A larger percentage of White students received teaching assistantships, as well: 48 percent, compared to 31 percent of African Americans, 39 percent of Hispanics (35 percent of Puerto Ricans), 39 percent of Asian Americans, and 42 percent of Native Americans.

There are several issues in financial support of minority doctoral students that continue to need attention: the low percentage of research assistantships received by African American, Hispanic, and Native American students; the low percentage of teaching assistantships received by Hispanic and Asian American students; the low percentage of university support received by Native American Students (22 percent, compared to 29 percent for Whites, 32 percent for African Americans, 31 percent for Hispanics, and 30 percent for Asian Americans); and the disproportionately high support by universities for foreign students.

Given that as a group African Americans, Hispanics, and Native Americans all have lower family incomes than Whites, it is reasonable to assume that they have greater need for assistance. Greater emphasis on need would increase financial support for these students and, ultimately, their doctoral degree attainment. Similarly, greater availability of grants and fellowships, instead of loans, should have a positive impact on doctorate attainment.

Among the recommendations made in "Meeting the National Need for Minority Scholars and Scholarship: Policies and Actions" (Adams, 1989) was a policy to "ensure that, where financial aid programs exist for graduate students, there is a mix of merit aid with aid based on financial need and targeted to underrepresented groups."

Traditional sources of funding for graduate education include federal and nonfederal fellowships and scholarships; institutional resources (including fellowships, research and teaching assistantships, and work study programs); loans (federally and state guaranteed, and market-rate loans); and the family. For all groups, the bulk of funding for graduate education comes from family resources. For African Americans, Native Americans, and Hispanics, the next most significant source of support comes from loans; on the contrary, for whites and Asian Americans, research and teaching assistantships represent the next most important source of funding (Coyle, 1986).

SUPPORT PROGRAMS TO INCREASE MINORITY PARTICIPATION IN GRADUATE EDUCATION

Throughout the last 20 years, many programs have been implemented to provide financial support to minorities pursuing doctoral studies. These programs have been launched by the federal and state governments, as well as by private foundations, corporations, and individual institutions of higher education. It would appear that these programs have had a measure of success for all minority groups, although for African Americans, as shown above, there has been a decline since the peak of 1,109 doctorates attained in 1977 that has never again been achieved.

Funding for federal programs has been reduced at the same time that tuition has increased dramatically. The decline in doctorates awarded to African Americans, presented above, is very likely related to the significant reduction in funds. Between 1970 and 1981 federal funds for fellowships, scholarships, and traineeships declined by more than half, and the number of federal stipends for graduate study declined from nearly 80,000 to 40,000 (National Commission on Student Financial Assistance, 1983).

Federal Programs

The United States government spends over $200 million annually to support graduate studies. Many departments, such as the National Institutes of Health and the Department of Agriculture support graduate education. The Higher Education Act also supports graduate education through specific fellowship and loan programs. Some of the federal programs are intended to increase the number of practitioners, faculty, and or researchers in fields in which the government has a specific interest, such as science, mathematics, foreign languages and international studies.

While many such programs do not target any funds for minorities, universities need to be held accountable for equitable distribution of such funds. Minority students should have equal access to all federally funded programs. Programs targeted to minorities should be seen as supplementing other programs, not supplanting them.

Fellowships and Grants Administered by the U.S. Department of Education. The **Patricia Roberts Harris Graduate and Professional Fellowship Program** awards tuition allowances to the institutions, which must make up the difference if costs are higher, and stipends to the students for a maximum of three years. The FY 1994 budget authorizes $21.8 million, an increase of $1.4 million over 1993, reflecting increases authorized in the 1992 Higher Education Amendments. Institutional grants were increased to $9,000 and student stipends to $14,000.

Women and Minority Participation in Graduate Program is a program that provides grants to institutions, which then provide need-based fellowships for talented undergraduate students who are underrepresented in particular fields of graduate study. Special emphasis is given to mathematics and the sciences. The fellowships help prepare students for graduate study by means of summer research internships, seminars, and other educational experiences. The 1994 budget request for this program was $6 million.

The **Faculty Development Fellowships** is a new program, authorized in the 1994 budget at $8.5 million, to help create a more culturally diverse professorate. Grants will be awarded to institutions to assist faculty from underrepresented groups attain their doctorate, and to assist college graduate members of underrepresented groups to obtain doctorates and enter the professorate. Funds in 1994 would support approximately 700 fellows.

Contact:
U.S. Department of Education
7th and D Streets, SW, ROB-3, Rm. 3514
Washington, DC 20202-5251
(202) 708-8395

The **Center for International Education** funds two programs that include support for graduate study. Although the programs do not have grants targeted to minority students, students from backgrounds other than English, who have a good command of their native language, may find these programs appropriate.

The *Foreign Language and Area Studies Fellowships* are awarded to academic departments that in turn select the students they will support for study in foreign languages and international studies. Stipends of $7,000 plus a tuition grant are awarded.

The *Fullbright-Hays Doctoral Dissertation Fellowships* awards stipends for six months to one year of research toward the dissertation. Awards range from $5,000 to $50,000.

Contact:
Advanced Training and Research Branch
Center for International Education

U.S. Department of Education
7th and D Streets, SW, ROB-3
Washington, DC 20202-5331
(202) 708-9298

Other Federal Fellowship Programs. The **National Aeronautics and Space Administration (NASA)** operates four financial assistance programs: The Graduate Students Researchers Program, the National Space Grant College and Fellowship Program, the Global Change Research Fellowships, and the Graduate Cooperative Education Program. Amounts of assistance, length, and purpose vary, except that they are all awarded for work in some aspect of research of interest to NASA.

In addition, NASA has a program to increase the participation of underrepresented minorities in space science and technology.
Contact:
NASA Headquarters
Code XEU
Washington, DC 20546
(202) 453-8344

The **National Science Foundation Minority Graduate Fellowships** program awards fellowships for graduate study in science and engineering. Awards include $6,000 toward tuition and annual stipends of $12,900 for up to three years.
Contact:
The Fellowship Office
National Research Council
2101 Constitution Ave., NW
Washington, DC 20418
(202) 334-2872

The **National Institutes of Health** provide funding for minority students in the biomedical sciences through the *Minority Access to Research Careers* (MARC). Awards includes tuition and annual stipends of $8,500 for up to five years. Participation in the MARC Honors Undergraduate Training Program is required.
Contact:
U.S. Department of Health and Human Services
Bureau of Health Professions
Health Resources and Services Administration
5600 Fishers Lane
Rockville, MD 20857
(301) 443-4776

The Bureau of Indian Affairs provides support for graduate study to Native Americans who have one-fourth or more Indian blood.

Contact:
Office of Indian Education
Bureau of Indian Affairs
18th and C Streets, NW
Washington, DC 20240
(202) 343-4879

In addition to the above, many federal government agencies provide fellowships and grants not specifically targeted to minority students, many of which are available on the basis of need.

Loans. The federal government funds several loan programs, the payment of which it guarantees. The most widely used and best-known are the Perkins and Stafford loan programs.

Perkins. Funds are provided to institutions of higher education and administered by the financial aid office. Loans to citizens or residents, based on need, of up to $18,000 may be borrowed for graduate study and are payable over 10 years at 5 percent interest. Perkins Loans were formerly known as the National Direct Student Loan program.

Stafford. Available to citizens and residents, and formerly called the Guaranteed Student Loan Program, this program provides up to $7,500 per year, for a total of $54,750, for undergraduate and graduate study. Loans are administered by banks and other lending institutions and are based on financial need. Interest rate is 8 percent through the fourth year and 10 percent in year five.

Supplemental Loans for Students (SLS). These loans are available in addition to other loan programs and provide up to $4,000 per year for a total of $20,000 for graduate study. Available to citizens and residents, SLS loans are guaranteed by the government but are not subsidized while the students are in school and are often payable during the students' school years. Interest varies and is dependent on the Treasury Bill rate, but there is a maximum of 12 percent interest that may be charged.

SLS loans do not require demonstration of need and are usually payable over five to ten years. Some banks require that payments begin while students are in school, but some banks will defer payment of either principal or both principal and interest.

Contact:
Any bank or other lending institution.

State Funded Programs

The Council of Graduate Schools (1990) reported that over half of the states provide funding for graduate study at approximately $48 million per year. Approximately two-thirds of the awards are need based and one-third is merit based. Only residents of the states are eligible and some programs are not transportable outside the state.

Contact:

Financial Aid office of any institution.

Private Funds

There are several national fellowship programs that target minority doctoral students. The following programs all emphasize teaching and research.

The Ford Foundation Fellowships. The Ford Foundation has been involved in funding minority graduate study since 1967 when it initiated a program to assist African American faculty from traditionally Black institutions (TBI) to take a year off to complete their doctoral studies. In 1968, the program focused on African American faculty at TBI's, and in 1969 it was extended to include African American faculty at any institution of higher education. In 1970, the program was again expanded to include Mexican Americans, Puerto Ricans, and Native Americans. Between 1967 and 1973, 826 awards were made, including 181 renewal awards.

In 1969, the foundation initiated the Doctoral Program for the purpose of increasing the number of African Americans studying for careers in higher education. In 1970, Puerto Ricans, Mexican Americans, and Native Americans were added to the list of eligible groups. Awards were renewable for up to five years.

By 1981, the foundation had awarded 2,306 fellowships as follows: 1,396 to African Americans, 470 to Mexican Americans, 300 to Puerto Ricans, and 140 to Native Americans. Arce and Manning (1984), in a study of the fellowship program, reported that 61.5 percent of all fellows enrolled in graduate school through 1979 had completed their degree programs.

The Ford Foundation Fellowship Program for African Americans, Hispanics, and Native Americans ended in 1980. In 1985, the foundation initiated another program of doctoral fellowships for minorities that focused on fields in which they are underrepresented. These awards provide institutional grants of $6,000, in return for which the institution waives tuition and fees, and annual stipends of $11,000 for up to three years, and a twelve-month dissertation award of $18,000.

Contact:
Ford Foundation Pre-doctoral and
Dissertation Fellowships
National Research Council
2101 Constitution Avenue
Washington, DC 20418
(202) 334-2872

Other Fellowship Programs. The **National Hispanic Scholarship Fund** provides grants for graduate study to Hispanic students, based on a combination of merit and need.

Contact:
National Hispanic Scholarship Fund
P.O. Box 728
Novato, CA 94948

The **National Consortium for Graduate Degrees for Minorities in Engineering (GEM)**, a consortium of 50 universities and 48 business organizations, provides fellowships for doctoral studies in the natural sciences or engineering. In addition to paid summer research internships, the program pays tuition, fees, and a stipend of $12,000 for the first year. Universities assume support of fellows beyond the first year.

Contact:
GEM
Box 537
Notre Dame, IN 46556
(219) 287-1488

The **McKnight Doctoral Fellowship Program** provides up to $5,000 toward tuition and fees and $11,000 stipends to African Americans to obtain a doctorate in a Florida institution of higher education. The program supports the first three years, and if necessary the universities support years four and five. A significant majority of McKnight fellows are pursuing degrees in science fields.

The **McKnight Minority Junior Faculty Development Fellowship Program** supports nontenured minority faculty, especially African Americans and women, in underrepresented fields to attain the doctorate degree. The program provides $15,000 to the institution to cover the costs of replacing the faculty member during the fellowship year and provides the normal salary and benefits to the fellow.

Contact:
Florida Endowment Fund for Higher Education
201 East Kennedy Blvd., Ste. 1525

Tampa, FL 33602
(813) 272-2772

The **Dorothy Danforth Compton Fellowships Program** awards grants to 10 institutions to support minority doctoral study for the purpose of increasing minority faculty. The fellowships are awarded by the institutions. The program provides $100,000 per year for tuition and stipends, plus $5,000 to the institutions to "create a supportive environment."

Contact:
The Danforth Foundation
231 South Bemeston Ave.
St. Louis, MO 63105-1903
(314) 862-6200

Professional Associations

Some professional associations have initiated fellowship programs to increase the number of minorities in the field.

The **American Psychological Association Minority Fellowship Program**, funded by the National Institute for Mental Health, supports 30 minority doctoral students in research and psychology, and 15 in neuroscience. Although financial need is not a criterion, it is considered in the award decision. Fellows receive stipends of up to $8,800 per year for a maximum of three years. The association will enter into cost-sharing agreements with the universities on the tuition and fees. To date 689 fellowships have been awarded in psychology and 71 in neuroscience.

Contact:
American Psychological Association
750 1st Street, NW
Washington, DC 20001
(202) 955-7761

The **American Sociological Association Minority Fellowship Program** awards approximately 10 fellowships annually. Awards include tuition and fees plus a $8,800 stipend, for a maximum of three years. Recipients are required to engage in research and/or training for a period equal to the length of support in excess of one year. A total of 328 awards have been made.

Contact:
American Sociological Association
Minority Fellowship
1722 N Street, NW
Washington, DC 20036
(202) 833-3410

The **American Political Science Association** funds six fellowships yearly, two to Hispanic students and four to other minority students. Fellows receive awards of approximately $6,000 for one year. Awards are given on the basis of need and potential for success.

Contact:
American Political Science Association
1527 New Hampshire Avenue, NW
Washington, DC 20036
(202) 483-2512

CONCLUSION

Minority educators, federal and state governments, institutions of higher education, and philanthropic institutions have been working for almost three decades on finding solutions to the underrepresentation among the ranks of doctorate-holding faculty and researchers of African Americans, Hispanics, and Native Americans. It has been demonstrated that the explicit policies of targeting programs and funds to that end were somewhat successful in increasing the numbers of minority doctorate holders. It has been demonstrated, as well, that momentum has been lost, growth has been slowed (and for African Americans reversed), and we are facing a backlash against race-specific policies.

We cannot afford complacency if we are to move forward again in minority doctoral attainment. While the cost of higher education, undergraduate and graduate, has been increasing at a rate higher than the annual inflation rate, the real income of African Americans and Hispanics has declined. Simultaneously, funds for financial aid have declined, and what funding is available has largely shifted from grants and fellowships to loans.

In recent years, we have seen many challenges to programs to aid minorities, not only in education, but in employment and contracting as well. The latest appointees of the last administration to the Department of Education declared scholarships given only to minorities illegal and unconstitutional. "Liberal" and "politically correct" became pejorative terms.

And yet, the demographics continue in an apparently inexorable trend toward a nation where all the major cities are populated by a majority of "minority" residents; where the urban schools are already populated by a majority of students of color; where the most populous state may become a "minority majority" state within a decade or so; where the family income of people of color continues to lose ground compared to whites; and where minorities continue to lag behind in educational attainment. Furthermore, all these trends continue at time when the labor market requires higher levels of education and skills.

We have learned something from our experiences of the last three decades about how to increase minority educational attainment, including doctorates. We need a renewed commitment to the strategies that have been effective. History has shown us that left to our own devices, without incentives or sanctions, we tend to do "business as usual." While we would all like to arrive at a time when "special" programs are unnecessary because we will have attained a "race-blind" society, only self-delusion would allow us to believe that we are there. We continue to need leadership from the top at institutions of higher education. We continue to need legislation and funding. We continue to need enforcement of the legislation and policies in place. Perhaps, most importantly, we need a shared conviction that we have to do better for the good of the country.

REFERENCES

Arce, C., and W. Manning. 1984. *Minorities in academic careers: The experience of Ford Foundation fellows.* A report to the Ford Foundation.

Adams, H. G. May 1986. Successfully negotiating the graduate school process: A guide for minority students. In *National Consortium for Graduate Degrees for Minorities in Engineering, Inc.* Notre Dame, IN.

Adams, M. C. 1989. *Meeting the national need for minority scholars and scholarships: Policies and actions.* Stony Brook: SUNY Press.

Carter, D., and R. Wilson. 1991. *Minorities in higher education.* Washington, DC: American Council on Education.

Council of Graduate Schools. 1990. *Graduate student financial support: A handbook for graduate deans, faculty, and administrators.* Washington, DC.

Coyle, S. L. 1986. *Summary report 1984, doctorate recipients from United States universities.* Washington, DC: Office of Scientific and Engineering Personnel, National Research Council.

Kidwell, C. S. March 1986. Motivating American Indians into graduate studies. *ERIC Digest.* Las Cruces, NM: ERIC Clearinghouse on Rural Education and Small Schools.

Minorities in higher education: Fourth annual status report. 1985. Washington, DC: American Council on Education, p. 17.

National Commission on Student Financial Assistance. 1983. *Signs of trouble and erosion: A report on graduate education in America.*

Nettles, M.T. 1990. *Black, Hispanic, and White doctoral students: Before, during, and after enrolling in graduate school.* Princeton, NJ: Educational Testing Service.

CHAPTER 7

• • • • • • • • •

Clearing the Pathway: Improving Opportunities for Minority Students to Transfer

Laura I. Rendón and Amaury Nora

To what extent do minority students find viable opportunities to initiate college-parallel studies in community colleges and to ultimately transfer to senior institutions? Currently, this question is receiving increased attention, given the fact that for large numbers of Hispanics, Blacks, Asians, and American Indians, community colleges are the main entry points to higher education. Of all Hispanics enrolled in higher education in fall 1991, fully 55 percent were enrolled in two-year colleges. About 43 percent of Blacks and 40 percent of Asians who enrolled in college attended two-year colleges in 1991, compared to 55 percent of American Indian college students (*Chronicle of Higher Education*, 1993).

For about half of minority students, completion of baccalaureate studies is conditioned by transfer from a community college to a four-year institution (Richardson and Bender, 1987). Yet, today there is mounting concern that over the years, the community college transfer function has lost its strength and vitality, and that, relative to their proportionate enrollment, minority students simply are not transferring in numbers high enough to create optimism that significantly more students will eventually earn bachelor's degrees (Nora and Rendon, 1988; Richardson and Bender, 1987; Cohen, Brawer and Bensimon, 1985). The warning signs are apparent. Transfer rates often fall lower than 10 percent, and some states with high two-year college minority enrollments have reported transfer declines in recent years. The colleges are often accused of providing students with inadequate counseling and substandard academic preparation, and student expectations have declined so that higher-order thinking skills receive limited attention. There is also concern that community college transfer losses are highest in colleges with high proportions of minority students (Rendon, Justiz, and Resta, 1988; Bernstein, 1986; Hayward, 1985; Richardson and Bender, 1987; Richardson, Fisk, and Okun, 1983; Rouche and Comstock, 1981).

These declines are coming at a time when minority students' access to college is declining relative to their overall precollege enrollments. In spite of the fact that the K-12 system is increasingly becoming more non-White, very high minority dropout rates have been registered in urban high schools. Further, studies document that higher education enrollments for Blacks and Hispanics are decreasing in proportion to their high school enrollments. Conversely, college enrollments for White students have been increasing. These trends are cause for concern given the fact that high school enrollments have been declining for Whites and increasing for Blacks and Hispanics (Orfield and Paul, 1987-1988; Wilson and Melendez, 1987). Moreover, proportionately fewer American Indians have enrolled in college since 1972. These declines have occurred even though the Indian birthrate is very high (Harris Tijerina, and Blemer, 1987-1988). Making college an attractive option for minorities is a critical challenge for the nation's educational system. Yet, there is now concern that the devaluation of the transfer function in community colleges may not afford students the opportunity to advance toward the baccalaureate.

THE DECLINE OF THE TRANSFER FUNCTION

Since their inception, two-year colleges offered a curriculum that prepared students to transfer to senior colleges and universities. The transfer program, also known as the college-parallel or the college-preparatory program, was the first curriculum to be offered in junior colleges, and the two-year college was identified simply as the first two years of a four-year college. Before 1950, the transfer program overshadowed all other functions (Monroe, 1977). Through the 1950s, approximately 65 percent of students in two-year colleges participated in transfer programs (Lombardi, 1980). However, as the colleges grew and became concerned with providing access and equal opportunity to people with diverse academic, social, and racial backgrounds, more functions were added to the colleges' missions. These included nondegree occupational programs and post-high school terminal programs for students who sought to enter jobs or prepare for family living. After World War II, junior colleges became community colleges, and added two more functions. Community services were an array of cultural and educational programs that did not lead to transfer. Remedial studies programs were designed to strengthen the weak academic skills of high school graduates.

By the late 1960s and 1970s, multiple functions allowed community colleges to become people's colleges. In the process, they underwent a major philosophical shift from institutions providing a traditional college preparation to flexible colleges that prepared students to find a job, adapt to life, and get the most for their money in a short period, without leaving home and without having to give up a full-time job (Rendon, 1984; Cohen, 1985; Monroe, 1977). Factors contributing to the decline of transfers during this period included increased enrollments in career and vocational programs; the growth of remedial education; the addition of adult, community, and continuing education functions; an increase in the proportion of part-time students and increased competition from four-year institutions for students who in the past had enrolled in community colleges. Consequently, by 1973 less than 43 percent of students in two-year colleges were participating in transfer programs, and by 1980 the proportion had dropped to about 30 percent (Friedlander, 1980). Today, estimates of students who transfer range from 5 to 15 percent, and if present trends continue, it is expected that the number of those in transfer programs may decline to about 3 to 5 percent of total enrollments (Richardson and Bender, 1985).

In an important article tracing the development of the community college and its possible links to social stratification, Karabel (1986) asserts that in the early 1980s the most fundamental change to have occurred in the history of the American community college was the "transformation from an institution primarily offering college-parallel liberal arts programs to one emphasizing terminal vocational programs." While the share of associate degrees awarded in arts and sciences declined from 57.4 percent in 1970-71 to 37.4 percent in 1980-81, the share of associate degrees awarded in occupational programs rose from 42.6 percent to 62.6 percent (Cohen, 1984). In 1985 the largest number of associate degrees awarded was in business and management (26.6 percent). The second largest degree area was liberal/general studies (23.6 percent), although approximately 3 percent fewer degrees were awarded in this area in 1985 than in 1983 (El-Khawas, Carter, and Ottinger, 1988).

According to Karabel (1986), this rise in vocationalism was due to declining labor markets for graduates of four-year colleges, especially in the liberal arts; the leveling off of the process of educational inflation; and internal organizational interests of community college administrators who wanted to carve out a distinct niche and identity. Interestingly, while the rise in vocationalism was associated with striking declines in the rate of community college transfers, it also became apparent that vocational curricula sometimes led to transfer into four-year institutions. But whether the vocational student rate of transfer is high or low, there appears to be consensus that transfer education has declined substantially during the past 15 to 20 years (Karabel, 1986; Friedlander, 1980; Cohen, Brawer, and Bensimon, 1985; Richardson and Bender, 1987; Rendon, Justiz, and Resta, 1988).

Yet, while many believe that vocational programs are what community colleges can and should do best, the jury is still out on what happens to students when they seek to enter the labor market. Nonetheless, a few existing studies do not support the view that vocational education is a path to upward mobility and economic security. These studies suggest that community college graduates often cannot secure employment in the fields for which they were trained, that economic returns are modest, and that the most successful training programs place graduates in low-status jobs (Pincus, 1980; Karabel).

Thus, the criticism of transfer programs and vocational curricula is double jeopardy for community colleges. It appears that not only has the transfer function been reduced to a very low priority on many two-year college campuses, but that vocational programs may lead to low-level, dead-end jobs that perpetuate a stratified class structure, with minorities and the disadvantaged occupying the bottom stratum. Reversing this situation will require a major breakthrough in revitalizing the transfer function, attracting students to transfer programs, and stopping the slippage of students as they flow through the educational pipeline.

ACCESS IN JEOPARDY

Given the differential representation of Hispanics, Blacks, and American Indians in community colleges, it is important to question whether the colleges are having a negative effect on minority students and to what extent the colleges have assisted minorities to make progress toward the baccalaureate. Several studies, descriptive as well as theoretical, provide some insights with regard to minority student participation in community colleges.

Aspirations

One should begin by emphasizing that despite declines in priority given to the transfer function, it is apparent that minority students do have transfer aspirations. For example, in a national study of urban community colleges with large Black and Hispanic enrollments, more than 74 percent of students sampled expressed a desire to obtain a B.A. or higher at some time in their lives (Bensimon and Riley, 1984). Similarly, a study of six community colleges located in Texas, Arizona, and California (Rendon, Justiz, and Resta, 1988) with large Hispanic student enrollments found that students were interested in and committed to transferring. Specifically, the study indicated that 87 percent of Hispanic students and 94 percent of Whites had plans to transfer to one or more four-year institutions. Half of the students planned to transfer after receiving an associate and one-fourth planned to transfer before earning an associate. Further, nearly three-fourths of students thought transferring was important and over 60 percent felt it was more important than getting a job. In another study (Richardson and Bender, 1987) urban community college faculty and counselors estimated that 40 to 50 percent of entering students had transfer aspirations. But perhaps more important than assessing how many students initially intend to transfer is what happens to Hispanics, Blacks, and American Indians after they enroll in a community college, for there is concern that enrolling in a two-year college may have a negative effect on minority students.

Hispanic Students

As a whole, Hispanic students rely heavily on two-year colleges for access to higher education but generally exhibit low transfer rates. A comprehensive study examining the transfer function in community colleges with large Hispanic enrollments in Texan, Arizona, and California (Rendon, Justiz, and Resta, 1988) revealed a number of barriers that impede the transfer process. Interviews with faculty, counselors, and administrators highlighted student-centered barriers, which included a lack of motivation and academic preparation; unfamiliarity with the costs and benefits of the higher education system; unwillingness to leave community and families; difficulties meeting timelines; lack of family involvement in education; the necessity of having to work to help the family survive; the pattern of initiating education by selecting small, seemingly attainable goals; unawareness of knowing they were capable of earning degrees; and failure to understand the consequences of changing programs and financial pressures, among others. At the community college level, there was some faculty resistance to advise students or to deal with students with basic skills problems. Moreover, despite numerous interventions such as remedial programs and assessment practices, community college staff expressed frustration that many programs had failed to help students, and that remedial students often took three to four years to earn an associate degree.

In general, the same study revealed that community college articulation with senior institutions was weak, in terms of exchanging data about transfer students and comparing curriculum and expectations. College catalogs were often a poor source of information about transfer, and there was concern that minority students often got channeled into vocational-technical tracks. Further, students faced multiple barriers at senior institutions. These included paperwork involved in application forms, costs such as tuition and moving, assessment policies, impacted programs with limited space, and varying university general education requirements. Further, community college staff expressed concern that universities often did not accept transfer courses, and university faculty were often unwilling to negotiate curriculum changes.

The same study included a student survey that provided information about why Hispanic and White students might not be transferring. According to student responses, the least encouragement to transfer came from community college faculty, counselors, and the registrar's office. Indeed, only one-third of the students felt community college teachers had encouraged them to think seriously about transferring. On the other hand, it was interesting to note that while students rated their academic and career preparation experiences very positively, felt that the community college offered excellent information on transfer opportunities, and knew that they could get assistance about transferring from faculty and counselors, for the most part students were not involved in counseling or academic-related behaviors. The vast majority did not participate in academic or career counseling or in meetings with four-year college recruiters. Further, about half never or rarely made appointments to meet with faculty, over 60 percent never or rarely asked faculty for advice, and over 50 percent never or rarely asked faculty for additional references or for help with writing skills (Rendon, Justiz, and Resta, 1988).

These findings suggest that while most students plan to transfer and think transfer is important, they are not taking advantage of services that could facilitate transfer. This lack of academic integration is coupled with limited social integration. Few students saw faculty outside of class, participated in extracurricular activities, had informal conversations with faculty, or participated in freshman orientation. Variables measuring student predisposition to transfer revealed similar inconsistencies. While the majority of students planned to apply for transfer to at least one institution and generally had positive perceptions about transferring, their transfer behavior was limited. Few students sought information about transferring from the counseling office, community college faculty, or four-year institutions. Instead, it appeared that students were getting assistance from friends who planned to transfer or had already transferred (Rendon, Justiz, and Resta, 1988).

Finally, the study (Rendon, Justiz, and Resta, 1988) included a survey of faculty who taught college transfer courses in math, English, history, and business. The study provided evidence that most faculty were not involved in a close working relationship with students and that faculty/student interactions were minimal. Further, faculty expectations of students were quite low.

Faculty overrelied on objective tests and minimally involved students in activities that required higher-order thinking skills, making it doubtful that transfer students would be able to compete with native four-year college students who had been exposed to these activities. Also, most faculty were not involved in helping students to transfer, nor were they involved in activities designed to facilitate the transfer process. Interestingly, 67 percent of faculty disagreed that the transfer function should be the colleges' most important function, and 50 percent disagreed that students who began work at a community college had a good start toward the baccalaureate.

In another study, McCool (1984) conducted a multiple regression analysis of factors that were hypothesized to influence Hispanic student retention in two-year institutions. The researcher found that number of credit hours completed, identification of positive and negative reasons for withdrawal, experience perceptions, and goal selection affected students' ability to achieve educational objectives.

A recent study of Hispanic students enrolled in six community colleges in Texas, Arizona, and California (Nora and Rendon, 1988) provides additional insights. Findings revealed that students with a high level of commitment to attending college and to attaining their educational goals had applied to more four-year institutions and sought more information about transferring from counselors, faculty, friends, four-year institutions, and community college catalogs. They also had high levels of social and academic integration. Further, students who exhibited high levels of social and academic integration tended to have positive attitudes about transferring and to exhibit transfer-related behavior. Ethnic origin, however, was not found to be related to any of the factors in the study.

In another study, Nora (1987) found that Hispanic students entering college with high levels of institutional and goal commitments had high levels of academic and social integration and, consequently, high levels of retention. A separate study (Nora, 1990) revealed that Hispanic community college students who received high levels of noncampus and campus-based financial aid were enrolled for more semesters, earned more semester hours, and received some form of college credential. Moreover, Hispanics who received high levels of campus-based resources earned high grade point averages.

American Indians

With their own system of 27 tribally controlled community colleges (25 in the U.S. and 2 in Canada), American Indians also rely heavily on two-year colleges for access to higher education. Yet, this group has received very limited research attention. Nonetheless, a few descriptive studies illuminate some of the factors that influence the progress of American Indians in two-year colleges.

A study at Glendale Community College (Arizona) revealed that faculty mentoring had a positive impact on American Indian student retention, and that the risk of attrition was greatest for first-time minority students who did not apply for financial aid. At Mesa Community College (Arizona) 94.2 percent of American Indians expressed concern about financing their education, with about half working either full or part-time (McIntosh, et al., 1987).

It is also apparent that tribally controlled community colleges provide an alternative method of education to Indian students. Indian colleges are focused on Indian philosophy and history, which are believed to add to students' senses of self-worth and beliefs that they are capable of making academic progress. In a study of Montana's tribally controlled community colleges, 94.7 percent of students were somewhat or very satisfied with tribal colleges. Among students who left before completing their educational goals, home responsibilities were the most frequently cited reason, followed by personal problems and insufficient financial resources (Wright, 1986).

Black Students

In general, Black students also depend heavily on community colleges, but to a lesser extent than Hispanics and American Indians. Yet, their participation in transfer programs is important, given that transfer students add to the pool of Blacks with potential to earn bachelor's degrees. In a study of Black and White students from the 1972 National Longitudial Study (NLS) data set, Levin and Clowes (1986) found not only that low-aptitude Blacks were overrepresented at four-year schools compared to two-year schools, but that for blacks of all aptitude levels, ". . . those who initially attended a two-year college were significantly less likely to complete their planned four years of college work during the four years subsequent to high school graduation, compared to those who initially attended a four-year college."

In a study of transfer students enrolled in nine universities (Richardson and Bender, 1987), it was noted that Black students were older than members of other racial groups and that they were the last to decide about transferring, suggesting the importance of counseling and identifying transfer students at an early stage. More than one in five Blacks decided to transfer after leaving the community college, and only about one-third made that decision before arriving at the community college. In contrast, about one-half of Hispanics and Whites knew they were transferring before entering the community college.

Of Blacks who transferred, nearly three out of every four students lost some credit. Those Blacks who lost most credits were the last to decide about transfer. In comparison to other ethnic groups, Blacks were significantly more likely to have been "C" students. Further, the study revealed that Blacks tended to enter nonscience fields. The researchers noted that "the fact that Black students reported the least loss of grade point average reflected their lower grades before transferring, the fields they entered, and the number who transferred to universities with a predominantly minority student body" (Richardson and Bender, 1987). Interestingly, the study noted that a majority of students transferred without benefit of direct contact with professionals from either their community college or university. Thus, loss of credits seemed more a function of lack of institutional and state interventions than of race.

In a separate study of urban community colleges (Cohen, Brawer, and Bensimon, 1985), it was shown that students who appeared to be indifferent or disengaged from the academic and social system of the college were unlikely to develop high transfer attitudes and behaviors. Further, the study showed that Black and Hispanic students (relative to Asians and Whites) were less likely to exhibit high transfer predispositions. According to the researchers, "this finding may reflect a failure of community colleges to recognize that initial transfer predisposition among these students is lower than for other groups and that institutional climate conditions may inhibit the type of enrollment in the academic and social systems most likely to induce an increase in transfer predisposition" (Cohen, Brawer, and Bensimon, 1985).

Summary

While more race/ethnic-specific research, especially that of a theoretical (as opposed to descriptive) nature, is needed to substantiate the effect of enrolling in community colleges, the studies cited above provide important clues toward a better understanding of the educational experience of minorities in two-year colleges. Certainly, one must consider the socioeconomic background of these students. In particular, being naive about the world of higher education, having attended inferior schools, and lacking financial resources can combine to have a devastating impact on students, both in selecting clear, viable options and having the monetary resources to continue academic studies. How community colleges can reverse or at least reduce the socioeconomic limitations of students remains a challenge. Most studies attest to the fact that community colleges are keenly aware of the students they serve, want to do a better job to prepare them for the future, and are constantly trying and testing new policies and practices, though they have yielded mixed outcomes. The fact that minorities have a difficult time staying in college and attaining their educational goals is not simply a matter of race or ethnicity. It is also a matter of what institutions and states do to promote student academic progress.

Certainly, enough evidence is available to document that institutions have serious gaps in their educational service delivery, as evidenced by limited student/faculty interaction, lack of mechanisms that engage students in the academic and social fabric of the college, as well as lack of policies that promote high expectations and facilitate higher-order learning skills. Similarly, states could be doing more with regard to promoting intersegmental collaboration and facilitating the transfer of credits among the sectors. The fact that the colleges are tailored to accommodate stopouts does more to perpetuate ruptures in the pipeline than to promote the smooth flow of students among the sectors. One wonders whether minority students stop out because they really don't want to continue college at the time or because no one has taken the time to explain the benefits and consequences of staying in college, as well as to design a suitable financial aid package (grants and work-study) that encourages full-time attention to studies and increased contact with the institution. Stopping out may indeed be a good deal for many students, but if disproportionate numbers of minorities start stopping out, the effect on the pool of minorities qualified to complete baccalaureate studies could be devastating. Further, if the transfer function continues to decline, minorities will be left with no visible alternative to initiate an education leading to a bachelor's degree. To improve the participation of minorities in higher education, nothing short of a major breakthrough in salvaging baccalaureate opportunities for students is needed.

TOWARD NEW POLICIES THAT FACILITATE BACCALAUREATE ATTAINMENT

Over the years, two-year colleges have responded to changing social and economic conditions by modifying their mission and by adopting new policies and strategies that can best address student goals and needs. As the nation prepares to enter a new century and accommodate growing numbers of special populations, it is a critical time for two-year colleges to reassess their mission and programs. The weight of the evidence derived from empirical research suggests that minority students are not finding viable opportunities to transfer in community colleges, rendering the transfer function in peril. This may have occurred because the colleges have adopted too many functions and assigned less importance to transfer education.

Yet, for minority students, the community college represents a pivotal institution. This is especially true for Hispanics who, unlike Blacks, do not have a set of historically Black colleges they can turn to to complete a four-year education. American Indians, with their own network of tribally controlled two-year colleges, may also be expected to turn to these colleges to initiate baccalaureate studies. Moreover, Blacks residing outside the South and Northeast, where Black colleges are not available, can also be expected to swell two-year college enrollments. These students will turn to community colleges, as they have in the past, in search of opportunities for upward academic and social mobility. Thus, much is at stake for students who can only connect to the world of higher education by enrolling in a community college.

STATE RECOMMENDATIONS

States should take an aggressive, proactive role to ensure that its growing minority population finds full access to opportunities to earn baccalaureate degrees. To this end, the following proposals are recommended.

Middle College

States should consider funding the middle college concept. The Middle College High School was initiated at La Guardia Community College in New York. The Middle College, an alternative high school at the two-year college, recruits only high-risk students. Students attend Middle College in the tenth grade and take the next three years of schooling at the college site. About 85 percent graduate and 75 percent go on to college at La Guardia or elsewhere. Components of the model include: 1) students go to high school on a college campus; they don't have to graduate from high school to go to college; 2) classes are small; 3) counselors and teachers know students on a personal basis; 4) nobody fails, when students don't pass a course there is no grade and the course is repeated; 5) tutoring is available before and after school in every course, every day; and 6) students spend one-third of their time working outside school on unpaid internships. The success of this model indicates that at-risk students are capable of learning and can be helped to move forward with their academic careers.

In addition to the middle college model above, states should give serious consideration to supporting the following measures:

1. **Grants and Scholarships for Minority Transfer Students.** Financial aid sufficient to help students survive without taking a full-time job that reduces time spent on studying should be made available.
2. **State Transfer Student Monitoring System.** More effective means to track the flow of transfer students among the sectors are needed for two basic reasons: 1) to understand student college enrollment patterns and

2) to ascertain the academic progress of students after they complete the transfer process. For example, a student's social security number could be used to track enrollment. In Texas a new system was recently implemented requiring senior institutions to send back transcripts of transfer students to community colleges so that colleges could determine whether students were making satisfactory academic progress.

3. **Institutional Incentives.** State agencies should consider awarding special incentives to community colleges that demonstrate extraordinary success retaining minority students and facilitating successful transfer. For example, states can create grants to colleges that can document student progress and the effectiveness of measures that promote minority student retention and transfer. The state of New Jersey is doing some of the leading work in this area, where funding formulas take into account an institution's previous year's progress.

4. **Academic Partnership Programs.** Efforts that promote intersegmental collaboration among the K-12 system, community colleges, and senior institutions should receive state support. Coordinated action that can arrest the leaks in the pipeline are needed at every juncture. For example, in 1985, the California legislature created the California Academic Partnership Program (CAPP), which promotes academic partnerships between postsecondary and secondary institutions to improve student academic preparation. The legislature provided funding so that curriculum enhancement models and diagnostic testing projects could be established throughout the state.

5. **Research on Students.** State agencies should conduct longitudinal studies of students as these students flow through the educational pipeline. Studies that desegregate data by gender and ethnicity are needed to assess student retention rates at each institutional level and to determine student transfer rates and student achievement (degrees earned, GPAs, etc.). Data should be collected to document the factors that impede or enhance the flow of students throughout the educational pipeline. States should also begin to ask hard questions, i.e., require community colleges to document why minority student retention and transfer rates are so low and what colleges intend to do to remedy the situation.

6. **Reform Assessment.** On a yearly basis, states should assess and evaluate the effectiveness of new reforms such as high school graduation and college admissions' requirements, as well as test policies and their impact on minority student populations.

7. **Transfer Centers.** A Transfer Center provides a central location for students to get information about transferring. Transfer counselors and

paraprofessionals could be available to assist students with selecting majors, courses, and potential institutions to which students can transfer. California has funded numerous Transfer Centers throughout the state.

8. **Academic Alliances.** Special state grants should be made available to institutions where faculty wish to participate in the design and implementation of academic alliances. The alliances provide the mechanism by which faculty from each tier can meet to develop a coherent system of coursework in specific disciplines. Alliances are built on the concept that teachers who teach the same subject in the same geographical area share a collective responsibility for the quality of each other's teaching and learning.

INSTITUTIONAL RECOMMENDATIONS

In community colleges with large numbers of minority students, the transfer function should be assigned a high priority. Action strategies are needed to fulfill the transfer mission of the college. Special activities for transfer students include the following.

Support Services

1. **Year of the Transfer Student.** An aggressive campaign should be launched by both state agencies and community colleges to promote opportunities for transfer students. Efforts should be made to fund and support activities that promote early identification of transfers, special counseling and advisement, information dissemination, and other strategies that target minority transfer students.

2. **Transfer Catalog/Newsletter.** The colleges should issue a special transfer student catalog that includes a step-by-step guide to transferring, a description of the difference between entering a general education and a vocational-technical track, an explanation of different programs of study, financial aid opportunities, a list of state universities and major programs of study, and examples of general education requirements, among others. The catalog should include photos of minorities studying, visiting universities, and interacting with faculty and staff. Similarly, a transfer newsletter can provide up-to-date information about transferring. Also a film or video about transferring can be developed and used in orientation courses.

3. **Transfer Centers.** Students should have access to Transfer Centers, central places where students can get counseling, information, and assistance throughout the transfer process.

4. **Financial Aid and College Awareness.** Access to information about financial aid and college opportunities should be widely available to minority students and their parents. Minority families need to be involved in education, and be aware of its importance and benefits. Students and parents should be assisted to explore options in the world of work and in the higher education system. Counselors should help students and parents to deal with the trauma of leaving home to transfer to distant universities. Financial planning should also be incorporated to assist students to budget their money and understand the consequences of selecting grants, loans, work-study, and scholarships.

5. **Visits to Four-year College Campuses.** Two- and four-year colleges should work collaboratively to sponsor field trips so that prospective transfer students have the opportunity to visit universities and interact with students and faculty.

Freshman Year Experience for Transfer Students

The freshman year is a critical time for all students. To enhance student retention, community colleges should build residential components into their programmatic offerings. These include the following:

1. **Cluster Programs in Major Field of Study.** Freshman students in selective majors should take 2-3 courses in their program together each semester and be assigned a mentor who can assist them in every phase of their community college experience. For example, students majoring in teaching could be in a teaching cluster; those majoring in business should form a business cluster.

2. **Faculty Transfer Mentors.** Each transfer student should be assigned a faculty transfer mentor—someone who knows and understands the major the student has selected. This faculty mentor would also be responsible for following the student's academic progress, helping the student select appropriate coursework and make the successful transition to the senior institution.

3. **Extracurricular Activities.** Students should be afforded opportunities to be socially integrated in an academic environment. For example, a Transfer Student Club can be formed. Students can take field trips to selective four-year institutions. Social events for transfer students can also be made available.

4. **Transfer Student Orientation.** Special orientation for transfer students should be made available, both when students enroll for the first time and at the time students prepare to transfer. In particular, it is important to explain the different general education patterns available, the differences peculiar to enrolling in a vocational, as opposed to an academic, track, and the steps (including admissions, financial aid, and housing forms) necessary to transfer.

Faculty Involvement

Improving student transfer involves more than just raising the absolute number of students who transfer to senior institutions. It also involves devoting attention to the quality of teaching and learning. Faculty are responsible for instruction, and must ensure that the quality of students who transfer is sufficiently high that students can compete fairly with native four-year college students. To this end, the following measures are proposed:

1. **Faculty Development.** Institutions should allocate a special fund to help faculty develop new curricula and materials, conduct classroom research, serve on articulation committees, participate in academic alliances, and/or present classroom teaching research and instructional innovations at state and national conferences.

2. **Articulation Committees.** Faculty should be supported to participate in articulation committees to hammer out core curriculum requirements in selective programs of study with faculty in senior institutions.

3. **Student Assessment.** Few faculty in higher education are test experts. Yet, the higher education reform movement has been largely focused on student assessment. Resources should be available to help faculty obtain, use, interpret, design, and apply tests to evaluate and improve their classroom practices, as well as to assess student performance from the beginning to the end of the semester.

   Since community colleges are primarily teaching institutions, faculty are evaluated on their teaching effectiveness. One measure of effectiveness is the extent that students learn what is supposed to be mastered. Classroom teaching research should be added to the criteria for faculty promotion, pay increases, and tenure.

4. **Faculty Incentives.** Faculty who already feel overburdened will need special incentives to be able to participate in new initiatives. Special funding could be made available to faculty who participate in developing articulation agreements with four-year college faculty. Release time could allow faculty to conduct special projects. Awards should be given to faculty who demonstrate extraordinary results working with minority students.

Up-and-Down Articulation

Program-by-program articulation should occur with both high schools and senior institutions. For example, math and science community college faculty should articulate their coursework with high school and university faculty, so that math and science teacher education majors can pursue a clear path toward the baccalaureate. Further, articulation agreements between two- and four-year institutions should aim toward guaranteed admissions for students who complete required coursework and meet GPA requirements. Articulation with junior highs and high schools should aim toward enhancing student academic preparation at the precollege level, developing a coherent system of coursework, and setting clear expectations for students as they flow through the pipeline.

Evaluation and Research

To document student and institutional outcomes, community colleges need to conduct evaluation and research. Examples include the following:

1. **Institutional Research.** On a yearly basis, the colleges should collect data, stratified by ethnicity and gender, on student retention rates, student GPAs, associate degrees awarded, and student transfers to selective institutions, as well as follow-ups on college alumni. The data should be compiled in a yearly "State of the College Report" and shared with faculty and staff so that research-based data can be employed to improve and modify mechanisms that facilitate student learning, retention, and transfer.

2. **Cooperative Research Internship Program.** Most community college faculty and administrators are not researchers, and often funds for institutional research are in short supply. A Cooperative Research Internship Program should be designed to link a community college with graduate students from nearby universities. The focus of this program would be to provide doctoral students with opportunities to conduct institutional research in a community college setting and to provide a vehicle through which nonresearch institutions can obtain reliable information about student and institutional outcomes.

3. **College Program Evaluation Project.** Evaluation should be conducted to assess the effectiveness of special projects such as transfer centers, remedial studies programs, and special projects designed to improve minority participation and achievement. Research-based information is needed to provide empirical information about what accounts for the "success" of these projects—the factors that make exemplary programs

work and the conditions under which projects can be replicated in other institutional settings.

CONCLUSION

To a large extent, access has lost much of its meaning for minority students, for the decline of transfer translates to a decline in access. This decline is exacerbated when viewed in the context of diminishing high school graduation and college entrance rates, as well as exceedingly low college completion rates for minority students. If any postsecondary institution can play a pivotal role in salvaging baccalaureate opportunities for minority students in the next decade, it will be the community college. However, to do so will require a new vision of what community colleges can and should do for minorities, as well as new policies that clear the pathway toward the baccalaureate.

By the next decade, two-year colleges will have to make a critical decision as to what extent they wish to become terminal or transfer institutions. The answer will be carefully watched by legislators concerned with how to best spend tax dollars targeted at minority student populations, by foundations concerned with reversing the ghettoization of minority youth, and by minority policy makers who will make recommendations as to which institutions can give students better returns on their financial and time investments. If community colleges want to regain their legitimacy as viable members of the academic community; if they want to receive increased public support; if they want to prosper by providing viable baccalaureate opportunities for minority students, then the answer is clear: They must work vigorously to revive and restore the vitality of the transfer function.

REFERENCES

American Council on Education. 1988. *One-third of a nation*. Washington, DC: American Council on Education

Arnold, B. 1988. *Summary of joint hearing of the Quality Education for Minorities Project and the Senate Committee on School Performance*. Unpublished paper prepared for hearing in Anchorage, Alaska.

Bensimon, E. M., Riley, M. J. 1984. *Student predisposition to transfer: A report of preliminary findings*. Los Angeles, CA: Center for the Study of Community Colleges. ERIC Document No. 247 963.

Bernstein, A. 1986. The devaluation of transfer. Current explanations and possible causes. *New Directions for Community Colleges 54*: 31-40.

Chronicle of Higher Education. August 25, 1993. *Almanac Issue*. Washington, DC.

Cohen, A. M. 1985. The community college in the American educational system. In *Contexts for learning*, edited by C. Adelman, pp. 1-16. Washington, DC: National Institute of Education.

Cohen, A. M., F. Brawer, and E. Bensimon. 1985. *Transfer education in American community colleges*. Los Angeles: Center for the Study of Community Colleges.

Commission on the Higher Education of Minorities. 1982. *Final report on the higher education of minorities*. Los Angeles, CA: Higher Education Research Institute.

El-Khawas, E. H., D. J. Carter, and C. A. Ottinger. 1988. *Community college fact book*. Washington, DC: ACE/McMillan

Friedlander, J. 1980. An ERIC review: Why is transfer education declining? *Community College Review* 8, no. 2: 59-66.

Harris Tijerina, K., and P. Blemer. 1987 and 1988. The dance of Indian higher education. *Educational Record* 68, no. 4 (Fall)/69, no. 1 (Winter): 79-85.

Hayward, G. 1985. *Preparation and participation of Hispanic and Black students: A special report*. Sacramento, CA: California Community Colleges, Office of the Chancellor. ERIC Document No. ED 254-85.

Hodgkinson, H. L. 1985. *All one system: Demographics of education—kindergarten through graduate school*. Washington, DC: Institute for Educational Leadership, Inc.

Karabel, J. June 1986. Community colleges and social stratification in the 1980s. In *The community college and its critics*, edited by L. S. Zwerling, pp. 13-29. San Francisco: Jossey-Bass, Inc.

Levin, B., and D. Clowes. 1980. Realization of educational aspirations among Blacks and Whites in two- and four-year colleges. *Community/Junior College Research Quarterly* 4: 186-93.

McCool, A. C. 1984. Factors influencing Hispanic student retention within the community college. *Community/Junior College Quarterly* 8: 19-37.

McIntosh, B. J., et al. 1987. *Native American academic, financial, social, psychological and demographic implications for education: A challenge to community college administrators, faculty and support service personnel*. Mesa: Mesa Community College, Office of Research and Development.

Monroe, C. 1977. *Profile of the community college*. San Francisco: Jossey-Bass, Inc.

National Commission on Secondary Schooling for Hispanics. 1984. *Make something happen*. Washington, DC: Hispanic Policy Development Project.

Nora, A. 1987. *Campus-based old programs as determinants of retention among Hispanic community college students*. Paper presented at the American Educational Research Association, New Orleans.

Nora, A. 1990. Campus-based aid programs as determinants of retention among Hispanic community college students. *Journal of Higher Education*, 61, 3: 312-31.

Nora, A., and L. I. Rendon. 1988. *Determinants of pre-disposition to transfer among community college students: A structural model*. Paper presented at the American Educational Research Association, St. Louis, Missouri.

Orfield, G., and F. Paul. 1987 and 1988. Declines in minority access: A tale of five cities. *Educational Record* 68, no. 4 (Fall)/69, no. 1 (Winter): 79-85.

Pincus, F. 1980. The false promises of community colleges. *Harvard Educational Review* 50: 332-61.

Rendon, L. I. 1984. *Involvement in learning: A view from the community college perspective*. Washington, DC: National Institute of Education. ERIC Document No. ED 255 268.

Rendon, L. I., M. J. Justiz, and P. Resta. 1988. *Transfer education in southwest community colleges*. Columbia, SC: University of South Carolina.

Richardson, R. C., and Bender, L. W. 1971. *Fostering minority access and achievement in higher education.* San Francisco: Jossey-Bass, Inc.

Richardson, R. C., and L. W. Bender. 1987. *Students in urban settings. Achieving the baccalaureate degree.* Report 6. Washington, DC: ERIC Clearinghouse on Higher Education.

Richardson, R., E. Fisk, and Okun. 1983. *Literacy in the open access college.* San Francisco: Jossey-Bass, Inc.

Rouche, S. D., and U.N. Comstock. 1981. *A report on theory and method for the study of literacy development in community colleges.* Contract No. 400-780-600. Washington, DC: National Institute of Education. ERIC Document No. ED 182 465.

U.S. Bureau of the Census. August 1987. *The Hispanic population in the U.S. March 1986 and 1987.* Advance Report. Series p-20, No. 416. Washington, DC: U.S. Government Printing Office.

Wilson R., and M. Justiz. 1987 and 1988. Minorities in higher education: Confronting a time bomb. *Educational Record* 68, no. 4(Fall)/69, no. 1(Winter): 8-14.

Wilson R., and S. Melendez. 1987. *Minorities in higher education.* Washington, DC: American Council on Education.

Wright, B. 1986. *An assessment of student outcomes at tribally controlled community colleges.* Paper presented at the annual conference of the National Indian Education Association, Reno.

CHAPTER

The Transfer Function: Building Curricular Roadways across and among Higher Education Institutions

Alison R. Bernstein and Judith S. Eaton

While there have been many efforts—special programs, special financing, special recruitment—directed to minorities in colleges and universities, few of these efforts have been focused on the *structure* of higher education. This structure is characterized by, first and foremost, a longstanding and powerful commitment to decentralization of the enterprise.

The nation's 3,400 institutions insist upon autonomy. They have widely varying admissions practices. In spite of the billions of dollars of public financial support, neither the state nor the federal government exerts a strong influence on their institutional independence. This decentralization, while neither undesirable nor inappropriate, does have a significant impact on students. Student use of educational sites, for example, increasingly involves attendance at two, three, or even four colleges on the way to the baccalaureate. In the case of minority students, the likelihood of success of the various special initiatives that have been so painstakingly developed is at stake. Decentralization is powerful: it affects the conditions for both access and persistence in a collegiate setting.

Transfer is the primary means by which students navigate decentralization to achieve the baccalaureate. To be successful, they need to be able to move within the decentralized enterprise with ease, avoid any loss of credit for work already completed, and be reasonably assured that their educational experience at one institution is roughly comparable in cognitive complexity to the work at another institution. They need access and maximum portability without penalty.

Transfer as the primary means of navigating within the decentralized higher education enterprise is especially crucial in the relationship between the nation's 1,200 community colleges and the 2,200 four-year institutions. Over the years, students in community colleges have consistently affirmed that they attend the two-year institution as their path to the baccalaureate. Even more important, community colleges enroll 45 percent of all minority students, more than any other sector of higher education (Carter and Wilson, 1993). It is not too much to say that the country's decentralized higher education system works well for minorities *only if* they are able to move from the two-year to the four-year institution and routinely achieve the baccalaureate.

While there are few national data to describe the current scope of the transfer phenomenon, the information that is available, however limited and equivocal, is a warning and cause for concern. First, the transfer function is not as generally effective as it might be (Brint and Karabel, 1989; Palmer and Eaton, 1991; Pincus and Archer, 1989). Second, students of any race whose educational career involves transfer are less likely to achieve the baccalaureate than their colleagues who do not transfer (Astin, 1979). Third, transfer is not as likely to result in academic success for minority students as for the general college population (Astin, 1982; NCES, 1992; Pincus and Archer, 1989). According to *High School and Beyond*, the federal government's ongoing tracking of high school seniors of 1980, the educational attainment for Blacks and Hispanics who begin their collegiate careers in the community college is even less than that of their white counterparts (NCES, 1992).

Given that institutions will remain fiercely independent in their admissions practices, and thus that transfer will remain a routine need for many students, strengthening transfer is important and desirable. More successful transfer is needed if a decentralized higher education enterprise is to be more effective than it presently is.

To deal with this need, The Ford Foundation, in the 1980s, began to focus particular attention on low-income and minority students, the transfer function, and the relationship between community colleges and public and private four-year schools. It funded, between 1982 and 1992, several major projects to strengthen the transfer relationship between two- and four-year institutions. The foundation sought to overcome obstacles that decentralization could cause by building *roadways* from the community college to all sectors of the four-year world: the less selective public colleges, highly selective four-year public institutions, and highly selective private institutions. No other foundation, set of institutions, or government has devoted such significant resources to this challenge.

The Ford projects all had the same goal: to increase the extent of baccalaureate degree attainment for low-income and minority students who began their collegiate education at the community college. Ford did not seek to change the decentralized structure of higher education but, instead, sought to widen the roadways among institutions, relying primarily on the strategy of *strengthening the interinstitutional educational environment* for low-income and minority students through more and better transfer-related programs and services. This effort, it believed, should lead to more low-income and minority students transferring and obtaining the baccalaureate. This policy may be contrasted with, for example, a strategy of direct financial assistance to students that Ford has used in a variety of other settings. These projects were really two kinds of *investment*: 1) investment in the enhancement of two-year and four-year student services to aid minorities such as counseling, advising, course equivalency guides, recruitment, and academic support; and 2) investment in the academic programs of two-year and four-year institutions to strengthen similarities among courses and programs so that students experienced some intellectual continuity as they moved between institutions. This paper will reflect on transfer efforts that centrally addressed academic and curriculum development between two-year and four-year institutions.

BUILDING THE ROADWAY AND STRENGTHENING TRANSFER TIES: FOCUS ON HIGHLY SELECTIVE INSTITUTIONS

While the past decade has seen a virtual explosion of collaborative projects between high schools and colleges, it is striking to discover very few partnerships exist between community colleges and four-year institutions which go beyond paper agreements, commonly known as "two plus two" or "articulation" agreements. One might have thought that the concern to enhance minority student access to baccalaureate degrees, which gave rise to many, if not a majority, of these new high school/college efforts, would have similarly given rise to a range of innovative academic projects in which community college faculty and university faculty join forces to help able students transfer to more intellectually demanding institutions.

The absence of strong, vibrant interinstitutional transfer programs is perplexing. If one is concerned about the minority "pipeline," community colleges are the higher education institutions that serve as the point of entry for a majority of Hispanics and Native Americans into higher education. They also enroll approximately 43 percent of all Blacks in colleges and universities. And, while the majority of these minority community college students may not be prepared for, or even be interested in enrolling as juniors at schools like Vassar, UCLA, and the University of Chicago, there is, nevertheless, an untapped pool of minority students in community colleges whose educational horizons ought to expand to include this option. Transfer could be, thus, strengthened academically by linking urban community colleges with highly selective liberal arts colleges and universities. Efforts to achieve this goal were mounted with Ford Foundation support in the 1980s in New York, Los Angeles, and Chicago. LaGuardia Community College and Vassar College, the Los Angeles Community College District and University of California-Los Angeles, and Loop Community College and University of Chicago, participated, respectively, in these programs.

The three projects employed strategies that differ considerably from project to project, but there were similarities in the overall design of each project which make it appropriate to discuss them as a group. The oldest of the three projects, the Vassar College Summer Institute for Community College Students, was begun in 1984, and the first group of students from LaGuardia Community College in Long Island City, New York, arrived at Vassar in the summer of 1985. The second project, the Transfer Articulation Program (TAP) was begun in 1985 as an outreach effort of UCLA's Office of Interinstitutional Programs. The third, entitled the Partnership Program, involved the University of Chicago with two summer programs, one for high school students enrolling at Loop College, a Chicago-based community college, and another for already-enrolled Loop students. These summer programs were launched at the university in 1989.

The UCLA project ran all year long, and it involved several community colleges in the greater Los Angeles area. It differed from the other two in several respects. First, TAP provided a UCLA-approved general education curriculum at the community college level, which functions almost as a "college within a college." It was designed to meet the needs of able community college students who were originally planning on enrolling at UCLA. Many were even eligible to attend as freshmen, but because of increasing student competition for limited spaces, could not be accommodated. TAP also was designed to provide a transfer track for able minority students who were ineligible to apply to UCLA as freshmen, but who, upon successful completion of the TAP curriculum, could automatically transfer as juniors to UCLA two years later.

Because TAP was conceived as providing the equivalent of the first two years of a UCLA degree program in the arts and sciences, it functioned largely as an extension program of the university which was housed at the community college. The TAP faculty were community college teachers, but the curriculum and quality control measures were determined at UCLA. Thus, students who elected a TAP curriculum at L.A. City College or Santa Monica City College were assured that they were experiencing a UCLA-type education, at least at the lower-division general education level. Hundreds of community college students enrolled in TAP, and the first cohort of students who began the two-year course of study in 1987 have successfully transferred to the university. Early evaluations of student performance and persistence suggest that the program succeeded in easing the transition from the community college to UCLA. Unfortunately, minority student participation in the program was lower than project planners had hoped. Despite this fact, TAP remains an important model of cooperation between urban community colleges and a distinguished research university. The community college faculty who were chosen to teach in the program reported enhanced levels of satisfaction with their work and a renewed commitment to teaching. Administrators at the cooperating institutions have built a level of trust and pride in their joint accomplishments.

The key element that made TAP successful was its identity as a UCLA-sponsored community college initiative. It carried a legitimacy that a similar program developed solely at the community college level would not enjoy. The negative aspect of this model is that it was not, in the truest sense, a real partnership. The community colleges proved that they could deliver education UCLA's way. There was little room, however, for the community colleges to shape UCLA's freshman- and sophomore-level core courses.

Unlike UCLA, the University of Chicago's joint venture with Loop College began as a collaboration between faculty at both institutions. Importantly, the Loop faculty who initially sought the assistance of the university were themselves Chicago graduates. In this respect, the Partnership Program had the advantage of involving community college faculty whose training and perspectives could not be dismissed by the research university. Moreover, Loop's president, Berenice Miller, was also a University of Chicago alumnus. The goal of the program was to provide a summer school experience for first-time Loop students before they entered in the fall, and an opportunity for already-enrolled Loop students to take courses at Chicago during the summer which were taught by regular university faculty. Two groups of 20 students participated in the summer sessions. The recent high school graduates enrolled in noncredit tutorial classes to strengthen their analytical reading, writing, and mathematical skills. These classes were taught by Loop faculty and University of Chicago graduate students. A second group of 20 students, selected by an advisory committee composed of faculty and administrators from Chicago and Loop, audited University of Chicago core courses taught in the summer by regular university faculty. This audit experience provided an opportunity for the students to gain an understanding of the university's academic expectations. Importantly, in the first summer, 5 of the 20 students enrolled in the core courses completed the work and received regular Chicago credit. One of the expectations of the project is that all 40 Loop students who participated would transfer either to Chicago or to other four-year institutions after the completion of their associate's degree. Those who transferred to Chicago applied all credits earned during the summer program toward their university degree.

In contrast to the UCLA model, this partnership project did not strive for four-year college course equivalency at the two-year college level. The goal instead was to expose students early to the rigors of a Chicago course through either tutorials aimed at strengthening students' cognitive skills or their involvement in the course itself. Also, unlike the UCLA effort, the Loop/ University of Chicago project focused exclusively on enhancing transfer opportunities for Black students. Loop is approximately 70 percent Black, while the Black enrollment of the University of Chicago is less than 3 percent. While both models of community college/university collaboration have strengths, they also have weaknesses. For example, few of the 40 Loop students in either summer program interacted with other Chicago students. Moreover, there was little follow-up from the university to the Loop summer students once the fall academic term began. Nevertheless, this partnership signaled Chicago's commitment to improve its relationship to the local Hyde Park community and to its local community college.

The most far-reaching model of collaboration between a community college and a selective four-year institution is located at Vassar College in Poughkeepsie, New York. It too is a summer program. Unlike UCLA's or Chicago's projects, however, the Vassar Summer Institute is a residential effort in which approximately 40-50 community college students live in dorms for five weeks and take two courses for regular Vassar credit, which are team-taught by Vassar and community college faculty. The institute was designed by Vassar and LaGuardia Community College faculty and staff, but it now enrolls students from several community colleges in New York City and upstate. The Vassar Summer Institute, which is called "Exploring Transfer," has received considerable attention in the national press. In 1989, the originators of the program, Dr. Janet Lieberman at LaGuardia Community College and Dr. Colton Johnson at Vassar, were co-recipients of the prestigious Dana Award for Innovation in Higher Education. The Association of American Colleges (AAC) has received funds from Ford and the AT&T Foundation to help other teams of colleges replicate the Vassar model. Thus, Smith College has a similar effort with Hartford Community College, Lewis and Clark has developed a joint program with Portland Community College, and Agnes Scott College in Georgia has begun working with Georgia Junior College.

Because the Vassar program is the oldest of the three models described in this paper, there is more longitudinal data about students who have participated. Approximately 60 percent of the 200 students who have enrolled at the summer institute are minority students. Over 70 percent of those community college students who attended Vassar and graduated from their home community colleges (Dutchess County Community College and Borough of Manhattan Community College have also participated) have transferred successfully to senior colleges. A number are attending out-of-town residential liberal arts colleges and universities like Middlebury, Wesleyan, and Cornell. By 1990 Vassar itself had accepted 22 transfers who had attended the summer institute. In one graduating class, three transfers were elected to Phi Beta Kappa.

While it is still too early to know which factors definitely account for the success of the Vassar effort, some tentative conclusions are possible. First, the program was built upon several themes of collaboration. Students are selected by a joint community college/four-year college admission committee. This selection process ensures that the community college faculty and administrators have a role in determining which of their students can benefit most from the program and have the best chance of succeeding. Second, courses that carry Vassar credit are jointly developed by a two-person teaching team composed of a community college faculty member and a faculty member from Vassar. Third, because the curriculum is jointly developed and taught, the expectations for student performance are the same for both faculty members, thus diminishing the gap between institutional cultures that have often sidetracked this type of partnership. While students initially report that they begin the five-week program with real concern over whether they can complete their course work, they invariably gain greater academic confidence over the weeks and produce a higher quality of work than they or their teachers thought possible. In contrast to the often-heard critique that community college education "levels-down" student and faculty expectations, this program appears to "level-up" the students' sense of their academic ability. Finally, it would be hard to overestimate the importance of the residential experience to the success of the Vassar program. For the first time in the lives of many of these community college students, they have had the opportunity to attend college full-time without worrying about work or family. Small wonder that many institute participants report taking themselves seriously for the first time as college students capable of B.A.-level work.

BUILDING THE ROADWAY AND STRENGTHENING TRANSFER TIES: FOCUS ON CURRICULUM

In 1989, Ford expanded its efforts to strengthen transfer through a curriculum development model. While remaining urban based, it expanded the four-year institutions with which it was working to include less selective institutions. And, it intensified its focus on teaching and learning as central to strengthening transfer. The National Center for Academic Achievement and Transfer was established in Washington, DC, to build curricular partnerships between community colleges and their primary four-year receiving institutions through grant funds for curriculum development, through strengthening institutional capacity to determine transfer effectiveness, and through attention to the policy framework needed to support a more viable transfer effort.

The Transfer Center Grant Program

The multi-year, multi-million-dollar grant program of the National Transfer Center was targeted to community colleges with significant enrollments of low-income, Black and Hispanic students and their receiving institutions. During 1989–93, the Transfer Center provided $1.7 million in grants to 54 institutional partnerships to implement what the center called an "Academic Model" for transfer. The Academic Model focused on curricular realignments between sending and receiving institutions so that students were able to transfer with ease. It is based on the assumption that similarity in course content and academic tasks between institutions would make transfer easier and more successful. The model has five elements:

- primary focus on curriculum and performance expectations;
- faculty leadership;
- two-year/four-year faculty collaboration;
- administrative leadership and support for faculty-led collaborative efforts;
- systematic tracking of the transfer student population to determine transfer effectiveness.

Based on the work of the first phase of Partnership Grants, the Academic Model displayed the following strengths:

- Institutions *were* willing to articulate the transfer challenge in terms of what happens in the classroom: what is taught and how it is taught.

- Faculty in two- and four-year institutions *were* willing and able to work together across institutions, in spite of years of little contact between the schools, even among faculty in the same disciplines.
- Lower-division courses at both two- and four-year institutions *were* redesigned, new courses were created, and alternative teaching methodologies were explored.
- Faculty at two- and four-year institutions *were* willing to do the political work necessary to gain institutional support for the new curricular initiatives.
- Senior academic administrators *did* provide the needed leadership for institutional change.

The following concerns also surfaced:

- Transfer data collection and analysis capacity on the campus needed to be strengthened.
- Effectiveness measures to determine the success of transfer efforts needed to be established.
- Institutional data collection needed to be unimpeded by state or other external system demands.
- The institution needed to realize that the Academic Model efforts were intended as long-term, systemic changes in institutional functioning.

Research

The Transfer Center's research efforts focused on describing the extent of transfer activity nationally, exploring the relationship between curriculum and transfer, analyzing the role of the community college and baccalaureate degree acquisition, and examining academic tasks in equivalent courses at sending and receiving institutions. Another ambitious project, examining student attendance patterns and transfer, is not yet complete. These research projects were undertaken after a survey of all community colleges and their current transfer practices.

These research projects could not have been successful without the important work of the Center for the Study of Community Colleges (CSCC) on transfer activity throughout the country. This center, also with support from the Ford Foundation, has done groundbreaking work in establishing a definition of the community college transfer population and assisting institutions in monitoring their transfer progress. The transfer population was defined as those students who were first-time college attendees who enrolled in a community college and earned, in a four-year period, at least 12 college-level credits and then enrolled in a four-year institution. Transfer rates for the 164 institutions with which the CSCC has worked is 23.4 percent: of those students who were first-time college attendees and earned at least 12 college-level credits, 23.4 percent were enrolled in a four-year institution within four years of their initial attendance at a community college.

The CSCC's research into transfer rates also enabled them to directly address the issue of minority transfer. Based on the data collected by the CSCC, minority transfer at the institutions participating in the survey mirrored the transfer activity of the colleges' general student population. That is, their research shows that transfer is an institutionally driven phenomenon: schools with high transfer rates sustain this transfer activity across all races and schools with low transfer rates are low for all races.

Building on this quantitative description of transfer activity, the Transfer Center, again working with the CSCC, was able to document the pivotal role of the liberal arts in transfer. The greater the presence of the liberal arts in the curriculum, the higher the transfer rate—establishing a curricular basis for community colleges to strengthen their curricular offerings in this area.

The Transfer Center's inquiry into transfer success—the earning of the baccalaureate—revealed that there is no single way that community colleges function as part of the baccalaureate experience. The community college role is diverse and idiosyncratic, with students using the community college in a highly unstructured manner, mainly to take arts and sciences courses. For example, students were equally likely to take six credits as they were sixty. This research lays an important foundation for reconsideration of curriculum structure at the community college level.

Efforts to establish a relationship between similarity of academic tasks and transfer is in their early stages. Thus far, researchers have been able to document that similarity or differences in tasks is driven by the individual disciplines. Further study is needed to confirm that similarity actually assists transfer students. This research also provides a valuable service by establishing a mode of inquiry for comparing academic tasks across institutions.

FOR THE FUTURE

The Ford Foundation projects make it clear that while decentralization of the higher education system works to the disadvantage of its students—and minority students in particular—steps can be taken to overcome these obstacles through effective transfer. Seven points are especially important here, particularly to the future success of minorities in higher education.

1. The building of *interinstitutional* intellectual community to offset the potential difficulties of decentralization *can* be successful. Faculty and

administrators are willing, under certain circumstances, to work together across institutions to build a roadway of academic programs and services to aid students who attend two institutions.

2. Community college students can and should be encouraged to "level up" their academic skills and expectations and aim for transfer to highly selective institutions.

3. Agreements about cognitive complexity are important. Lower-division education in two- and four-year institutions should be governed by shared understandings about course content, scope of work, and level of student performance. To the extent that faculty are willing to establish this intellectual community across institutions, these communities need to house common expectations about the academic work students are to undertake.

4. Both public and private four-year institutions are important to community college transfer students, especially minorities. The conventional wisdom that minorities, especially low-income students, cannot be effectively served by private higher education is mistaken.

5. Because of the increasing mobility of the society, state controls on interinstitutional arrangements are increasingly irrelevant. State-level articulation agreements are especially weak forces in managing the transfer experience. And, because societal mobility takes place independent of state lines, these agreements do not assist students moving across institutions on a nationwide basis.

6. The effectiveness of institutional commitments to transfer can and should be measured. The transfer definition enables institutions to set transfer goals, include transfer in their strategic planning, and document student flow to determine how many students are benefiting from transfer efforts, what "works" in transfer, and whether additional institutional efforts are needed.

7. The higher education community cannot continue to have it both ways. Higher education has sought to sustain its decentralization while, at the same time, ignoring the actual attendance patterns of students. The increasing mobility of students, their atypical use of various institutions at various times, argues strongly for the sanctioning of the portability of the academic experience. If higher education wishes to remain decentralized, it has a responsibility to build more roadways and thereby ease access and portability.

CONCLUSION

Transfer emerges as a major roadway through the decentralized complex of higher education institutions. The efforts of the Ford Foundation make it clear that decentralization *need* not prove problematic for students and that, for the minority student, strong reliance on the community college need not be deleterious in relation to the earning of the baccalaureate.

REFERENCES

Astin, A. 1979. *Four critical years*. San Francisco: Jossey-Bass.
———. 1982. *Minorities in higher education*. San Francisco: Jossey-Bass.
Brint, S., and J. Karabel. 1989. *The diverted dream: Community colleges and the promises of educational opportunity in America, 1900–1985*. New York: Oxford University Press.
Carter, D., and R. Wilson. 1993. *Minorities in higher education: Eleventh annual status report 1992*. Washington, DC: American Council on Education.
Community college factbook. 1990. Washington, DC: ACE/Macmillan.
Kintzer, F. C., and J. H. Wattenbarger. *The articulation/transfer phenomenon: Patterns and directions*. AACJC.
National Center for Education Statistics. October 1992. *Digest of education statistics 1992*. Washington, DC: United States Department of Education, Office of Research and Improvement. NCES 92–097.
Palmer, J., and J. Eaton. 1991. *Setting the national agenda: Academic achievement and transfer*. Washington, DC: American Council on Education.
Penny, S. 1987. Final report of SUNY Transfer Project to The Ford Foundation.
Pincus, F., and E. Archer. 1989. *Bridges to opportunity: Are community colleges meeting the transfer needs of minority students?* New York: The College Entrance Examination Board and the Academy for Educational Development.
Report to the Ford Foundation on the Upper Division Scholars Program, the Academy for Educational Development (AED). 1990. Washington, DC.
Warren, J. 1985. The changing characteristics of community college students. In *Renewing the American community college: Priorities and strategies for effective leadership* edited by W. L. Deegan and D. Tillery. San Francisco: Jossey-Bass.

CHAPTER

Hispanic Student Achievement

Richard Durán

INTRODUCTION

The limited educational attainment of Hispanic youth is a major national policy issue tied to the changing demographics of the United States and to its economic and social well-being. By the year 2000, one-third of the United States population will consist of non-White minorities, most of whom are not currently well served by the education system and who are likely to be ill prepared to contribute to the growing need of the United States economy for technically skilled workers and professionals (Hodgkinson, 1985; Griffith, Frase, and Ralph, 1989).

Hispanics are growing in rapid numbers in the United States. In 1990 nearly 22.5 million Hispanics resided in the United States, accounting for 8.2 percent of the total population. During the period 1980-88, the Hispanic population grew by 5½ million, with one-half of this growth arising among new immigrants to the country. The most rapid growth rate is occurring among young Hispanics. Projections indicate that by the year 2030 Hispanics will contribute 18 percent of the 10-24-year-old population, up from 10 percent today (Children's Defense Fund, 1990).

The rapid growth in Hispanics in the population is coupled with depressing data on their economic well-being. In 1987 more than one-quarter of all Hispanic families earned incomes below the poverty line as compared to less than 10 percent of all non-Hispanic families, and Hispanics in the labor force were 50 percent more likely to be unemployed than non-Hispanics (Children's Defense Fund, 1990).

The demographic and economic conditions of Hispanics call attention to a range of societal issues that affect their educational outcomes and aspirations and that should be taken into consideration when devising educational reforms benefiting this population and other underserved populations. Indeed, one can begin by questioning whether the educational reform movement in the United States is appropriately oriented to deal with minority population issues. Following the release of A Nation at Risk (National Committee for Educational Excellence, 1983), the bulk of attention has been on greater accountability of school systems and teachers as evaluated by students' achievement test scores and teachers' scores on competency tests. The hope is that greater use of tests will result in more rigorous setting of standards for students and teachers, and that compliance with these standards means that schools and teachers will ensure that students will receive higher quality instruction. Unfortunately, as this chapter argues, the educational problems besetting Hispanic youth are not resolvable in this manner. The education of Hispanic and other underserved minority students will require more radical reforms in teacher preparation, the conduct of instruction, and outreach to Hispanic families and communities.

Recently, innovations in the educational reform movement have emerged that have questionable promise for Hispanic students. One innovation involves parents exercising greater "choice" in selecting the schools students attend and the programs serving students (Association for Supervision and Curriculum Development, 1990). This innovation will likely lead more economically well-off parents to move their children from low-achieving schools populated by increasing numbers of African American, Hispanic, and other underserved students. Rather than aiding students overall, greater school choice may create greater ethnic and socioeconomic segregation among students, abandoning inner-city schools to the poor without increasing resources for these schools and their teaching staff.

Another educational reform innovation argues for increased school-based management. One source of support for school-based management has come from parental and community advocacy groups concerned with increasing their voice in the selection of textbooks and the content and structure of the curriculum. Parent and community groups have also expressed concern about the economic burden of local- and state-level taxation to support schools and the high cost of staffing and maintaining separate categorically funded programs for students.

Two other sources informing educational reform stem from research on effective schools. First, research has found that schools with strong local leadership, and in particular, a strong principal show higher school achievement than otherwise comparable schools (Smith and Andrews, 1989). Second, research in socioeconomically depressed inner-city schools has found that strong local school leadership coupled with increased parental involvement in children's schooling deters low school achievement (Comer, 1988).

Increased local school-based management is both promising and problematical for Hispanics. Poor Hispanic parents with limited or no English proficiency are not likely to be represented in local community power structures advocating school-based management, unless special efforts are made to include them in advocacy and decision-making groups. Another complication is that parents and local school staff need district, state, and federal technical assistance in providing Hispanic pupils, and particularly bilingual students, with curriculum materials, curriculum design, and staff development programs meeting students' needs.

As a supplement to existing reform initiatives, this chapter proposes implementation and evaluation of additional educational interventions for Hispanic students coupled with reforms in teacher training. One important form of intervention involves creating support systems that promote contact and collaboration among students and persons in home, community, and school settings. A second form of intervention should focus on the use of pedagogical techniques that ensure immediate learning benefits to students in everyday classroom activities. Appropriate attention to the language and cultural resources of students are essential in this process. A third intervention involves creation of cross-tier educational intervention. These interventions bring together students at-risk for attaining the next tier in their education, such as high school or college, with students and teachers performing successfully at this next tier. All three forms of intervention are intended to stimulate students' further aspirations for schooling and are intended to develop students' self-identity as successful school learners. The three forms of intervention suggest modifications that should be made in the training of teachers.

The rationale underlying the forms of intervention outlined is motivated by an analysis of Hispanic school achievement and attainment patterns and explanations of factors influencing Hispanics' success in schools.

EDUCATIONAL ATTAINMENT AND ACHIEVEMENT: TRENDS

One of the most salient indicators of Hispanics' lack of progress through the education system is their high dropout rate from high school. Census Bureau estimates in 1988 indicated that 36 percent of Hispanics age 16 to 24 had dropped out of high school—a rate nearly triple that of White students and double that of African American students (Johnson, 1989). The data also showed that nearly one-third of Hispanic students drop out at or before completing the sixth grade, compared to about 5 percent of non-Hispanic students.

Other analyses of Hispanic dropout rates suggest that up to 50 percent of Hispanics of high school completion age fail to complete high school and that high rates of absenteeism, lack of academic success, repeated suspensions, low parent involvement, teenage pregnancy, low self-esteem, and low average grades are associated with dropping out of school (Orum, 1986; Howe, 1987; Hispanic Policy Development Project, 1989).

Access to college among Hispanics is obviously affected by the high school dropout rates cited and points to numerous factors extending beyond school performance per se. Nonetheless, the study of achievement patterns of Hispanics in verbal, mathematics, and science skill areas from the elementary through high school years is revealing.

National survey studies using achievement tests, such as the National Assessment of Educational Progress (NAEP) and the High School and Beyond Longitudinal Survey (HS&B), show a clear pattern of results. They indicate that Hispanic students' educational achievements begin to fall behind that of white students during the elementary grades and that this gap continues throughout the high school years. The gap remains despite the fact that Hispanics drop out of school at a higher rate than Whites.

NAEP reading achievement test scores of 9-, 13-, and 17-year-old Hispanic, White, and African American students for 1971 through 1988 indicate a steady rise in the reading test scores of Hispanics and African Americans at all three age levels. Rises have also occurred in the reading test scores of White students, but these rises are not as great as for Hispanic and African American students. Despite these achievement gains over the period in question, it is important to note that in 1988 Hispanic and African American students scored far below the average for Whites. For example, in 1988, Hispanic 17-year-old students scored only a little better than White students aged 13 years and far below White students aged 17 years (National Assessment of Educational Progress, 1990).

The NAEP reading test score scale can be interpreted in terms of score levels indicating "Adept" and "Advanced" reading skill levels. Adept readers score above 300 on the NAEP scale. Adept readers are identified as follows:

> Readers with adept reading comprehension skills and strategies can understand complicated literary and informational passages, including material about topics they study at school. They can also analyze and

integrate less familiar material and provide reactions to and explanations of the text as a whole. *Performance at this level suggests the ability to find, understand, summarize, and explain relatively complicated information.* (National Association of Educational Progress, 1990.)

In turn, advanced readers who score above 350 on the NAEP reading scale are described as:

Readers who use advanced reading skills and strategies can extend and restructure the ideas presented in specialized and complex texts. Examples include scientific materials, literary essays, historical documents, and materials similar to those found in professional and technical working environments. They are also able to to understand links between ideas even when those links are not explicitly stated and to make appropriate generalizations even when the text lacks clear introductions or explanations. *Performance at this level suggests the ability to synthesize and learn from from specialized reading materials.* (National Association of Educational Progress, 1990.)

Hispanic 17-year-old students are far less likely than White students to earn NAEP reading test scores in the score ranges pertaining to adept and advanced readers in 1988. Nearly half of all White 17-year-old students (46 percent) were classified as scoring at or above the adept level on the NAEP reading achievement test. In contrast, only about 24 percent of Hispanic 17-year-old students were classified as adept readers.

NAEP data for 1988 also indicate the absence of advanced reading skill among Hispanics and, as might be expected, the discrepancy with Whites is even greater at this level. Only 6 percent of White 18-year-old students scored at this level on the NAEP reading test, but this rate exceeded that of the other groups by a considerable extent. Less than 2 percent of African American and Hispanic students scored at this level. If one is willing to assume the validity of the NAEP reading test, the results as a whole suggest that Hispanic (and African American) students who are near to completing high school are far less skilled in reading than their White counterparts.

The main thrust of the NAEP data is clear: Overall, Hispanic students appear to be less able to read well in English than their White peers at the same grade levels.

NAEP data on mathematics achievement trends of 9-, 13-, and 17-year-old White and minority students have been compiled for the period 1978-1982. With one exception, the data suggest gains in the mathematics performance on all those students (Plisko and Stern, 1986). However, these gains were found to be statistically significant only for 13-year-olds: The gains in performance among Hispanic and African American 13-year-old students were larger than for their White counterparts. Despite this evidence of gains at one age level, Hispanic students' performance fell far below that of White students overall in 1981-82.

The High School and Beyond Longitudinal Survey of high school sophomores in 1980 and the subsequent follow-up survey of these students in 1982 assessed students' reading and science achievement at both points in time, excluding students who were not enrolled in high school in 1982, two years after the initial assessment. The data indicate that Hispanic sophomores earned lower reading and science test scores than their White and Asian American/Pacific Islander counterparts both in 1980 and in 1982. Data for African American and Native American students show a similar pattern. Further examination of the data indicates that the increased reading and science achievement test scores of Hispanic, African American, and Native American students during this period were smaller than those attained by White and Asian American/Pacific Islander students. This evidence needs to be examined for statistical significance; it suggests the possibility that Hispanics were falling further behind in reading and science achievement as students approached the completion of high school—despite the exclusion of students who dropped out of school between 1980 and 1982.

ACADEMIC COURSEWORK OF HISPANIC HIGH SCHOOL STUDENTS

The High School and Beyond Longitudinal Survey also provided data on the average number of Carnegie units earned by students while in high school for five ethnic groups of students in nine academic areas: English, foreign language, mathematics, natural science, social science, arts, business, trade and industry, and "other." Overall, Hispanics showed a slightly lower number of total Carnegie study units than White students and about one less Carnegie unit than Asian American/Pacific Islander students. The largest differences between Hispanic students and White and Asian American/Pacific Islander students in amount of study units occurred in pursuit of mathematics and natural science study: in both of these areas, Hispanic students studied almost one-half year less than White students and nearly a year less than Asian American/Pacific Islander students.

The evidence also indicates that Hispanics did not earn as high academic grades as White and Asian American/Pacific Islander students in mathematics and natural science coursework. A little over 11 percent of Hispanics earned an "A" average in mathematics study in high school as compared to about 18 percent of White students and about 28 percent of Asian American/ Pacific Islander students. Hispanics were much more likely to earn barely passing or failing grades in mathematics: Over 35 percent of Hispanic high school students averaged "D" or "F" grades in mathematics as compared to about 22 percent of White students and 20 percent of Asian American students. Hispanic students (more than 34 percent) also were more likely than White or Asian American/Pacific Islander students (18 and 16 percent, respectively) to earn "D" or "F" grades in natural science study (Plisko and Stern, 1986).

The data cited imply that Hispanic students completing high school are likely to be underprepared in language arts, mathematics, and science study areas and that efforts to improve their access to college will benefit from improving their educational progress in these areas prior to the completion of high school and as early as possible.

An underlying problem facing Hispanic students in high school is that they become tracked into nonacademic-oriented coursework not suitable for college preparation. An excellent summary of evidence from the High School and Beyond survey supporting this conclusion is provided by Orum (1986):

> Data from the 1980 High School and Beyond Study indicate that by their senior year in high school, 73.8% of Hispanic youth have been enrolled in curricular programs that make a college education impossible. Other data indicate that in 1980:
>
> - over 40% of Hispanic youth were enrolled in a general high school curriculum;
> - more than 30% were enrolled in vocational programs, with the majority taking courses in business or office occupations; and
> - only 26% of Hispanic high school seniors were following a college preparatory curriculum, as compared to 39% of Whites, 32% of Blacks, and 52% of Asians. With only 24% enrollment in college preparatory programs, American Indians were the only group less likely than Hispanics to receive the instruction needed to attend college.
>
> The 1982 Follow-Up to the High School and Beyond Study reported that the percentage of Hispanic high school seniors in academic curricula had declined slightly to 25%. Enrollment in vocational programs had increased from 31% to 35%, and enrollment in general programs remained approximately the same at 40%.

STATE MANDATED TESTING AND HIGH SCHOOL PERFORMANCE

The introduction of competency tests and other forms of mandated testing programs has been viewed as a potentially damaging force in improving Hispanic students' school performance (Navarro, 1985). The use of these tests has been encouraged by state legislatures and by the public at large as ways of evaluating the effectiveness of the education provided students. Hispanic and other minority students have earned lower scores on these tests, but the outcomes and implications of these testing programs in practice of Hispanic education have not been investigated intensively. In particular, apart from the field of special education and gifted and talented education involving general intelligence tests and not competency tests or subject matter achievement tests, we have little empirical evidence of how curriculum tracking decisions for Hispanic students are affected by teachers' use of test results. There is a clear need for such research. In particular, research needs to address the question of whether Hispanic students have actually had the opportunity to learn the material included on competency and achievement tests used in making tracking decisions. The danger that Hispanic and other minority students are being tested on material they have not been taught at all or adequately well is a serious policy issue, particularly since civil rights of students may be being abrogated by the state (Snider, 1988).

Empirical studies of state-mandated test scores and their relation to Hispanic students' schooling are just beginning to emerge. The California Assessment Program (CAP), during 1986-87, gathered achievement test score data on 3rd, 6th, and 12th graders in the four areas of reading, writing, spelling, and mathematics. CAP data is reported at the school-level, and it is not intended to provide information about the achievement of individual students. The data indicate that Hispanic and African American 12th graders solve approximately 5 to 15 percent fewer test items than White and Asian American students in each academic area cited. These percentage differences indicate lower achievement on the part of Hispanic and African American students, but the meaning of this achievement gap is difficult to evaluate in terms of its educational implications.

A study of CAP data by Espinosa and Ochoa (1986) sheds light on school and socioeconomic factors related to White and minority students' 1977-78 CAP reading performance. Espinosa and Ochoa divided the CAP reading scores into 4 quartiles representing high to low achievement performance. They then examined the number and proportion of students in each ethnic group that scored within each quartile. The data indicated a very different distribution of CAP reading achievement test scores for the ethnic groups. The data indicated that the higher the CAP quartile, the greater the proportion of the Whites scoring in a quartile. In contrast, the data showed for Hispanics and African Americans, that the lower the test-score quartile, the greater the proportion of students scoring in a quartile. Further investigation of the data indicated that Hispanic students who attended the most segregated schools were the most likely to earn lower CAP reading scores.

The above findings are important to consider, given other research (Arias, 1986; Orfield, 1983) that suggests school segregation is increasing among Hispanics in urban settings and evidence that segregated schools are likely to have less fiscal and material resources and more poorly prepared teachers and administrators than less-segregated schools.

Data on the relationship between a state's use of minimum competency tests and the 1982-84 NAEP reading achievement test performance of Hispanic students has recently become available. The results seem somewhat surprising given an expectation that minimum competency testing would lead to lower academic achievement among Hispanic and other minority students. Winfield (1987) found that 11th grade White, African American, and Hispanic students from states requiring minimum competency tests earned higher NAEP reading scores than students from the same groups in states not requiring competency tests. These effects were small, but statistically significant. And they were found after statistically controlling for the influence of student variables (sex, age, student and parent academic values) and school-level variables (geographical region, SES, racial composition, remedial program offering, and instructional dollars per pupil) on NAEP reading achievement test scores.

How can we interpret the foregoing results? One possibility is that states' use of competency tests is tied to other educational reforms affecting the structure of the curriculum and the attention given to students' learning needs. If this is so, then Hispanic and other minority students might be receiving higher quality instruction in states using minimum competency tests. However, given what we know about the negative academic effects of tracking students, and what we know about Hispanic high school dropout rates, it seems very unlikely that the educational reforms currently being undertaken by states are having a serious positive impact on Hispanics' school achievement (Oakes, 1985). The results of the Winfield study do not address how tracking might affect Hispanic student achievement. The ennactment of the Goals 2000 federal legislation in 1994 and the movement to establish standards for curricula, performance testing, and delivery of curricula will no doubt affect our understanding of Hispanic students' progress. Frameworks for equitable assessment of language minority students have just begun to emerge (Lacelle-Peterson and Rivera, 1994).

COLLEGE ADMISSIONS TEST SCORES AND COLLEGE ENTRY

SAT test score data for the period 1969-92 show that Hispanic test takers score well below White test takers and that during the past 10 years there has been only a modest reduction in test score differences (Shea, 1992). The gap in SAT test scores between Hispanics and Whites, if taken at face value, indicates that Hispanics are less competitive for admission into selective colleges than Whites. The test score differences between Hispanics and

Whites are consistent with evidence cited earlier on the weaker academic preparation of Hispanics for college.

The legitimacy of SAT test scores as predictors of Hispanics' college success has undergone extensive analysis, and some evidence exists that SAT and ACT test scores may not predict the early college grades of Hispanics as well as it does for White students (Durán, 1983). While the issue of bias in college admissions tests for Hispanics is unsettled, the patterns of test scores shown by Hispanics is quite consistent with evidence that they are not served as well as White students by the education system. Perhaps the strongest criticism of college admission testing of Hispanic and other students is that the information provided by test scores has little systematic connection with instructional efforts to strengthen students' academic skills. This conclusion is consistent with the final report of the National Commission on Testing and Public Policy (1990). The Commission report forcefully argues that existing testing practices in education and other areas do not address the development of the human potential of those assessed by tests.

National education statistics indicate that Hispanic college enrollment is at an all-time high and that there has been a 23 percent increase in the number of Hispanics attending college between 1984 and 1986. However, closer inspection of these patterns shows that the proportion of Hispanic students attending college after completing high school dropped by 4 percent during the same period (American Council on Education, 1988). It is likely that the growth in the United States Hispanic population as a whole has increased the number of Hispanics attending college, yet the evidence also indicates that the education system is not improving the chances of Hispanic high school students going on to college, and four-year colleges in particular.

EXPLAINING HISPANICS' LIMITED SCHOOL SUCCESS

There is no dearth of possible explanations for Hispanics' lack of opportunity to benefit from schooling. Valencia (1989), e.g., cites connections between numerous factors and limited educational outcomes of Hispanics. Factors mentioned include 1) racial and ethnic segregation in the schools, 2) language and cultural biases in school practices, 3) limited academic achievement of students, 4) dropping out of school, 5) limited school financing, 6) poor- or low-quality teacher-student interaction, 7) tracking and curriculum differentiation, 8) lower college eligibility and enrollment rates, 9) psychological stress, 10) special education practices, and 11) absences of Hispanics in the teaching force. Making sense of such a litany of causes and antecedents of educational failure is no easy matter.

Walker (1987) analyzes the development of research on Hispanic education outcomes and concludes that regardless of explanatory focus, research shows increased attention is being paid to the needs of Hispanic students and less research is being done on alleged shortcomings and failures of students. She also suggests that there is an increase in both macro- and micro-oriented research on the relationship between Hispanics and schooling. Macro-oriented research has sought relationships between broad cultural, societal, and economic system factors and opportunities for Hispanics' schooling success. Such work is being done by Ogbu and Matute-Bianchi (1986). These investigators pursue evidence that Hispanics' low school attainment is influenced by parental and familial setting of low education expectations among children, a belief that Hispanics' job market salary will not be lower than that of nonminority persons with the same level of education.

Micro-oriented researchers have as a goal understanding how integration of Hispanic children in specific schooling contexts affects their opportunity to learn. A number of investigators in addition to Walker (e.g., Trueba, 1987; Gumperz, 1982; Mehan, 1989) suggest the importance of conducting micro-oriented studies sensitive to the ways in which broader societal inequities might affect interaction in the classroom. Mehan, for example, proposes that children from different sociocultural backgrounds enter schools with different "cultural capital" that affects children's ability to benefit from and learn in classroom interactions.

As a result of their familial and community upbringing, students acquire a self-identity, perceptions of the world, and ways of communicating, thinking, and interacting within the world as they perceive it. The cultural capital of children may or may not be congruent within the knowledged beliefs of institutional settings, such as school, that have evolved their own sense of cultural capital. According to this account, Hispanics' lack of success in schools can be attributed to the discrepancy between children's sociocultural repertoire (or cultural capital) and that expected by schools. The major education reform issue stemming from this perspective is that "bridges" must be created between the repertoire of students and forms of knowledge and behavior accepted within classrooms and the school. Mehan (1989) suggests that failure to create such bridges leads to a reinforcement of schools as agencies reproducing social inequity. For example, placement of low-achieving Hispanic children in low academic tracks with no accommodation to children's sociocultural resources leads to further low academic achievement and alienation from school. A vicious and pernicious effect of such school failure is that institutional values and accommodations to Hispanic children remain unquestioned, reinforced, and thereby re-created.

EFFECTIVE INTERVENTIONS FOR HISPANIC STUDENTS

Historically, the move to establish bilingual education for limited English proficient students stands out as the most marked attempt to make instruction and schooling effective for some of the neediest Hispanic students. Regardless of whether transitional or maintenance programs were at issue, bilingual education has sought to ensure that Hispanic children with limited English proficiency have an opportunity to benefit from instruction in Spanish while learning English. While there has been a lot of public debate about the efficacy of bilingual education, the preponderance of evidence suggests that bilingual instruction modestly improves the achievement of limited English proficient children (United States General Accounting Office, 1987; Willig, 1985). However, there is good reason to believe that use of an appropriate language for instruction is not a sufficient guarantee for children's learning. And it must be recognized that bilingual instruction in isolation does not systematically address the learning needs of those Hispanic children for whom English is the language of greatest proficiency and who show low school achievement.

Socioculturally sensitive accounts of schooling and learning, such as those drawing on Vygotsky's theories of teaching and learning, propose that individuals' learning is inseparable from, and indeed founded upon, social interaction (Tharp and Gallimore, 1988; Moll, Velez-Ibáñez, and Greenberg, in press). Cross-cultural and comparative studies of thinking and problem solving (Scribner, 1979; Heath, 1983) show that individuals' everyday thinking is intimately imbedded within their perceptions of immediate social and cultural contexts and that individuals actively interpret these contexts in terms of their previous knowledge or "cultural capital." Sociolinguistic and ethnography of communication studies of classroom communication (see Durán, 1981; Trueba et al., 1981; Cook-Gumperz, 1986) amply illustrate that the ability of language and ethnic minority students to interact in the classroom is directly affected by children's socially constructed beliefs about the nature of classroom activities, their pertinence to students' previous experiences, and the social and cultural norms for interaction negotiated between students and teacher. Effective education interventions for Hispanic students need to be founded on this sensitivity. They need to cultivate the self-identity of Hispanics as learners and to draw upon knowledge and ways of using language familiar to their experience. They also require that the teachers of Hispanic students employ instructional activities and teaching strategies that foster competence and confidence among Hispanic students. Reliance on instructional activities that allow students to build meaning out of their world is at the center of such an effort.

Home-Community and School Connections

Building connections between schools and Hispanics' homes and communities is likely to be a necessary component in improving Hispanics' schooling success. There is a need to build multiple forms of connections. Two important goals are to strengthen parents' and community members' participation in the education of children and to improve the quality of instruction offered students. Yet a third goal may emerge as very important and that is to devise learning opportunities for parents so that they may improve their literacy and schooling knowledge and opportunity to help their children progress in school (Delgado-Gaitán, 1990).

Attention is here focused on an example of connections between home/community and the school system that may have an impact on designing better instructional activities for Hispanic children. This focus is not meant to imply lesser importance to parental and community involvement in schooling decisions and indeed the latter deserves separate attention in a broader, more systematic discussion of interventions.

Moll, Velez-Ibáñez, and Greenberg (1989) describe a program of research exploring ways in which Hispanic children's school and out-of-school learning can be promoted by drawing on the social and cultural capital of family and community members. The work is premised on the idea that children will benefit from schooling that builds upon an awareness of learning and sharing of knowledge as intrinsic to the survival of the family and community. Everyday survival is dependent upon "funds of knowledge" or sociocultural capital that is exchanged among community members as they go about everyday activities. Funds of knowledge are exemplified by skills required in everyday activities and chores of life, such as childcare, purchasing goods and appliances, repairing equipment and cars, dealing with institutions such as hospitals, banks, etc. The survival of family and community in the everyday world requires making sense out of the world and requires cooperation among community members in resolving everyday needs and problems. Schools are critical. They are settings where many of the skills for real world survival are learned. This appreciation is missing for Hispanic students because of the failure of schools to draw these connections into the curriculum and because Hispanic students do not see the ways in which their own family-community experiences are related to schooling.

Moll et al. (1989) examine how different funds of knowledge are distributed among family and community members according to different social roles and intergenerational relationships. They go on to investigate in- and out-of-school learning activities that help Hispanic students and their teachers appreciate that learning is vital to personal development and making sense of the world. Students get to experience, for instance, that school mathematics learning has direct and immediate connections to the behavior of community members engaged in activities such as carpentry or tending a shop.

Building ties between funds of knowledge in families, communities, and schools appears promising in that it can provide Hispanic students with a way to see how school learning fits into the everyday experiences of family and community members. Extensions of such work to bridge connections between Hispanic students and other communities and institutions would also appear to be just as promising. Other institutional contexts worthy of attention include college and university connections to elementary and high schools and industry connections to home and community settings. Such efforts to create connections between external institutions and Hispanics' schooling are not new, but work by investigators such as Moll, Velez-Ibáñez, and Greenberg brings out the importance of making such connections meaningful to the everyday life, welfare, and motivations of students.

Warren, Rosebery, and Conant (1989), for example, have undertaken a project to teach middle-school-language minority science by conducting research projects in the community. While the students in question are Haitian rather than Hispanic, their research indicates that students acquire important scientific reasoning and inferencing skills by conducting hands-on investigation of everyday issues such as pollution in local water supplies.

Improving Classroom Interaction

More attention to ways in which the everyday world of Hispanic students is connected to schooling in and of itself will not ensure that students learn in classroom settings. The very nature of classroom activities needs to be reconceptualized and cast from within more effective models of teaching and learning. Tharp and Gallimore (1988) point out that recent policy-level concern for educational reform has largely presumed that there is no inherent pathology in the way instruction is conducted in most classrooms. While research on effective instruction has highlighted the importance of maximizing the time students spend in instructional activities that have specific objectives, it has largely avoided the question of how students are expending their time, and how teachers and students monitor learning progress apart from results conveyed by periodic achievement tests.

Tharp and Gallimore propose a strong definition of teaching that addresses these concerns. They propose that true teaching can only occur when a teacher actively assists each and every student in accomplishing a task or learning activity that could otherwise not be accomplished independently by a student. In order for assistance to be most effective, it must be given as immediately as possible and there needs to be a progression of active assistance that makes it possible for students to show greater autonomy and independence in their learning. This definition of teaching as *assisted performance* contrasts sharply with the predominant instructional strategy of teachers in whole group instruction. In the latter form of instruction, a teacher lectures to students while students passively listen. Subsequently, the teacher poses questions and selectively calls upon students to answer questions. This form of instruction is what Cummins (1986) has termed a "transmission" orientation to teaching. Such instruction will be of benefit to students who have sufficient prior knowledge and skills, but will not benefit students who are incapable of independent learning of the materials and tasks at hand.

The key question becomes: How can we assist the students who can progress in learning only if they are provided with active help in learning? Tharp and Gallimore suggest that this goal should be central to the everyday behavior of teachers in the classroom and that it should be central to the pedagogical models that teachers acquire in their early training.

Placement of low-achieving Hispanic students in remedial learning does not comply with the goals for teaching as assisted performance, because students in remedial tracks are typically asked to carry out drill and practice forms of instruction involving worksheets and because these activities have no real connections to meaningful learning.

The notion of teaching as assisted performance may seem unrealistic given the realities of teacher-student ratios in the classroom; however, it is workable in practice by utilization of collaborative and cooperative learning activities. These practices rely on small groups of students working together. Research on use of cooperative learning methods with Hispanic children suggests that cooperative activities can be structured so that children take more charge of their own learning and also so that they take on an effective role in helping other students learn (Cohen and DeAvila, 1983; Kagan, 1986; Slavin, 1990). This body of research has found preliminary evidence of achievement gains among students, but ways to maximize these gains and to adopt cooperative learning methods to the sociocultural and language characteristics of students is undergoing intensive research.

Calderón (1989) and Durán et al. (1990), for example, are conducting an implementation and evaluation of a cooperative learning intervention known as CIRC (Cooperative Integrated Reading and Composition) with 2nd and 4th grade Hispanic bilingual children. CIRC has been found to be a highly effective intervention raising the reading and writing achievement of nonminority elementary school children, but until recently was not investigated for use with Hispanic language minority children. The CIRC curriculum includes a wide variety of small group activities helping students acquire skill in comprehending stories, answering and exploring questions about stories, making predictions about story outcomes, and related writing exercises. Attention is also given to acquiring pronunciation and vocabulary skills. The CIRC research on Hispanic bilingual children has required modifications in the materials and procedures used to implement CIRC.

For example, the CIRC curriculum must be enriched in the area of English-language arts to help students change from a Spanish-only curriculum to one involving use of both Spanish and English. Other adaptations of CIRC have included enriched vocabulary building strategies and use of alternative grouping strategies for children to ensure that children check each other's learning more accurately.

While collaborative and cooperative learning can help ensure that the teaching of Hispanic children actually assists their learning performance, the need to adapt such procedures to the particular characteristics of students must be localized to specific classrooms and community-school settings. The finding that CIRC cannot be effectively implemented without such considerations is similar to earlier findings that effective reading and literacy interventions for Hawaiian school children (KEEP) required modification before it was successful with Navajo school children in a northern Arizona setting (Tharp, 1989).

Two other examples of interventions for children exemplifying use of collaborative and cooperative learning techniques are found in the OLE curriculum and AIM FOR THE BEST curriculum for Hispanic children deemed eligible for placement in special education (Ruiz, 1989; Ortiz, 1990). Hispanic students at risk for placement in special education consitute a particularly troublesome population. Special education categories such as "learning disabled" and "learning handicapped" are artificial constructions with no real diagnostic connection to instruction. Students are labeled and placed into these categories based upon a discrepancy between their school achievement and performance on standardized ability tests with no real attention to their true learning needs and the need for language services.

The OLE and AIM FOR THE BEST interventions sidestep the usual special education placement process. Both programs initiate the intervention with an intensive assessment of the learning needs of students that includes clinical observation of students' classroom performance in addition to use of traditional testing procedures. The clinical observations examine how well students perform authentic learning tasks and ways in which students use communicative and thinking skills. Based on the outcomes of the initial student assessment, the OLE and AIM FOR THE BEST interventions go on to provide students with meaning-centered collaborative learning activities that emphasize use of literature-based texts and authentic writing and communications tasks consistent with the findings of their assessment and students' capabilities in English and Spanish.

The long-range success of collaborative and cooperative learning with Hispanic children is likely to be founded upon the "democratization" of the learning process that it represents as well as upon the active assistance to learning that occurs. Collaborative and cooperative learning activities replace the teachers as the sole authority for teaching in the classroom. Students develop a responsibility for their own learning and for the learning of other students. Future research on these interventions must ask the question: Do children actually learn a self-identity as teachers and learners that persists into other schooling and learning contexts and into school learning contexts that will arise in the future en route to college preparation?

Interventions across Tiers of the Educational System

While attention to the connections between home/community and school and the conduct of teaching as assisted performance can be critical to Hispanic children's schooling success, an additional form of intervention incorporating these two interventions is necessary. The additional intervention is to create opportunities for students to develop new academic skills while simultaneously connecting their self-identity and goals at one educational tier or grade level with other educational tiers or grade levels.

The reality that nearly one-third of Hispanic school dropouts leave school before the end of the 6th grade creates a climate that reinforces the irrelevance of advanced schooling for Hispanic children. This negative climate for schooling is reinforced by the selective absence of Hispanics as teachers and as role models in institutional settings at all levels and especially those involving higher education. Attention to bridging these social and institutional barriers requires specific interventions that circumvent the status quo and that require a talent development model of the mission of educational institutions.

The Mathematics, Engineering, Science, and Achievement Program (MESA) is one example of such an outreach program serving large numbers of Hispanic students in California and other states. MESA serves junior high and high school students who are potential candidates for undergraduate and graduate study in the sciences and engineering. College and university staff, faculty, and students affiliated with MESA conduct a wide range of activities with targeted students. These activities include advising and counseling students on coursework for college preparation, career counseling, field trips to college campuses and local industry sites, and workshops with invited speakers. In addition, college and university students—often minority students—tutor MESA students in mathematics and science-related coursework. One important aspect of MESA is that substantial portions of its budget are supported by science-related industry. Evaluations of the MESA program indicate that 80 percent of MESA participants go on to enroll in college (MESA, 1988).

Another program, Partners for Valued Youth: Learning by Teacher, exemplifies ways in which at-risk Hispanic middle school students can develop academic skills and school self-esteem by tutoring elementary school children in subject matter areas (Robledo, 1990). The participating middle school students are matched with one or two elementary students for an entire year and are expected to meet four times per week in tutoring sessions. The middle school students receive training on mentoring students, and they also participate in field trips to explore economic and cultural opportunities, and they hear distinguished speakers on topics related to career planning. Students also receive recognition in the form of awards and media coverage regarding their contributions to education. Preliminary data from the program indicates that it strengthens middle school students' motivation to stay in school and that it raises the reading grades earned by participating students.

Interventions such as MESA and Partners for Valued Youth share in common a talent development approach to Hispanic education. They emphasize ways in which Hispanic students can become more meaningfully involved in their long-term education.

CONCLUSIONS AND IMPLICATIONS FOR TEACHER EDUCATION

All three intervention types mentioned in this chapter (Home/Community to School Connections, Improvements in Classroom Interaction, and Interventions across Tiers of the Education System) have important implications for teacher education. Two foci for improvements seem a priority. First, it is all too clear that Hispanics are underrepresented in the teaching force and that we need to improve this representation. Hispanics make up roughly 8 percent of all students enrolled in the nation's primary and secondary schools, but they constitute only 3.7 percent of the teaching force. Each form of intervention cited in this chapter would benefit from the greater presence of Hispanics in the teaching force (Alston, 1988). For education to work for Hispanics, they must become greater stakeholders in the process at every educational level and the community and family values of Hispanics must be allowed to be represented within the range of cultural and social capital available to schools as resources for the education of children.

A second focus for improvements in teacher education concerns the development of a new professional identity for teachers that is sensitive to the range of social, cultural, and linguistic characteristics of Hispanic (and other) children and to effective pedagogies and interventions assisting at-risk students. Consistent with Tharp and Gallimore (1988), teachers must be trained so that they do not shy away from the goal that instruction can only be effective if students benefit directly from it as it occurs. Further, teachers must develop an appreciation for the nature of students' family and community and ways in which these resources can help stimulate students' classroom learning and involvement in their education.

The goal of developing sociocultural and linguistic sensitivity for Hispanic children among teachers and of making instruction work for students will not be achieved by mere exposure to reading materials, teacher training courses, and workshops (Casden and Mehan, 1989). Extensive evidence exists that such forms of training will produce only superficial results at best in teachers' actual behaviors (Joyce and Showers, 1980; Calderón, 1984; Tharp and Gallimore, 1988). Research on teacher training and staff development indicate that effective programs require long-term commitments to assist teachers in acquiring and using new skills under the active mentorship of more-experienced teachers, professional development staff, and cooperating principals and other school leaders.

Perhaps the greatest challenge facing the teachers of Hispanic children is the need for teachers to adopt a constructivist approach to teaching and learning in contrast to existing reductionist approaches (Poplin, 1988). Teaching as assisted performance will only be effective to the extent that it empowers students to make sense out of their world. Reductionist approaches to instruction stress the teaching of isolated pieces of knowledge and skills to students with the belief that students will learn how to assemble these pieces into larger elements of knowledge and skills required in real world problem solving and learning of new subject matter areas. Current research on acquisition of cognitive skills does not support such a view. In contrast, increasing attention is being given to teaching in contexts requiring that students actively construct their own learning as part of an effort to provide a meaningful analysis of problems they encounter (Resnick, 1987). Constructivist approaches to learning stress this form of cognitive skill acquisition and the importance of situating learning in activities that make everyday sense to the lives and self-identity of learners. The foregoing concern once again brings us back full circle to the need for teachers to better understand the everyday lives, families, and community of Hispanic students and to make education relevant to students.

REFERENCES

Alston, D. 1988. *Recruiting minority classroom teachers: A national challenge.* Washington, DC: National Governers' Association.

American Council on Education. 1988. *Seventh annual status report on minorities in higher education.* Washington DC: Office of Minority Concerns.

Arias, M. B. 1986. The context of education for Hispanic students. *American Journal of Education* 95, 1: 26-57.

Association for Supervision and Curriculum Development. 1990. *Issues analysis: Public schools of choice.*

Calderón, M. 1989. Cooperative learning for LEP students. *Interculteral Development Research Association Newsletter* 16, 9.

Calderón, M., and D. Marsh. 1988. Applying research on effective bilingual instruction in a multi-district inservice teacher training program *NABE Journal* (Winter): 133-52.

Cazden. C. B. and H. Mehan. 1989. Principles from sociology and anthropology: Context, code, classroom and culture. In *Knowledge base for beginning teachers* edited by M. C. Reynolds, American Association of Colleges of Teacher Education. pp. 47-57. New York: Pergamon Press.

Children's Defense Fund. January/March 1990. *Latino youths at a crossroads.* Washington DC: CDF's Adolescent Pregnancy Prevention Clearinghouse.

Cohen, E., and E. DeAvila. 1983. *Learning to think in math and science: Improving local education for minority children.* Stanford, CA: Stanford University Center for Educational Research at Stanford.

Comer, J. P. 1988. Educating poor minority children. *Scientific American 259*, 5.

Cook-Gumperz, J. ed. 1986. *The social construction of literacy.* New York: Cambridge University Press.

Cummins, J. 1986. Empowering minority students: A framework for intervention. *Harvard Educational Review* 56: 18-36.

Delgado-Gaitan, C. 1990. *Literacy for empowerment.* Bristol, PA: The Falmer Press.

Durán, R. P. ed. 1981. *Latino language and communicative behavior.* Norwood, NJ: Ablex.

Durán, R. P. 1983. *Hispanics' education and background.* New York: College Entrance Examination Board.

Durán, R. P., M. E. Calderón, and P. L. Olmos. April 1990. *Implementing CIRC in fourth grade bilingual classrooms: Student and teacher outcomes.* Paper presented at the Annual Meeting of the American Educational Research Association, Boston.

Espinosa, R., and A. Ochoa. 1986. Concentration of California Hispanic students in schools with low achievement: A research note. *American Journal of Education 95*, 1: 77-95.

Griffith, J. E., M. J. Frase, and J. H. Ralph. 1989. American education: The challenge of change. *Population Bulletin 44*, 4.

Gumperz, J. J. 1982. *Discourse strategies.* New York: Cambridge University Press.

Heath, S. B. 1983. *Ways with words: Language, life and work in communities and classrooms.* New York: Cambridge University Press.

Hispanic Policy Development Project. 1989. *The Research Bulletin 1, 3* (Fall). New York: Hispanic Policy Development Project.

Hodgkinson, H. L. 1985. All one system. *Demographics of education, kindergarten through graduate school.* Washington, DC: Institute for Educational Leadership, Inc.

Howe II, H. 1987. 1980 high school sophomores from poverty backgrounds: Whites, Blacks, Hispanics look at school and adult responsibilities. *The Research Bulletin 1, 2:* 1-11. New York: Hispanic Policy Development Project.

Johnson, J. 1989. Hispanic dropout rate is put at 35%. *New York Times National Edition,* September 15.

Joyce, B., and B. Showers. 1980. Improving inservice training: The messages of research. *Educational Leadership 37*: 379-85.

Kagan, S. 1986. Cooperative learning and sociocultural factors in learning. In *Beyond language: Social and cultural factors in schooling language minority students*, edited by California State Department of Education. pp. 231-298. Los Angeles: Evaluation, Dissemination, and Assessment Center, California State University, Los Angeles.

Lacelle-Peterson, N. W., and C. Rivera. 1994. Is it real for all kids? A framework for equitable assessment policies for English language barriers. *Harvard Educational Review*, 64, 1: 55-75.

Mehan, H. 1989. Understanding inequality in schools: The contribution of interpretive studies. A revision of the paper invited for presentation at the ASA meetings, August, San Diego.

MESA. 1989. *1989 Report*. Berkeley: The Regents of the University of California.

Moll, L. C., and J. B. Greenberg. 1990. Creating zones of possibilities: Combining social contexts for instruction. In *Vygotsky and education* edited by L. C. Moll. Cambridge: Cambridge University Press.

Moll, L. C., C. Velez-Ibáñez, and J. Greenberg. 1989. *Community knowledge and classroom practice: Combining resources for literacy instruction*. Tucson: University of Arizona, Bureau of Applied Research Anthropolgy.

National Assessment of Educational Progress 1990. *Learning to read in our nation's schools: Instruction and achievement in 1988 at grades 4, 8 and 12*. Washington DC: Educational Testing Service.

National Commission on Teaching and Public Policy. 1990. *From gatekeeper to gateway: Transforming testing in America*. Chestnut Hill, MA: Boston College.

National Committee for Educational Excellence. 1983. *A nation at risk: The imperative for educational reform*. Washington DC: Government Printing Office.

Navarro, M. S. 1985. The quality education movement: New state standards and minority access to college. *Educational standards, testing, and access*. Proceedings of the 1984 ETS Invitational Conference, 15-22, Princeton: Educational Testing Service.

Oakes, J. 1985. *Keeping track*. New Haven: Yale University Press.

O'Brien, E. 1989. Some gains, some losses in minority test scores. *Black Issues in Higher Education* 6, 14: 1, 12-13.

Ogbu, J., and M. Matute-Bianchi. 1986. Understanding sociocultural factors: Knowledge, identity, and school adjustment. In *Beyond language: Social and cultural factors in schooling language minority students*, edited by California State Department of Education, pp. 73-142. Los Angeles: Evaluation, Dissemination, and Assessment Center, California State University, Los Angeles.

Orfield, G. 1983. *Public school desegregation in the United States, 1968-1980*. Washington, DC: Joint Center for Political Studies.

Ortiz, A. 1990. *Assessment and intervention model for the bilingual exceptional student: An innovative approaches research project*. Paper presented at the Annual Meeting of the American Educational Research Association, Boston (unpublished).

Orum, L. S. 1986. *The education of Hispanics: Status and implications*. Washington, DC: National Council of La Raza.

Plisko, V., and J. Stern, eds. 1986. *The condition of education, 1985 edition*. Statistical Report. Washington, DC: National Center for Education Statistics.

Poplin, M. S. 1988. Holistic/constructivist principles of the teaching/learning process. *Journal of Learning Disabilities*. 21, 7: 401-16.

Resnick, L. 1987. *Education and learning to think*. Washington, DC: National Academy Press.

Robledo, M. 1990. *Partners for valued youth: Dropout prevention strategies for at-risk limited English proficient students.* Presentation at The Innovative Approaches Research Project Symposium, Development Associates, June, Washington, DC.

Ruiz, N. 1989. An optimal learning environment for Rosemary. *Exceptional Children* 56, 2: 130-44.

Scribner, S. 1979. Modes of thinking and ways of speaking: Culture and logic reconsidered. In *New directions in discourse processing,* edited by R. O. Freedle, pp. 223-43. Norwood, NJ: Ablex.

Shea, G. 1992. SAT scores rise 1 point on verbal section, ending steady drop. *The Chronicle of Higher Education* (September 2).

Slavin, R. E. 1990. Cooperative learning and language minority persons. Paper presented at the Annual Meeting of the American Educational Research Association, Boston (unpublished).

Smith,W. F., and R.L. Andrews. 1989. *Instructional Leadership: How principals make a difference.* Association for Supervision and Curriculum Development.

Snider, W. 1988. State mandates, equity law: On a collision course? *Education Week* 7, 20 (February 10): 1, 15.

Tharp, R. G. 1989. Psychocultural variables and constants: Effects on teaching and learning in schools. *American Psychologist* 44: 349-59.

Tharp, R. G., and R. Gallimore. 1988. *Rousing minds to life.* New York: Cambridge University Press.

Trueba, H. T. 1987. The ethnography of schooling. In *Success or failure? Learning and the language minority student,* edited by H. T. Trueba. New York: Newbury House.

Trueba, H. T., G. P. Guthrie, and K. H. Au, eds. 1981. *Culture and the bilingual classroom: Studies in classroom ethnography.* Rowley, MA: Newbury House.

United States General Accounting Office. 1987. *Bilingual education. A new look at research evidence.* GAO/PEMD-87-12BR. Washington, DC.

Valencia, R. R. 1989. For whom does the schoolbell toll? *Chicano school failure and success: Research and policy agendas for the 1990s.* Keynote address presented at Chicano School Failure and Success Conference.

Walker, C. L. 1987. *Hispanic achievement: Old views and new perspectives.* Unpublished manuscript, University of Minnesota, Department of Curriculum and Instruction.

Warren, B., A. S. Rosebery, and F. R. Conant. 1989. *Cheche Konnen: Learning science by doing science in language minority classrooms.* Bolt, Beranek and Newman, Inc.

Willig, A. 1985. A meta-analysis of selective studies on the effectivenes of bilingual education. *Review of Educational Research* 5, 3: 269-317.

Winfield, L. 1987. *The relationship between minimum competency testing programs and students' reading proficiency: Implications from the 1983-84 National Assessment of Educational Progress of Reading and Writing.* Princeton: Educational Testing Service.

CHAPTER 10

Progress of Hispanics in American Higher Education

Alfredo de los Santos Jr. and Antonio Rigual

INTRODUCTION

At first glance the figures seem impressive:

- 954,000 Hispanics* enrolled in higher education in 1992 (an increase of 129 percent since 1978) (O'Brien, 1993);
- over 49,000 bachelor's degrees awarded to Hispanics in 1991 (a growth of 81 percent since 1977) (National Science Board, 1993);
- a 146 percent increase in the number of doctoral degrees in science and engineering awarded to Hispanics from 1977 to 1991 (National Science Board, 1993);
- a 58 percent increase in the number of Hispanic college faculty members from 1981 to 1991 (O'Brien, 1993).

Should we declare victory and call off the struggle? Hardly. Yes, there are ample reasons to celebrate the accomplishments of the Hispanic men and women whose efforts are responsible for these statistics. However, their triumphs exist within an environment in which:

---

*The term "Hispanic" is used throughout this chapter. The authors acknowledge the preference for other terms by many members of the Hispanic community. The U.S. Bureau of the Census defines a Hispanic individual as "a person of Mexican American, Puerto Rican, Cuban, Central or South American, or other Spanish culture, or origin, regardless of race."

- the high school completion rate of Hispanic 18-to-24-year-olds in 1992 was 26 *points less* than the rate for White non-Hispanics (57.3 percent to 83.3 percent) and only slightly ahead of the 15-year (from 1978 to 1992) average rate for Hispanics of 56.9 (Carter and Wilson, 1994);
- the 49,000 bachelor's degrees awarded to Hispanics in 1991 represented only 4.5 percent of all bachelor's degrees awarded in the U.S. (National Science Board, 1993);
- the 478 doctoral degrees awarded in science and engineering to Hispanic U.S. citizens and permanent residents in 1991 amounted to just under 2 percent of the total number of science and engineering doctoral degrees awarded in the nation that year (National Science Board, 1993); and
- Hispanic full-time faculty members accounted for only 2.2 percent of the professoriate in 1991 (O'Brien, 1993).

Statistically, little is known about the status of Hispanics in higher education prior to 1972, a fact reflective of the almost complete neglect accorded the group by the majority population until recently. Thus, the focus of this chapter is the period from 1972 to 1992. The data reveal loudly and clearly that although Hispanics have made real progress in the educational arena during these 20 years, they are far from reaching proportional representation in any meaningful way.

THE HISPANIC POPULATION—GENERAL CHARACTERISTICS

Any discussion of the status of Hispanics in higher education must be framed by, at the very least, an understanding of some basic characteristics of this segment of the U.S. population. According to the 1990 Census, there were some 22.4 million Hispanics living in the U.S., representing approximately 9 percent of the total population. While the non-Hispanic U.S. population grew by 6.8 percent from 1980 to 1990, the Hispanic group increased by 53 percent (U.S. Bureau of the Census, 1993a).

The rapid rise in the size of our nation's Hispanic population is even more dramatically apparent when the 1970 figure—9.1 million—is compared to the 22.4 million of 1990: an increase of 146 percent in just 20 years (U.S. Bureau of the Census, 1993.). Census Bureau projections (the 1992 middle series) suggest continued rapid growth for the remainder of this century and into the next (U.S. Bureau of the Census, 1993d). (See Figure 10.1.)

Currently one of every 11 persons in the U.S. is Hispanic; in the first half of the twenty-first century the proportion will be between one of six and one of five (U.S. Bureau of the Census, 1993a). Because Hispanics are not evenly

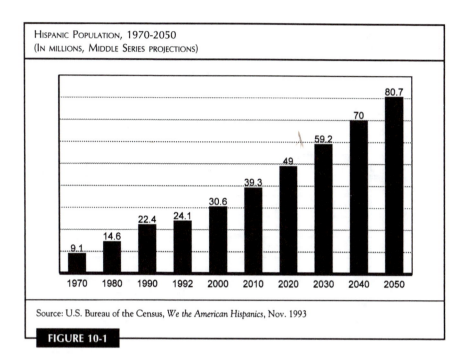

HISPANIC POPULATION, 1970-2050
(IN MILLIONS, MIDDLE SERIES PROJECTIONS)

Source: U.S. Bureau of the Census, *We the American Hispanics*, Nov. 1993

FIGURE 10-1

spread across the nation, colleges and universities in certain regions of the U.S. will see this demographic trend reflected in their applicant pools earlier than those of other areas. Even so, Hispanics will constitute a growing proportion of the student body at institutions of higher education throughout the nation.

Nearly 90 percent of Hispanics live in 10 states. California, Texas, New York, and Florida have the largest Hispanic populations. Nearly 4 of 10 persons in New Mexico are Hispanic, and Hispanics constitute over one-fourth of the population of California and Texas (U.S. Bureau of the Census, 1993a). (See Table 10-1.)

Hispanics are highly urban (90 percent lived in a metropolitan area in 1990) (U.S. Bureau of the Census, 1993a), accounting for at least 20 percent of the population of nine of the nation's largest cities (U.S. Bureau of the Census, 1991). Hispanics constitute 40 percent of the population of Los Angeles; San Antonio is a majority Hispanic community, as are a number of smaller cities, such as El Paso and Miami (U.S. Bureau of the Census, 1991). (See Figure 10-2.)

Diversity is an important characteristic of the U.S. Hispanic population. Hispanics are not a monolithic group. When the Hispanic population is studied and discussed—as will be the case in some sections of this very

TABLE 10-1

HISPANIC POPULATION, 1990 SELECTED STATES

State	Total Population	Hispanic Population	% Hispanic
Arizona	3,665,228	680,628	18.6
California	29,760,021	7,557,550	25.4
Colorado	3,294,394	419,322	12.7
Florida	12,937,926	1,555,031	12.0
Illinois	11430602	878682	7.7
New Jersey	7,730,188	720,344	9.3
New Mexico	1,515,069	576,709	38.1
New York	17,990,455	2,151,743	12.0
Texas	16,986,510	4,294,120	25.3

Source: U.S. Bureau of the Census, *Statistical Abstract of the United States: 1991*

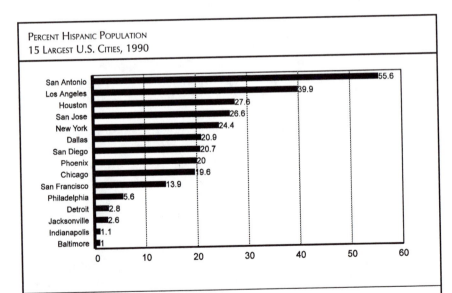

PERCENT HISPANIC POPULATION
15 LARGEST U.S. CITIES, 1990

San Antonio — 55.6
Los Angeles — 39.9
Houston — 27.6
San Jose — 26.6
New York — 24.4
Dallas — 20.9
San Diego — 20.7
Phoenix — 20
Chicago — 19.6
San Francisco — 13.9
Philadelphia — 5.6
Detroit — 2.8
Jacksonville — 2.6
Indianapolis — 1.1
Baltimore — 1

Source: U.S. Bureau of the Census, *Statistical Abstract of the United States: 1991*

FIGURE 10-2

chapter—subgroup differences often are not presented. It is incumbent on institutions of higher education to be aware of and take into account those distinguishing features as they design programs and services that match the needs of their evolving student populations.

Hispanic persons of Mexican origin make up almost 64 percent of the U.S. Hispanic population; other Hispanic subgroups include persons of Puerto Rican (10.6 percent), Cuban (4.7 percent), Central and South American (14 percent), and other Hispanic (7 percent) origin (U.S. Bureau of the Census, 1993b). (See Figure 10-3.)

Characteristics such as educational attainment, length of residence in the U.S., and English-speaking ability, for example, vary among the different Hispanic communities (U.S. Bureau of the Census, 1993d). These factors, either individually or in combination, may affect standardized test scores, readiness for college-level work in English, and college participation rates. (See Figures 10-4, 10-5, and 10-6.)

The age of the Hispanic population closely relates to the increases that have occurred in the group's college enrollment patterns. Such increases will continue well into the next century because Hispanics as a group are relatively young. In 1992 the median age of the Hispanic population was 26.4

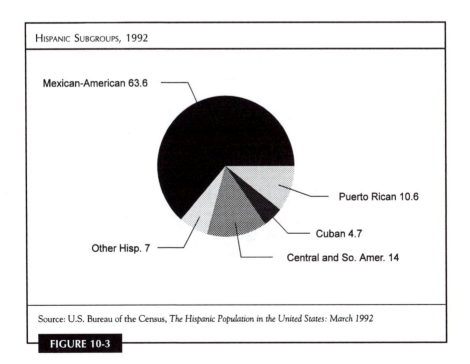

HISPANIC SUBGROUPS, 1992

Mexican-American 63.6

Puerto Rican 10.6

Cuban 4.7

Other Hisp. 7

Central and So. Amer. 14

Source: U.S. Bureau of the Census, *The Hispanic Population in the United States: March 1992*

FIGURE 10-3

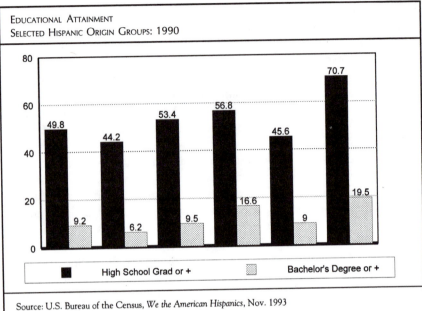

EDUCATIONAL ATTAINMENT
SELECTED HISPANIC ORIGIN GROUPS: 1990

Source: U.S. Bureau of the Census, *We the American Hispanics*, Nov. 1993

FIGURE 10-4

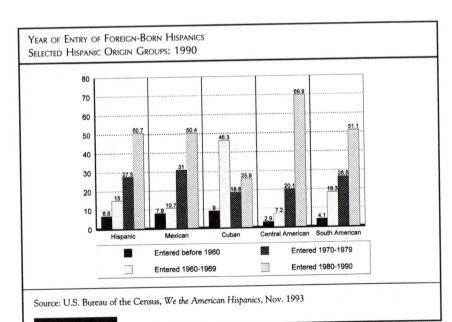

YEAR OF ENTRY OF FOREIGN-BORN HISPANICS
SELECTED HISPANIC ORIGIN GROUPS: 1990

Source: U.S. Bureau of the Census, *We the American Hispanics*, Nov. 1993

FIGURE 10-5

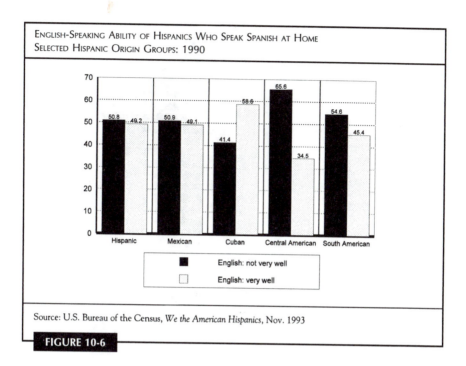

ENGLISH-SPEAKING ABILITY OF HISPANICS WHO SPEAK SPANISH AT HOME
SELECTED HISPANIC ORIGIN GROUPS: 1990

Source: U.S. Bureau of the Census, *We the American Hispanics*, Nov. 1993

FIGURE 10-6

years, while the median age of the non-Hispanic population was 34.1 years (U.S. Bureau of the Census, 1993b). (See Figure 10-7.)

As a percentage of the total number of 18- to 24-year olds, the Hispanic representation will continue to increase, a fact of special significance to colleges and universities that draw the majority of their undergraduate enrollments from this pool. Current population projections indicate that the number of Hispanic 18- to 24-year olds will increase from some 13 percent of the total in 1995 to about 20 percent of all persons in this age group by the year 2020 (U.S. Bureau of the Census, 1993b).

Three Hispanic population socioeconomic indicators vividly underscore the critical role that financial assistance plays in making access to higher education truly meaningful for Hispanics:

- Hispanic median family income in 1991 was $23,900 (compared to $37,000 for non-Hispanic families) (U.S. Bureau of the Census, 1993a);

- nearly 15 percent of all Hispanic households in 1990 had six or more persons (compared to 3.4 percent for non-Hispanic households) (U.S. Bureau of the Census, 1993c); and

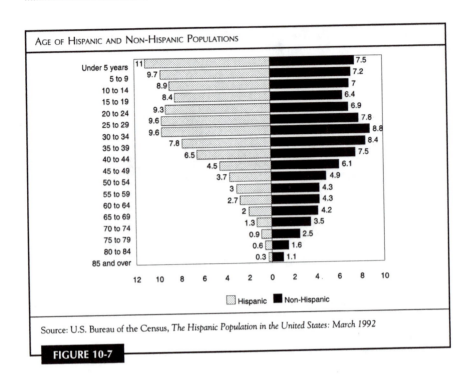

AGE OF HISPANIC AND NON-HISPANIC POPULATIONS

Source: U.S. Bureau of the Census, *The Hispanic Population in the United States: March 1992*

FIGURE 10-7

- about 27 percent of Hispanic families lived below the poverty level in 1991 (compared to 10 percent of non-Hispanic families) (U.S. Bureau of the Census, 1993a).

Lower family income levels and larger numbers of persons per household are only two of the many socioeconomic factors that mitigate against further increases in Hispanic college participation rates. Further increases will not occur without a corresponding expansion of financial assistance to defray higher education expenses. The overall share of federal government support—by far the largest source of financial aid for higher education—actually declined during the 10-year period between 1982 and 1992 (from 80 percent of all aid to 74 percent) (National Science Board, 1993).

HISPANIC COLLEGE STUDENTS

When financial considerations are set aside, two factors have an obvious direct relationship to the number of Hispanic students enrolled in higher education: high school completion rates and college participation rates. As has been noted previously, the Hispanic high school completion rate of 18- to 24-year olds has not improved markedly over the 15-year period from 1978 to

1992. (In fact, the 1992 rate of 57.3 percent was only 0.4 percentage points ahead of the 15-year average rate of 56.9) Although the Hispanic enrolled-in-college participation rate of 18- to 24-year olds fluctuated over the same span, the 1992 rate of 37.1 percent was the highest of the 15-year period and 6.9 percentage points above the 15-year average rate of 30.2 percent. Even at this high level, the Hispanic enrolled-in-college participation rate was 5.1 percentage points lower than the White non-Hispanic rate of 42.2 percent (Carter and Wilson, 1994). (See Figure 10-8.)

When seen in this light, it is evident that the growth in Hispanic higher education enrollments is due primarily to two factors: the overall increase in Hispanic population and gains in the rate at which Hispanic high school graduates enroll in college. Also noteworthy is the fact that the growth in the Hispanic enrolled-in-college participation rate over the last 15 years reflects a much larger increase in the participation of Hispanic women in higher education (a remarkable gain of 14.6 percentage points) than of Hispanic men (a gain of 4.3 percentage points) (Carter and Wilson, 1994). (See Figure 10-9.)

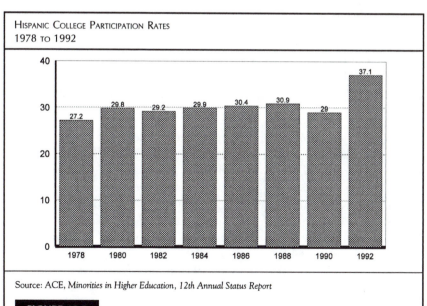

HISPANIC COLLEGE PARTICIPATION RATES
1978 TO 1992

Source: ACE, *Minorities in Higher Education, 12th Annual Status Report*

FIGURE 10-8

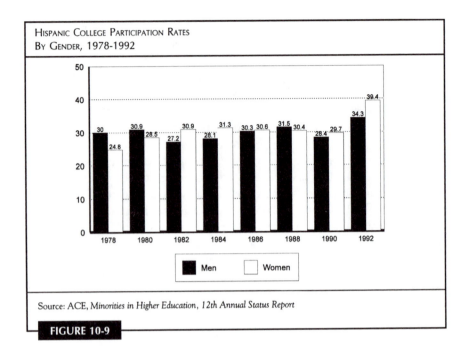

HISPANIC COLLEGE PARTICIPATION RATES
BY GENDER, 1978-1992

Source: ACE, *Minorities in Higher Education, 12th Annual Status Report*

FIGURE 10-9

In 1992, a total of 954,000 Hispanics were enrolled in U.S. institutions of higher education, an increase of 84 percent over the 1982 figure of 519,000 (Carter and Wilson, 1994). (See Figure 10-10.)

A profile of Hispanic college students in 1992 shows the following characteristics:

- undergraduates—93 percent; graduate students—6 percent; professional school students—1 percent
- 55 percent women
- 61 percent of undergraduates were at two-year colleges
- 86 percent enrolled in public institutions (Carter and Wilson, 1994)
- 44 percent attended on a part-time basis in 1991 (O'Brien, 1993)
- 34 percent of 1992 freshmen chose majors in science/engineering fields (National Science Board, 1993)
- approximately 40 percent of 1992 freshmen reported a need for remedial work in mathematics (National Science Board, 1993)
- 62 percent of full-time undergraduates received support from federal financial assistance programs in 1990 (O'Brien, 1993)

Hispanic college students accounted for 6.6 percent of the total enrollment in higher education in 1992 (Carter and Wilson, 1994). Although this signifies an improvement over the 1980 level of 4 percent (Carter and

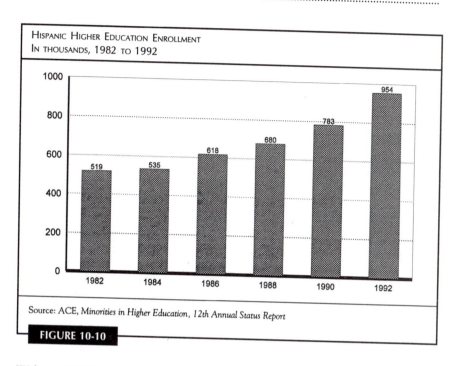

HISPANIC HIGHER EDUCATION ENROLLMENT
IN THOUSANDS, 1982 TO 1992

Source: ACE, *Minorities in Higher Education*, *12th Annual Status Report*

FIGURE 10-10

Wilson, 1993), it is far short of Hispanics' proportional representation within the total U.S. population (9 percent) and farther short still of the representation of Hispanics within a group traditionally very important to higher education, the 20- to 24-year old population (11.8 percent Hispanic) (U.S. Bureau of the Census, 1993b).

Only at two-year institutions do Hispanics participate at a rate that closely mirrors their representation in the U.S. population: 9.5 percent of all students at two-year colleges in 1992 were Hispanic. Hispanic students comprise only 4.7 percent of the total enrollment at four-year colleges; they constitute 3.4 percent of the enrollments of graduate and professional schools (Carter and Wilson, 1994). The higher participation rate for Hispanics at two-year colleges is a result of several factors, including those institutions' location in the communities where Hispanics live; their relatively lower cost when compared to four-year institutions and, in particular, to four-year private institutions; their more liberal admission policies; and their traditional egalitarian orientation.

Hispanic access to higher education is but one of the indicators on which to measure the progress of this growing segment of the U.S. population. Although educational "inputs" are important, "outputs" (graduates) are even more critical. Not as much is known about the persistence-to-graduation rates of Hispanic students as is known of their enrollment patterns. Available data sources indicate that, by and large, institutions of higher education are not coming close to achieving the desired results in retaining and graduating Hispanic students (O'Brien, 1993).

At best, the four-year retention rate for Hispanic students who follow the "traditional college path" (defined as entering a four-year institution on a full-time basis in the fall immediately following high school graduation) is 42 percent. Moreover, since most Hispanics (84 percent) do *not* keep to the "traditional" path, it is reasonable to assume that the *overall* Hispanic rate of retention-to-graduation is considerably less than 42 percent. Currently the six-year college completion rate for Hispanic students can only be expressed as a range: from 4 percent for students who start on a nontraditional path to about 31 percent for those who follow the traditional route (Carter and Wilson, 1994). Such statistics foretell dire circumstances for the nation's productivity in the twenty-first century. It is doubtful that the U.S. will be able to remain competitive globally if 20 percent of its population (by around the year 2050) still exhibit today's low educational attainment levels.

The small percentage of Hispanic students who "made it" through the various levels of the U.S. system of higher education in 1991 earned the following degrees:

TABLE 10-2

DEGREES EARNED BY HISPANICS, 1991
BY LEVEL OF DEGREE

Degree Level	Number Awarded to Hispanics	% of total number of degrees awarded
Associate's	29,019	6.0%
Bachelor's	49,027	4.5%
Master's	9,684	3.2%
Doctoral	843	3.2%

Source: National Science Board, *Science & Engineering Indicators, 1993*

The "degrees earned" figures mirror the case with enrollment statistics; although there has been significant growth in the number of degrees earned by Hispanics at all levels in the 15-year period between 1977 and 1991, only at the associate's degree level does the number even come close to a proportional representation of the Hispanic population. (See Table 10-3.)

TABLE 10-3

Degrees Earned by Hispanics
By Level of Degree, 1977-1991

Degree Level	1977	1981	1985	1989	1991	Increase 1977-1991
Associate's	19,808	22,088	22,783	23,475	29,019	46.5%
Bachelor's	27,043	33,167	36,391	41,361	49,027	81.3%
Master's	7,071	7,439	7,730	8,133	9,684	37.0%
Doctoral	474	526	634	694	843	77.8%

Source: National Science Board, *Science & Engineering Indicators, 1993*

More Hispanic women earned associate's, bachelor's, and master's degrees in 1991 than Hispanic men, and, although Hispanic men still outnumber women in the number of doctoral degrees earned, the gap has narrowed considerably. At the bachelor's, master's, and doctoral levels, the distribution of degrees earned by Hispanics by academic areas in 1990 was as follows:

TABLE 10-4

Degrees Earned by Hispanics — 1991
By Level and Academic Area

Academic Area	% of Bachelor's	% of Master's	% of Doctoral
Education	14.6	42.1	25.1
Business	36.6	27.1	*
Social Sciences	20.8	4.7	23.5
Health Professions	8.2	7.5	*
Biological/Life Sciences	6.6	11.2	14.3
Engineering	13.2	7.5	5.4
Physical Sciences	*	*	11.8
Humanities	*	*	15.5
Professional-Other	*	*	4.3

*Data source did not use this category in reports.
Source: National Science Board, *Science & Engineering Indicators, 1993*

For the period from 1981 to 1990, the number of bachelor's degrees earned by Hispanics increased in all academic areas except education; the greatest gains were in business and engineering. During the same period, the number of master's degrees awarded to Hispanics grew, once again, in all fields except education, with business and health professions experiencing the greatest increases. At the doctoral level, the number of degrees earned by Hispanics increased in all areas during the 1980-90 period, with gains in the physical sciences and life sciences leading the way (Carter and Wilson, 1994; National Science Board, 1993).

HISPANICS EMPLOYED IN HIGHER EDUCATION

From 1975 to 1991, the number of Hispanics serving as full-time faculty members in institutions of higher education in the United States increased by 81 percent, from 6,323 to 11,424 (Carter and Wilson, 1989; Carter and Wilson, 1993; O'Brien, 1993). (See Figure 10-11.) Even with such substantial growth, Hispanic faculty members constituted only 2.2 percent of the professorate in 1991 (O'Brien, 1993). (See Figure 10-12.)

Hispanic women faculty members accounted for 36 percent of the total number of Hispanic faculty in 1991, a gain of three percentage points over the 1989 proportion. Hispanic men and women full-time faculty had lower tenure rates (61 percent) than non-Hispanic faculty (70 percent) and were less well represented within the full professor rank (one in six) than their non-Hispanic colleagues (one in four) (O'Brien, 1993).

The number of Hispanic full-time higher education administrators increased at an even faster rate than did Hispanic full-time faculty. In 1975 there were 1,203 Hispanics employed in higher education administration; by

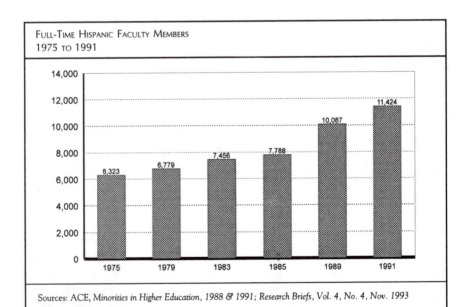

FULL-TIME HISPANIC FACULTY MEMBERS
1975 TO 1991

Sources: ACE, *Minorities in Higher Education, 1988 & 1991; Research Briefs,* Vol. 4, No. 4, Nov. 1993

FIGURE 10-11

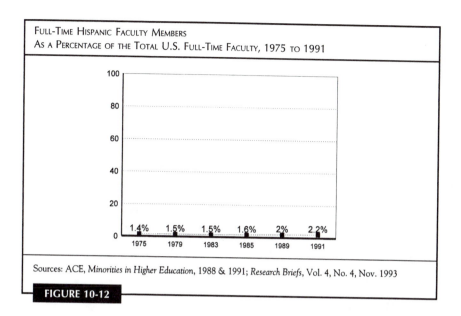

FULL-TIME HISPANIC FACULTY MEMBERS
AS A PERCENTAGE OF THE TOTAL U.S. FULL-TIME FACULTY, 1975 TO 1991

Sources: ACE, *Minorities in Higher Education*, 1988 & 1991; *Research Briefs*, Vol. 4, No. 4, Nov. 1993

FIGURE 10-12

1991 the number had grown to 3,453, a gain of 187 percent during the 15-year period. And yet, 97.5 of our nation's college and university administrators in 1991 were non-Hispanic persons (Carter and Wilson, 1989; Carter and Wilson, 1992; O'Brien, 1993). (See Figures 10-13 and 10-14.)

In 1993, only 2.6 percent of the presidents of the 3,611 U.S. colleges and universities were Hispanic (O'Brien, 1993; National Science Board, 1993). Relatively little is known about the professional training, social origins, and career mobility of Hispanic higher education administrators throughout the nation. A regional study focusing on Mexican American administrators in five Southwestern states (Arizona, California, Colorado, New Mexico, and Texas), first conducted in 1976 and replicated in 1991, determined that 85 percent of respondents in 1991 were employed in administrative positions that were classified as being of "moderate," "moderate to low," and "low" prestige level. This same study found that there had been substantial increases in the numbers of administrators at all levels (except for department chair) and identified 1,325 Mexican American administrators at the department chair/director level and above in 1991, a gain of 152 percent in 15 years (Esquibel, 1992).

Rarely, then, do Hispanic students see affirming reflections of themselves in their instructors or in the administrative leadership of their campuses. Hispanic women, who now constitute the majority of Hispanic college students, encounter even fewer Hispanic faculty and administrators of their

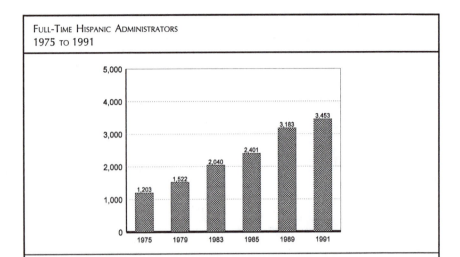

FULL-TIME HISPANIC ADMINISTRATORS
1975 TO 1991

Sources: ACE, *Minorities in Higher Education, 1988 & 1991; Research Briefs*, Vol. 4, No. 4, Nov. 1993

FIGURE 10-13

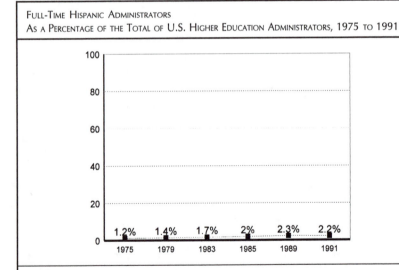

FULL-TIME HISPANIC ADMINISTRATORS
AS A PERCENTAGE OF THE TOTAL OF U.S. HIGHER EDUCATION ADMINISTRATORS, 1975 TO 1991

Sources: ACE, *Minorities in Higher Education, 1988 & 1991; Research Briefs*, Vol. 4, No. 4, Nov. 1993

FIGURE 10-14

own gender who could serve as role models or mentors. Academe in 1994 is still largely a non-Hispanic environment at every level.

INSTITUTIONS OF HIGHER EDUCATION

Most Hispanic faculty members and administrators employed by institutions of higher education and most Hispanic students enrolled in 1990 at colleges and universities in the 50 states and the District of Columbia could be found at so-called majority institutions in which Hispanic students constitute a relatively small number and/or percentage of the student body. Of the 3,611 U.S. colleges and universities, approximately 3,350 could be classified as institutions of this type. Additionally, 102 institutions are historically Black colleges and universities (HBCUs)—where less than one percent of all Hispanic students enrolled in 1991—or other institutions in which non-Hispanic minority group students predominate (such as colleges that are not HBCUs, but where African American students are the majority, and tribal colleges).

A fairly recent development in U.S. higher education (since the early 1970s) involves the concentration of Hispanic students at colleges and universities now commonly referred to as "Hispanic-serving institutions" (HSI), those that qualify for membership in the Hispanic Association of Colleges and Universities (HACU). Established in 1986, HACU's membership is drawn from the institutions of higher education where Hispanic students represent at least 25 percent of the enrollment.

Outside of Puerto Rico, 89 colleges and universities qualify for HACU membership. These institutions, approximately 2.5 percent of the total number in the mainland U.S., account for a disproportionately large number of Hispanic students—31 percent of the total higher education Hispanic mainland enrollment. Thirty-four campuses in Puerto Rico also qualify for HACU membership (O'Brien, 1993). An unfortunate characteristic of many "national" studies, and one that Hispanic and other leaders need to address, is their tendency to deal only with the 50 states and the District of Columbia, thus excluding data from/about Puerto Rico. People born in Puerto Rico are U.S. citizens, but their characteristics and attitudes are not included in many studies of the U.S. population.

In contrast to HBCUs, which were established to educate and train African Americans, most HSIs were not founded for the specific purpose of serving Hispanics or of addressing their educational needs. As the Hispanic population grew and as federal government financial assistance programs in the 1970s made it economically feasible for students from low-income backgrounds to afford a college education, larger numbers of Hispanics overcame the barriers that had prevented them from accessing higher education. The institutions to which Hispanics often turned were those in their own communities, mostly lower-cost two-year colleges and four-year public universities. However, some four-year private institutions also were in the vanguard of colleges providing higher education opportunities to Hispanic students.

Just as with institutions in Puerto Rico, continental U.S. HSIs are both public and private, two-year and four-year. The Hispanic enrollments of mainland HSIs range from the 25 percent threshold for HACU membership to 99 percent. HSIs are found in the same 10 states where 90 percent of the Hispanic population lives. (See Table 10.1.)

Since HSIs were, with few exceptions, not created as Hispanic institutions, they find themselves at different stages in the development of their Hispanic "identities." Although generally higher than at non-HSIs, the representation of Hispanics as a proportion of HSI faculty and administration far from mirrors the Hispanic composition of the institutions' student bodies. Of 94 college presidents identified in 1993 by the American Council on Education as Hispanic, 73 headed HSIs; however, some HSIs do not have even one Hispanic senior administrator (president or vice president) (O'Brien, 1993).

As demographic trends involving the growth of the U.S. Hispanic population unfold, more colleges and universities will become HSIs, and Hispanic students will increase as a proportion of the total student body at current HSIs. The degree to which these institutions are willing and able to redefine and reshape themselves, to undergo the transformation into truly "Hispanic-serving institutions" and, thus, respond effectively to the needs of their ever-increasing Hispanic clientele, will have much to say about how successful Hispanic college students are in the late 1990s and in the next century.

STRATEGIC DIRECTIONS

The trends of the last 15 years in Hispanic enrollment, degrees earned, and faculty and administrative representation demand that policy makers and higher education leaders make a new commitment to equal opportunity across the various levels of education. As society searches for solutions to its pressing problems, Hispanics must be part of the problem-solving process. Such involvement is unlikely, however, without an improvement in educational attainment levels.

If Hispanics are to achieve proportional representation in higher education by the end of this century or shortly after the beginning of the next, the Hispanic community in general *and* the higher education community in particular need to devise new strategies. Four such strategic directions are recommended: redefining the question, building community, leadership development, and accountability.

Redefining the Question

Problem statements have inherent constraints: how one states the problem often limits the options for solving it. By defining a problem rather narrowly, the solutions considered conform to the limited definition. The question of minority participation in higher education has gone through two "stages" of definition; it is time for a redefinition.

In the 1960s and early 1970s, the problem of minority participation in higher education was defined as an issue of *access*. The dilemma was seen merely as one of bringing minorities to the institutions, in other words, making the colleges and universities *accessible*. The institutional response was, thus, limited to outreach, recruitment, and related activities.

By the middle 1970s, outreach and recruitment were deemed to be insufficient. Minority students recruited to the campuses were dropping out before graduation. Institutions of higher education then redefined the basic issue of low minority participation as one of *retention*. Once again, the "solutions" were limited to this new, but still narrow, definition of the problem. During this era tutorial services, learning assistance centers, child care, and other similar "solutions" were established or implemented in hopes of increasing the *retention* of minority students. Still, these students dropped out in droves before graduation.

Clearly, institutional responses based on access or retention definitions of the problem have not been successful in eliminating race/ethnicity as a factor in college completion.

To increase minority participation in higher education in the 1990s and in the twenty-first century, the issue must be viewed in two new ways. The first new approach should be to focus on *achievement*. That is, emphasis has to be placed not only on the number of students who *enroll* but, more importantly, on the number who *graduate*—a question, then, of not just *access*, but also *success*. This success must extend beyond the associate's and bachelor's degrees and concentrate on achievements at the master's, first professional, and doctoral levels.

The problem of low minority participation in higher education also should be defined by *quantifying* objectives. Quantifying must be of the sort adopted by the trustees of the College Board at their March 1989 meeting:

> By the end of the twentieth century, individuals from traditionally underrepresented groups will have access to and complete two-year and four-year college education at the same rate as traditional students (Personal Correspondence: Donald Stewart to Alfredo de los Santos, 1989).

A second example of quantifying comes from the report of the National Task Force on Minority Achievement in Higher Education, sponsored by the Education Commission of the States, which was issued in December 1990. The Task Force recommended:
Every state should adopt and strive to reach two goals:

- Minority enrollment in higher education should be at least proportional to the minority population in each state.
- Minority graduation rates should be comparable to those of other students (*Policies for Change*, 1990, p.2).

Higher education needs to specify more clearly and with more precision what it wants as outcomes both in terms of minority *achievement* and numbers of graduates—the *quantity*.

Clearly, restating the problem does not remove race and ethnicity as factors in college completion. Enlightened leadership, commitment and accountability over time are also crucial to solving the problems faced by our nation.

Building Community

The second strategy for improving minority participation in higher education is *community building*. Community building begins with listening, understanding, and communicating.

Higher education needs to listen more carefully to understand what is happening in Hispanic communities. Community leaders need to communicate better with each other, with those whose aims are allied, and even with those whose interests are different or opposed. In addition, legislative and other political leadership must be kept informed about community problems and about options for solving them legislatively, politically and fiscally.

The Hispanic community must assume a portion of the communication burden and become more involved in the process of change. Hispanic organizations need to learn to form coalitions across interests and across the different Hispanic subgroups to work more effectively on community and higher education issues. By complementing and supplementing the work that the various organizations do, Hispanic and higher education leaders can be much more effective.

In addition, those who work in institutions of higher education must take a much more active role with the public schools. School-college programs are imperative in the effort to help Hispanic students graduate from high school with the preparation they need to succeed in college and beyond, to the first professional and doctoral degrees. And, as recommended by a 1993 report of the Tomas Rivera Center, teacher-training institutions must increase their efforts to help build community by preparing more Hispanics to teach in public school systems with high Hispanic enrollments.

Finally, Hispanics need to work with the legislative leadership to encourage state policies that foster and sustain college/school partnerships.

Leadership Development

Leadership development is another necessary element for fostering minority success in higher education. Programs to develop young Hispanic leaders are extremely important. Hispanic students must learn leadership skills early on and then refine them through advanced programs such as the Institute for Educational Management at Harvard University and the Fellows Program of the American Council on Education. Institutions of higher education need to assume a more aggressive posture in recruiting and developing Hispanic administrators. Special efforts need to be made to prepare, recruit, and retain Hispanic faculty members and to help them develop into leaders in their own right.

Institutions need to prepare "more of our own" who will become leaders and who will help shape the policies that will influence the future.

Accountability

Accountability is the fourth and final strategy to achieve Hispanic educational success. Hispanics must, as a community, hold themselves accountable in a disciplined way for the solutions of their problems and also hold those who make decisions that affect them and their children more accountable.

Hispanics need to understand how the system works and find effective ways of working within it when it works *for* them. When the system does not work, they need to provide options to improve it, and then implement these changes.

To summarize, *we* Hispanics need to help plan *our* future. We need to redefine the question as one of *achievement.* We need to quantify our objectives, to specify how many should *graduate* and not focus only on enrollment numbers.

We can be successful if we *build community* and if we continue to develop more *leaders.*

We have to assume more *accountability* for our own solutions to problems, while also holding others accountable. We need to act more aggressively, more wisely to "build the ark," rather than to lament about the rains and the floods.

REFERENCES

Carter, Deborah, and Wilson, Reginald. 1993. *Eleventh annual status report on minorities in higher education.* Washington, DC: American Council on Education.

————. 1989. *Seventh annual status report on minorities in higher education.* Washington, DC: American Council on Education.

————. 1992. *Tenth annual status report on minorities in higher education.* Washington, DC: American Council on Education.

————. 1994. *Twelfth annual status report on minorities in higher education.* Washington, DC: American Council on Education.

Education Commission of the States. 1990 December. *Policies for Change.* Denver, CO: National Task Force for Minority Achievement in Higher Education.

Esquibel, Antonio. 1992. *The career mobility of Chicano administrators in higher education.* Boulder, CO: Western Interstate Commission for Higher Education.

National Science Board. 1993. *Science and engineering indicators-1993.* Washington, DC: U.S. Government Printing Office.

O'Brien, Eileen. 1993. *Latinos in higher education.* (Research Briefs, Vol. 4, No. 4). Washington, DC: American Council on Education.

U.S. Bureau of the Census. 1993a. *Hispanic Americans today* (Current Population Reports P23-183). Washington, DC: U.S. Government Printing Office.

————. 1993b. *The Hispanic population in the United States: March 1992* (Current Population Reports P20-465RV). Washington, DC: U.S. Government Printing Office.

————. 1993. *Persons of Hispanic origin in the United States* (1990 Census of the Population). Washington, DC: U.S. Government Printing Office.

————. 1993d. *We the American Hispanics* (1990 WE-2). Washington, DC: U.S. Government Printing Office.

————. 1991. *Statistical abstract of the United States: 1991.* Washington, DC: U.S. Government Printing Office.

CHAPTER 11

The Participation of African Americans in American Higher Education

Reginald Wilson

HISTORICAL BACKGROUND

African American participation in higher education in America's majority institutions, in any substantial numbers, is a relatively recent phenomenon. As recently as two decades ago the majority of African Americans in college were in historically Black colleges and universities (HBCUs). However, two revolutions in federal initiatives, Supreme Court actions, and congressional laws gave considerable impetus to African American and other minority participation in higher education that dramatically changed both the number of those participants and their geographic distribution throughout American higher education institutions.

The first revolution in minority access to higher education occurred with the passage of the first GI bill for educational benefits in 1945. That bill was followed by the Korean War and the Vietnam War GI bills. The first GI bill was passed primarily to keep millions of veterans from flooding the job market after the war in 1945 and seriously disrupting the national economy. Nevertheless, despite its utilitarian intent, that GI bill enabled hundreds of thousands of veterans, including thousands of African American and Hispanic veterans, many the first in their families, to attend college independent of scholarship or previous educational achievement. The GI bill was a true educational revolution that structurally changed American higher education.

The second revolution in minority access to higher education began in 1964. The 1964 Civil Rights Act built on the previous beginnings of John F. Kennedy's Great Society programs such as the Office of Economic Opportunity. All the programs that are now familiar to us on campuses flowed from those efforts: the TRIO programs—Upward Bound, Special Services, Talent Search, Executive Order 11246 establishing Affirmative Action, and so forth. One statistic will suffice to document that revolution: as recently as 1965, 600,000 African Americans were in college and 65 percent of them were in historically Black colleges. By 1980 African American enrollment had doubled to 1.2 million but only 20 percent were in historically Black colleges.

African American participation, however, was more tenuous than permanent during this period of expansion. Wilson and Melendez (1988) note that most of the increase in African American undergraduate student enrollment was in community colleges from which transfer rates to four-year schools and ultimate attainment of baccalaureate degrees is minimal (see chapters 7 & 8). Moreover, many African American faculty were in ethnic studies and compensatory programs that were often not tenure track positions. Many African American administrators were directors of TRIO programs and special services. Thus, progress prior to the 1980s, while impressive, was marginal, specially funded with federal grants rather than with institutional funds, and subject to the vagaries of the political process and fluctuating federal policies.

As Tables 11-1 and 11-2 indicate, African Americans were over 4 percent of the American faculty and over 7 percent of the administrators by the end of the 1970s; however, two observations are in order. One, it is important to note that half of these professionals were in historically Black colleges, thus making their presence in mainstream institutions somewhat less impressive.

TABLE 11-1

PARTICIPATION IN FACULTY BY RACE AND ETHNICITY—1979 AND 1981

	Total	White	Black	Hispanic	Asian Pac. Is.	Amer Ind. Alaska
1979						
Number	451,348	410,933	19,494	6,799	13,086	1,056
Percent	100	91.0	4.3	1.5	2.9	0.2
1981						
Number	467,304	424,071	19,670	7,247	14,381	1,431
Percent	100	90.7	4.2	1.6	3.1	0.3

Source: U.S. Equal Employment Opportunity Commission: EEOC, Higher Education Staff Information, 1981

TABLE 11-2

PARTICIPATION IN ADMINISTRATION BY RACE AND ETHNICITY—1979 AND 1981

Exec./Adm./Mgr.

	Total	White	Black	Hispanic	Asian Pac. Is.	Amer. Ind. Alaska
1979						
Number	107,448	96,668	7,969	1,522	959	330
Percent	100	90.0	7.4	1.4	0.9	0.3
1981						
Number	116,557	104,849	8,021	1,973	1,207	510
Percent	100	89.9	6.8	1.7	1.0	0.4

Source: U.S. Equal Employment Opportunity Commission: EEOC, Higher Education Staff Information, 1981

Two, already by 1981 the numbers had peaked and begun to decline (Wilson and Melendez, 1985).

HISTORICALLY BLACK COLLEGES AND UNIVERSITIES (HBCUs)

HBCUs played a unique role in the education of African Americans that had not been experienced by any other ethnic group, and therefore their history is deserving of separate elaboration to augment the revolutions in African American higher education discussed in the preceding section. Historically Black colleges and universities have for over 125 years provided higher education access for the overwhelming majority of African Americans. (See chapter 12 for a more detailed discussion.)

Most public Black colleges in their early years were true "colleges" in name only. Most began as primary schools and added upper grades and collegiate divisions as students progressed over the years. For example, as late as 1917, Florida Agriculture and Mechanical College enrolled only 12 students at the collegiate level. In contrast, all the other Black public colleges combined enrolled 7,500 students in elementary and secondary grades and only 24 in the collegiate curriculum (Holmes, 1934). Until well into the twentieth century, private colleges carried the substantial responsibility of educating African Americans at the college level, accounting for 72 percent in 1926. By 1935, however, public colleges accounted for 46 percent of Black college enrollments and shortly thereafter surpassed the private colleges (Wilson, 1990). (See Table 11-3.)

TABLE 11-3			
BLACK COLLEGE ENROLLMENT FOR SELECTED YEARS			
	1915	**1926**	**1935**
Public	36	3,800	10,500
Private	2,462	10,000	12,000
TOTAL	**2,474**	**13,800**	**22,500**
Source: General Education Board (Approximations)			

In 1862, Justin Morrill, member of Congress from Vermont, succeeded in getting legislation passed which established grants of land to each state (30,000 acres for each member of Congress) the proceeds of which were to be used to establish universities for education primarily in the mechanical arts and the agricultural sciences. Because of the strict educational segregation of the Southern states, a subsequent Morrill Land Grant Act, enacted in 1890, established 16 Black colleges to serve the same purpose for the African American population. Some existing and some new public institutions for African Americans became what are known as the "1890 colleges" to distinguish them from the 1862 land grant colleges. At the same time, private Black colleges were being established primarily by missionary societies and Black Baptist and Methodist Churches. These schools were instrumental in the training of ministers, teachers, and administrators (Anderson, 1988).

Before desegregation these institutions educated the overwhelming majority of African American college graduates in the nation including the majority of physicians, lawyers, and teachers. Indeed, up to as recently as 1965, nearly 65 percent of African Americans in college were in the HBCUs. These institutions were meritoriously cited for extraordinary achievement "in the face of considerable obstacles, such as discriminatory public funding, hostility of the white power structure, low church support, minimal response from the white philanthropic community and foundations" (LeMelle and LeMelle, 1969).

During their over one-hundred-year history, HBCUs not only were the nearly exclusive avenue of access to higher education but, with their nearly open door policies, took in both the best prepared students and many who would not have been readily admissible to any college. And, by disregarding customary admission criteria, they were able to successfully educate scholars in defiance of the predictive validity of traditional standardized tests. Moreover, the HBCUs provided a major source of employment for the educated African American middle class in professional positions and, second only to the church, were the most respected institutions in the African American community.

While HBCUs also experienced enrollment growth during the periods of educational expansion previously described, their share of that enrollment diminished as a consequence of two factors: the increase in community colleges and the *Adams* decision desegregating higher education in the South.

COMMUNITY COLLEGES

The substantial portion of the dramatic enrollment increase of African Americans during the 1960s and 1970s had been in the community colleges. The most astonishing development in post-World War II higher education, the community colleges grew from approximately 200 at the turn of the century to nearly 1,100 institutions by 1975. Because of their traditionally "open admissions policies," community colleges were more accessible to minorities whose primary and secondary educational preparation was often not sufficient for entrance into selective four-year colleges. Moreover, since a majority of these institutions were developed in the northern and western United States, the trend of African American enrollment during the past two decades has increasingly been outside of the South and into community colleges.

TABLE 11-4

RELATIVE AFRICAN AMERICAN ENROLLMENT TRENDS IN BLACK COLLEGES, WHITE COLLEGES, AND COMMUNITY COLLEGES FOR SELECTED YEARS (IN THOUSANDS)

	1982	1986	1990	1992
HBCU	177	176	207	225
PWI	851	906	1016	1,168
Total	1,028	1,082	1,223	1,303
HBCU%	16%	16%	17%	16%
C.C.%	44%	43%	42%	43%

Source: Annual Status Report, 1993 (American Council on Education)

Community colleges, while significantly increasing access, did not substantially contribute to increasing baccalaureate degree production because of low transfer rates of African American students to four-year schools (see chapters 7 and 8). Despite most African American community college students expressing a desire to complete a B.A. degree, less than 15 percent transfer to a four-year school and fewer still graduate. Moreover, emphasis in community college programs is to a considerable extent focused on terminal vocational programs. This comment is not intended to denigrate vocational programs, which often lead to meaningful employment, but to suggest that increasing the already minimal supply of African American B.A.'s is not significantly improved by community college enrollment. Indeed, of two equally prepared students, one entering a community college and the other a four-year school, the latter enrollee is most likely to ultimately complete a baccalaureate degree (Karabel, 1986).

HIGHER EDUCATION DESEGREGATION

When Judge John H. Pratt's order to dismantle 10 previously segregated state higher education systems was upheld by the U.S. Court of Appeals in 1973 (*Adams v. Richardson*), plans were required to be filed indicating how these states would integrate the student bodies, faculties, and administrations of their public colleges and how they would "enhance" their historically Black colleges. In the 17+ years since that order, the states have moved with various degrees of compliance to implement those plans. Nine other states subsequently were added to the Adams mandate bringing the total number of states under the court order to 19. In 1985 and 1986 the plans of the original 10 states expired, and they were to submit evaluations of their degree of compliance or noncompliance to convince the Office of Civil Rights of the Education Department and the court that, indeed, these states were in compliance and should be removed from the order's jurisdiction, or that they should not be. Several organizations have reviewed those state plans.

For example, the NAACP Legal Defense Fund (LDF), which filed the original *Adams* suit, maintained that "on virtually every measure, [the] states have failed to meet their desegregation targets" and their goals for enhancing traditionally Black institutions, "goals they themselves set in plans approved by the Department of Education Office of Civil Rights." Moreover, LDF charges, "the disparity in college-going rates between Blacks and Whites have consistently worsened in the last decade." African American participation has declined at all levels and that decline is compounded by the "states' aggressive efforts in reform at elementary and secondary levels [which] has hurt Blacks' college enrollment; the reform movement has escalated high school graduation requirements without emphasis on getting Black and disadvantaged students into college preparatory tracks" ("Right Activists Call OCR Inactive," 1987).

The mandate of the *Adams* case called for: 1) the dismantling of the segregated and dual systems of higher education; 2) enhancement of the underfunded traditionally Black institutions; 3) the elimination of duplicative programs; and 4) the increase conversely in each set of schools of African American and White students, faculty, and administration.

In 1970 when the LDF filed the *Adams* case against the Secretary of Health, Education, and Welfare, African American enrollment in predominantly White institutions was 4.3 percent. In 1982 this number had increased to 9.4 percent, which represented approximately 63 percent of the total African American enrollment in the 19 *Adams* states. In 1976, 12 percent of HBCU enrollments comprised students from other races. In 1982 that figure had increased to 18 percent: 11 percent White; 6 percent nonresident aliens; with Asian Americans, Hispanics, and Native Americans, combined, comprising 1 percent. The increase of non-African Americans in HBCUs during this period accounted for most of the overall growth in their enrollment.

Comparison of total enrollment figures in public institutions between 1980 and 1984 in *Adams* states indicates that only 4 states had increased the overall African American enrollment at both two-year and four-year institutions. Those states were Georgia, North Carolina, Oklahoma, and Texas. Alabama and Louisiana had increased enrollments at four-year institutions but those at two-year schools had declined.

African American participation in faculty positions between 1977 and 1983 declined in all but 7 *Adams* states—Florida, Georgia, Kentucky, North Carolina, Oklahoma, Ohio, and Pennsylvania. African American participation in administration for this same period increased in 11 of the 19 *Adams* states—Arkansas, Delaware, Florida, Georgia, Louisiana, North Carolina, Ohio, Oklahoma, Pennsylvania, Texas, and West Virginia.

Although state appropriations to public HBCUs increased during the 1970s, they increased in a lesser proportion when compared to appropriations to predominantly White institutions. Among four-year public institutions in the *Adams* states, appropriations increased 62 percent for non-HBCUs and 48 percent for HBCUs between 1971 and 1981. State appropriations to public four-year and two-year HBCUs varied greatly from state to state in the amount and percentage of change from 1971 to 1981.

The aforementioned date indicates that although most of the *Adams* states are making progress in enrolling more African American students in traditionally White institutions, the increase is not commensurate with their growth in the population.

It also appears that fewer than half of these states are making progress in employing additional African American faculty.

Although in December 1987 Judge Pratt dismissed the *Adams* case on technical grounds, the Appeals Court, in a favorable response to an LDF challenge, remanded the case to Judge Pratt's jurisdiction. The Department of Education has since ruled that, despite meeting none of their goals, all of the states have made "good faith" efforts and are, thus, said to be in compliance. The *Adams* case is now closed.

Further address of issues of profound philosophical and legal consequences of higher education desegregation will continue to occur: Can a substantive case be made for maintaining African American racially identifiable public institutions in an alleged desegregated system? Can a "remedy" which places the greater burden of desegregation on Black institutions be considered legally fair? Despite Judge Pratt's specific order that desegregation plans take "into account the special problems of minority students and of Black colleges . . . [which] fulfill a crucial need," can states, none of which achieved their own self-imposed desegregation goals, be seen as in compliance? These and other knotty questions will confront institutions and observers of desegregation for some time to come. With the ruling in the *Fordice* case (see chapter 12) and continued questions raised by cases in Georgia and Louisiana, there will be further complex adjudication.

Higher education desegregation did not provide the solution to African American access to higher education that some optimists in the 1970s had expected. Indeed, more stringent requirements for access to higher education (higher test scores, more academic courses) have been enacted in the *Adams* states than in all other states. The imposition of these standards, combined with the Reagan/Bush administrations assault on equal opportunity programs, has had a substantially deleterious effect on minority participation in higher education during the 1980s.

REAGAN ADMINISTRATION IMPACT ON EQUAL OPPORTUNITY

The election of Ronald Reagan as president of the United States and the decline of civil rights and affirmative action were not accidentally correlated but were causal in relationship. Reagan ran for president on a platform of opposition to desegregation and affirmative action and, once elected, proceeded to either dismantle or neglect initiatives intended to empower minorities and women with more ideological consistency and measurable effect than any president in the twentieth century. Examples of that impact abound: one case that Reagan's Education Department inherited from the Carter administration was a threatened cutoff of federal aid to the state of North Carolina for noncompliance with desegregation requirements. Not only did the department under Reagan withdraw the threatened cut, but it allowed North Carolina to adopt a much more modest plan as well. Indeed, the Reagan Justice Department opposed the court's jurisdiction of higher education desegregation altogether and filed a brief that ultimately persuaded the federal District Court to dismiss the *Adams* case (Haynes, 1978). It is important to remember that the *Adams* ruling on higher education desegregation was handed down in 1973; after litigation most state plans were approved by 1980, with implementation begun in 1982 and 1983. Thus, the actual impact of *Adams* enforcement in higher education was only felt for about five years before Judge Pratt dismissed the case.

The Reagan administration reduced the staff and budget of the Education Department's Office of Civil Rights (OCR) by one-fourth, and even then the office underspent its budget, due to inaction in enforcement and ignoring its responsibilities, and *returned* funds to the Treasury! The Reagan Justice Department considered intervening in 51 affirmative action plans in order to overturn them even though they had been voluntarily entered into. The administration opposed federal intervention to assure state compliance with desegregation requirements and ignored states, like Virginia, where "the disparity in college-attendance rates between Black and White high school graduates jumped from 9 percent in 1978 to 21 percent in 1985." OCR reduced its collection of statistical data that would have documented the consequences of Reagan administration policies, and agency staff were ordered not to provide such information to inquirers even when requested through the Freedom of Information Act (Orfield, 1989).

The Reagan administration attempted to seek tax-exempt status for segregated schools; opposed busing to achieve school desegregation; and decreased the amount of student financial aid available in grants while increasing the onerous burden of student loans. It cannot be said that the intent and consequences of these actions was serendipitous. These policies were deliberate, consistent, and devastating in their impact. Moreover, these policies were continued unabated by the Bush administration and Secretary of Education Lamar Alexander. The advent of the Clinton administration coincided with a rise in African American enrollment. Also Education Secretary, Richard Riley, has made positive comments about his commitment to minority education, but with Clinton's emphasis on the budget deficit, there is little expectation of substantial new funding for minority programs.

CURRENT STATUS OF AFRICAN AMERICAN PARTICIPATION

In addition to the impact of Reagan/Bush administrations' policies, certain other measurable factors have affected the participation of African Americans in higher education including the following facts:

FACT: There are more Native Americans, Hispanics, and African Americans below the poverty line today than there were 10 years ago.

FACT: Hispanic unemployment is about 50 percent higher than the rate for Whites, and African American unemployment is two and one-half times as high.

FACT: The gap in life expectancy between African Americans and Whites has grown worse for African Americans since 1984.

FACT: Infant mortality for African Americans has grown worse in the past 10 years.

In addition to these devastating socioeconomic factors, the Reagan/Bush administrations' recommended cuts in student aid grants created the increasing reliance on loans, which is a disincentive to poor minority students; the doubling of tuition in the past 15 years made the cost of higher education even more prohibitive; and the policies of many state institutions raising admission requirements either through additional course requirements, higher test scores, or both made access even more difficult. We have, then, the paradox of a greater pool of minority high school graduates, better prepared than previously, and a decline in completion of college.

We are also concerned about the regressive effects on degrees granted to African Americans at the graduate and doctoral levels. (See Tables 11-6, 11-7, and 11-8.)

The only area where African Americans have shown slight degree increases is at the first professional degree level. These increases, however, were insufficient to offset losses at the lower degree and doctoral levels. (See Table 11-9.)

NEEDED REFORMS IN COLLEGIATE EDUCATION

It must be insisted that there be no reduction in the commitment to improving minority access by institutions of higher education. Such commitment can be greatly enhanced through utilizing variable admission criteria, strong support and retention programs, and counseling minority students into nontraditional disciplinary majors. In the future, however, improving primary and secondary education must also be stressed so that African American high school graduates are not only better able to meet rigorous admission criteria but also to significantly improve their college retention and graduation rates as well.

Focus on Precollegiate Education

What factors must be addressed in improving African American academic achievement in elementary and secondary schools that will enhance collegiate access?

TABLE 11-6

BACHELOR'S DEGREES BY RACE/ETHNICITY FOR SELECTED YEARS

	1976		1981		1985		1987		1989
	Total	%	Total	%	Total	%	Total	%	Total
African American	59,122	6.4	60,673	6.5	54,473	5.9	56,554	5.7	58,016
Men	25,634	5.1	24,511	5.2	23,019	4.8	22,498	4.7	22,365
Women	33,488	8.0	36,162	7.8	34,455	7.0	34,056	6.7	35,651

	% Change 1976–87	% Change 1985–87
African American	-4.3	-1.6
Men	-12.2	-2.3
Women	1.7	-1.2

TABLE 11-7

MASTER'S DEGREES BY RACE/ETHNICITY AND SEX FOR SELECTED YEARS

	1976		1981		1985		1987		1989
	Total	%	Total	%	Total	%	Total	%	Total
African American	20,345	6.6	17,133	5.8	13,939	5.0	13,867	4.8	14,076
Men	7,809	4.7	6,158	4.2	5,200	3.7	5,153	3.6	5,200
Women	12,536	8.7	10,975	7.4	8,739	6.2	8,717	5.9	8,876

	% Change 1976–87	% Change 1985–87
African American	-31.8	-0.5
Men	-34.0	-0.9
Women	-30.5	-0.3

TABLE 11-8

TRENDS IN DOCTORAL AWARDS TO U.S. CITIZENS BY SEX: 1978-1988

	1980	1982	1984	1986	1988	1990
African American	1,032	1,047	953	823	805	828
Men	499	483	427	322	311	320
Women	533	564	526	501	494	508

First, we know that minorities take fewer high school academic courses in preparation for college than do Whites.

Second, the quality of education in inner-city and in predominantly minority schools is markedly inferior to that in suburban and middle-class schools. It is still true, as it has always been, that those with the most resources are provided the best education, and those requiring the most help are given the poorest resources and have of them the lowest expectations.

TABLE 11-9

FIRST-PROFESSIONAL DEGREES BY RACE/ETHNICITY AND SEX FOR SELECTED YEARS

	1981		1986		1987		1989		1991	
	Total	%	Total	%	Total	%	Total	%	Total	%
African American	2,931	4.1	3,029	4.3	3,402	4.8	3,148	4.4	3,575	5.0
Men	1,772	3.4	1,623	3.4	1,836	3.9	1,618	3.6	1,672	3.8
Women	1,159	6.1	1,406	6.0	1,585	6.3	1,530	5.9	1,903	6.8

% Change 1981-91	
African American	22.0
Men	-5.6
Women	64.2

Source for Tables 11-6–11-9: U.S. Department of Education, Equal Employment Opportunity Commission
Data on Earned Degrees conferred from institutions of higher education by race/ethnicity 1975-76
U.S. Department of Education, Center for Education Statistics, Digest of Education Statistics, 1983-84, pp. 122-23
U.S. Department of Education/Center for Education Statistics. "Degrees Conferred" Surveys, 1985, 1987, 1990

Not only educational practices but teachers' attitudes and expectations of students differ between schools that are effective and schools that reinforce subordinate status and expectations of failure. *These facts remain true despite the massive amounts of money we have spent on school reform in the last decade.* "In 1982, federal, state and local governments were spending $2,726 per pupil in our public schools. By 1987, that figure had jumped 26 percent after adjusting for inflation. In the past two years per pupil spending has accelerated even faster to a current level of $4,527. Teacher salaries have also been increasing far faster than inflation, and are now at record levels and rising. But since then, as reforms have really kicked in, student performance has stagnated. Despite the self-congratulation surrounding the reform movement, the record has been one of occasional success and widespread failure" (*The Wall Street Journal*, 1989).

Study after study documents that neither increased per pupil expenditures, nor better facilities, nor lower student-teacher ratios nor increased teacher salaries resulted in any significant improvement in student achievement; yet those are the areas where most school reform is directed and where most educators are urging change. These reforms did not make a difference because they did not change our beliefs about student potential or about what we do to increase pupil performance.

"In 1988, Dr. Antoine Garibaldi, Dean of Education at Xavier University in Louisiana, conducted a national study on education and the African

American male that yielded some disturbing results. Asked if they thought their African American male students would go to college, six of ten teachers said 'no.' At the same time, 95 percent of the African American male students said they expected to graduate from high school, and eight out of ten expected to go to college. Obviously, teacher expectations make a significant difference in teacher practices with students in the classroom" (Wilson, 1989).

Similarly, parents' expectations have a significant impact on student performance as well. A study in June 1989, at Johns Hopkins University found that "Black and White Children . . . enter first grade with almost identical computational skills as measured by the California Achievement Test." Yet, by third grade their performance was markedly different. The researchers tested to determine if race, parent education, economic resources, family type (e.g., single parent families), or parent expectations and teacher behavior made any difference in pupil achievement. Despite our belief in the influence of all the other factors, the only ones that made any significant difference were parental expectations and teacher behavior.

The report concluded: "Parent expectations have large effects on performance in computation for both Black and White children," especially if these expectations are followed by visits to the library and reading to children daily. The research found that teachers "reported they expected all parents to fulfill a number of specific parent involvement responsibilities ranging from teaching children to behave, to knowing what children are expected to learn each year, to helping them on those skills."

Yet few teachers had practices in place to help parents produce the desired behaviors at home. And most teachers were resistant to close parental involvement in the school program.

Our expectations of pupil and school performance is very much determined by the socioeconomic characteristics of students and their families. If you were told that one child was the son of Dr. Huxtable and the mother was a lawyer, you would expect better school performance from that child than the daughter of a single parent in a welfare family. But you would often be wrong.

Elementary and secondary schools that are educationally effective adopt a comprehensive approach in which there is collaborative involvement of administrators, parents, teachers, and support staff, all committed to improving the school climate, pupil academic performance, and teaching staff development. This approach includes

1) A learning model that is characterized by a set of high, purposive, and accelerated goals

2) Increased time devoted to learning, achieved by eliminating such chores as school announcements, attendance taking, unnecessary room changes, and other tasks that do not contribute to learning

3) Contracts with parents to assist in school governance by identifying acceptable school behaviors and enforcing them, while also identifying expected afterschool activities that parents will monitor

4) A heavily language-based curriculum for all subjects, including mathematics, to increase student conceptual and analytic skills

5) Periodic and systematic assessments to assure that students are achieving goals and to assure accountability of school staffs

6) In-service training of teachers in classroom organization and management, and in techniques of positive reinforcement to increase desirable classroom behavior of pupils.

[The foregoing was adapted from a longer essay, Wilson, 1989]

CONCLUSION

African American participation in higher education has gone through many dramatic changes from the postbellum period to the present. For over 150 years, until well past the mid-twentieth century, African American collegiate education was confined to the historically Black colleges, mainly in the South. With the GI bills of World War II and subsequent wars, thousands of African Americans appeared on previously exclusively white campuses. Following the 1964 Civil Rights Act and the Pell Grant legislation, African American enrollments burgeoned numerically and shifted geographically. Whereas previously African American education had been essentially a Southern phenomenon, by the 1970s its greatest increases in numbers were in the East and West and had shifted to predominantly White colleges, particularly community colleges.

African American participation during this period of the 1970s and 1980s continued to be plagued by high attrition and lack of degree completion. With most state colleges and universities throughout the country tightening admission criteria, there was a strong likelihood that the declining college enrollments of African Americans during the 1980s would continue to slide. But fortunately the decline has halted in the 1990s and is now showing an upturn. However, those previous declines were further exacerbated by restrictive policies affecting equal opportunity under the Reagan/Bush administrations which continue to have a lingering impact. With the advent of the Clinton administration, it is expected that more positive policies favorable to minority advancement in higher education will be forthcoming.

Part of the impediment to improving precollegiate education is restricted resources in large urban school systems where minorities are overwhelmingly enrolled. Much can be done, however, to improve African American student achievement that does not require additional finances but can be effectuated by changes in attitudes and expectations, and changes in the teaching-learning environment in inner-city schools. The incentives for such change are not strong at present. Considerable research on effective schools, however, shows that there are some models of school practice currently operational which have contributed to astonishing gains in the academic achievement of African American students. It is imperative that these models be replicated widely, for it is primarily with substantial improvement of the education of African American children in the elementary and secondary schools that we will see significant increases in higher education enrollments.

REFERENCES

Anderson, J. D. 1988. *The education of Blacks in the South, 1860-1935.* Chapel Hill: The University of North Carolina Press. 238.

Haynes, L. L. 1978. *A critical examination of the Adams case: A sourcebook.* Washington, DC: Institute for Services to Education.

Holmes, D. O. W. 1934. *The evolution of the Negro college.* New York: Bureau of Publications, Columbia University, Teachers College.

Karabel, J. June 1986. "Community colleges and social stratification in the 1980s." In *The community college and its critics,* edited by L. Steven Zwerling, no. 54. San Francisco: Jossey-Bass, Inc.

LeMelle, T. J., and W. J. LeMelle. 1969. *The Black college: A strategy for achieving relevance.* New York: Frederick A. Praeger. 17.

Orfield, G. 1989. Reagan's blind eye to civil rights. *Focus* (The Joint Center for Political Studies, January-February).

Rights activists call OCR inactive, college desegregation marginal. 1987. *Education Daily* 20, 150 (August).

The Wall Street Journal. June 27, 1989.

Wilson, R., and S. E. Melendez. 1985. *Minorities in higher education: Fourth annual status report* (American Council on Education).

Wilson, R., and S. E. Melendez. 1987. *Minorities in higher education: Sixth annual status report* (American Council on Education).

Wilson, R., and S. E. Melendez. 1988. Strategies for developing minority leaders. In *Leaders for a new era: Strategies for higher education,* edited by Madeleine F. Green. New York: Macmillan Publishing Co.

Wilson, R. 1989. Affirmative action: Yesterday, today and tomorrow. *CUPA Journal* (December).

———. 1989. Gaining momentum: Increasing minority participation in higher education. Paper presented at the Council on Higher Education. December 8, Richmond, Virginia.

———. 1990. Can Black colleges solve the problem of access for Black students? *American Journal of Education.*

CHAPTER 12

Maintaining the Competitive Tradition

N. Joyce Payne

INTRODUCTION

Since the mid-1970s, references to global interrelationships and "the twenty-first century are so prolific in discussions among forward looking minds in our society, that you might refer to it as an international theme song" (McClure, 1989). Most thoughtful analysts have concluded that the new world society will be a mix of progress and concomitant social and economic problems. America's conceptual frame of reference will be challenged by new social, economic, and political structures; catastrophic ecological shifts; major health epidemics; changing family configurations; dramatic socio-demographic changes; reunification of world powers; dominance of multinational corporations and world managers; and the "soft landing of the cold war." These monumental shifts will have a profound impact on the business of higher education and particularly Black colleges and universities.

Today, mankind is faced with the challenge of medical, toxic, and human waste. The inability to control the world environment has become a preoccupation in the scientific community given the wonders of Hurricanes Gilbert and Andrew, the fury of Hugo, the California earthquakes of 1989 and 1994, and the greenhouse phenomenon. Increasingly the dictates of man's ability to control his physical and human environment are in direct conflict with the shifting balance in economic power.

By the year 2000, China will become the leading textile producer and the Third World will manufacture as much as 30 percent of the world's goods. More than $10 billion worth of the nation's real estate will be controlled by the Japanese and about $1 trillion or 10 percent of all U.S. assets will be in the hands of private Japanese investors and the government by 1995. In Atlanta alone, the Japanese have invested around $1 billion in business ventures ("Eastern Capital of Asia," 1988). Today, Japan is the number one automaker in the world substantially exceeding U.S. production and controlling a large number of U.S. manufacturing companies with operations in more than 42 states. Moreover, foreigners own a substantial portion of all U.S. banking assets and control a large number of U.S. banks.

The internationalization of the nation's economy will profoundly influence the way Americans live, work, and educate future generations. Moreover, these changes are likely to have an enormous impact on the economic growth of the African American community and the fiscal and political stability of public Black colleges.

These changes also will affect the quality and quantity of production, consumption, and the nation's standard of living. Today, Americans enjoy the luxury of more than 5,000 television cable systems; we have the capacity to store trillions of words a minute on a disk smaller than a note pad; we produce nearly 3,000 kinds of fruits and vegetables including designer qualities; we perform delicate eye surgery with a laser; and we have created artificial intelligence for use in education as well as the workplace. Through artificial intelligence and telecommunications, higher education institutions have extended educational opportunities to private homes for personal convenience and to inaccessible communities.

Given these enormous economic, political, and social shifts, higher education will be forced to make radical changes in the production of students for the twenty-first century. Wesley C. McClure, former president of Virginia State University, speculates that "in the year 2001 the young entrepreneur is likely to find himself or herself negotiating a contract in the morning with an Asian supplier, discussing profit margins with a European investor in the afternoon, and sharing a late dinner with a Virginia banker who will finance his next project. The phrase, 'all in a days work,' will take on new meaning as we crisscross the international dateline" (McClure, 1989).

As higher education prepares to meet these challenges, African American students must become more cognizant of the fact that historically, education has fostered "inequality through the ostensibly meritocratic manner by which they reward and promote students, and allocate them to distinct positions in the occupational hierarchy" (Bowles and Gintis, 1976). Thus, the poor and disenfranchised should treat inequality in the world enterprise as deliberate and systematically applied aberrations in the American economy. These realities should become an essential part of the learning process from pre-school to higher education. Indeed, the core of academic pursuits should be based on a world curriculum that views education as a powerful instrument for economic change.

The impact of these changes offers all the conditions for creating new education and economic policies, domestically and internationally. This nation still has the power and extraordinary wealth to create a progressive inclusive social agenda. The U.S. economy is twice the size of Japan's, the American standard of living is one of the highest in the world, and the nation's multinationals continue to transform the global economy in developed as well as developing countries. Yet, although our economic dominance has altered the social landscape of the world, domestically we continue to "think global and act local" in terms of making a sustained national investment in the full development of African American higher education with a resultant change in the economic status of Black America.

EDUCATION AND ECONOMIC STABILITY

America's capacity to compete as a major industrial nation is inextricably tied to its ability to invest in the future of millions of young men and women. Yet, today nearly a million students graduate each year who are dysfunctional in basic skills, while corporate America spends $75 billion annually on social problems derived from miseducation.

"The average Black 17-year-old reads at the same level as the average White 13-year-old" (MDC and Charles Mott Foundation, 1988). Forty percent of all African American high school students drop out of school annually, less than 20 percent of all children eligible for Head Start are engaged in the program, and more than 2 million children have been forced out of school lunch programs since 1980.

As new global paradigms become evident, recognition is growing that all sectors of the nation have an important stake in contributing to the economic renewal of the American economy. Despite this recognition, the connection between education and the economy remains unchanged for a critical segment of the African American community. Congressional voices and policy makers preach competition, innovation, and the importance of building a highly skilled and knowledgeable workforce, while cutting student financial assistance, the lifeblood of African American higher education; we generate new international trade and investment policies while rendering deprived sectors of our community null and void; we provoke human rights challenges all over the world while dismantling 50 years of liberal policies under the

Reagan/Bush administrations; and we talk access and opportunity while undermining the full development of Black colleges and universities as social equalizers of the nation.

The all too familiar rhetoric suggests that policy makers fully accept the premise that America's capacity to compete as a major industrial nation is inextricably tied to its ability to invest in the future of millions of young men and women. Yet, today more than 30 percent of all high school students drop out; nearly 50 percent drop out in urban centers; more than 60 percent remain in segregated classrooms (Coalition for National Science Funding); college enrollment for African Americans dropped to 44 percent while White enrollment increased to 55 percent between 1975 and 1985; and the poverty rate for African Americans increased by 2 points to 33.1 percent while White families experienced an increase of half a percentage point ("New Untouchable," 1990; Rich, 1988). The National Alliance of Business estimates that in 1986 dropouts cost the economy more than $147 million (Business Week, 1989).

An editorial in the *Washington Post* suggests that there are chronic problems with the distribution of poverty with an increasing number of ethnic groups being left too far behind (*Washington Post*, 1987). The richest fifth of American families controlled 43.7 percent of all income while the bottom fifth received 4.6 percent of national income in 1987 (*Washington Post*, 1987). Today, more than 33 million people in America are locked in the wicked cycle of poverty including 13 million children. Children are being abandoned on "a lonely island of poverty in the midst of a vast ocean of material prosperity" (King, 1963).

While a national consensus is emerging on how to reform and restructure the economy, the challenge to move beyond the injustices of society are magnified by miseducation, poverty, and the absence of a national investment in African American higher education. Shortsighted economic policies continue to widen the gap between poverty and productivity; the growing permanent underclass and the massive waste of human talent continue to grow; and unemployment, crime, and drug abuse are endemic in the escalating misery of urban communities.

The essential relationship between an educated citizenry and a strong global economy is evident when the chairman of Xerox Corporation announced that private industry will be forced to spend nearly $25 billion annually to produce an educated productive workforce (*U.S. News and World Report*, 1989). Increasingly, major corporations with 10,000 or more employees offer some form of remediation; an estimated 25 million Americans are illiterate; and SAT scores are at a historic low (*Business Week*, 1989). In the absence of a radical change in economic policies, millions of Americans will remain trapped in dependency with no sense of a decent future and few resources to transcend the barriers of poverty and its iniquitous complements.

In 1987, one in three African Americans was living below the poverty level; between 1973 and 1987, the average real income for African American men age 20 to 29 declined by 27.7 percent; and nearly six of ten African American families with children 18 years or younger were headed primarily by women ("Worsening Problems," 1989). The state of Black America is a major indictment of our national education and economic policies. Uneven distribution of wealth, the lack of socially responsible leadership, years of conservative federal presence in higher education, and the void of basic common sense all mitigate against the creation of full access, equality, and economic opportunity for the common good of the nation.

A recent report issued by the Education Commission of the States (1986-87 to 1989-90) suggests that progress toward full participation of African Americans and other minorities in all sectors of higher education has become distressingly stalled. Another article based on Jonathan Kozol's recent book, *Racheal & Her Children* (1988), suggests that "we see the need to train the poor but educate the children of the middle class and rich" (*Newsweek*, 1990). Kozol sees few solutions to the growing plight of the underclass. In urban communities all over America a sense of fatalism and destitution is far too pervasive.

The nation cannot continue to relegate African American and poor children to underclass status while at the same time attempting to build the critically essential ingredients of a strong world economy—human capital. Education must become an integral part of our economic agenda as we bargain for greater world power in the global arena of the twenty-first century.

BLACK HIGHER EDUCATION IN AN EXPANDING ECONOMY

The ability of Black colleges to sustain their record of achievements in technology and the physical and social sciences is tied to the nation's investment in equality of opportunity with a resultant growth in U.S. performance and productivity in world markets. An administration that spends $32 billion to build a space station, $8 million a month to warehouse the Hubble Telescope for nearly 13 years, and $1 million to put a single person in orbit should recognize both the legitimacy and the desirability of investing in Black colleges and universities as a national resource.

The relationship between economic growth and educational equality is of major concern to historically Black public colleges and universities (HBPCUs). These institutions tend to be concentrated in politically conservative states with marginal public school systems and some of the lowest per capita incomes in the nation. For example, in 1988, Mississippi ranked 50 at $10,992; Arkansas ranked 47 at $12,172; Louisiana ranked 46 at $12,193; and Alabama ranked 43 at $12,604. Only three states with public Black colleges, Maryland, Delaware, and Virginia, were in the top 10. Obviously, the fiscal barriers imposed on state-assisted institutions and the students they serve become clearly evident in such regressive circumstances.

There are numerous national reports calling for greater recognition of the expanding role of higher education in the economic growth of the nation. Few, if any, however, speak to the relationships between economic and educational equality. Even fewer acknowledge the indispensable contributions and role of African American higher education in strengthening the economy in general and particularly in economically depressed areas with a disproportionate share of African American and poor families.

To alter erosion of the U.S. economy, the vast resources of Black colleges and universities should be utilized in retraining the underemployed, creating new technologies, diffusing information through new communications technology, increasing human aptitude, and furthering our knowledge of the nature of our environment.

While a national consensus is emerging pertinent to altering economic trends, the involvement of Black colleges and universities as full partners in economic renewal remains unresolved. African American higher education should become an indispensable adjunct to the American economy. With the cost of higher education increasing about 8 percent annually or twice the rate of inflation, the nation can ill afford the mindlessness of underutilizing public Black colleges and universities as economic instruments of the states and the nation. Historically, these institutions have created new frontiers for social equality and shaped the economic future of millions of Americans. Linking Black colleges to the condition of economic life, domestically and internationally, is more than a moral issue. It is an issue of vision, of rational economic sense, of enlightened self-interest. The benefits are clear, given the vibrant tradition of Black colleges and universities.

What is sorely needed is recognition of and attention to the unequal representation of Black colleges among major research institutions, innovators of new technologies, and producers of Ph.D.'s in progressive fields of science and technology.

The most striking testimonial to the resilience and value of public Black institutions is the prominence of the leaders they produce in all fields of research and endeavors—leaders such as the late Associate Supreme Court Justice Thurgood Marshall, Lincoln University of Pennsylvania; Barbara Jordan, former member U.S. House of Representatives, Texas Southern University; Jesse Jackson, former presidential candidate and civil rights leader,

North Carolina A&T State University; the late Reginald F. Lewis, major international business executive, Virginia State University; Wilma Rudolph, first American woman to win three Olympic gold medals, Tennessee State University; Ernie Barnes, official artist, 1984 Olympiad, North Carolina Central University; Ed Towns, member U.S. House of Representatives, North Carolina A&T State University; Harold Ford, member U.S. House of Representatives, Tennessee State University; and, Walter Payton, all-time leading ground-gainer in National Football League (NFL) history, Jackson State University. Two graduates of public Black colleges recently sacrificed their lives in the service of others: astronaut Ronald McNair (North Carolina A&T State University) died aboard the space shuttle, exploring the infinity of space, while Congressman George "Mickey" Leland (Texas Southern University) died on an Ethiopian mountainside in an airplane crash, trying to bring aid to the famine stricken in Africa.

These colleges and universities have been what Martin Luther King, Jr., would have referred to as "creative extremists" in that they have been successful in turning around a whole nation of people who bring all the educational and social impediments of an inequitable economy. They have performed what no other social institution could accomplish. While enduring the injustices of society, Black institutions have provided exemplary role models; influenced the dreams of young geniuses; served as a fertile source of professional leadership; and fostered an unyielding commitment to academic excellence, social equality, and the assurance of a decent future for students from the lowest economic strata of the nation. The extraordinary influence of Black colleges and universities on the lives of African Americans has "no precedent." As a national resource, they offer profound lessons for higher education and for the larger society.

Since the time of Reconstruction, the nation's Black colleges and universities have been a consistent beacon of success in promoting opportunity. Each year, these institutions educate more than 54 percent of those African Americans who go on to graduate school and beyond. With limited fiscal resources and against nearly insurmountable odds, these institutions have made great strides in building competitive academic programs in engineering, business, mathematics, computer sciences, environmental sciences, nursing, and journalism. They possess broad expertise in teaching, research, technical assistance, and community development to help counter the probability of 12 million children dropping out of school by the year 2000 (Charles Mott Foundation, 1988).

Consider what public Black colleges accomplish each year despite limited fiscal resources. The nation's 35 public Black colleges and universities annually enroll more than 160,000 students and more than 70 percent of those are enrolled in four-year historically Black institutions. Between 1986 and 1991 enrollments increased by more than 4.8 percent and nearly 32 percent of all baccalaureate degrees awarded to African Americans came from public Black colleges and universities. Seventy-two percent or 32 of the 43 historically Black colleges listed as the top producers of baccalaureate degrees conferred in 1989 were HBPCUs.

With substantially limited resources, few political options, and marginal state support, Black colleges find ways to balance competing priorities while maintaining the integrity of academic programs. Like all institutions, they will continue to make improvements in the quality and productivity of their students while exploring new ways to contribute to the nation's economic strength and vitality.

DYNAMICS OF HISTORICAL CHANGE

Black colleges and universities were conceived and developed in a whirlwind of political, economic, and social cross-currents. The history of these institutions is a richly textured chronology of ecstasy and agony, of hope and desperation, of victory and vulnerability. It is a classic history that deserves world attention. It is a history that must live for future generations. It is a history of freedom, justice, and democracy. It is a history etched deeply in the archive of African Americans—a history marked by portraits of achievement, progress, and preeminence in virtually every aspect of the American experience.

At the core of this profound story of social struggle emerges a community of public higher education institutions that seized the opportunity to transform the lives of the rural, poor, and disenfranchised. In the abyss of oppression, these colleges emerged as a monumental tribute to Black America's inexorable struggle for educational justice. As DuBois stated in 1903:

> [T]hey founded colleges, and up from the colleges shot normal schools, and out from the normal schools went teachers, and around the normal teachers clustered other teachers . . . . It was a miracle—the most wonderful peace-battle of the 19th Century, and yet today men smile at it, and in fine superiority tell us that it was all a strange mistake (DuBois and Washington, 1903).

For African Americans, higher education, more than any other social institution, became the liberating force in spite of political oppression and economic opposition. A commitment to improving the vitality and quality of life in poor and isolated communities became an essential part of the pedagogic experience of public Black colleges. Thus, there was and still is an organic relationship between the political ideology of the democratic movement and the academic imperatives of the academy.

The creation of higher education institutions exclusively for African Americans was an outgrowth of a tenaciously segregated society. For decades, African American students were concentrated in inferior public schools lacking all the fundamental imperatives of even a marginal education. Indeed, to fully appreciate the magnitude of this extraordinary transformation, one must acknowledge the malignant effect of economic oppression as a by-product of segregation. Despite the adverse human consequences of segregation, African American education was viewed as the panacea for social and economic reform. Yet, even today, the tyranny of segregation continues to choke the ability of Black colleges and universities to create systemic change at every level of the academy and beyond.

Out of humble beginnings, Black institutions emerged at a time when the highest hopes and dreams of liberal America were embodied in bold ideals of equality of opportunity—ideals that thrust the country into a new era of profound social change and created a deeper appreciation for the consequences of equal opportunity for the masses. Amid great resistance and deeply rooted elitism, a philosophical revolution took place that altered the social milieu of education and challenged the notion that institutions of higher learning were exclusive domains for wealthy landowners. While irrevocable shifts were taking place in higher education, enlightened Americans were rising in rebellion against repression and the remnants of slavery.

Public Black colleges can be traced back to 1837 when a Quaker group in Philadelphia established a school that became Cheyney State College (Cheyney State University of Pennsylvania since 1983). At a time of great controversy and struggle, Cheyney State College became a potent new force, challenging elitism in American higher education. This unparalleled time in history also influenced passage of the Morrill Act of 1862, which established white land-grant institutions, and more than 32 years later the 1890 Act, which led to the creation of Black land-grant institutions exclusively for African Americans. Ironically, the 1890 Morrill Act essentially sanctioned the separate but equal doctrines of the nation, yesterday and today.

THE LAND-GRANT MOVEMENT

Today, the rich legacy of the land-grant tradition remains prominent on the campuses of 17 public Black colleges and universities established in accordance with the Morrill Land-Grant Acts of 1862 and 1890. The 1862 act established White land-grant institutions (with the exception of Alcorn State University), and the 1890 act created Black land-grant colleges and universities. Thus, they are commonly referred to as 1862s (White land-grant institutions) and 1890s (Black land-grant institutions). Alcorn State University is the only historically Black public institution accorded land-grant status under the 1862 federal legislation.

America's land-grant system represents a revolutionary philosophy that has a long and eminent history. The notion of people's universities has served as the guiding standard for assuring equality of opportunity within the confines of the land-grant mission. Often referred to as the "educational Bill of Rights," the first and second Morrill Acts constitute a revolution in educational philosophy—"a philosophy that boldly asserts that education should be open to the sons and daughters of the industrial classes" (Aaron, 1987).

The land-grant story is a story of class and ideological struggles; a story of the richness of choice and freedom; a story of a progressive social paradigm in higher education. This bold democratic movement created new relationships, powerful allies, reconciliation of obvious contradictions in higher education, and a profound world perspective of liberal educational reform. With this renaissance came recognition of the land-grant system as an economic instrument essential to world prosperity, national security, and state and nation building for the common good.

While Black land-grant institutions have become a national resource, their beginnings were humble. The University of Arkansas at Pine Bluff held its first class in 1875 for 7 students in a rented frame school house. Kentucky State University received a donation of $1,500 in 1886, which led to the opening of a new school with 3 teachers and 55 students. In 1896, South Carolina State University had 13 faculty members and a campus of 135 acres. In 1885, Tuskegee University graduated its first class of 10 students. Alcorn University was created on a campus consisting of 225 acres with a $50,000 appropriation.

Today, the University of Arkansas at Pine Bluff has produced more African American legislators, business owners, educators, lawyers, dentists, doctors, and army officers in the state of Arkansas than the combined total of all other higher education institutions in the state. Kentucky State University has graduated around 7,000 students and reached a milestone in 1983 when the highly progressive Whitney M. Young, Jr., College of Leadership Studies was founded. South Carolina State University has around 260 faculty members and an impressive campus of more than 436 acres. More than 55,000 students have graduated from the prestigious Tuskegee University and the first agricultural experiment station at a Black college was established under the leadership of the renowned George Washington Carver of Tuskegee. Today, Alcorn State University has an annual operating budget of around

$29 million, thrives on more than a 1,700 acre campus, and has more than 150 faculty and nearly 3,000 students.

Today, land-grant universities enroll more than 2.7 million students and award more than 450,000 degrees annually; including nearly 60 percent of all U.S. doctorates (Aaron, 1987). Black land-grant colleges and universities constitute some of the largest and most prestigious systems of higher education in the nation. These institutions contribute immeasurably to agricultural science and technology, human ecology, and other essential academic fields. Teaching, research, and extension remain prominent on these 17 campuses.

These institutions have been in the forefront of educating youth at risk, in conducting research vital to the quality of life and the environment, and in addressing the social and economic needs of both urban and rural communities. The ability of "1890s" to sustain their land-grant mission is intimately linked with their ability to exploit new opportunities while moving toward parity with majority land-grant colleges and universities. Increasingly, policy makers are recognizing that the nation's agricultural industry needs the human and capital resources of the entire land-grant enterprise.

In a white paper on the nation's agricultural enterprise, the National Association of State Universities and Land-Grant Colleges (1989) states that "although the food and agricultural system is the largest source of renewable wealth in the country, serious problems must be overcome for the agricultural industry to be restored to its previous robust position . . . the 1980s has been devastating for the majority of U.S. agriculture, the 1990s offer promise for recovery." While the promise for recovery looks good in 1993, state and national legislators will be forced to focus greater attention on transforming the entire land-grant enterprise. Incremental federal assistance and less than marginal state funding will continue to diminish the capacity of Black land-grant universities to bridge the widening gap between "1890s" and "1862s." In the absence of "1890s" as integral partners in strengthening the world agriculture enterprise, decline in the agriculture economy and beyond will continue unabated.

The distinguished record of teaching, research, and public service in the field of agriculture and beyond symbolizes the legacy of 1890 land-grant institutions and complements the traditional relationship between the "1890s" and the U.S. Department of Agriculture. USDA awarded research funds to the "1890s" in 1967 followed by federal support for cooperative extension in 1977, thus, strengthening the land-grant mission at the "1890s." Engaging "1890s" as full partners in the growth of agriculture will require a sustained infusion of state and federal dollars and a far-reaching legislative agenda that is responsive to new demographic trends and economic realities of world markets. It also will require recognition that the nation has an important stake in creating a superlative research infrastructure, strengthening productivity and processing of food and fiber, innovating the commercialization of new food products, and producing new and highly skilled talent for the twenty-first century.

America's capacity to maintain preeminence in agriculture sciences and technology will be largely dependent on its willingness to engage "1890s" as a dynamic new force in the "Third Land-Grant Movement." As major centers of teaching, research, and extension, the "1890s" need policy makers to promote equal state funds and provide more federal assistance for the creation of new undergraduate and graduate programs in high-demand disciplines, massive modernization and construction of academic and research facilities, federally sponsored research labs and centers, targeted public service programs, and a system architecture for strengthening research networks.

In response to expanding opportunities in domestic and world agriculture industries, the presidents/chancellors of Black land-grant colleges and universities organized a Council of 1890 Presidents/Chancellors. For several decades, this policy-making council has exerted great influence on congressional and federal policies and positioned the "1890s" to enlarge their resource base in public and private sectors while creating new alliances with government, industry, and the scientific community. Under the council, more than six major "1890" associations are central in mobilizing support toward strengthening the land-grant mission. These associations have become a powerful network for undergirding teaching, research, extension, home economics, libraries, and international affairs. Increasingly, the council in conjunction with the "1890" associations are building an enviable position in the body politics of higher education.

Given the growing influence of the council and the "1890" associations, even greater attention will be devoted to shifting state and national priorities in the interest of fiscal and social parity with "1862s." Stimulating a stronger commitment to the emerging demands of Black land-grant colleges and universities as full partners in sustaining a competitive economic enterprise will be the driving force toward impacting public policy. As Black land-grant colleges and universities celebrate more than 100 years of progress, a strong thread of social activism permeates every level of these institutions and beyond. Most will agree that the future of "1890s" looks promising.

THE ROLE AND ACHIEVEMENTS OF PUBLIC BLACK COLLEGES

Black colleges and universities constitute the birth of educational opportunity, the struggle for political and economic parity, and the dreams and aspirations of millions of young men and women. As stated by William P.

Hytche, former chairman of the 1890 Council of Presidents/Chancellors and president of the University of Maryland Eastern Shore (UMES), during the recent celebration of 100 years of service at the UMES, "Something extraordinary happens here." Black state colleges and universities transformed the consciousness of the nation and stimulated a new social era of defiance and dedication. The convergence of powerful social and political movements led to the creation of 19 public institutions for African Americans between 1866 and 1887, and another 15 campuses were founded between 1890 and 1950.

The historical development of these institutions is embodied in the appointment of William Hooper Councill, a former slave, and first president of Alabama A&M University. The audacity of Inman E. Page opening the doors of Langston University with a $9,000 budget, 4 faculty members, and 41 students is symbolic of the early beginnings of public Black colleges and universities. During World War II, Tuskegee University became the first aviation training center for all African American fighter pilots, which constituted a major historical event in the development of the Black land-grant movement. The brilliant historical roots of Kentucky State University's survival in 1886 in the depth of racial turmoil or the success of Alfred Harris, a member of the Virginia General Assembly, in obtaining a $20,000 appropriation for the founding and operation of Virginia State University in 1882 constitutes a dramatic shift in the political power of African American higher education. In the midst of a primitive social society, this history is about the ability to influence the aspirations of Bridges Alfred Turner, the first African American to earn a doctorate in education from Pennsylvania State University in industrial education. Turner graduated from the University of Arkansas at Pine Bluff in 1935 at a time when the entire state of Arkansas had the lowest per pupil and per capita costs for education of 16 southern states.

Since Reconstruction, these institutions have fostered the American concept of universal education dedicated to ensuring academic freedom, social equality, and the assurance of a decent future for widely diverse ethnic and economic groups. Public colleges and universities continue to serve as the great social equalizers in an educational system replete with social contradictions.

To speak of social change is tantamount to the history of public Black colleges. Historically, these colleges have institutionalized what John Dewey was talking about when he said that "education is the means of social continuity of life, . . . each individual gets an opportunity to escape from the limitations of the social group in which he was born, and to come into living contact with a broader environment" (Dewey, 1966). Giving rise to the correspondence between social responsibility and higher education, these institutions are places where social consciousness and equal opportunity are "built in" the fabric of academic and research programs; where great minds engage in democratic social relationships unalienated by ethnic and economic differences; where intellect, talent, and creativity elevate man beyond the social malaises of the world; and where strong precedents exist for the advancement of progressive ideology and liberal thought.

While these institutions continue to advance equality of opportunity, they struggle to overcome enormous inequities in political and fiscal support both at the state and federal levels. Although the rhetoric of equal opportunity remains a dominant theme in higher education, equality of opportunity for Black colleges and universities is profoundly illusory. These institutions of higher learning have had to come to grips with the well-intentioned failure of the state and the nation to invest in social equality and reform. While the nation has used the law-and-order stick to force some modicum of equity, there are entrenched barriers in higher education coexisting with the inequities of society. Thus, the "American Dream" of higher education is a panorama of persistent social injustices when viewed from the perspective of African Americans. This assertion is supported by the lack of comparable state appropriations, meager private support, and marginal federal dollars.

Black land-grant institutions are disproportionately underfunded given the general lack of state support to carry out the tripartite mandate of teaching, research, and extension. Unlike, the 55 majority land-grant institutions, which receive more than $200 million annually to serve as economic instruments of the state, the 17 Black land-grant institutions including Tuskegee University receive less than $20 million (Hines, 1989).

ACADEMIC PROGRAMS

Knowledge, discourse, and scholarship are the essential conditions for democracy in modern society—a society that is made more humane, more flawless, and immensely more fulfilling through teaching and learning. The teaching process helps us clarify our purpose in life and define our roles as citizens of the world. Merilyn Ferguson says that "the teacher liberates the self, opens the eyes, makes the learner aware of choice. . . . The true teacher is also learning and is transformed by the relationship" (Ferguson, 1980). The profound influence of the learning process permeates the African American higher education community and reinforces an irrepressible belief in the empowerment of African Americans.

Although Black colleges continue to redefine themselves to meet new political and social exigencies, the one persistent philosophy is the sense of purpose that grew out of the historical events and tumultuous social struggles of the 1950 and 1960s. An enlightened observer may compare the intellectual climate on Black campuses of yesterday with the collective sense of purpose paramount today on campuses in Black South Africa. Like Professor Jakes Gerwel, vice-chancellor and rector of the University of the Western Cape, many African American scholars view teaching as a politically liberating process. A process that requires "the integration of academic and intellectual life with and the development of it out of the reality of people's social experience and world is essential both for the order of our functioning and, more importantly, for the vitality and quality of our intellectual environment" (Gerwel, 1987).

In fostering "a more perfect union," public Black colleges are preoccupied with the economic well-being of African Americans. Thus, they are creating new opportunities to assure competitiveness in world markets of the future. Drawing on centuries of success, one of the great strengths of public Black colleges lies in their academic richness and diversity.

The growth of new course offerings, as well as expansion of areas of specialization, indicate continued support for the "tradition of excellence." In strengthening academic programs, public Black colleges have capitalized on innovative instructional methodology and made considerable use of information technology. In the early 1970s, these institutions expanded opportunities for students to utilize advanced technology in day-to-day academic endeavors. Computerized academic enrichment centers were created, personal computers were increasingly made available to students in dormitories, and a large number of institutions strongly encouraged students to enroll in computer science courses as a prerequisite for academic success. During this same period, a number of campuses engaged in major efforts to integrate information systems throughout the institution. To remain academically competitive, the importance of computer literacy remains a paramount concern for students and faculty.

Public Black colleges have made great strides in building competitive academic programs in engineering, business, mathematics, animal sciences, biotechnology, and systems information. In 1989, more than 300 different majors leading to undergraduate and graduate degrees were offered at public Black colleges. Information systems management, architectural engineering, and fisheries biology are just a few of the new majors.

Bowie State University offers more than 35 majors, including master's degrees in computer science, public and business administration, and management information systems. To assure that African Americans play a larger role in international trade, Grambling State University offers a master's degree in international business and trade. The University of Arkansas at Pine Bluff plans to propose a master's degree and Ph.D. program in fisheries. During the 1987 school year, 97 Jackson State University undergraduates received computer science degrees, representing the largest number of minority computer science graduates from any U.S. campus. Alabama A&M University has established a $1 million endowed chair in physics.

In 1984, Florida A&M University (FAMU) was granted the authority to offer its first Ph.D. in pharmacology and today has six advanced degree programs in pharmacology and chemical and mechanical engineering. The College of Pharmacy at FAMU produces more African American pharmacists than any U.S. campus. FAMU experienced substantial growth during the 1970s with 11 schools and colleges and a division of graduate studies, research, and continuing education. "FAMU has grown to a record 7,508 students—up 26 percent in the last two years and 47 percent since 1985" (Cooper, 1990). In 1992, FAMU enrolled nearly 8,500 full-time students. FAMU's School of Business and Industry is internationally recognized for the quality of its academic program, reinforced by the performance of its graduates and the creation of a $1 million Eminent Scholar's Chair. Given the success of the School of Business, it attracted nearly $200,000 in corporate support in 1989 and Bill Cosby awarded the university $325,000 in 1988.

Elizabeth City State University has constructed a $5 million science complex that will house an aquarium and planetarium. The creation of the complex has strengthened the university's recruitment program and enhanced enrollments substantially in science and technology.

In 1986, North Carolina A&T State University established a School of Technology; North Carolina Central's School of Law and School of Library and Information Sciences offer a dual-degree program to train law librarians; North Carolina Central produces more than 70 percent of all African American lawyers in North Carolina; Southern University Law Center graduates more than 90 percent of all African American lawyers in the state of Louisiana; and Texas Southern's Law School graduates around 50 percent of all African American attorneys in the state.

Grambling State University was featured in a national PBS television documentary series, "Learning in America," for its success in producing between 40 to 60 education majors annually with a 100 percent passage rate on the National Teacher's Examination. In response to the success of the series, the executive producer (1989) said, "For a long time we have thought of Grambling as a place where recruiters come for men and women with athletic prowess. . . . But now with a nationwide shortage of teachers, particularly minority teachers, we really wanted to show a different type of recruiting at Grambling—the recruitment of talented teachers."

Alcorn State University's Division of Nursing is nationally recognized for "maintaining a cumulative passing rate on the nursing state board examination of 93 percent. . . . The national mean score for baccalaureate nursing students is 100; Alcorn's is 118. The national mean score for associate degree nursing students is 1600; Alcorn's is 2000" (Alcorn State University, 1987). In recognition of the university's success, the W. K. Kellogg Foundation awarded Alcorn's Division of Nursing a $1.1 million grant to improve access to health services for adolescents and their families. Winston-Salem State University's School of Nursing is well known for similar achievements. Today, they enroll more than 105 students in the upper level and maintain a cumulative passing rate on the nursing state boards examination of 80 percent.

One of the fastest growing academic programs at North Carolina A&T State University (NCA&T) is computer and information sciences with a steady overall enrollment of more than 6,500 students. NCA&T has established a Silicon Fabrication Laboratory and expanded student-faculty involvement in the university's research on the space shuttle program. NCA&T had the distinguished honor of graduating a chemistry major in 1989 who was offered more than $178,000 in awards for graduate study. The recipient plans to pursue doctoral studies at Carnegie-Mellon University in biochemistry with a $55,000 five-year fellowship.

In 1988, four of the five Black colleges that produced the largest number of bachelor's degrees in engineering were public Black institutions and North Carolina A&T State University, Prairie View A&M University, and Southern University ranked second, third, and fourth. In the same year, six public Black colleges produced 16.5 percent or 350 of all African American bachelor's degree recipients in engineering. North Carolina A&T State and Morgan State Universities have created Ph.D. programs in engineering.

Delaware State College has the only graduate social work program in the entire state and Alabama A&M University offers Ph.D.'s in plant and soil science, food science, and physics. Tuskegee University's School of Veterinary Medicine and the School of Graduate Studies at Meharry Medical College developed a partnership to offer the first combined Ph.D. program in veterinary medicine at Black universities. Tuskegee University created an aerospace science engineering program in 1982 and graduated its first class in 1987. It is noteworthy, that on the eve of World War II, Tuskegee University began a civilian pilot-training program, which subsequently trained all 99 African American pilots who served in the U.S. armed forces during the war. In 1987, Delaware State created a new airway science program and in 1988 awarded its first M.B.A. and M.S. degrees in chemistry. It is noteworthy that less than one half of 1 percent of all American pilots in the nation are African American. In 1987, the American Institute of Physics reported that Lincoln University (PA) graduated 23.5 percent of the nation's African American physics majors.

Interestingly, in 1939 a graduate studies division was organized at Virginia State University by John McNeil Hunter, a physicist who was a Massachusetts Institute of Technology graduate. He was credited with teaching more African Americans who earned doctorates in physics than any other U.S. professor. One of Hunter's graduates, James Stith, became the first African American to serve full time on the faculty of the U.S. Military Academy at West Point.

If current trends continue, public Black colleges and universities will offer a vastly expanded range of opportunities at the Ph.D. level and beyond, while the quality and range of undergraduate programs continue to serve as a magnet attracting highly motivated students from an increasingly diverse cultural and economic mix.

GRADUATE EDUCATION

Given the disproportionate underrepresentation of African American doctorates in the sciences, more public and private support will be needed to make some radical changes in the business of producing minority talent for the twenty-first century. In 1991, only 3.8 percent of doctoral degree recipients in the nation were African American in sharp contrast to over 74 percent of Ph.D.'s being White Americans. As the report *One-Third of a Nation* (1988) notes, of 355 doctorates awarded in computer science in 1986, only one was awarded to an African American. These data are compelling in a society that is losing its competitive edge in domestic and international markets. The nation has an important stake in creating superlative graduate programs, significantly enlarging the production of African American Ph.D.'s in the sciences, and increasing financial assistance for graduate studies in areas of national need such as biotechnology, organismal and molecular biology, mathematics, computer science, engineering, and environmental and atmospheric sciences.

Federal and private support is essential in stimulating a realignment of academic programs at the undergraduate and graduate levels at public Black colleges. As economic instruments of the state and the nation, public Black colleges must bring academic programs into line with the realities of the market place. At the same time, public colleges must build academic and research programs in ways that intensify and politicize the oppressive contradictions of higher education and society. They should be in the forefront of exploring the underpinnings of discrimination and barriers in the production of Ph.D.'s. National forums should be convened to rally higher education and the nation around issues concerning the critical need for African American talent in the twenty-first century.

While the nation has used the legislative stick to force some modicum of equal opportunity at Ph.D.-granting institutions, little has been done to build doctoral programs in the Black higher education community. A first step is to create and expand legislative initiatives to encourage support of Black colleges in programs administered by the National Science Foundation, Department of Defense, National Institutes of Health, National Oceanic and Atmospheric Administration, National Aeronautics and Space Administration, and other federal agencies with substantial research dollars. In addition, Title III, Institutional Aid, Higher Education Act, should be amended to include support solely for the expansion of professional and doctoral programs, particularly in areas of national need. Current federal and state programs offering graduate support should be substantially enlarged to include "race specific" provisions. The supply, demand, and production of African American Ph.D.'s should serve as the driving force in targeting public Black colleges as major contributors to the graduate pipeline.

In a 1983 study published in *The Journal of Negro Education*, Brazziel reported that 7 of the top 10 Black institutions contributing to the production of African American doctorates were public Black universities with Southern University, Florida A&M University, Morgan State University, and Tennessee State University among the top 5. In 1989, 54 percent of the nearly 13,000 graduates of public Black institutions enrolled in graduate studies (Brazziel, 1983).

Ensuring the availability of scientific and technical know-how will require an assertive federal role and a sustained national investment in Ph.D. programs complemented by strong research and financial support for graduate students and faculty.

The report, *A Nation at Risk: The Imperative for Education Reform*, released in 1983, stimulated a national debate on the decreasing numbers of minority faculty and challenged the nation to rectify the problem through social reform. The report noted that the higher education enterprise had failed to come to grips with the importance of creating a culturally diverse community, not just as a matter of fairness but as a valued objective in its own right. The production and inclusion of greater numbers of African American faculty enriches the academy, broadens the nation's intellectual resources, and reflects the highest ideals of a progressive society (National Commission on Excellence in Education, 1983).

Although more than two-thirds of the nation's aging professoriate will have to be replaced by the end of the century, the production of African American Ph.D.'s in research dropped from 1,095 in 1976 to 820 in 1986. African Americans earned 28 doctorates in engineering in 1990 and a total of 21 in computer science; in sharp contrast, non-Americans earned 2,191 engineering doctorates and 263 Ph.D.'s in computer science during the same year. In 1990, there were no Ph.D.'s awarded to African Americans in applied mathematics, materials sciences, biophysics, and other critical scientific fields. These numbers take on a more sinister cast in light of figures that show that less than half of the African American 1986 Ph.D. recipients planned careers in higher education, as opposed to more than two-thirds of the class of 1975 (Educational Testing Service, 1989). Thus, the few African Americans in the pipeline provide only a decreasing flow of African Americans to America's higher education classrooms and research laboratories. This, despite the fact that minorities now comprise 21 percent of the U.S. population, a figure predicted to rise to 35 percent by the year 2020.

A former administration that supported a possible $200 billion bail-out for savings and loan enterprises and failed to scrutinize waste and abuse at the Department of Housing and Urban Development at the cost of $4 billion managed to overlook the seriousness of an investment in Black colleges as one of the primary sources of faculty. To address this problem, the nation should move beyond traditional models for the production of faculty and create national efforts to bring about a dramatic change in the immediate future. If a major difference is anticipated, Black colleges and universities must be in the forefront of this endeavor.

ENROLLMENT

Time Magazine article (1989), "Black by Popular Demand," notes that Black colleges are experiencing a renaissance with students deserting Ivy League campuses and returning to academically competitive Black colleges and universities. Current enrollment trends suggest that "Black students are rediscovering the nurturing atmosphere and pride in a shared heritage that made Black campuses attractive to their parents' generation" ("Black by Popular Demand," 1989). The article also cites low tuition and new political vitality as reasons for increased popularity. It is noteworthy that 8 of the top 10 producers of baccalaureate degree granting institutions in 1989 were HBPCUs.

Public Black colleges report that other key factors credited with affecting enrollment growth are the offering of more competitive academic programs, improved enrollment management, and expanded recruitment and public awareness efforts.

There is general consensus that the quality of academic programs is one of the major factors driving increased enrollments. For example, one of the highly marketable academic additions at Delaware State College is the airway science program. During the first year of the program, students on the

Precision Flight Team came in fourth place in regional competition. Other newly established courses at Delaware State College include forestry, dendrology, hotel/management, and dietetics. To increase enrollments in mathematics, science, and engineering, the college received a substantial grant from General Foods to create "Project Access." Thus, enrollment at Delaware State reached an all-time high in 1987 with a 2.7 percent increase over 1986 and an estimated 2,600 in 1990 (Delaware State College, 1987-88).

Similar recruitment programs are conducted on nearly every public Black college campus including after-school remediation, weekend enrichment programs, or more intensive summer intervention programs. A large number of public Black colleges have established enrollment management offices that have been highly successful in promoting recruitment and retention as a university-wide responsibility, from the football coaching staff to the chemistry professor.

In a report (1992) published by the American Association of State Colleges and Universities and the National Association of State Universities and Land-Grant Colleges, estimated enrollments for 1991 at public Black colleges increased in every full-time category except first-professional students. Among full-time students, first-time freshmen experienced a 9.6 percent increase. As shown in Table 12-1, overall public Black colleges reported a 6.3 percent enrollment increase.

TABLE 12-1

ESTIMATED ENROLLMENTS AND PERCENT CHANGE—FALL 1991 PUBLIC HISTORICALLY BLACK COLLEGES AND UNIVERSITIES

Enrollment Categories	1990 Totals	Estimated 1991 Totals	Percent Change
Full-Time Students			
Undergraduate	104,385	111,856	7.2%
First-Time Freshmen	26,295	26,453	.6%
Graduate	3,883	4,371	12.6%
First-Professional	1,429	1,395	-2.3%
TOTAL	**111,453**	**121,111**	**8.7%**
Part-Time Students			
Undergraduate	18,902	19,648	3.9%
First-Time Freshmen	1,509	1,432	-5.1%
Graduate	10,879	10,963	.8%
First-Professional	94	199	112.2%
TOTAL	**35,466**	**35,020**	**-1.3%**
GRAND TOTAL	**146,919**	**156,131**	**6.3%**

Source: "Special Report," American Association of State Colleges and Universities and National Association of State Universities and Land-Grant Colleges, Washington, DC, April 1992

Among the four-year public colleges, the HBPCUs reported the largest full-time enrollment increase of 8.7 percent with the greatest growth among undergraduates (7.2 percent) and graduate students (12.6 percent).

In 1987 Bowie State University reported an enrollment increase of 15 percent, which constitutes the highest level of enrollment since 1975 and nearly a 30 percent increase since 1982. Increased public awareness, greater community support, more high-demand courses, and improved marketing contributed significantly to Bowie's success. In 1986, Pepsi-USA awarded the university $50,000 for producing the best marketing plan nationally in its "Excellence in Education Marketing Program." Today, Bowie has around 4,200 students and continues to experience steady growth in graduate enrollment.

In 1988, the University of Arkansas at Pine Bluff (UAPB) reached its highest level of enrollment in 21 years with 9 percent growth over 1987, 25 percent growth in new freshmen, and the largest increase among all institutions in the Arkansas system. The late Chancellor Charles Walker noted, "Not only has the quantity of students increased at UAPB, the quality of ACT averages improved substantially as well. We are being deluged with students from all over the country and pressed to the wall for dorm space. It's a problem we plan to convert into solutions in terms of greater state support and continued growth. We are ecstatic." (Personal conversation, Walker, July 1989). Today, the university serves more than 3,600 students with a significant increase in average ACT scores for 1989 over 1988.

Enrollment at the University of Maryland Eastern Shore (UMES) increased by more than 63 percent from 1980 to 1990 with the largest freshman class in the history of the university in 1990.

Elizabeth City State University experienced a 10 percent increase in enrollment between 1985 and 1989 and an average increase of 200 points on the SAT. Elizabeth City State University is the only public Black institution in North Carolina to receive state support for an "Incentive Scholars Program." As a merit scholarship program, academically talented freshmen are awarded $12,000 for a four-year period. This program has had a significant impact on the quality and quantity of students at Elizabeth City State.

Over a six-year period, Prairie View A&M University experienced more than a 25 percent increase and an average growth of 120 points on the SAT. The majority of public Black colleges have reported similar patterns over the last five years.

With an enrollment of more than 8,000 students in 1992, Florida A&M University is experiencing extraordinary growth in enrollment. In 1989, FAMU reported more than a 45 percent increase in the number of new applicants and a 17 percent increase in freshman enrollment. Further, FAMU

ranked 5th in the nation in 1988 in the recruitment of 21 National Achievement Scholars, immediately following Harvard, Yale, Stanford, and the
University of Texas.

With more than 8,000 students, Norfolk State University increased its
enrollment by 2 percent in 1989 and anticipates even greater growth over the
next five years.

Southern University and A&M College, the largest historically Black
public university, serves more than 14,000 students on three major campuses
with an African American enrollment of more than 90 percent.

In 1990, positive enrollment trends continued with most campuses reporting 5 to 48 percent increases in the number of new applicants. A number of
campuses are attracting more second-generation college students who frequently attribute their commitment to Black colleges to their parents' success
as graduates of Black institutions. Four of the 5 largest historically Black four-
year institutions in 1992 in the nation were Southern University and A&M
College, Texas Southern, Florida A&M University, and Norfolk State University, all public institutions.

In the absence of a national effort to promote public Black colleges, the
Thurgood Marshall Scholarship Fund was created in 1987 in cooperation
with the Miller Brewing Company. The fund's mission is to provide merit
scholarships at the nation's public Black colleges including the University of
the District of Columbia and University of the Virgin Islands. Scholarships
are awarded to students in recognition of their demonstrated exemplary
achievement in academic studies or exceptional talent in the creative and
performing arts. The first four-year awards of $16,000 were made in 1989. The
creation of the fund also was spurred by the lack of a broad-based national
effort to attract a greater number of talented students. Thus, Thurgood
Marshall Scholars must be U.S. citizens; be full-time entering freshmen; be
pursuing a bachelor's degree in any discipline; have a high school grade-point
average of not less than 3.0; have a combined verbal/math score of 1,000 or
more on the SAT or a score of 24 or more on the ACT; and be recommended
by their high school. Ideally, the fund will create opportunities in which the
collective talents of Thurgood Marshall Scholars can be used to enhance
greater access to higher education.

Although a number of positive enrollment patterns are emerging on Black
campuses, persistent declines among African American men is becoming a
critical concern. As reported by the American Council on Education, despite
increases in the number of African American high school graduates, enrollment of African American men in higher education declined between 1976
and 1986 by 34,000 or 7.6 percent, the highest drop for any group. However,
in 1991 African American men increased their enrollment in higher educa-

tion by 6.5 percent compared to 7.3 percent for African American women. According to 1991 data, there are about 517,000 African American men and 818,000 African American women on college campuses today. It is noteworthy that, while African American men are underrepresented in higher education, the prison population hit an all-time high in 1988 with an increase of 257,589 or 81 percent since 1980, which includes a significant number of African American inmates (U.S. Department of Justice, 1989).

DISTINGUISHED GRADUATES

Through graduates of distinction, the nation's public Black colleges have been the chief agents of social change for African Americans. Black colleges have given wings to the aspirations of young leaders who may have languished unchallenged, unrevealed, and possibly shattered by racism and social neglect. These institutions have served as social satellites in the Black community—nurturing leadership while extending educational opportunities to the masses.

In reflecting on the future of North Carolina Central University, Tyronza Richmond, former chancellor, said, "You cannot study the history of this institution without feeling the presence of the giants who walked this campus before us."

Giants like Julius L. Chambers, nationally recognized civil rights attorney and recently appointed president of, and graduate of, North Carolina Central University; Ernie Barnes, internationally known artist, North Carolina Central University; Katie Hall, former member U.S. House of Representatives, Mississippi Valley State University; Jesse Hill, president and chief executive officer, Atlanta Life Insurance Company, Lincoln University of Missouri; Ed Bradley, former White House correspondent and veteran newsman on top-rated news-magazine 60 Minutes, Cheyney University of Pennsylvania; and Parren Mitchell, former member U.S. House of Representatives, Morgan State University. The extraordinary accomplishments of the late Ronald McNair of North Carolina A&T State University and George "Mickey" Leland of Texas Southern University stand as a monument to the achievements of public Black colleges.

Other distinguished graduates include Moneta J. Sleet, Jr., 1969 Pulitzer Prize winner in feature photography and nationally known photographer for Johnson Publishing Company, and the late Whitney Young, Jr., highly acclaimed national leader and executive director of the National Urban League from 1961 to 1971, both graduates of Kentucky State University. Grammy Award-winning composer and vocalist Lionel Ritchie is a graduate of Tuskegee University; Earl "The Pearl" Monroe and Timothy Newsome, both graduates of Winston-Salem State University, are nationally recognized professional basketball stars; Selma Hortense Burke, sculptor and distinguished graduate of Winston-Salem State University, is best known for her portrait of F. D. Roosevelt that appears on the U.S. dime; and Harold Barnes, the attorney who successfully challenged the at-large system of voting in Elizabeth City, North Carolina, is a recognized graduate of Elizabeth City State University.

Jackson State University's list of distinguished graduates includes such notables as Walter Payton, retired professional football player; Robert G. Clark, first Black state legislator in Mississippi; and Elwyn M. Grimes, head of obstetrics and gynecology at Truman Medical Center.

Retired Major General Leo A. Brooks; retired Brigadier General Alfred J. Cade; Brigadier General Alonzo Short; and retired Major General Ernest R. Morgan are all highly respected graduates of Virginia State University.

As an all-male institution for the first century of its existence, Lincoln University (PA) has produced an endless list of distinguished graduates and established a highly enviable record of distinction. Langston Hughes, poet, playwright, and novelist graduated from Lincoln University as did Thurgood Marshall, the late U.S. Supreme Court Justice; Roscoe Lee Browne, former professor at Lincoln, actor, director, poet, and two-time A.A.U. track star; Benjamin Nnamdi Azikiwe, first president of the Republic of Nigeria and founder of the University of Nigeria; Judge Barrington D. Parker, U.S. District Court, highly acclaimed for presiding over the case of would-be presidential assassin John Hinkley; Richard Helms; former congressman Otto Passman; Kwame Nkrumah, the first prime minister of Ghana; Horace Mann Bond, writer, scholar, educator, and father of Julian Bond; Franklin H. Williams, president of the Phelps-Stokes Fund and former ambassador to Ghana; W. Beverly Carter, former ambassador to the Republic of Liberia and to United Republic of Tanzania and deputy assistant secretary of state for African Affairs; James L. Usry, first Black mayor of Atlantic City; and Horace G. Dawson, Jr., former ambassador to the Republic of Botswana.

"As an institution where excellence is expected and distinction is the goal, the tradition of prominence at Lincoln continues" (Sudarkasa, 1988). An article in Ebony (1988) notes that president Sudarkasa, the first female CEO of Lincoln University of Pennsylvania, is preoccupied with transforming her students into stellar academicians who can compete on the very cutting edge. Over the last 10 years, over 61 percent of all Lincoln's graduates and more than 80 percent of all physical science graduates entered graduate programs in highly prestigious universities throughout the nation and beyond.

Similarly, Texas Southern University produced 80 percent of the African American and 30 percent of the Hispanic lawyers in the state of Texas. The

College of Pharmacy produced more than 45 percent of all African American pharmacists in the nation and has the proud distinction of a 80 to 90 percent first-time passage rate on the National Association Board of Pharmacy Licensure Examination. In the Houston Independent School District, more than 3,000 teachers and 200 administrators are graduates of Texas Southern.

In "Celebrating 100 Years of Excellence," Florida A&M University highlighted such distinguished graduates as LaSalle Leffall, Jr., a leading cancer surgeon; Senator Carrie Meek, the first African American woman to be elected to the Florida senate and recently elected to the U.S. Congress; and Bob Hayes, who in 1963 was called the fastest human in the world ("They Made a Difference," 1987).

Art Shell, the head coach of the Los Angeles Raiders is a graduate of the University of Maryland Eastern Shore; Jerry Rice of the San Francisco 49er's, acclaimed as one of the most extraordinary football stars in the nation, is a graduate of Mississippi Valley State University; and Edward V. Woods, the highly respected deputy commissioner of police in the city of Baltimore, is a graduate of Coppin State College. Tennessee State University Tiger Belles won the first national women's Amateur Athletic Union (AAU) track and field championship in 1955 and through 1968 won 25 of 40 American women's track and field Olympic medals.

Lincoln University (MO) boasts several graduates in top corporate positions: Earl Wilson, vice president, International Business Machines (IBM); Jesse Hill, president and chief executive officer, Atlanta Life Insurance Company; and, Thomas Shropshire, retired senior vice president, Miller Brewing Company.

In 1987, the late Reginald Lewis, a product of Virginia State University, became the owner of the largest Black-owned business in the nation and "orchestrated a one-two punch of dazzling financial maneuvering by securing a 90-to-1 return on the sale of the McCall Pattern Co., for a $95 million profit, and followed up that move with the $985 million acquisition of Beatrice International Foods" (Edmond, Jr., 1988). His accomplishments as a world entrepreneur are central to former President McClure's vision of Virginia State University in the twenty-first century when he states that "graduates of Virginia State University will possess the skills and insights necessary to make meaningful contributions in the context of the global economy" (*Telegraph Register*, 1989).

OVERVIEW

Prudent education and economic policies cannot overlook the fact that progressive societies run on talent—talent prominent among graduates of public Black colleges and universities. Talent that can produce innovations in laser propulsion research, superconductor technology, remote sensing, disposal of nuclear waste, and robotics. The ability of Black colleges to continue to produce graduates in the physical and social sciences is tied inextricably to the nation's willingness to invest in equality of opportunity with a resultant growth in U.S. performance in world markets. The economy demands that the decade of the '90s provide opportunities for higher education to develop new directions for leadership, new consensus for change, and new energy for ameliorating uneven access and opportunities.

Like the communities they serve, Black institutions have been exceptionally resilient in seeking solutions to serious challenges in an increasingly competitive enterprise. Like most institutions, they are faced with critical questions of governance, academic standards and performance, faculty entrenchment, decline in student financial aid, accountability, fiscal constraints, and education reform, all compounded by escalating operational costs. Yet with substantially fewer resources and limited political alternatives, they find ways to balance competing priorities while maintaining the integrity of academic programs in a continuous state of change. Like all institutions, they will continue to make improvements in the quality and productivity of their students while exploring new ways to contribute to the nation's economic strength and vitality.

What is sorely needed in the future is recognition of and attention to the unequal representation of Black colleges among major research institutions, providers of graduate programs, innovators of new technologies, and producers of talent in progressive fields of science and technology.

For more than a century, these institutions have fostered a hardy optimism that education can alleviate social inequality and produce a free enterprise that respects knowledge and talent. Although the contradictions of America's social agenda are pervasive, these institutions have persisted in their reaffirmation that the future holds great promise for those who are willing to engage in the attainment of knowledge as a liberating force. The principles of success, hard work, and excellence characterized by intrinsic economic rewards for those who attain the highest level of achievement permeate these academic centers. As stated in Alabama State University's "Education for Success," "These universities are institutions where success stories begin . . . . They offer a veritable wealth of knowledge and experience embracing the past, the present, and the future."

REFERENCES

Aaron, B. 1987. *Serving the world.* Washington, DC: National Association of State Universities and Land-Grant Colleges.

Alcorn State University. August 28, 1987. News Release.

American Association of State Colleges and Universities and National Association of State Universities and Land-Grant Colleges. April 1992. Special Report. Washington, DC.

MDC, Inc., and the Charles Stewart Mott Foundation. 1988. *America's Shame, America's Hope—Twelve Million Youth at Risk.*

Black by popular demand. 1989. *Time,* March 20.

Bowles, S., and H. Gintis. 1976. *Schooling in Capitalist America,* Basic Books, Inc. New York.

Brazziel, W. F. 1983. Baccalaureate college of origin of Black doctorate recipients. *The Journal of Negro Education.* 52, 2 (Spring).

Business Week, October 20, 1989.

Business Week, October 29, 1989.

Cooper, K. J. 1990. Quality, marketing lure students to Black colleges. *The Washington Post,* April 3.

Delaware State College. 1987-1988. *President's annual report.*

Dewey, J. 1966. *Democracy and education: An introduction to the philosophy of education.* New York: Macmillan.

DuBois, W. E. B., and B. T. Washington. 1903. *The Negro problem.* James Pott & Company.

The Eastern Capital of Asia. 1988. *Newsweek,* February 22.

Ebony. February 1988.

Edmond, Jr., A. June 1988. Dealing at the speed of light. *Black Enterprises.*

Education Commission of the States, American Council on Education, Washington, DC. May 1988. *One-third of a nation.*

Ferguson, M. 1980. *Aquarian Conspiracy.* Los Angeles, CA: J.P. Tarcher, Inc.

The Genesis of Genes. 1989. *The Economist,* September 3.

Gerwel, J. 1987. *Inaugural Address,* June 5. University of the Western Cape, South Africa.

Grambling State University. 1989. News release. March 30.

Hines, E. R. 1989. *Appropriations: State tax funds for operating expenses of higher education,* 1988-89. Washington, DC: National Association of State Universities and Land-Grant Colleges.

Investment for the Future. Washington, DC: The Coalition for National Science Funding. U.S. Department of Justice. December 1989. News Release.

King, Jr., M. L. August 1963. I Have a Dream, Washington, DC.

Made to order babies. 1990. *Newsweek.* p. 94.

Kozol, J. 1988. *Racheal and her children.* NY: Fawcett Book Group.

McClure outlines VSU of the 21st century. *Telegraph-Register.* Virginia State University. 1, no. 2 (October).

McClure, W. C. 1989. A global society demands a global education. *Opportunities.* 1, 1, (Spring).

The National Commission on Excellence in Education, U.S. Department of Education, April 1983. *A nation at risk: The imperative for education reform.*

The national initiative for agricultural research. 1989. Washington, DC: National Association of State Universities and Land-Grant Colleges.

The New Untouchable. 1990. *Newsweek.* (Spring). Special Issue. p. 48.

The Pacific Century. 1988. *Newsweek*, February 22.

Rich, S. 1988. U.S. family income is up slightly. *The Washington Post*, September 1.

Sudarkasa, N. Lincoln looks ahead. 1988. *The Lincoln Journal*, (Summer).

Three-Year Plan. Education Commission of the State, 1986-87 to 1989-90, Denver, CO.

They made a difference. 1987. *Legacy*, Florida A&M University, (Spring).

US News and World Report, May 18, 1989.

The Washington Post, August 3, 1987.

Worsening problems bring fatalistic attitude. 1989. *The Washington Post*, December 28.

CHAPTER

Higher Education Issues in Native American Communities

Clara Sue Kidwell

Native Americans have participated in higher education virtually from its inception in America. Harvard College had a special Indian college, established in 1655. "A dozen or more Indian youths were sent to Master Corlet of the Cambridge Latin School to be prepared for college; but not more than four or five ever managed to enter, and of those but one, Caleb Cheeshahteaumuck, took his degree; and he died of tuberculosis within a year" (Morrison, 1936). Dartmouth College in New Hampshire began as Moor's Charity School for Indians. Its headmaster, Eleazor Wheelock, solicited funds in England to expand his school and renamed the institution after his chief patron, Lord Dartmouth. Part of his fund-raising appeal turned on his proposal to educate Native Americans, although not long after its founding the college was serving mainly the sons of the landed gentry of the Connecticut River Valley, rather than the sons of the forest (Szasz, 1988).

The fate of the first Native American college students is echoed disturbingly in the status of Native American students in higher education today. There are few in colleges and universities, and those who begin drop out at alarming rates. One study showed that 72.7 percent of Native American students in 79 colleges and universities left school before graduating, most after their first year. Although such statistics must be interpreted in light of the small samples and the problems of surveys, they dim the hope that most Native American students will be successful in higher education (Wells, 1989).

Native Americans in contemporary communities see higher education primarily as a means of improving their economic conditions, but the conditions on Native American reservations and the low-income levels of many Native Americans who live in urban areas mean that the financing of higher education is a significant barrier to their participation. High dropout rates also indicate that higher education does not necessarily meet the needs of Native American students.

Native American people have, nevertheless, begun to adapt formal education to their own uses to enhance their economic development and, as important, their cultural survival. There are three major issues that face Native American communities today. What can be done to improve retention rates of Native American students who attend colleges and universities away from their home communities? How can they create opportunities to attract those students back to the communities? And how can communities take control of their own educational institutions to meet their needs without isolating themselves from the sources of power that mainstream education offers?

The development of academic programs in Native American/American Indian Studies at major universities increased institutional sensitivity to the history and cultural diversity of Native American communities. Support services for Native American students at colleges and universities have begun to address the retention issue. The establishment of Native American-controlled community colleges on or near reservations is leading to greater community investment, intellectually and financially, in higher education.

EDUCATION AND ACCULTURATION IN NATIVE AMERICAN COMMUNITIES

If Native American people view mainstream higher education with some suspicion, the history of their involvement with it makes the reasons clear. Education has been used by the United States government as a form of often-forced acculturation for Native American people. Although Native Americans have gone to college since colonial times, the experience has not been particularly profitable for their communities. In one exchange between the representatives of a colonial government and leaders of the Iroquois nations, the commissioners offered college educations to the young men of the tribe, but the leaders replied that "it was remembered some of their Youths had formerly been educated in that College" and after their return "they were absolutely good for nothing being neither acquainted with the true methods of killing deer, catching beaver or surprizing an enemy." Nevertheless, the offer indicated good will on the part of the English and deserved a return, and "if the English Gentlemen would send a dozen or two of the Children to Onondago the great Council would take care of their Education, bring them up in really what was the best manner and make men of them" (Labaree et al., 1961).

In 1819 the federal government appropriated $10,000 to prevent the "final extinction of the Native American tribes" by "introducing among them the habits and arts of civilization" and "teaching their children in reading, writing, and arithmetic" (U.S. States at Large II, 1819). Although the stated purpose of the Civilization Act was benevolent by the white man's standards, its implementation was disastrous for many Native American children and had a profound impact on native cultures. The act supported schools established by Christian missionaries whose aim was to convert as well as teach their students. Such Christian education became a force for acculturation, leading ultimately to suppression of native languages and sometimes forced separation from community and culture.

Many treaties required tribes to cede land, in exchange for which the government would provide annuities, school buildings, and teachers to instruct them in agricultural and mechanical arts. The Chippewas in Michigan in 1819 were to be furnished "with such farming utensils and cattle, . . . and such persons to aid them in their agriculture, as the President may deem expedient." The Creeks were provided with "instruction in agriculture" in 1825. Christian missions among the Osage in 1825 were to be funded "so long as said Missions shall be usefully employed in teaching, civilizing, and improving the said Native Americans." Native Americans in Florida were guaranteed a school in 1832 (Deloria, Jr., 1975).

Some tribes, however, came to view education as a way of protecting themselves from the encroachment of White civilization. The Choctaws negotiated a provision in the treaty of Doaks Stand in 1820 that set up a fund for the education of 20 youths each year in schools outside the nation (Kappler, 1904-41).

Treaties established a fiduciary relationship between tribes and the federal government. In exchange for Native American land, the government agreed to provide payments and services, including education. That relationship is the basis for federal educational services for Native Americans to the present day.

In the 1870s, the government decided that off-reservation boarding schools should be established for Native American children so that they could be removed completely from their tribal surroundings, the better to inculcate them with the culture and values of the dominant society. Hampton Institute in Virginia accepted Native American students, and Carlisle Institute was established in Pennsylvania, both with the aim of educating Native Americans to be economically self-sufficient (Pratt, 1964). Students in boarding schools had their hair cut, their traditional dress replaced with school uniforms, and were often punished for speaking their native languages (LaFlesche, 1963; Standing Bear, 1975). If education led to employment, it also often resulted in loss of tribal identity.

Some Native American students still went to college during the late 1800s and early 1900s. College-educated Native Americans such as Charles Eastman (Ohiyesa), Carlos Montezuma, Laura Cornelius, and Arthur Parker were politically active on behalf of Native American people and formed the Society of American Native Americans to promote Native American causes (Hertzberg, 1971). For the most part, however, the vocational boarding schools sponsored by the Bureau of Native American Affairs for Native American students provided the only real access to "higher" education, i.e., post-high school, for most Native Americans until the 1950s, when government policy called for relocation of Native Americans from reservations to urban areas and provided allowances for vocational training programs. It was not until the 1960s that the bureau made a conscious decision to emphasize academic training as well as vocational training in its high schools so that students would have the option of going to college (Szasz, 1974).

Despite the negative impacts of government-sponsored education, Native American tribes still view educational opportunities as a right guaranteed to them on the basis of treaties. If formal education has been used to destroy Native American cultures, Native American communities also recognize its value as a source of social and economic power and are seeking to take advantage of the opportunities it affords.

THE DEMOGRAPHICS OF CONTEMPORARY NATIVE AMERICAN HIGHER EDUCATION

There is no comprehensive source of statistics on American Native American students in higher education. Statistics are reported in federal sources and in the U.S. census, but they are not necessarily comparable because of differences in collection and reporting. Definitions of Native American identity vary across sources. The rise in Native American population between the 1970 and 1990 censuses, from approximately 763,000 in 1970 to almost 1.4 million in 1980 (a 43 percent increase) to 1.9 million in 1990 (a 38 percent increase over 1980), raises questions about the nature of Native American identity and how Native Americans are counted. It also casts suspicion on the comparability of the data (U.S. Bureau of Census, 1987).

From such disparate data, we can still derive a picture, however fuzzy, of the status of Native Americans in higher education and see that their participation and achievement levels lag behind those of white students. If the number of Native Americans in colonial colleges was minute, their enrollment in colleges today is still small, and comparison of figures in 1970 and 1980 shows that it did not grow appreciably during the 1970s, despite the apparent increase in population.

In 1970, about 3,000 Native American high school graduates (18 percent of the age cohort) entered college or some other form of postsecondary school. The rate for the White population was 40 percent. The projected graduation rate for Native American students was about 25 percent, which meant that 4 percent of the Native American age cohort would graduate, compared with approximately 22 percent of the White population (Fuchs and Havighurst, 1973).

By about 1979 only 55 percent of Native American students graduated from high school, as compared to 83 percent of White students. Only 17 percent entered college, as compared with 38 percent of White students. Only 6 percent completed college, as compared with 23 percent of White students. Those who graduated from college with a bachelor's degree were about as likely as White students to go on to graduate school, but only 2 percent completed a graduate or professional degree, as compared with 8 percent of White students (Astin, 1982).

The 1980 census and the *Digest of Educational Statistics* give a snapshot of the demographics of Native American higher education in the early 1980s. In 1984, 83,571 Native Americans (approximately 6 percent of the total Native American population in 1980) were enrolled in college. Their distribution by level was 83 percent undergraduate, 4.6 percent graduate, 1.2 percent in first-professional programs (law, medicine, theology, and health sciences), and 11 percent unclassified. For White Americans in 1984, the number enrolled in higher education programs was also approximately 6 percent. The distribution by level was 77 percent undergraduate, 9 percent graduate, 2.4 percent in first-professional programs, and 11 percent unclassified. About 15 percent of Native American students were in universities, 31 percent in other four-year institutions, and 54 percent in two-year institutions. For White Americans, almost 25 percent were enrolled in universities, about 40 percent in other four-year institutions, and 36 percent in two-year institutions (Center for Education Statistics, 1988; "Racial and Ethnic Makeup," 1986).

By 1990, 103,000 Native Americans were enrolled in college, but they did not make any gains in their proportional enrollment in higher education. They still account for only 0.8 percent of all college students (O'Brien, 1992). In a departure from past trends, however, Native Americans enrolled in greater numbers at four-year colleges. Their enrollments increased at those institutions by 14.3 percent over 1988, while enrollments at junior colleges increased by only 8 percent (Carter and Wilson, 1992). At the graduate level, the Council of Graduate Schools reported 3,343 Native American students enrolled in 1990 in graduate programs in its 389 member institutions (0.4 percent of the total enrollment at those schools) (Syverson, 1992).

Although the data may not be comparable, the trend is clear. Native American students are more likely than their non-Native American counterparts (except Hispanics) to attend a junior college, although that trend seems to be changing, and less likely to attend graduate school. These trends are of some concern since national statistics show that students who attend junior colleges have very low rates of transfer into four-year institutions, and students without bachelor's degrees cannot go to graduate school (Mingle, 1987; Brown, 1987). (See chapters 7 and 8.) Thus, Native American students may not have as great an access to bachelor's and graduate degrees as White students.

The factors mitigating against greater participation of Native Americans in higher education are often socioeconomic ones. Although many Native American parents value education for their children, their expectations of the results of education are often vague because they themselves have limited educational experiences. According to the 1980 census, only 5.2 percent of Native American people in the 40-69 age range had completed 17 years of school, while 14.2 percent of the White population (almost three times as many) had completed that much. Thus, as a percentage of their respective populations, Native Americans who were in the age range to be parents of college age children in 1980 were much less likely to have completed graduate education themselves and to be able to tell their children what graduate education might demand or what opportunities it might present (U.S. Bureau of the Census, 1980).

Nevertheless, studies show that parental encouragement is a strong motivating force for Native American students to succeed in college, even when parents have not had a college education (Rindone, 1988). Even when parents cannot prepare their children with information, their encouragement and moral support are important factors for students who seek higher education.

The financial burden of college education is a significant deterrent to Native American students, especially as the costs of education escalate. In 1989 the median income of Native American families was $20,025, while that of White families was $31,435 (U.S. Bureau of Census, 1990). As college costs escalate at rates faster than inflation, higher education costs constitute a greater percentage of family income. The differential between Native American family incomes and White family incomes indicates how difficult it is for an average Native American family to afford the costs of college education.

Low enrollments and high attrition contribute to low graduation rates relative to the White population. The high school achievement levels of Native American students affect their representation in college. Approximately 20,000 Native American students took the standard college entrance examination in 1990. Their mean Scholastic Aptitude Test scores were 388-verbal and 437-mathematical. For those who took the American College Testing program, their average score was 18. The national mean scores were 424-verbal and 476-mathematical. The average ACT score was 20.6. Those rates, in turn, contribute to very low rates of representation in graduate programs (O'Brien, 1992).

Another factor affecting the status of Native Americans in graduate education is that the achievement levels of Native American undergraduates lag behind those of White students on the measure of Graduate Record Examinations. In 1987/88, 1,023 students who took the GRE identified themselves as Native American. Their mean scores on the verbal, quantitative and analytical parts of the test were 471, 472, and 487, respectively, as compared with scores for white test takers of 516, 541, and 554 and scores for *all* test takers of 505, 531, and 541 (Educational Testing Service, 1988).

The Native American students who took the GRE came from families where the parents' educational levels and family incomes were less than those of the White test takers. Although there is no definitive study to show a direct statistical correlation between educational and income levels and test scores for American Native American students, socioeconomic status must be an important variable in determining how well students perform on the tests. Since many universities use GRE scores as part of the decision-making process on graduate admissions, Native Americans are at a disadvantage in gaining access to graduate education.

Native Americans in graduate school tend to be concentrated in certain areas. At the doctoral level, the number of degrees earned by Native Americans declined from a high of 130 in 1981 to 99 in 1986, but rose to 128 in 1991 (Center for Education Statistics, 1988; O'Brien, 1992). The existence of special programs and fellowship support probably accounts for the fact that the largest number of doctoral degrees awarded to Native Americans has been in education. In 1991, 39 percent of the 128 doctorates awarded to Native Americans were in some area of education (Summary Report 1986). At the master's degree level, 1,108 Native Americans earned degrees in 1990, 465 men and 643 women. Again, the largest number of these degrees were in education (405) (Syverson, 1992).

If Native American people receive few doctoral degrees, they are even more underrepresented on college faculties. The *Digest of Educational Statistics* showed only 1,307 Native Americans (0.27 percent) on the faculties of institutions of higher education in the fall of 1983 (Center for Education Statistics, 1988). That number had risen to 1,498 in 1989 (0.3 percent), but Native American faculty have tenure at a slightly lower rate that non-native faculty, and their share of administration and management positions remained relatively unchanged during the 1980s. Although 31 Native Americans held college presidencies in 1991, 27 of those were the presidents of institutions in the American Indian Higher Education Consortium, the group of tribally controlled community colleges (O'Brien, 1992; Carter and Wilson, 1992).

The statistics on Native American participation in higher education reveal some numerical growth, but a virtual stagnation of the percentage representation of Native Americans in undergraduate, graduate, and faculty populations. The numerical size of these Native American populations is such that a small increase or decrease in the numbers can cause a large increase or decrease in percentages relative to total Native American population while causing little if any change relative to the overall population. Given census statistics showing rapid numerical growth and high percentage changes for the Native American population in the United States (a 38 percent increase between 1980 and 1990, compared with 9 percent growth for the U.S. population as a whole), it appears that Native American percentages in higher education should have risen at a proportional rate. They have not.

Higher education is the key to socioeconomic mobility in American society. Income levels rise with years of education. Native Americans participate in higher education at relatively low levels. Their lack of participation is partly a result of lack of access because of socioeconomic constraints. But there are other constraints—language skills for those whose native language is not English; separation from the social and cultural support systems of family and community; and lack of understanding of the whole process of higher education.

THE FEDERAL ROLE IN HIGHER EDUCATION FOR NATIVE AMERICANS

Formal education has been a major focus of federal Native American policy since the first treaties in the 1780s. Federal legislation has established programs and provided funds to carry out that responsibility. For better or worse, the relationship between Native Americans and the government continues to exist.

The social and economic conditions of Native American tribes have prompted ongoing concern and periodic investigations by the federal government. All have dwelt at some length on the historic consequences of education for Native American people, and all have made recommendations designed to correct perceived problems. The Meriam report in 1928 recommended that Native American students attend colleges and universities for higher education rather than the bureau's establishing special post-secondary programs for them. It also recommended adequate scholarships and loans for college students (Institute for Government Research, 1928). The Kennedy Subcommittee report of 1969 recommended that stipends for Native American students receiving Bureau of Indian Affairs scholarships and fellowships be brought into line with other federal support programs, and that more funding be provided for graduate fellowships (Committee on Labor and Public Welfare, 1969). The American Native American Policy Review Commission recommended in 1976 that funds be provided for the establishment of Native American-controlled colleges and specialized training centers for areas such as Native American law (Schierbeck et al., 1976). In 1991, the Native American Nations at Risk Task Force, established by the U.S. Department of Education, recommended that the federal government seek legislation authorizing a set-aside of Native American students in the Special Programs for Disadvantaged Students (Title IV of the Higher Education Act) programs to ensure increased access to and completion of higher education. The task force also recommended that the government assess the unmet financial needs of Native American students and coordinate the development of budgets that would increase the number of Native American students attending and graduating from colleges and universities. It encouraged particularly the training of Native Americans to teach at all levels of the educational system, including college (Indian Nations at Risk Task Force, 1991).

Presently there are three major federal agencies that provide support for Native American students in higher education: the Bureau of Native American Affairs, the U.S. Office of Education, and the Public Health Service.

The Bureau of Native American Affairs grew out of the Office of Native American Trade, one of the earliest federal bureaucracies, and it was formally established as a branch of the government in 1834. For Native American communities, the Bureau of Native American Affairs represents an acknowledgment of the government's responsibility to carry out promises it made in exchange for Native American land. From the government's perspective, its responsibility has been to prepare Native Americans to function in the dominant society, which in many cases has meant changing cultural values and native languages.

Although the bureau's responsibility for Native American tribes is based in treaty rights, its legislative responsibility for current Native American education is authorized in the Snyder Act of 1921, which allows the government to provide services to all Native Americans without restriction on residence or degree of Native American blood (Tyler, 1973). Since 1975 the federal government has begun to emphasize the role of Native American people in decisions that affect their communities. The Native American Self-Determination and Education Improvement Act (P. L. 93-638) of that year allowed Native American tribes to assume management of programs from the bureau on a contract basis. Health care, education, and social services have been contracted by many tribes.

The bureau is the primary funding agency for Native American students who want to go to college. During the 1993 fiscal year, Congress appropriated $11,171,000 to the bureau for postsecondary education (including vocational education) and $2,469,000 for special higher education scholarships, most of which is administered through American Indian Scholarships, Inc., of Albuquerque, New Mexico. Tribes received $29,031,000 for scholarships for higher education (National Advisory Council on Indian Education, 1993).

The U.S. Department of Education assumed its role in Native American education with passage of Title IV of Public Law 92-318 in 1972 (and its subsequent amendments). The act is mainly concerned with primary and secondary education; however, one section provides for "fellowship programs leading to an advanced degree." The Office of Indian Education administered $1,600,000 in fellowship monies in 1987-88 (National Advisory Council on Indian Education, 1989). The Indian Fellowship Program has provided funding for Native American students, but in only a limited number of professional degree programs—law, business administration, education, medicine, engineering, natural resource management, and psychology and related fields. It has provided access for students in areas where there is a perceived need in Native American communities for trained professionals, and in that way it has played an important role in advancing the well-being of Native American communities. But in a subtle way, it has also continued the policy of pushing Native American students toward vocational, now professional, areas, rather than allowing them a range of choices.

The Indian Health Service financial aid program has had a significant impact in increasing the number of Native American health care professionals. For 1987-88 it had a budget of $6,000,400 and supported 438 students (both undergraduate and graduate) in various health professions curricula (National Advisory Council on Indian Education, 1989).

To meet needs for Native American school administrators, a special program established in 1971 has also provided fellowships and special support programs for Native American students at Harvard, Pennsylvania State University, Arizona State University, and the University of Minnesota. These institutions have established programs for Native American students leading to master's and doctoral degrees in educational administration.

Besides the financial role that federal agencies play in Native American higher education, they also shape policy. The Indian Education Act of 1972 laid the basis for greater involvement of Native American parents in the education of their children through a provision for Native American parent advisory committees at the local elementary school level. It also provided for the establishment of the National Advisory Council on Native American Education, whose members are appointed by the president of the United States. The council reports to the president, the U.S. Congress, and the U.S. secretary of education and makes recommendations on personnel matters, legislative matters, and policy issues that affect Native American education. Its existence is an important recognition of the role that Native American people should play in shaping the education of their children.*

Although Native American people have been guaranteed a greater voice in the administration of programs that serve their communities, their effectiveness is diminished by the fragmentation of their audience. For higher education, the Bureau of Indian Affairs, U. S. Office of Education, and Indian Health Service reside in different agencies, and there is virtually no formal communication among them. Collectively in 1988-89 the three agencies provided approximately $30,676,400 in financial support for Native American students, and their potential constituency numbered about 93,000 students (Schantz and Brown, 1990). They do not, however, speak with any unified voice about major policy issues with regard to Native American higher education. If higher education for Native American students is to produce results in terms of representation and success rates, there must be a stronger Native American voice at the national level, more funding, and more systematic attention to higher education for Native American students.

NATIVE AMERICAN STUDENTS IN COLLEGE

A major issue in Native American communities is the effect that college education has on Native American students. The Iroquois leaders who

---

*The Indian Education Act is an Amendment to the Higher Education Act of 1965, the Vocational Educational Act of 1963, and related acts. It constitutes Title IV of the Higher Education Act, and programs under its authority are generally referred to by Native American people as Title IV programs.

complained to the British agent in the eighteenth century that young men who went away to college were useless to the tribe might find a sympathetic ear in many communities today. Formal education in colleges and universities away from reservations is often viewed as too abstract and not practical enough to meet the needs of communities (Guyette and Heth, 1985).

The attrition rate for Native American students who attend colleges and universities indicates that the experience is not always productive for them. Dropout rates for Native American students are higher than for Whites and similar to or higher than those for other minority groups at all levels of education from high school through college and graduate school. In the early 1980s, the estimated rates was 75 percent to 93 percent across a range of institutions (McNamara, 1982). In the late 1980s, the study mentioned earlier showed that only 27.3 percent of Native American students graduated from 79 institutions surveyed (Wells Study, 1988).

There are many factors affecting the success rates of Native American students in colleges and universities. Some are socioeconomic—low parental income and educational levels. Some are social—the scarcity of Native Americans as role models in professional and academic areas, and peer group pressure that exacerbates the high dropout rates for high school students. Some are cultural—language problems for students whose native language is not English, a sense of obligation to family and community rather than the academic world.

The academic world stresses rational thought and constant questioning of what constitutes "truth." Native American communities stress acceptance of common values and belief in long-held traditions and customs, and participation in the day-to-day life of the community. Power is not in abstract theories about truth but in knowledge of the on-going social relationships and activities of family and friends (French, 1987). The cultures of the non-Native American academic world and the Native American community are quite different. Native American students face the challenge of mastering a new environment and, in many cases, justifying the existence of their own cultures in the academic world where they find themselves (Ferron, 1989).

Native American studies programs at major universities began to emerge in the early 1970s as a way of validating Native American cultures and the presence of Native American students on their campuses. At the University of Minnesota, the establishment of the American Indian Studies Department proceeded by negotiation (Miller, 1971). At the University of California at Berkeley, the Native American Studies program was created as part of the Ethnic Studies Department, whose establishment was the result of a massive student strike percipitated by the administration's decision to cancel a class that was to have been taught by Black activist Stokeley Carmichael.

These programs flourished at colleges and universities throughout the country in the 1970s. In 1977 there were 100 institutions with some courses on Native American history and culture that constituted some kind of formal Native American studies program (Locke, 1978). In 1981, 105 institutions reported some academic courses and more or less formally recognized an Indian studies or Native American studies program. They generally provided some student support services, if only a counselor with part time responsibility for Native American students (Guyette and Heth, 1985).

Native American/American Indian studies programs have persisted since the early 1970s, and they have indeed established the legitimacy of the study of Native American cultures on college and university campuses. The Native Americans who serve on university faculties will undoubtedly be found overwhelmingly in Native American/American Indian studies programs. There are a number of Native American/American Indian studies programs or centers at major universities that provide a nexus for student activities, academic programs, and outreach to Native American communities. Montana State University has a program to encourage Native American students to pursue undergraduate and gradute degrees in biological sciences. MSU also works with Native American-controlled community colleges in neighboring communities to enhance transfer to the university.

Some programs have gained academic legitimacy with bachelor's degree programs and have established their own journals at major research universities. Arizona State University has a Center for American Native American Education and publishes *The Journal of American Native American Education*, which is a major source for scholarly articles on Native American higher education. The University of California at Los Angeles publishes the *American Native American Culture and Research Journal*. The University of Oklahoma publishes *The American Native American Quarterly* (Washburn, 1975).

Despite the existence of the studies programs and support services for Native American students throughout the decade of the 1970s, the enrollment of Native American students in higher education declined from 1982 to 1986, and the number of doctorates awarded to Native American fell between 1981 and 1986. The numbers had rebounded by 1990, but the percentages have remained virtually unchanged. Although Native American studies programs persist, their existence alone cannot increase the number of Native American students attending college (Kidwell, 1991).

The societal factors of the 1960s and 1970s that led to the establishment of Native American studies programs and easy access to higher education for Native American students have largely disappeared. The fervor of the civil rights movement of the 1960s has subsided. The militancy of the American Indian Movement has been suppressed. The highly visible activities surrounding Native American causes have diminished, but the Native American lawyers, doctors, teachers, social workers, business owners, accountants, and other professionals who are working at colleges and universities, with tribal governments, and in urban Native American communities are there because of the militancy of the 1960s and the opening of higher education during the 1970s. The skills and knowledge that they acquired allow them to continue to serve their communities. The Native American students of the 1980s and 1990s may not be involved in such dramatic events as those of the 1960s and 1970s, and their representation in numbers may not be as significant, but Native American students are still in colleges and universities, and their achievements continue to contribute to their communities.

NATIVE AMERICAN COMMUNITY COLLEGES

The growing force in Native American higher education since the 1980s is the Native American Higher Education Consortium, which is comprised of 28 Native American-controlled community colleges, 23 of which are located in reservation communities, 3 of which serve several Native American communities from an urban area, and 2 of which are in Canada (Oppelt, 1984; O'Brien, 1992). The colleges are a result of the desire of Native American people to control their own educational institutions. The oldest college in the consortium is Haskell Indian College, established by the federal government as a trade and vocational school in 1884. Haskell initiated a formal academic college-transfer program in 1970 and has recently begun a four-year education curriculum. The first Native American-controlled community college was Navajo Community College, which was established in 1969 (Szasz, 1974). Since then the number of Native American-controlled community colleges has grown rapidly. By 1988 one college, Sinte Gleska in South Dakota, was offering some four-year and graduate programs.

The enrollment in consortium institutions for the 1988-89 academic year was 4,975 students (Tier, 1989). By 1990, it had risen to approximately 13,000 (a full-time-equivalent enrollment of 6,024), and the colleges enrolled approximately 14 percent of all Native American college students (O'Brien, 1992). The main financial support for these colleges comes through the Bureau of Native American Affairs, which in 1988-89 received an appropriation of $12,968,000 for their support (National Advisory Council on Indian Education, 1989). The level of funding available from the government has not kept pace with the needs of the colleges, and per capita expenditures in 1991 were $2,672, compared with $5,129 at all public two-year colleges (O'Brien, 1992).

Consortium institutions are strongly oriented toward the immediate needs for job training for people living on reservations, although they also generally offer a basic liberal arts curriculum as well. Students tend to be adults who have family responsibilities and who are looking for a way to enhance their income levels. As a means of access to four-year institutions, the transferability of courses from the colleges is subject to the vagaries of state and institutional articulation policies and agreements, and there are no statistics that indicate rates of transfer for students from the tribal community colleges to four-year institutions. Anecdotal information from several presidents of these colleges indicates that very few students plan to go on to four-year institutions, and those who do often drop out (Tierney, 1992).

HIGHER EDUCATION AND NATIVE AMERICAN COMMUNITIES

Tribes and communities look at higher education in terms of their own requirements for trained persons to provide skills to solve immediate problems and to provide education to meet social needs in reservations and urban Native American communities. The only assessment of tribal needs for higher education was conducted in 1983 by the Native Indian Center at the University of California at Los Angeles. The intent of the survey was to assess the needs that tribes, communities, and urban groups wanted met. The educational needs most often expressed were those for professional expertise in tribal planning. Business administration was the second major priority, and teaching came in as a third priority. College teaching, a major career objective for graduate education in academic subjects, was ranked seventeenth (Guyette and Heth, 1985).

Tribal needs are perceived in short-range terms because they are so pressing. Tribes need to manage their own resources to build an economic base so their members can have jobs. The curricula of tribal community colleges are geared to meet these immediate needs. Short-term training for immediate goals, however, does not give students the broader skills of analysis and problem solving that they need to meet longer-term tribal goals. Native American professionals must also deal with non-Native American professionals and translate immediate community and tribal needs into terms with which the non-Native American world can deal.

Tribal leaders sometime feel that college does not adequately prepare students to deal with practical situations on reservations or in Native American communities. Native American students are sometime confronted with the situation of going away to college and not being able to find a job when they return home. Tribes and communities are struggling to deal with social conditions caused by lack of resources, physical isolation, high unemployment rates, and low income levels. Higher education outside their communities is not a high priority for Native American leaders in dealing with social problems. Nevertheless, the cadres of Native Americans who have gone away to get college degrees and who have returned to work with their communities is important. The suspicion of those who have gone away to school is gradually diminishing as those individuals have made valuable contributions to their communities.

SUMMARY

Native Americans are a young and rapidly growing population. The average age of the population in 1980 was 16 (Tijerina and Biemer, 1988; U.S. Department of Health and Human Services, 1984). Of that population, however, only about one-third of students who enter the ninth grade will eventually go beyond high school (Tierney, 1989).

Given the low levels of Native American participation in higher education, must we conclude that Native Americans are failing to take advantage of college, either by choice or because of inadequate preparation? Low grade point averages, high dropout rates, and low scores on standardized tests are taken as signs of failure for Native American students. However, those who opt out of college to return to their communities cannot be said to fail if they go back to play productive roles, which many do. Given tribal values concerning higher education, success in college is not necessarily perceived in the same way in tribal communities as it is in American society.

Native American communities are also setting their own standards of success in community colleges established to meet specific needs. And Native American students are completing courses, learning skills, and growing intellectually in both Native American-controlled and other colleges and universities. Failure of Native American students in higher education is defined as a problem in terms of the dominant society. It is not necessarily defined as failure in terms of Native American communities. The status of Native American students must include recognition of those who choose not to attend college, those who attend but opt to return to their own communities, and those who receive their degrees and make a decision to carry out a commitment to help improve the status of Native American people.

Although the history of higher education for Native American people has been associated with acculturation and loss of identity, over the years Native American communities have persisted and have found ways to use education as a bridge of communication between themselves and American society. Native American cultures have proven remarkably adaptable throughout the history of their contact with Europeans. The adaptation to higher education is still fraught with hazards, i.e., high attrition rates, but Native American students do persist, and they have more than succeeded in disproving the statement of the eighteenth century leader that those who go away to college are of no use to their communities.

REFERENCES

Astin, A. M. 1982. Minorities in American higher education: Recent trends, current prospects, and recommendations. San Francisco: Jossey-Bass.

Carter, D. J., and R. Wilson. January 1992. Minorities in higher education. Washington, DC: American Council on Education.

Center for Education Statistics. 1988. Digest of Education Statistics 1988. Washington, DC: U.S. Department of Education, Office of Educational Research and Improvement.

Deloria, Jr., V. 1975. Legislative analysis of the federal role in Indian education. U.S. Office of Education.

Educational Testing Service. 1988. A summary of data collected from Graduate Record Examinations test takers during 1986-87. Report no. 12. Princeton, NJ.

Ferron, R. 1989. American Indian women in higher education: Common threads and diverse experiences. In Educating the majority: Women challenge tradition in higher education. New York: American Council on Education/Macmillan Publishing; London: Collier Macmillan Publishers.

French, L. 1987. Psychocultural change and the American Indian: An ethnohistorical analysis. New York: Garland Publishing.

Fuchs, E., and R. J. Havighurst. 1973. To live on this earth: American Indian education. Garden City, NY: Anchor Press/Doubleday.

Guyette, S., and C. Heth. 1985. Issues for the future of American Indian studies: A needs assessment and program guide. Los Angeles: American Indian Studies Center, University of California.

Hertzberg, H. 1971. The search for an American Indian identity: Modern pan-Indian movements. Syracuse: Syracuse University Press.

Institute for Government Research. 1928. The problem of Indian administration. Baltimore: Johns Hopkins University Press.

Kappler, C. 1904-1941. Indian affairs: Laws and treaties. Vol. 2. Washington, DC: Government Printing Office.

Kidwell, C. S. 1991. The vanishing native reappears in the college curriculum. Change: The Magazine of Higher Learning 23, 2 (March/April).

Labaree, L. W., et al., eds. 1961. The papers of Benjamin Franklin. New Haven: Yale University Press.

La Flesche, F. 1963. The middle five: Indian Schoolboys of the Omaha tribe. Madison: University of Wisconsin Press.

Locke, P. 1978. A survey of college and university programs for American Indians. Boulder, CO: Western Interstate Commission for Higher Education.

McNamara, P. P. 1982. American Indians in higher education: A longitudinal study of progress and attainment. Ph.D. diss., University of California at Los Angeles.

Miller, F. C. 1971. Involvement in an urban university. In The American Indian in urban society, ed. J. O. Waddell and O. M. Watson. Boston: Little, Brown and Company.

Mingle, J. R. July 1987. *Focus on Minorities: Trends in higher education participation and success.* Denver: Education Commission of the States and the State Higher Education Executive Officers.

Morrison, S. E. 1936. *Three centuries of Harvard.* Cambridge: Harvard University Press.

National Advisory Council on Indian Education. 1989a. *NACIE Newsletter* (March).

———. 1989b. *NACIE Newsletter* 6, 2 (June 15).

———. 1993. *NACIE Newsletter* 9, 2 (January).

O'Brien, E. M. 1992. American Indians in higher education. *Research Briefs* 3, no. 3. Division of Policy Analysis and Research, American Council on Education.

Oppelt, N. T. 1984. The tribally controlled colleges in the 1980s: Higher education's best kept secret. *American Indian Culture and Research Journal* 8, 4: 27-45.

Payne, N. J. 1989. Personal communication with G. Tiger, June 9, Washington, DC.

Pratt, R. H. 1964. *Battlefield and classroom: Four decades with the American Indian 1867-1904,* ed. R. M. Utley. New Haven: Yale University Press.

Racial and ethnic makeup of college and university enrollments. 1986. *The Chronicle of Higher Education* (July 21).

Rindone, P. 1988. Achievement motivation and academic achievement of Native American students. *Journal of American Indian Education* 28, 1 (October): 1-2.

Schantz, N. B., and P. Q. Brown. June 1990. *Trends in racial/ethnic enrollment in higher education: Fall 1978 through fall 1988.* U.S. Department of Education. National Center for Education Statistics.

Schierbeck, H., et al. 1976. *Report on Indian education, Task Force Five.* Washington, DC: Government Printing Office.

Standing Bear, L. 1975. *My people the Sioux,* ed. E. A. Brininstool. Lincoln: University of Nebraska Press.

Summary report 1986: Doctorate recipients from United States universities. 1987. Washington, DC: National Academy Press.

Syverson, P. D. 1992a. Number of master's degrees granted surges in 1990. *Communicator* (August).

———. 1992b. Early returns from CGS/GRE enrollment survey indicate continued enrollment growth in fall 1991. *Communicator* 7 (September). Washington, DC: Council of Graduate Schools.

Szasz, M. C. 1974. *Education and the American Indian: The road to self-determination, 1928-1973.* Albuquerque: University of New Mexico Press.

———. 1988. *Indian education in the American colonies 1607-1783.* Albuquerque: University of New Mexico Press.

Tierney, W. G. 1989. Organizational aspects of Native American participation in postsecondary education. Unpublished paper, August.

———. 1992. *Official encouragement, institutional discouragement: Minorities in academe—the Native American experience.* Norwood, NJ: Ablex Publishing.

Tijerina, K., and P. Biemer. 1988. The dance of Indian higher education: One step forward, two steps back. *Educational Record* 68, no. 4/69, no. 1.

Tyler, S. L. 1973. *A history of Indian policy.* Washington, DC: U.S. Department of the Interior, Bureau of Indian Affairs.

U.S. Bureau of the Census. 1980. *1980 census of population, characteristics of the population, United States summary.* Washington, DC.

———. 1987. *We, the first Americans.* Washington, DC.

———. 1990. Minority economic profiles. Tables. No. CPH-L-94.

U.S. Congress. Senate. Committee on Labor and Public Welfare. Special Subcommittee on Indian Education. 1969. *Indian education: A national tragedy—a national challenge.* 91st Cong., 1st sess. Report no. 91-105.

U.S. Department of Education. Indian Nations at Risk Task Force. October 1991. *Indian nations at risk: An educational strategy for action.*

U.S. Department of Education. National Center for Education Statistics. 1991. *Digest of Education Statistics.*

———. 1992. *Race/ethnicity trends in degrees conferred by institutions of higher education, 1992.*

U.S. Department of Health and Human Services. Public Health Services, Health Resources and Services Administration, Indian Health Service, Office of Planning, Evaluation and Legislation, Program Statistics Branch. June 1984. *Indian health services, chart book series.*

U.S. States at Large II, sec. LXXV. March 3, 1819.

Vining Brown, S. 1987. *Minorities in the graduate education pipeline.* Princeton: Educational Testing Service.

Washburn, W. 1975. American Indian studies: A status report. *American Quarterly* 27, 3.

Wells, R. N. 1988. Study. St. Lawrence University, Canton, NY.

———. 1989. Press release of study by Wells. Office of University Communications, St. Lawrence University, Canton, NY, April 24.

CHAPTER 14

Higher Education Issues in the Asian American Community

Bob H. Suzuki

Aside from the recent controversy over the admission of Asian American students into some of the more prestigious academic institutions, higher education issues in the Asian American community have received scant attention. In the past, there was little interest in such issues because Asian Americans were small in number and considered a rather insignificant minority. Now that Asian Americans* have emerged during the past decade as the nation's fastest growing minority and number nearly 7 million, or almost 3 percent of the total U.S. population (U.S. Bureau of the Census, 1993), such issues have been attracting more interest, but it is still rather nominal. This relatively low level of interest may be due to the prevalent view that Asian Americans are a "model minority" who have enjoyed extraordinary success in American society and are supposedly even outdoing Whites (Peterson, 1978; Oxnam, 1986). Thus, in contrast to other minorities, Asian Americans are

---

*Pacific Islanders are frequently grouped with Asians and data for both groups are often aggregrated. While common issues confront both groups, there are vast language, cultural and socio-historical differences between them. In fact, the problems and needs of Pacific Islanders in higher education are more similar, in many respects, to those of other minorities than to those of Asians. Moreover, because Pacific Islanders are a relatively small group, their problems and needs tend to be slighted in comparison to those of Asians when both groups are treated together. For these reasons, this paper does not attempt to include Pacific Islanders in its coverage.

generally seen as a group that has few, if any, special problems and needs in higher education and, therefore, warrants little attention.

Due to the model minority stereotype, to even suggest that serious problems exist for Asian Americans in higher education may seem to border on the absurd to many people, especially educators. Asian Americans, both students and faculty, are viewed as "overrepresented" in higher education in comparison with their proportion in the general population. Moreover, Asian American students are almost universally seen as industrious, conscientious, and well-behaved high achievers whose educational attainments have been widely acclaimed ("A Formula for Success," 1984; Butterfield, 1986). Such a view, however, is both simplistic and naive and its perpetuation has led to widespread misconceptions that have impeded efforts to identify and meet the needs of Asian Americans in higher education.

In this chapter, I will summarize what I consider to be the most salient issues facing Asian Americans in higher education. These issues will be delineated by reviewing the extant research on Asian Americans in higher education. Because such research has been so limited, I will also discuss the additional research I believe is needed in the future. Before covering these topics, a brief historic overview of the Asian American experience in the United States will be presented, followed by a summary of current and projected demographic data on Asian Americans.

HISTORIC OVERVIEW

The first of the early Asian immigrants, the Chinese, began arriving in the United States in the late 1840s. By 1880, there were some 105,000 Chinese living in the western states, primarily in California, and another 12,000 in Hawaii. However, in 1882, as a result of a virulent anti-Chinese movement, the immigration of Chinese laborers was brought to a halt by an exclusion act passed by the United States Congress (Chinn, 1969; Lyman, 1974).

The Chinese were followed by the Japanese, of whom the major proportion arrived in Hawaii and on the United States mainland between 1890 and 1920. Japanese immigration was brought practically to a complete halt in 1924 when Congress passed the National Origins Quota Act. At the time, there were about 110,000 Japanese living in the United States mainland, mainly in the three Pacific Coast states, and an equal number in Hawaii (Ichihashi, 1932; Conroy, 1953; Daniels, 1962; Kitano, 1969).

Next to arrive, though in much smaller numbers, were the Koreans of whom a few thousand came to Hawaii during a short period starting in 1903 and abruptly ending in 1905 when Korea was annexed by Japan. Between 1910 and 1924, more than a thousand Korean immigrants were allowed to come to the United States mainland, where they joined about 2,000 other Koreans who had migrated from Hawaii. With the enactment of the National Origins Quota Act in 1924, the first phase of Korean immigration came to an end (Yang, 1982; Kim, 1986).

The last of the early Asian immigrants to arrive in the United States were the Asian Indians and the Filipinos. Between 1907 and 1920, over 6,000 Asian Indians entered and settled in the western states, predominantly in California. During this period, a small number of Asian Indians also arrived and settled on the East Coast, particularly in New York. The total Asian Indian population was probably less than 10,000 when immigration from India was stopped by the National Origins Quota Act of 1924 (Hess, 1974; Melendy, 1977).

The first major influx of Filipino immigrants occurred from 1907 through 1919 when the Hawaiian sugar plantations experimented with Filipino labor as a replacement for the Japanese. With the passage of the National Origins Quota Act of 1924 (which was not applicable to the Philippines since it was a protectorate of the United States at the time), Filipino immigration increased sharply both to the mainland and Hawaii. During the 1930s, however, Filipino immigration was reduced to a trickle in the face of demands for their exclusion and a development of a labor surplus. By this time, the Filipino population in Hawaii had reached a peak of about 60,000 and that on the mainland had leveled off at around 50,000 (Lasker, 1931; Melendy, 1977).

These early Asian pioneers made major contributions to the development of the American West and Hawaii. They provided much of the labor for the expanding agricultural industries of these areas and for building the vast network of railroads throughout the Western states. Others worked in fields such as lumbering, fishing, and mining, and in jobs in canneries, domestic work, and gardening, in which the demand for cheap, unskilled, and dependable labor was high.

These contributions are especially impressive when considered in light of the intense discrimination encountered by the early Asian immigrants. They arrived during a period when racism and violence were rather commonplace in the American West, and, furthermore, they were viewed as a competitive threat by White workers. As a consequence, they became victims of countless repressive, often violent, acts of racism (Daniels, 1962; Saxton, 1971; Melendy, 1977). The culmination of this "yellow peril" movement was perhaps reached during World War II when over 110,000 West Coast Japanese, mostly

American-born citizens, were imprisoned by the United States government in detention camps (Daniels, 1971; Weglyn, 1976).

Despite the fact that most of the early Asian immigrants were common laborers, poor peasants, or destitute small farmers in their countries of origin, they had surprisingly high levels of literacy and education. In fact, the Japanese and Korean immigrants probably had a higher level of education than the average American due to the institution of universal education in their homelands. The children of Asian immigrants had difficulty enrolling in the public schools and were often required to attend segregated schools, particularly in California (Lasker, 1931; Wollenberg, 1976; Kim, 1986).

By the 1930s, a few Asian Americans were beginning to enroll in institutions of higher education. Many of those who graduated, however, were not able to obtain jobs in their chosen fields of study. Consequently, these individuals had little choice but to make their living by taking menial jobs, running vegetable stands, or working as gardeners.

While discrimination against Asian Americans persisted into the post-World War II era, the more overt forms prevalent during the prewar period were now less frequently encountered, and American attitudes toward Asian Americans gradually improved. Increasing numbers of Asian American students enrolled in institutions of higher education with growing confidence that they would be able to obtain jobs commensurate with a college degree when they graduated. Most of the discriminatory immigration restrictions imposed in 1924 were finally lifted with the passage of the Immigration Act of 1965. Partly as a result of this new law, the rate of immigration from Asia, particularly from Hong Kong, India, Taiwan, South Korea, and the Philippines, increased enormously. More recently, since the withdrawal of the United States from Vietnam in 1975, over 800,000 Southeast Asians have entered the country.

CURRENT AND PROJECTED DEMOGRAPHIC DATA

As mentioned earlier, Asian Americans are the nation's fastest growing minority in terms of proportional growth in population. According to the 1990 U.S. Census, the Asian American population increased by a startling 97 percent, growing from about 3.5 million in 1980 to 6.9 million in 1990, and now constitutes 2.9 percent of the total U.S. population.

The 1990 Census also showed that foreign-born Asians numbered over 4.5 million, or 65 percent of the total Asian American population. For the nation as a whole, the total foreign-born population was enumerated to be about 20 million, or about 8 percent of the total U.S. population.

The populations of the six largest Asian groups in 1990 were enumerated to be the following:

Chinese	1,645,472
Filipino	1,406,770
Japanese	847,562
Asian Indian	815,447
Korean	798,849
Vietnamese	614,547

In 1985, the Asian American population was projected to grow to nearly 10 million by 2000, or almost 4 percent of the total U.S. population (Gardner, Robey, and Smith, 1985). The results of the 1990 census indicate that this projection is very likely to be exceeded.

The phenomenal growth in the Asian American population has been and will continue to be propelled primarily by the large influx of immigrants from the Asian countries—an influx that began with the lifting of the discriminatory immigration restrictions in 1965. Between 1980 and 1990, about 2.6 million Asian immigrants entered this country (U.S. Bureau of the Census, 1993).

SUMMARY OF THE EXTANT RESEARCH

The research on Asian Americans in higher education has been quite limited. Prior to the 1960s, no such research appears to have been conducted. Starting in the 1960s, a few small-scale studies began to appear on selected Asian groups, primarily the Chinese and Japanese. In the 1970s and 1980s, these studies increased in number and expanded in scope, encompassing a broader range of Asian American groups. In addition, regional and national studies on minorities in higher education sometimes included Asian Americans, usually as a single, aggregated group. A few studies, conducted during the past decade, have focused specifically on Asian Americans, including their participation in higher education, and provided disaggregated data on the larger Asian American groups.

The summary of the extant research to be presented in this section will focus on those studies that have implications for institutional, state, and/or federal policy. It categorizes these studies into the following seven areas: 1) college preparation; 2) access issues; 3) academic development and achievement; 4) curricular and instructional issues; 5) socio-psychological environment; 6) hiring and promotion issues; and 7) returns on higher education. For each of these areas, I will begin with a set of questions which I will try to answer by referring to the extant research.

College Preparation

Are Asian American students adequately prepared for college? How do they perform on standardized admissions tests, such as the SAT and ACT? Are they underprepared in any areas? These are among the questions I will try to answer by reviewing the findings of research on the college preparation of Asian American students.

Almost all of the extant research in this area indicates that Asian American parents place a great deal of emphasis on education and that Asian American students are generally well prepared for college (Kitano, 1971; Schwartz, 1971; Sigel, 1972; Young, 1972; Nakanishi and Hirano-Nakanishi, 1983). This assessment is supported by data compiled in the 1990 U.S. Census showing that all of the Asian American groups had a consistently higher rate of enrollment in educational institutions at practically all ages than that of other racial/ethnic groups, including Whites. In particular, they showed that 38 percent of Asian Americans, who were 25 years of age or older, had earned a bachelor's or higher degree compared with 20 percent of the general population in the same age bracket (U.S. Bureau of the Census, 1993).

An earlier study showed that a large proportion of Asian American high school graduates expect to go on to college (Peng, Fetters, and Kolstad, 1981). Perhaps because of this expectation, Asian American students prepare themselves better to enter college. According to a 1982 survey, Asian American students on the average earned more units in the core subjects preparatory to college than other racial/ethnic groups. In particular, the units they earned in foreign languages, mathematics, and natural sciences were considerably higher than those of other students (Snyder, 1987).

Over the past two-and-a-half decades, there have been a number of national studies which have analyzed the performance of Asian American students on standardized tests (Hsia, 1988). Among the findings of these studies are the following:

- A larger proportion Asian American students take the SAT than students in general. A study by Ramist and Arbeiter (1984) revealed that 33,062 of the 983,474 SAT candidates nationally in 1982-83 identified themselves as Asian Americans. This number was almost one-half of all 18-year-old Asian Americans; whereas, the total number of SAT candidates represented only about one-quarter of the total 18-year-old population.
- The average overall performance of Asian American students on standardized tests, such as the SAT and ACT, is comparable to that of White students. However, they have also consistently shown that

Asian American students score lower on verbal ability and higher on quantitative ability than their White peers. This was true even for Asian American students who reported that English was their best language (Ramist and Arbeiter, 1984).

■ A recent study of over 4,000 Asian American and 1,000 White college freshmen showed that: 1) high school GPA and SAT or Achievement Test scores could, to a moderate degree, predict the freshmen grades of both the Asian American and White students; 2) for both groups of students, high school GPA was the best single predictor; and 3) mathematics scores are a better predictor than verbal scores for Asian American students, but not for White students (Sue and Abe, 1988).

The research summarized above has important implications for the education of Asian Americans. Perhaps the most significant of these is that much greater attention should be paid by educational institutions to helping Asian students develop their verbal/linguistic skills. Because having such skills is essential for certain fields of study, especially the social sciences and humanities, and becomes even more important in one's professional career, Asian Americans have long been concerned about the underdevelopment of these skills among Asian American students (Watanabe, 1973; Sue, 1973; Ueda, 1974).

The problem is exacerbated by the large proportion of Asian American students who do not speak English as their first language. As noted earlier, the 1990 U.S. Census revealed that about 4.5 million Asian Americans, or 65 percent of the total Asian American population, were foreign born, indicating that a majority of Asian Americans have mother tongues other than English or live in households in which languages other than English are spoken. As the Asian immigrant population continues to grow, an increasing proportion of Asian American students will undoubtedly be limited-English speaking or non-English speaking and will need help in developing their verbal/linguistic skills.

While the dropout rate for Asian American students is still quite low, there is growing concern over the rise of Asian street gangs in recent years. Starting in a number of Chinatowns back in the 1970s (Sung, 1977), the most active gangs today have been formed by troubled Southeast Asian teenagers from immigrant families who have been alienated from American society and are pursuing a life of crime. Many of them have not developed proficiency in English and are dropping out of school (Arax, 1987). They represent a small, but significant segment of the Asian American student population who do not fit the model minority image. These students are struggling at home and in school and need special assistance to succeed in their academic pursuits.

As discussed earlier, the research has shown that Asian American students, regardless of their English proficiency, have consistently outperformed White students on quantitative tests. Their superior quantitative skills coupled with their lower verbal/linguistic skills may partially explain why they tend to major in fields requiring strong quantitative skills and shy away from fields requiring strong verbal/linguistic skills.

Access Issues

Do Asian Americans have any problems in gaining access to institutions of higher education? Or, are they, in fact, "overrepresented" in higher education? Due to the paucity of the extant research in this area, answers to these complex questions cannot be readily provided. I will, however, review the pertinent available data and what little research that does exist and try to draw some preliminary conclusions.

The statistics on Asian American enrollments in higher education would seem to suggest that Asian Americans have no problems of access to institutions of higher education. The dramatic increases in the Asian American population during the past decade have been paralleled by increases in Asian American enrollments in higher education. Between 1982 and 1991, Asian American enrollments in higher education increased by 81 percent from 351,000 to 637,000, or 4.4 percent of the total enrollment (Chronicle of Higher Education Almanac, 1993). If this trend continues, by 2000, there could be 1 million Asian American students enrolled in higher education, constituting as much as 10 percent of all students (Suzuki, 1989).

Despite these favorable statistics, there are at least two important access issues that are of concern to Asian Americans. The first is related to the aggregation of data for all of the 29 Asian groups identified by the 1990 U.S. Census. While certain groups, such as the Japanese and Chinese, may be "overrepresented" in comparison with their proportions in the general population, other groups, such as the Southeast Asians and Filipinos, may be underrepresented. However, the extent of this underrepresentation is currently difficult, if not impossible, to ascertain because most academic institutions do not disaggregate data on Asian Americans. Consequently, almost all of the research studies and national surveys on higher education have only been able to provide aggregated data on Asian Americans.

The aggregation of data on Asian Americans conceals important differences between the various groups. These groups differ substantially in their socioeconomic characteristics, cultural backgrounds, and historical experiences. For example, certain Southeast Asian groups, such as the Cambodian and Hmong refugees, who have only recently arrived in the United States and are still having a difficult time subsisting, are not only underrepresented in higher education, but also have more serious problems and needs in education than any of the other Asian American groups. Students from these and other underrepresented Asian American groups need to be recruited by educational equity programs and provided with financial aid, ESL assistance, and other supportive services to help them gain access and succeed in institutions of higher education.

The second access issue, which has generated heated controversy over the past five years, is whether some of the most selective and prestigious institutions of higher education have imposed unofficial "quotas" on the admission of Asian American students. During the past 10 years, Asian American enrollments have steadily increased in a number of such institutions and now comprise a substantial proportion of the total enrollments in those institutions. For example, in the fall of 1986 Asian American students comprised 26.5 percent of UC-Berkeley's freshman class, 33 percent of UC-Irvine's freshman class, and 8 to 19 percent of the freshmen at UCLA, Stanford, Harvard, Yale, Brown, and MIT (Nakao, 1987). These high percentages apparently created considerable concern in these institutions that Asian American students may be "overrepresented" and upsetting the "ethnic balance" of the student population (Hassan, 1986-87; Salholz, 1987). Many Asian Americans believe it was not coincidental that most of these institutions revised their admissions criteria about six or seven years ago in ways that work to the disadvantage of Asian American students.

Asian American student groups (Ho and Chin, 1983), community leaders (Asian American Task Force on University Admissions, 1985), and scholars (Sue, 1985) who researched the matter found that although Asian American applications to these institutions have increased substantially since 1983, the number of Asian American students admitted by most of them had remained about the same or decreased. Furthermore, they found that the admissions rate for Asian American students was anywhere from 65 to 85 percent of the rate for White students. Yet, the combined SAT scores of the admitted Asian American students were found to be as much as 112 points higher than those of the White student admittees (Bunzel and Au, 1987).

It has been argued that since Asian Americans constitute 2.9 percent of the total U.S. population, they should be considered overrepresented and their enrollment curtailed if their proportion of the student enrollment in an institution substantially exceeds this percentage (East-West, 1985; Alleyne, 1987). Such a position presumes that affirmative action was instituted merely to maintain "ethnic balance"; when, in fact, it was actually implemented to overcome the effects of historic discrimination against certain groups in our society. These effects were often clearly manifested by such observable outcomes as the underrepresentation of minorities in higher education. It was convenient and practical, therefore, to gauge the effectiveness of affirmative action efforts by determining the extent to which the proportion of minorities in academic institutions was increasing; i.e., the extent to which ethnic balance was being achieved.

However, when the enrollment proportion for a given minority group reaches or exceeds their proportion in the general population, it may be presumed in some, but not all, cases that parity has been reached and affirmative action efforts are no longer needed for that group. At this point, it would seem reasonable to adopt a "color blind" admissions policy and admit both whites and members of that minority group on the same basis. Any other policy would move us backward to the 1920s when admission quotas were applied to Jewish students, presumably for the sake of ethnic balance (Hechinger, 1987). If such an admissions policy were reinstituted and applied to all overrepresented groups, quotas should be established not only for Asian Americans, but also for Jewish people and other White ethnic groups who may also be overrepresented. Such a policy would be regressive and repugnant and should surely be rejected by institutions of higher education.

These admissions issues should be addressed objectively and fairly and with some urgency by institutions of higher education. As the projections presented earlier indicate, Asian American student enrollments in higher education could nearly double over the next 10 years and constitute as much as 10 percent of the total college student population. Although this would still be a small fraction of the total college student population, Asian Americans could foreseeably constitute as much as 25-40 percent of the enrollment in many institutions. Consequently, the controversy over Asian American admissions could become even more heated and acrimonious in the absence of well-reasoned, equitable, and clearly articulated policies by institutions of higher education.

Academic Development and Achievement

Are Asian American students being adequately educated in institutions of higher education? How do their retention and graduation rates compare with those of other students? Are they appropriately represented in all fields of study? Do they need help in their academic development in any area? I will attempt to answer these questions by reviewing the available data and research on the academic development and achievement of Asian American students.

If we look only at the statistical data on Asian Americans in higher education, we would have to conclude that Asian Americans have been well served by institutions of higher education. During the 1980-81 academic year, when Asian Americans comprised 1.5 percent of the total population,

2.0 percent of all bachelor's degrees conferred by institutions of higher education were earned by Asian Americans (Vetter and Babco, 1984). In 1990, when Asian Americans comprised 2.9 percent of the total population, they comprised about 4.1 percent of the total enrollment in higher education (*The Chronicle of Higher Education Almanac*, 1993). Moreover, the 1990 census showed that the percentage of Asian Americans who had completed four or more years of college was almost twice that of Whites (U.S. Bureau of the Census, 1993).

Given these statistics, it should hardly be surprising that Asian American college students also have very high persistence rates. The High School and Beyond Survey (Peng, 1985) showed that the persistence of Asian American community college students in 1982, two years after they had graduated from high school, was 70 percent and that of Asian American students in four-year institutions was 86 percent. Clearly, Asian Americans are doing very well in terms of their participation, persistence, and completion rates in higher education. In fact, their rates are higher than those of any other racial or ethnic group.

Despite these highly favorable statistics, the academic development of Asian American students is seriously deficient in at least one major respect. There is clear evidence that the verbal/linguistic skills of Asian American students are underdeveloped not only among immigrant students but among U.S.-born students as well. As I have already discussed, on standardized tests, Asian American students score substantially below White students in verbal ability. In addition, the results of a number of studies, which have been summarized by Hsia (1988), show that the writing skills of Asian American students at both the high school and college levels are substantially below those of their White peers. After analyzing the research on Asian American high school students, Hsia arrived at the following cogent assessment:

> In order to optimize their chances for admission and financial aid, Asian American students concentrate on high-level courses in mathematics and sciences and take fewer courses than their classmates in English and social studies. This risk-adverse strategy is successful in keeping average rank in class high, at the cost of limiting opportunities to improve crucial reading, writing, and speaking abilities. This dilemma is one that needs to be confronted together by teachers, the Asian American students, and their parents. New curricula and innovative teaching and learning approaches need to be developed and tested to help "English not best language" Asian Americans master the multiple modes of communication skills necessary for life in the United States.

Hsia arrived at basically the same assessment of Asian American college students as well, especially those who are recent immigrants. She observed that the "contrast between Asian Americans' achievement in quantitative fields and their avoidance of and difficulties with fields that demand well developed verbal skills is stark among recent immigrants and still noticeable after several generations among the native born."

What can be done to help Asian American students develop their verbal/linguistic skills? A few programs for this purpose have been developed at institutions in different parts of the country (Tsuchida, 1982; Hsia, 1988). These programs appear to have been quite effective in helping Asian American students, including recent immigrants, improve their writing and speaking abilities. However, only a minuscule number of Asian American students are being helped by such programs. The vast majority of students who need this help are not receiving it. Most academic institutions have largely ignored the problem, and should be making much greater efforts to assist Asian American students in this critical area. Unless Asian Americans develop these essential skills in college, they are not likely to acquire them later on and will be at a serious disadvantage in pursuing their professional careers.

The relatively weak verbal skills of Asian American students and their relatively strong quantitative skills are reflected in the major fields of study they have pursued. The bachelor's degrees awarded to Asian American students in 1980-81 have been identified by survey data collected by the U.S. Department of Education (Vetter and Babco, 1984). The most popular field of study for both Asian American students and students in general was business/management. About one-fifth of the Asian American students and students in general earned bachelor's degrees in this major field of study. The next most popular field of study for Asian American students was engineering. Over 16 percent of the Asian American students earned degrees in this major field of study, compared with 8 percent of students in general. Education, the second most popular field of study for students in general, was pursued by nearly 12 percent of all students; however, less than 4 percent of the Asian American students pursued this field. In fact, paradoxically, given their strong emphasis on education, Asian Americans are quite underrepresented in the teaching profession, comprising less than 1 percent of all elementary and secondary school teachers in 1980 (Vetter and Babco, 1984).

The third most popular field of study for both Asian American students and students in general was social sciences, which was pursued by 8.8 percent of the Asian American students and 10.8 percent of all students. The fourth and fifth most popular fields of study for Asian American students were the biological sciences and the health professions, respectively. A higher proportion of Asian American students than students in general pursued degrees in the biological sciences, computer/information sciences, and mathematics;

while a lower proportion pursued degrees in letters and education. For other fields of study, the proportions of Asian American students and students in general pursuing these fields were not significantly different.

These data indicate that 51 percent of the Asian American students pursued bachelor's degrees in biological sciences, business/management, computer/information sciences, engineering, and mathematics; compared with 37 percent of all students. On the other hand, only 8.2 percent of the Asian American students pursued bachelor's degrees in communications, education, and letters; compared with 19.2 percent of all students. While these data support the common view that Asian Americans tend to major in the science/math-based fields and to shun fields that require well developed verbal/linguistic skills, such as the humanities, they also indicate that Asian Americans pursue a far more diverse range of majors than generally thought. For example, the proportions of Asian American students pursuing degrees in the fine and applied arts, psychology, and the social sciences are comparable to those of all students, a finding that may be somewhat surprising to many.

Nevertheless, the underdevelopment of their verbal/ linguistic skills, along with parental pressure and perceptions of where the best jobs will be, undoubtedly provide much of the explanation of why so many Asian American students major in the science/math-based fields. To enable Asian American students to pursue a wider range of career options, academic institutions should not only help Asian American students develop their verbal/linguistic skills, but also help them broaden their academic interests.

Curricular and Instructional Issues

What changes are needed in the college curriculum to respond to the increasing diversity of higher education? More specifically, what changes are needed to respond to the needs of Asian American students? Are traditional instructional practices effective in developing the full learning potential of Asian American students? The research in this area is mostly descriptive or conceptual in nature, but it will be useful to review to frame the relevant issues.

In view of the growing diversity of the student population in higher education, the need for curricular reform has never been greater. The situation was described well by Charles Muscatine of the University of California at Berkeley, who chaired the committee that produced the well-known Muscatine Report in the 1960s:

> One of the defects of our system is that it was originally designed for an ethnic elite and it still in many ways teaches assimilation into the White Male Anglo-Saxon Protestant culture. This culture has superb attributes, and many a generation of immigrants has been successfully drawn by

education into its fold. But it is far from perfect, and critical scrutiny of it from a variety of minority viewpoints has already brought about deep changes in our view of WASP civilization and of "Western Culture" generally. . . . Our axiom should be that minority students in many ways have the problems of traditional students—only more so. Addressing ourselves to them, making the curriculum for them, will be making a better curriculum for all (Muscatine, 1985).

Thus, in redesigning the college curriculum to respond to the changing demographics, the incorporation of minority viewpoints—of multicultural perspectives—becomes quite essential. Of course, most institutions have established ethnic studies departments or programs and offer specialized courses on minority groups through these units. On a few campuses, ethnic studies courses may even fulfill General Education requirements. While ethnic studies have contributed significantly in redressing the imbalance in the curriculum and should continue to be supported and maintained, they have not, for the most part, penetrated into the heart of the college curriculum (Endo, 1973; Liu, 1989).

This heart—the liberal arts core which includes the traditional disciplines in the arts, the humanities, and the sciences—continues to reflect, as noted by Muscatine, the perspective of WASP culture. While feminist perspectives have made some inroads into this core in recent years, the dominance of the WASP male perspective largely remains.

The incorporation of minority viewpoints should not simply be an additive process in which the contributions of minorities and their experiences as victims of oppression are merely added to the curriculum. It should also lead to the development of alternative conceptual frameworks that may significantly restructure a discipline or fundamentally alter the conventional interpretations in a field.

The point should also be made, however, that a truly multicultural perspective would include the viewpoints of women and White ethnic groups, as well as minorities. As I have discussed elsewhere (Suzuki, 1984), if we wish to fully understand the nature of our society, we must study the interrelationships between all groups in society—minorities, women, White ethnics, and, perhaps most importantly, the dominant WASP males. All of these interrelationships are influenced by the social structure and the culture of the society as a whole.

In addition to these curricular changes, institutions of higher education should also examine instructional practices. The standard lecture approach to teaching may have worked with the more selective group of students enrolled in higher education 30 years ago (and even that conjecture is open to question), but it is unlikely to be effective for the increasingly diverse student population entering our institutions now and in the future. For example, many Asian American students are reticent to respond to questions (if, indeed, any are asked) or engage in class discussions without special encouragement. Alternatives to the lecture approach, such as small group discussions, are more likely to be effective with these, as well as other, culturally different students.

More generally, institutions of higher education need to pay much greater attention to improving the quality of instruction for all students by gaining much more knowledge about the teaching and learning process in higher education. In far too many institutions, faculty have been rewarded primarily for their research and publications, while scant attention is paid to their effectiveness as teachers. They should also be equally rewarded for achieving excellence as teachers and encouraged to conduct research into the teaching and learning process in their particular disciplines. Unless we learn far more about this process, efforts to educate the increasing numbers of minority students who will be entering higher education may end in failure.

Socio-Psychological Environment

What psychological problems do Asian American students face in higher education? How serious are these problems and what can academic institutions do to address them? What is the nature of the social environment on campuses and how has it affected Asian Americans? To address the first two questions, I will review the considerable body of psychological research on Asian college students. Very little research exists to address the third question, but I will try to reach some preliminary conclusions based on descriptive reports and surveys.

A good deal of the psychological research on Asian Americans has been summarized by Sue and Morishima (1982). As they have noted, the vast majority of this research has been conducted on Chinese and Japanese college students, with a few of the earliest studies going back to the 1950s. Most of the studies have focused on the personality characteristics of Chinese and Japanese Americans. In general, these studies have shown that in comparison to whites, Chinese and Japanese "exhibit greater deference, abasement, and external locus of control and show less dominance, aggression, preference for ambiguity, and autonomy" (Sue and Morishima, 1982).

A number of the studies also examined the cultural and identity conflicts being experienced by Asian American college students and found that such conflicts have had serious adverse effects on the self-esteem and socioemotional adjustment of these students. Many of these students, especially recent immigrants, were found to be experiencing severe psychological stress and alienation. Recent immigrants, who have limited English proficiency and must study longer hours, were found to be more anxious, lonely, and isolated than other students. As a consequence, the academic performance of many of these students was detrimentally affected—sometimes to such an extent that they were forced to drop out of school (Sue and Sue, 1971; Sue and Frank, 1973; Sue and Zane, 1985).

These psychological problems have been exacerbated by incidents of racial harassment and even violence against Asian American students on several campuses across the country. Since 1982, there have been numerous reports of shootings, killings, physical assaults, widespread vandalism, and racial slurs and signs—all incidents in which the victims and targets were Asian Americans. Other minority groups have had similar experiences. The marked increase in such incidents, many of which have occurred on college campuses, have prompted investigations by the U.S. Commission on Civil Rights and the California Attorney General (U.S. Commission on Civil Rights, 1986; Attorney General's Asian/Pacific Advisory Committee, 1988).

As a number of recent news articles have reported, there is growing concern by Asian American students about many campus incidents that are not overt, blatant acts of racism, but are covert in form and, therefore, more difficult to substantiate and combat. These more subtle forms of discrimination can include such incidents as derogatory remarks by instructors about the limited English proficiency of Asian American immigrant students, subtly racist statements about Asian Americans by both instructors and students, or expressions of resentment by other students toward the achievement orientation of Asian American students. Such incidents can inflict serious psychological damage on Asian American students, affecting their social adjustment to campus as well as their academic performance. On some campuses, Asian American students have formed organizations to combat these, as well as more overt, forms of discrimination. African American and Hispanic students on many college campuses have also been targets of such discrimination (Greene, 1987; Farrell, 1988).

Institutions of higher education should address these serious and disturbing problems directly and immediately through the leadership of their top executive officers. Among other efforts, programs in cross-cultural counseling should be instituted, many more Asian American counselors should be hired, and the racial awareness and sensitivity of the entire campus should be raised through workshops, conferences, and staff training programs. Ultimately, the rising tide of racism can only be combated if students, faculty, and administrators are appropriately sensitized and spurred to take effective action (Loo and Rolison, 1986).

Hiring and Promotion Issues

Are Asian American faculty and administrators equitably represented in institutions of higher education? How do their tenure and promotion rates and salaries compare with those of other groups? Should they continue to be a protected class under federal affirmative action regulations? If so, are adequate affirmative action efforts being taken on their behalf? To address these questions, I shall review a number of studies and surveys on the hiring and promotion of Asian Americans in higher education.

According to a 1981 survey, there were 14,381 Asian American faculty and 1,207 Asian American administrators in institutions of higher education, constituting 3.1 percent and 1.0 percent, respectively, of the totals in these categories (Wilson and Melendez, 1985). These gross statistics make it appear that Asian Americans were adequately represented, if not overrepresented, among faculty in higher education. On the other hand, they appear to have been underrepresented among higher education administrators.

However, as often is the case for Asian Americans, the situation is far more complex than it may seem. In a detailed analysis of data on the status of Asian American faculty and administrators in higher education, Hsia (1988) found that Asian American faculty were more likely to be in nonteaching, nontenure track positions. They also tended to be concentrated in departments of engineering, physical sciences, and mathematics and were much less likely to be in the social sciences and humanities, except for Asian American studies and Asian languages. Despite having stronger academic credentials and more scholarly publications, they were paid less than both their White and African American counterparts. There is also considerable evidence that they have greater difficulty gaining tenure and promotion.

These findings strongly suggest that although Asian American faculty have gained access to academic institutions, they still have not achieved equity or parity. They also indicate that Asian American faculty are still underrepresented in the social sciences and humanities. Moreover, as in the case of students, faculty from certain Asian American groups, such as the Southeast Asians and Filipinos, are very likely underrepresented. Whether this is true or not cannot presently be determined because of the aggregation of data on Asian faculty.

Even among those Asian American groups that are well represented, such as the Japanese and Chinese, native-born Asian Americans are still underrepresented on the faculties of most college campuses. A 1979 survey showed that only 10 percent of the Asian American faculty in higher education were native born; the rest were foreign born (Maxfield, 1981). In addition, female faculty appear to be underrepresented among all Asian American groups. Affirmative action efforts to recruit these particular Asian

American groups are clearly needed, but have rarely been undertaken by institutions of higher education.

Finally, as mentioned earlier, Asian American administrators in higher education are still substantially underrepresented. Although Asian Americans comprise over 3 percent of all college faculty, they comprise only 1 percent of all college administrators. Even these few Asian American administrators are more likely to be in lower-level positions, in staff rather than line positions, and in student or administrative affairs rather than academic affairs (Hsia, 1988). Their underrepresentation is especially severe at the higher levels. For example, currently, there are only four Asian Americans who are chief executive officers of four-year institutions of higher education in the United States; and only five Asian Americans are chief academic officers of such institutions. When one considers that there are over 2,000 four-year institutions in the United States, the severity of this underrepresentation becomes very clear.

The results summarized above indicate that Asian American faculty and administrators still face discriminatory barriers in higher education. These barriers are often not recognized because of the apparent "overrepresentation" of Asian Americans and the pervasive influence of the "model minority" stereotype. Academic institutions should become far more sensitive than they have been to the problems of discrimination being encountered by Asian American faculty and administrators and pursue Affirmative Action efforts far more vigorously on their behalf. Such efforts are especially needed to redress the underrepresentation of native-born Asian Americans and Asian American women, both native born and foreign born, on the faculty and the underrepresentation of Asian Americans in general in administrative positions.

Returns on Higher Education

Have Asian Americans received adequate returns on their heavy investments in higher education? Are they really the "model minority" who are supposedly outdoing Whites? Have Asian Americans benefited from the model minority image promoted by the media? These questions will be addressed by reviewing a large body of research on the socioeconomic status of Asian Americans.

For the past two decades, Asian Americans have been touted by the media as the model minority who have enjoyed extraordinary success in American society despite their long history as an oppressed racial minority (e.g., Peterson, 1966; Newsweek, 1971; Los Angeles Times, 1977; Time, 1987). This view of Asian Americans has most recently been backed up by the 1990 U.S. Census data which showed that for the four largest Asian American groups—the

Chinese, Filipinos, Japanese, and Asian Indians, who comprised over two-thirds of the total Asian population, both median family and median individual incomes considerably exceeded those of their White counterparts. Moreover, the average years of schooling of these groups were found to exceed that of Whites. Thus, it would appear that Asian Americans have, indeed, been amply rewarded for investing so heavily in education.

However, these results, which are based on gross statistics, are misleading. Since the early 1980s, several researchers have conducted detailed studies into the socioeconomic status of Asian Americans based on the 1980 census data. Using sophisticated statistical techniques, such as regression and multiple classification analyses, these researchers assessed the effects of a number of factors on the earnings of Asian Americans and other ethnic groups. These factors included education, years of work experience, region of residence, age, generation (or native born vs. foreign born), ability to speak English, gender, weeks worked, and occupational status, among others. By statistically holding constant the effect of these factors on income, the researchers could calculate the extent to which a particular group's income was affected by the factor of race alone (Suzuki, 1977; Chun, 1980; Wong, 1982; Nee and Sanders, 1985: Cabezas, Shinagawa, and Kawaguchi, 1986-87; Jiobu, 1988; U.S. Commission on Civil Rights, 1988).

Among the many findings of these studies, the following are probably the most relevant to the present discussion:

- None of the Asian American groups, except the Japanese, had reached income parity with Whites when adjustments were made for the factors listed above.
- Whites consistently gained a substantially higher return on education than any of the Asian American groups; i.e., for same level of education, Whites were more likely to earn more, on the average, than Asian Americans.
- Native-born Asian American men were less likely to be in management positions than their White counterparts and highly-educated native-born Asian American men were earning less—in most cases, substantially less—than similarly qualified White men. One study suggested that although their relatively high levels of education enabled Asian American men to enter high-paying occupations and industries, they may encounter a racial barrier, the so-called glass ceiling, as they try to move upward.

Despite some disparities in the findings of various researchers, the vast majority of them have concluded that as a group, Asian Americans have not yet achieved full equality and participation in American society. The extant studies strongly suggest that they continue to face inequities in income and employment. Although many Asian Americans are well educated and gain relatively easy access to entry-level jobs, they appear to encounter subtle discrimination when they attempt to move up the occupational hierarchy to managerial, administrative, or executive positions (Yu, 1985; Jacobs, 1989).

Furthermore, many Asian Americans still live in poverty today. Overall, except for the Japanese and Filipinos, a larger proportion of Asian American families with school-age children live below the government's poverty line than comparable White families. The poverty rate is exceptionally high for the Chinese in the Chinatowns of New York, Los Angeles, and San Francisco, and for the Southeast Asians in several regions of the country. Government agencies, as well as community agencies such as United Way, have been slow to recognize the existence of this poverty and reluctant to fund Asian American community organizations that have been trying, often desperately, to assist the Asian American poor (Mann, 1988).

Moreover, the statistical data alone cannot tell the whole story. College-educated Asian American immigrants are often unable to obtain jobs commensurate with their education and are forced to make a living by becoming self-employed entrepreneurs (e.g., the Korean "green grocers" of New York), or by taking dead-end menial jobs as clerks, service workers, and operatives. Other college-educated Asian Americans, both foreign born and native born, may be drawing relatively good wages, but find themselves trapped in monotonous, low-level white-collar jobs that stifle their creativity and potential. The income figures of such college-educated workers would certainly not reveal their personal agonies over frustrated ambitions, broken dreams, and suppressed anger (Takaki, 1989).

In view of the widespread promotion of the model minority image of Asian Americans, most institutions of higher education have undoubtedly assumed the image is true, despite the foregoing evidence to the contrary. While the extent to which this image has influenced higher education policies and programs would be impossible to determine, most institutions of higher education seem to have the perception that Asian Americans are, indeed, outdoing Whites and have no serious problems or needs. This prevailing attitude may explain in part why Asian Americans are often excluded from or overlooked in programs designed to serve minorities.

As positive as the model minority image may seem, Asian Americans have suffered significant negative fallout from this stereotype. It has not only allowed institutions to neglect the many real needs of Asian Americans, but has also been used to admonish other minorities to follow the "shining example" set by Asian Americans, thereby pitting Asian Americans against these groups. Therefore, institutional officials should address the concerns of

Asian Americans as objectively and fairly as possible without being influenced by the model minority stereotype. Such consideration should lead academic institutions to develop more equitable and effective policies and programs and to do a better job of meeting the real needs of Asian Americans.

FUTURE RESEARCH

In this final section, I will first suggest ways by which the research on Asian Americans in higher education may be improved and extended. I will then suggest additional research I believe is needed in each of the areas delineated in the previous section.

General

To improve and extend the research on Asian Americans in higher education, the following suggestions are made for consideration by institutions of higher education, various higher education associations, and federal agencies that collect and/or report higher education data:

1. National surveys, which currently do not do so, should include Asian Americans as one of the specific groups for which data are collected and reported. Frequently, such surveys do not break out data on Asian Americans.
2. Whenever possible and feasible, data should be collected in ways that will allow the data on Asian Americans to be disaggregated. The data should be disaggregated for at least the six largest Asian groups, which are currently the following: Filipino, Chinese, Japanese, Asian Indian, Korean, and Vietnamese.
3. Whenever feasible, efforts should be made to select sufficiently large sample sizes of the various Asian American groups to enable researchers to conduct statistically meaningful analyses.
4. Much of the extant research focuses on the Chinese and Japanese. While research should be continued on these groups, much more research is needed and should be conducted on other Asian American groups, such as the Filipinos, Southeast Asians, Koreans, and Asian Indians.
5. Most of the extant research on Asian Americans in higher education has been based on quantitative survey data. To gain more insight into some of the issues, more qualitative studies should be conducted on smaller sample groups, using such techniques as in-depth interviews and participant observations.

Additional Research

There are numerous gaps in the extant research on Asian Americans in higher education. To fill these gaps, suggestions for additional research, including key research questions, are presented below.

College Preparation

6. Except in the area of verbal/linguistic skills, most Asian American high school students are well prepared for college. What are the important factors that enable them to be so well prepared? Can this information be used to improve the preparation of other minority students? By observing the study habits of Chinese American students at the University of California in Berkeley, Uri Treisman was able to develop strategies to help African American students succeed academically (Watkins, 1989). Further research of this type may also prove to be similarly fruitful.

7. Not all Asian American students are well prepared, however, especially those who are recent immigrants. Many immigrant students, who come from low-income families and have poor English proficiency, become alienated from school, drop out, and join street gangs. What can high schools do to strengthen the precollege social, personal, and academic preparation of these students?

8. In particular, why aren't Asian American high school students developing adequate verbal/linguistic skills? What can the schools do to help Asian American students develop these skills? More in-depth research is needed to shed light on this vexing problem. Pilot programs in the schools need to be started and evaluated to develop effective approaches to teaching these skills to Asian American students.

Access Issues

9. Certain Asian American groups may still be underrepresented on many campuses. What groups are these? Should they be among the targeted groups in campus educational equity programs? What efforts should be made to recruit and retain them?

10. Since studies have shown that the mathematics scores of Asian American students on standardized tests are better predictors of their future success in college than their verbal scores, should appropriate adjustments be made to the results of such tests in evaluating Asian American students for admission? This is a complex and difficult policy issue that deserves further examination.

11. What is a reasonable and equitable admissions policy for institutions in which Asian American students comprise a fraction of the total enrollment exceeding their proportion in the general population? Should

they be consider "overrepresented," or should a "color blind" admissions policy apply to these students? These are policy issues that should be addressed with some dispatch by institutions of higher education.

Academic Development and Achievement

12. How serious is the underdevelopment of the verbal/linguistic skills among Asian American students in higher education? Are there any other areas in which their academic development is deficient? What can academic institutions do to assist Asian American students in overcoming these deficiencies? These questions can probably be best addressed through small-scale, in-depth quantitative studies rather than through survey research.

13. Why does such a disproportionately large percentage of Asian American students pursue majors in the science/math-based fields? How can academic institutions help these students broaden their academic interests? Again, small-scale, in-depth quantitative studies are more likely to provide us with insight into these issues.

14. What is the subjective impact of an Eurocentric curriculum on Asian Americans and other minority students? How can multicultural perspectives be incorporated to improve the college curriculum for all students? Will such a curriculum enhance learning for Asian American and other minority students?

15. Can or should the traditional curriculum be targeted toward meeting the needs of ESL students? Most courses do not recognize differences in writing styles among students, especially ESL students. Linguistic specialists should be enlisted to study ways of teaching ESL that are sensitive to cultural and cognitive differences.

16. Should American history be taught the same way for immigrants as it is for native-born students? How do you help immigrant students learn about American culture, as well as language? The background knowledge of immigrant students may be quite different from that of native-born students, but the college curriculum is designed on the assumption that all students are native born.

17. How effective are the traditional approaches to teaching, especially the lecture approach, for the increasingly diverse college student population? Are there significant differences in the learning styles of various ethnic groups? If so, how should teaching approaches be tailored to these differences? Much more research on the pedagogy of all disciplines should be conducted to address these important questions.

Socio-Psychological Environment

18. Are Asian American students undergoing increased psychological stress as a result of the rise in incidents of racial harassment and violence in recent years? Is this having an adverse effect on their social adjustment and academic performance? Qualitative studies should shed more light on these issues than surveys.

19. Have any institutions developed effective strategies for improving the socio-psychological environment on campus? If so, what are these strategies and will they be effective at other institutions?

Hiring and Promotion Issues

20. Are the concerns of Asian American faculty over tenure, promotion, and salary issues being effectively addressed by campus affirmative action programs? How can we better establish the underrepresentation of certain Asian American groups, such as women, Southeast Asians, and native-born Asian Americans? Are these underrepresented groups being actively recruited through campus affirmative action programs? These issues have often been neglected by academic institutions and should be seriously addressed.

21. Why are Asian American faculty underrepresented in the social sciences and humanities? What can be done to remedy this underrepresentation? This is a complex problem that will doubtlessly require a long-term solution.

22. Why are Asian Americans so severely underrepresented in administrative positions in higher education? What is the nature of the "glass ceiling" that Asian Americans apparently encounter as they try to move upward to the higher levels of administration?

Returns on Higher Education

23. Why have Asian Americans invested so heavily in education despite the relatively weak returns on their investment? Some hypotheses have been proposed to answer this interesting question, but further study is needed.

24. To what extent has the "model minority" image influenced higher education policies toward Asian Americans? Have they been excluded from programs for minorities because of this stereotype? Studies of these questions should be quite revealing and may help academic institutions address the problems and needs of Asian Americans in a more objective and equitable manner.

The list of suggested areas of research presented above is not intended to be comprehensive. They will, however, provide a starting point for the development of a meaningful agenda for further research on Asian Americans in higher education.

CONCLUDING COMMENTS

This review of the issues facing Asian Americans in higher education was certainly not meant to be exhaustive. Limitations of space and time did not permit that. I have tried to cover what I consider to be the most salient issues and research findings. Other authors may have covered additional and/or different issues and cited other studies, depending on what they consider important. Notwithstanding such inevitable differences in viewpoints, I hope that a sufficiently comprehensive overview was provided to stimulate the necessary further thought and discussion needed to develop programs and to conduct future research studies that will be relevant to addressing the problems and meeting the needs of Asian Americans and other minorities in higher education.

REFERENCES

Alleyne, R. 1987. Everyone needs Affirmative Action. Los Angeles Times, February 15: V5.

Arax, M. 1987. Lost in L.A. Los Angeles Times, December 13: 10-16, 42-48.

Asian American Task Force on University Admissions. 1985. Task force report. San Francisco, CA: Asian Inc.

Asians. 1989. In Shaping Higher Education's Future: Demographic Realities and Opportunities, 1990-2000, edited by Arthur Levine and Associates. San Francisco: Jossey-Bass.

Attorney General's Asian/Pacific Advisory Committee. 1988. Final report of the Attorney General's Asian and Pacific Islander advisory committee. Sacramento, CA: Office of the Attorney General.

Bouvier, L. F., and A. J. Agresta. 1985. The fastest growing minority. American Demographics 7 May:31-33, 46.

Butterfield, F. 1986. Why Asians are going to the head of the class. The New York Times, August 3: Education, 18-24.

Bunzel, J. H., and J. K. D. Au. 1987. Diversity or discrimination?—Asian Americans in college. Public Interest Spring: 49-62.

Cabezas, A., L. Shinagawa, and G. Kawaguchi. 1986-87. New inquiries into the socioeconomic status of pilipino Americans in California in 1980. Amerasia Journal 13:1-21.

Chinn, T. ed. 1969. A history of the Chinese in California: A syllabus. San Francisco: Chinese Historical Society of America.

Chronicle of Higher Education Almanac. 1993. August 25: 13.

Chun, K. 1980. The myth of Asian American success and its educational ramifications. IRCD Bulletin 1 & 2: 1-12.

Conroy, H. 1953. The Japanese frontier in Hawaii, 1868–1898. Berkeley: University of California Press.

Curriculum transformation for multicultural education. 1984. Education and Urban Society, special issue edited by J. Goodlad and T. David, (May):294-322.

Daniels, R. 1962. The politics of prejudice: The anti-Japanese movement in California and the struggle for Japanese exclusion. Berkeley: University of California Press.

———. 1971. Concentration camps U.S.A.: Japanese Americans and World War II. New York: Holt.

Endo, R. 1973. Whither ethnic studies: A re-examination of some issues. In Asian Americans: Psychological perspectives, edited by S. Sue and N. Wagner. Palo Alto, CA: Science & Behavior Books.

Farrell, C. S. 1988. Black students seen facing "new racism" on many campuses. Chronicle of Higher Education (January 27):A1, A36-38.

A formula for success. 1984. Newsweek. April 23:77-78.

Gardner, R. W., B. Robey, and P. C. Smith. 1985. Asian Americans: growth, change, and diversity. Population Bulletin 40 (October).

Greene, E. 1987. Asian-Americans find U.S. colleges insensitive, form campus organizations to fight bias. Chronicle of Higher Education (November 18): A1, A38-40.

Hsia, J. 1988. Asian Americans in higher education and at work. Hillsdale, NJ: Lawrence Erlbaum Assoc.

Hassan, T. E. 1986-87. Asian-American admissions: Debating discrimination. College Board Review (Winter):18-21, 42-46.

Hechinger, F. M. 1987. The trouble with quotas. New York Times, February 10: C1, 10.

Hess, G. R. 1974. The forgotten Asian Americans: The East Indian community in the United States. Pacific Historical Review 43 November: 576-96.

Ho, D., and M. Chin. 1983. Admissions impossible. Bridge (Summer):7-8, 51.

Ichihashi, Y. 1932. Japanese in the United States. New York: Arno Press Reprint, 1969.

Immigration and Naturalization Service. 1986. Statistical yearbook of the Immigration and Naturalization Service. U.S. Department of Commerce.

Jiobu, R. M. 1988. Ethnicity and assimilation. Albany: State University of New York Press.

Jacobs, J. 1989. Asian-Americans are counted only when convenient. San Jose Mercury, August 14:7B.

Japanese in U.S. outdo Horatio Alger. 1977. Los Angeles Times . October 17:I1.

Kim, H. 1986. Koreans in the United States. In Dictionary of Asian American history, edited by H. Kim. New York: Greenwood Press, 13-22.

Kitano, H. H. L. 1969. Japanese Americans: The evolution of a subculture. Englewood Cliffs, NJ: Prentice-Hall.

Lasker, B. 1931. Filipino immigration to continental United States and Hawaii. Chicago: University of Chicago Press.

Liu, J. 1989. Asian American studies and the disciplining of ethnic studies. In Frontiers of Asian American studies, edited by G. M. Nomura, R. Endo, S. H. Sumida, and R. C. Long. Pullman: Washington State University Press.

Loo, C., and G. Rolison. 1986. Alienation of ethnic minority students at a predominantly white university. Journal of Higher Education 57:58-77.

Lyman, S. 1974. Chinese Americans. New York: Random House.

Mann, J. 1988. Koreans have difficulty adapting to U.S., research shows. Los Angeles Times, April 10:I22.

Maxfield, B. D. 1981. Employment of minority Ph.D.'s: Changes over time . Washington, DC: National Academy of Sciences.

Melendy, H. B. 1977. Asians in America: Filipinos, Koreans, and East Indians. Boston: Twayne Publishers.

Muscatine, C. 1985. Dimensions/challenges: Coherence in a new context. In *Addresses and proceedings of the 61st annual meeting of the Western College Association: Educational coherence in a multicultural society.* Long Beach, CA: The Association.

Nakanishi, D. T., and M. Hirano-Nakanishi. 1983. *The education of Asian and Pacific Americans: Historical perspectives and prescriptions for the future.* Phoenix: Oryx Press.

Nakao, A. 1987. Thorny debate over UC: Too many Asians? *San Francisco Examiner,* May 3:A1, A12

Nee, V. and J. Sanders. 1985. The road to parity: Determinants of the socioeconomic achievement of Asian Americans. *Ethnic and Racial Studies* 28 (January):281-306.

The new whiz kids. 1987. *Time,* August 31, 42-51.

Oxnam, R. B. 1986. Why Asians succeed here. *New York Times Magazine,* November 30, 74-75, 88-89.

Peng, S. S. 1985. Enrollment patterns of Asian American students in postsecondary institutions. Paper presented at the Annual Meeting of the American Educational Research Association, Chicago.

Peng, S. S., W. B. Fetters, and A. J. Kolstad. 1981. *High school and beyond: A national longitudinal study for the 1980s.* Washington, DC: Center for Educational Statistics.

Peterson, W. 1966. Success story, Japanese-American style. *New York Times Magazine,* January 9.

————. 1978. Chinese and Japanese Americans. In *Essays and data on American ethnic groups,* edited by T. Sowell. Washington, DC: Urban Institute.

Ramist, L., and S. Arbeiter. 1984. *Profiles, college-bound seniors, 1982.* New York: College Entrance Examination Board.

Salholz, E. 1987. Do colleges set Asian quotas? *Newsweek,* February 9: 60.

Schwartz, A. J. 1971. The culturally advantaged: A study of Japanese American pupils. *Sociology and Social Research* 55 (April):341-53.

Sigel, I. E. 1972. Developmental theory and preschool education: Issues, problems and implications. In *Early childhood education,* edited by I. J. Gordon. 75th Yearbook. Chicago: National Society for the Study of Education.

Snyder, T. D. 1987. *Digest of education statistics 1987.* Washington, DC: Center for Education Statistics.

Success story: Outwhiting the Whites. 1971. *Newsweek.* June 21:24-25.

Sue, D. W. 1973. Ethnic identity: The impact of two cultures on the psychological development of Asians in America. In *Asian-Americans: Psychological perspectives,* edited by S. Sue and N. N. Wagner. Palo Alto, CA: Science and Behavior Books.

Sue, D. W., and A. C. Frank. 1973. A typological approach to the psychological study of Chinese and Japanese American college males. *Journal of Social Issues* 29 (2): 129-48.

Sue, S. 1985. Asian Americans and educational pursuits: Are the doors beginning to close? *Asian American Psychological Association Journal* (Spring):16-19.

Sue, S., and J. Abe. 1988. *Predictors of academic achievement among Asian American and white students,* College Board Report No. 88-11. New York: College Entrance Examination Board.

Sue, S., and J. K. Morishima. 1982. *The mental health of Asian Americans.* San Francisco: Jossey-Bass.

Sue, S., and D. W. Sue. 1971. Chinese-American personality and mental health. *Amerasia Journal* 1 (July): 36-49.

Sue, S., and N. W. S. Zane. 1985. Academic achievement and socioemotional adjustment among Chinese university students. Journal of Counseling Psychology 32, 4: 570-79.

Sung, B. L. 1977. Gangs in New York's Chinatown. New York: Department of Asian Studies, City University of New York.

Suzuki, B. H. 1977. Education and the socialization of Asian Americans: A revisionist analysis of the "model minority" thesis. Amerasia 4:21-51.

Takaki, R. 1989. Asian newcomers who "get ahead so fast" may be far behind where they started. Los Angeles Times, August 20: B6.

Takeuchi, S. M. 1974. Verbal skills of the Asian American student. ERIC Document No. ED 097 395. Boulder, CO: University of Colorado.

Tsuchida, N. 1982. Support services and academic retention programs for Indochinese students at the University of Minnesota. Alternative Higher Education: The Journal of Nontraditional Studies 6 (Spring):160-71.

UCLA's Asian enrollment declines; Admissions discrimination charged. 1985. East/West. 19, 25: 1.

U.S. Bureau of the Census. 1993. Asian and Pacific Islanders in the United States, 1990 census of population. Supplementary report, 1990 G-3-5. U.S. Department of Commerce. 1992. Summary of social, economic, and housing characteristics, 1990 census of population. Report 1990 CPH-5-1. U.S. Department of Commerce.

U.S. Commission on Civil Rights. 1986. Recent activities against citizens and residents of Asian decent. Clearinghouse Publication No. 88. Washington, DC: Government Printing Office.

————. 1988. The economic status of Americans of Asian decent: An exploratory investigation.

Ueda, R. 1974. The Americanization and education of Japanese Americans. In Cultural pluralism, edited by Edgar G. Epps. Berkeley: McCutchan Publishers.

Vetter, B. M., and E. L. Babco. 1984. Professional women and minorities: A manpower data resource service. 5th edition. Washington, DC: Scientific Manpower Commission.

Watanabe, C. 1973. Self-expression and the Asian American experience. Personnel and Guidance Journal 51 (February):390-96.

Watkins, B. T. 1989. Many campuses now challenging minority students to excel in math and science. Chronicle of Higher Education (June 14):A15-18.

Weglyn, M. 1976. Years of infamy: The untold story of America's concentration camps. New York: William Morrow.

Wilson, R., and S. E. Melendez. 1985. Fourth annual status report on minorities in higher education. Office of Minority Concerns. Washington, DC: American Council on Education.

Wong, M. G. 1982. The cost of being Chinese, Japanese, and Filipino in the United States 1960, 1970, 1976. Pacific Sociological Review 25 (January):59-78.

Young, N. F. 1972. Socialization patterns among the Chinese in Hawaii. Amerasia 1 (February):31-51.

Yu, W. 1985. Asian Americans charge prejudice slows climb to management ranks. Wall Street Journal, September 11: 35.

CHAPTER 15

Assessment in Higher Education and the Preparation of Minority Teachers

Manuel Justiz and Marilyn Kameen

The assessment movement in the United States is the central force of a broader educational reform debate, precipitated in particular by the *Involvement in Learning* report. Accusations of mediocrity were leveled against higher education, as state policy makers called on colleges and universities to become more accountable for the achievement of their students. Representing public demands for accountability, an increasing number of states, either through direct legislation or through actions of statewide coordinating or governing boards, have officially addressed assessment in higher education. Fortunately, most current state initiatives are encouraging institutions to develop assessment methods consistent with their own institutional missions, their instructional settings, and their student types.

Assessment has taken on a variety of faces and meanings. On the positive side, it is a tool used to improve teaching and student learning. It can also refer to procedures generated by department faculty to measure educational achievement and to ensure accountability. On the negative side, it can mean the standardized tests used to determine access to higher education. Standardized tests are as entrenched as ever in college admission and retention procedures. For example, many institutions collect assessment data on students at major transition points in college, such as tests for placement in curricula or developmental programs, entrance tests for admission to teacher education, comprehensive junior-level exams for progression to upper division courses, and competency tests for graduation. But these measures are often used for screening and credentialing. As such, they cannot be compared to show changes in students' intellectual and personal development over time. Further, such measures can become barriers to minority access to higher education, particularly if used as the sole measure of a student's abilities. Rather than assisting students to enhance their possibility of success, this type of assessment can actually prevent them from participating in college at all.

Nowhere have the calls for higher education reform been more evident than in schools and colleges of education, where the drive to improve teacher education has resulted in mandated competency testing of preservice teachers, state specific tests, and national tests for exit and/or certification purposes. Placing a heavy emphasis on standardized tests to assure the public that prospective teachers possess adequate professional knowledge and skills to teach, policy makers in 46 states have adopted teacher testing for initial certification or recertification (Childs and Rudner, 1990). In fact, the number of states that require teachers to pass tests rose by more than 400 percent from 1980 to 1990. Twenty-seven states now use standardized tests for admission to teacher education and 38 states use certification tests. States commonly use commercially available tests rather than designing their own (Childs and Rudner, 1990). And, three-fifths of the member institutions of the Association of Colleges and Schools of Education in State Universities and Land Grant Colleges and Affiliated Private Universities reported that they require various forms of competency testing as part of their teacher education curriculum (Case, Shive, Ingebretson, and Spiegel, 1988).

The rapid growth in teacher competency testing has occurred when there are sharp declines in the minority teacher population, subjecting teacher testing to considerable debate and prompting allegations that some minority teacher candidates who would have been effective in the classroom are being denied access to the profession. And this trend is happening when the teaching profession needs a large number of college graduates, particularly minority graduates, to educate the rapidly increasing minority school-age population. This warning is not to suggest that academic standards should be lowered, but rather that higher education institutions, and particularly teacher education programs, should redesign their assessment efforts to eliminate the negative and unwanted side effects of assessment. To understand why a new approach to assessment must be taken, it is important to first examine the demographic changes occurring in the nation and their implications for educating minority youth.

A DEMOGRAPHIC OVERVIEW

The increasing numbers of minority youth in schools and the dwindling numbers of minority teachers signify a critical problem for the nation's educational system. As Zapata (1988) stated, "A situation where the vast majority of teachers is White and where most students are minority is not ideal for the psychological development of minority students." A vicious cycle is created where minority students, who often lack positive role models and mentors, are less likely to be exposed to challenging educational programs and to do well in school activities, which would facilitate their advancing in the educational system. The demographic indicators show quite clearly that at each level of education, greater proportions of the minority population than of whites are left behind, reflecting an apparent failure of the country's schools and colleges to educate minority students successfully.

MINORITY STUDENTS

Between 1968 and 1986, there was a 16 percent decline in the number of White children enrolled in public schools; whereas African American enrollment increased by 5 percent and Hispanic enrollment rose sharply by 103 percent (Rendon, 1989). In 1986, almost 30 percent of the total school population was minority, with projections that by the year 2000, 38 percent of the school-age youth will represent minority groups (Spellman, 1988).

Minorities already constitute the majority in many school districts. For example, in the 32 largest school districts in the country, 75 percent of the 5 million students are from minority groups, mostly African Americans. These students often attend segregated, inner-city schools characterized by overcrowded classes, inadequate counseling services, inexperienced teachers and inferior instruction, and a greater emphasis on vocational/technical education than on college preparatory curricula (Orfield and Paul, 1987-1988).

Although high school graduation rates for minority students have increased significantly over the last 10 years, their graduation rates are still well below that of White students. More than 50 percent of students in some urban school districts where there are large concentrations of minorities will drop out before graduation. Further, the proportion of minority high school graduates who enroll in college and successfully complete degrees has declined in the last decade, particularly for African Americans and Hispanics, as the gap in participation between Whites and minorities continues to grow.

MINORITIES IN TEACHING

In no state with a large minority population does the percentage of minority teachers come close to the percentage of minority students enrolled in elementary and secondary schools. The minority teacher shortage is especially critical in urban school districts that serve the largest concentration of at-risk students. The Carnegie Task Force on Teaching estimated that 23 percent of each college graduating class would be needed to meet the demand for teachers in the 1990s. Yet, the current increase in the number of college graduates annually wanting to teach is 0.5 percent (Thomas and Hirsch, 1989). Gregory Anrig, president of the Educational Testing Service, predicted that the percentage of minorities in the national teaching force, currently about 12 percent, could be cut in half by the year 2000, especially if there is not a significant change in their pass rates on teacher certification tests (Anrig, 1986).

Dramatic declines in the number of minorities choosing education as a college major and entering the teaching profession are well documented. Academically talented minorities, once limited to teaching as a professional career, are now choosing other occupations that promise greater financial rewards, better working conditions, and more opportunities for advancement. Today African Americans are the least likely segment of the population to choose teaching as a career, with a reported 52 percent decline in education degrees awarded to them for the years 1976 to 1982 ("At Risk," 1986).

Teacher competency testing has exacerbated the shortage of minorities in teaching. As Gifford (1986) stated, disproportionate failure rates of minorities on these tests can discourage minority youth from choosing teaching as a career. If minority youth learn that prospective minority teachers are judged not competent to teach, they may lose confidence in their own abilities to pursue higher education or teaching as a career, reducing even further the representation of minorities in higher education and in the teaching profession.

INADEQUACIES OF STANDARDIZED TESTS FOR SCREENING TEACHER CANDIDATES

Concerns about discriminatory access to higher education and particularly to teacher education, where assessment programs rely heavily on standardized tests have been voiced across the country. A high percentage of minority high school graduates compared to Whites perform poorly on standardized college admission and placement tests. For example, in 1985, 9 percent of the 1.05 million high school seniors taking the SAT were African American and 3 percent were Hispanic. Seventy-three percent of the African American test takers scored below 400 on the verbal portion and 64 percent scored below 400 on the math portion. Of the Hispanic students who took the SAT, 59 percent scored below 400 on the verbal and 45 percent scored below 400 on math. In contrast, 31 percent of the White students scored below 400 on verbal and 22 percent scored below 400 on the math portion of the SAT (Ramist and Arbeiter, 1986). As Haberman (1988) reported, even though the SAT scores for African Americans rose between 1975 and 1986, they have not yet narrowed the gap with Whites. This trend can be observed for Hispanics' performance on the SAT as well.

Standardized tests can also control who enters and remains in the teaching profession. Minorities, who are much more likely than Whites to fail standardized tests for admission to teacher education and for certification are being screened out of teaching at alarmingly high rates. For example, a recent national survey reported the failure of nearly 38,000 minorities on teacher tests in 19 states (Fields, 1988). In Florida, where prospective teachers must pass six different competency assessments before becoming certified, five of which are paper-pencil tests, disproportionate numbers of minorities are eliminated from teaching at each point of testing. The situation is most severe for African American students. Smith, Miller, and Joy (1988) reported that only 37 percent of the African American teacher candidates had passed the Florida Teacher Certification Examination in the last seven years. In 1987, 48.7 percent of the Hispanics taking Florida's teacher certification exam passed, while 87.5 percent of White teacher candidates passed the exam (Fields, 1988). In Texas, for 1988-89, 76.3 percent of the Hispanics and 58.6 percent of the African Americans taking the state's certification test passed it on the first attempt compared with 91.6 percent of White and other race teacher candidates who passed the test on the first attempt (Texas Education Agency, 1990). These trends have been observed across the country as states have established testing requirements for initial teacher certification or recertification.

The barriers that prevent even academically capable minorities from performing adequately on standardized assessment instruments are varied and include poor reading and analytical skills due to inadequate prior educational experiences, lack of sophistication about the importance of standardized tests, and poor test-taking skills. A single low test score, which is not necessarily an indicator of achievement or potential, can hurt minority students by labeling them failures. Compounding this problem is the fact that current teacher assessment methods may not adequately measure demonstrated teacher competence, which is observable in the classroom. To date, there is no factual evidence that any of the tests used with preservice or inservice teachers can differentiate between competent and incompetent teachers. While teacher tests may measure the knowledge and skills gained in a teacher education curriculum, no standardized test can accurately measure the full range of instructional skills and human qualities necessary for effective teaching (Madaus and Pullin, 1987; Spellman, 1988).

Policy makers have begun to recognize the inadequacies of a single test to screen candidates for programs and to measure individual capabilities. The NAACP has gone on record to oppose testing as the single criterion for certifying teachers, and it is legally challenging what it claims to be abuse of teacher competency tests (Cole, 1986). The Educational Testing Service (ETS) and National Evaluation Systems (NES) have publicly opposed use of a single test for decision making about admission to teacher education, certification, or recertification of teachers (Educational Testing Service, 1988b; National Evaluation Systems, 1988). Also, ETS and the National Teacher's Exam (NTE) Policy Council refused to allow use of NTE tests for mandatory one-time testing of experienced teachers (Anrig, 1986).

In keeping with the growing recognition that multiple measures are needed to adequately assess teaching abilities, the National Commission on Testing and Policy (1990), an interdisciplinary group supported in part by the Education and Culture Program of the Ford Foundation, issued a call for reform in testing which included the recommendation that "test scores are imperfect measures and should not be used alone to make important decisions about individuals, groups, or institutions; in the allocation of opportunities, individuals' past performance and relevant experience must be considered."

APPROPRIATE EDUCATIONAL RESPONSES

A new approach to assessment in higher education would increase the probability of success of aspiring minority teachers by focusing not only on learning outcomes, but also on the processes for bringing about those outcomes. Teacher education programs in colleges and universities should assume leadership to initiate changes necessary to provide minority college students the educational tools they need to enter the teaching profession. Colleges of education should address two major areas: 1) the development of a comprehensive process for assessing prospective teachers that will provide valid measures of the affective as well as cognitive factors constituting effective teaching and 2) comprehensive learning assistance programs implemented collaboratively with testing companies and educational institutions to help teacher candidates acquire the knowledge and skills they need to be certified and retained in the profession.

COMPREHENSIVE TEACHER ASSESSMENT PROGRAMS

Haberman (1988) posed a question to teacher education institutions, "Are we, in effect, seeking to recruit and admit students who don't need us to teach them about teaching?" Colleges and universities must emphasize teaching and learning, not just judging. This orientation provided the framework for Richardson's description of an adaption process through which higher education institutions could change their cultures to improve the enrollment and achievement outcomes of minority students (Richardson, 1989). A comprehensive approach to teacher assessment would be one aspect of this larger effort to restructure campus learning environments to support minority achievement.

A comprehensive approach to teacher assessment and learning is based on the beliefs that assessment should improve the process of teaching and learning in higher education and that the goal of teacher preparation is to improve teacher competence and to increase not restrict access to the profession. A comprehensive program should increase the probability of success for aspiring minority teachers by providing processes for developing the knowledge and skills covered in the assessment program. Comprehensive assessment of teacher candidates should consist of profiles composed of multiple sources of information collected at different points in the prospective teacher's education. In addition to standardized test scores, these profiles should include essays, interviews, and performance-based assessments that can compensate for the limitations of any single assessment.

Information collected on students entering teacher education should include their abilities, family and educational background, motivation and goals, learning style, financial needs, and other factors that impact learning. Assessment during the student's teacher education program should consist of multiple measures from a variety of situations that yield a profile of cognitive and affective development. Examples of such assessments include writing samples, oral presentations, assessment center exercises, documentation of performance during supervised field experiences, and direct observation by trained observers. Assessments should include criterion-referenced measures that provide information on the knowledge and skills each student has mastered during college. Feedback to students should show specifically what has and has not been learned, and what is needed next to improve.

Two approaches to comprehensive assessment for teacher certification have recently been developed. Beginning in 1993, ETS redesigned the NTE, the most frequently used test for teacher certification nationally. The replacement, called the Praxis Series: Professional Assessment for Beginning Teachers, is a comprehensive teacher assessment process that includes three stages.

The first stage involves diagnostic assessment of basic skills in reading, writing, mathematics, and using computers, and it is gathered very early in the student's undergraduate career. The second stage includes an assessment of subject-matter knowledge and knowledge about teaching and learning, using multiple choice and short answer tests, and conducted at the completion of teacher training. The third stage, perhaps implemented collaboratively with educational institutions and state education agencies, involves assessments of teaching performance, after the individual has had substantial opportunity to practice teaching. A profile consisting of classroom observation, assessment center exercises, and portfolio documentation of teaching accomplishments is being explored.

The assessment program being conducted for national certification is also based on a comprehensive approach. Shulman (1989) proposed an ongoing strategy of teacher assessment that combines the following elements: 1) written examinations of knowledge and reasoning, both multiple choice and open ended; 2) performance assessments in the form of simulation exercises, computer-based problems, and structured interviews; 3) observations of teaching, both direct and via videotape; and 4) documentation through reflective portfolios of classroom work. A program combining portfolio development and subsequent assessment of performance has already been field tested.

COMPREHENSIVE LEARNING ASSISTANCE PROGRAMS

The ability to take standardized tests, rather than the ability to acquire knowledge, leads to a differentiation in test scores between minority and White students. Research has shown that the knowledge and skills assessed in standardized competency tests used for admission to teacher education or for certification are learnable (Gifford, 1986). Several model programs across the country have shown that minorities can learn test-taking skills and the content to be tested (Greer, 1986; Zapata, 1988). Further, both ETS and NES have initiated joint programs with schools/colleges of education and school districts to help minorities prepare for tests (Educational Testing Service, 1988a). The collaboration between Grambling State University and ETS to help faculty develop workshops on the skills Grambling students needed to pass Louisiana's certification test is one example of a successful program for helping minority teacher candidates become certified. Almost 100 percent of Grambling University's students now pass the state's teacher certification test, up from 10 percent in the late 1970s (Fields, 1988).

Colleges of education are in a key position to initiate collaborative and comprehensive learning-assistance programs with testing companies, education agencies, and school districts to help minority teacher candidates become certified. These programs should address the variety of problems that contribute to low scores on standardized tests. At a minimum such programs should include test preparation and review sessions, as well as diagnostic reporting of results and remediation for candidates with deficiencies.

Test preparation sessions should focus on 1) techniques for coping with test anxiety; 2) the development of testwiseness by providing diagnostic, self-paced tutorials and study guides with practice exercises on the skills to be measured, as well as explanations of right and wrong answers and references for further study; and 3) the development of strategies for analyzing information and responding to questions requiring higher level cognitive skills. To prepare minority teacher candidates for teacher certification tests, test review sessions should be offered that clarify the test objectives and build their confidence in test-taking by providing them with information on 1) the development of the tests; 2) the purposes of the tests; 3) the knowledge and skills to be measured; 4) the test format; 5) the time allotted; 6) procedures for reporting results; and 7) the interpretation and use of the results. ETS and the Southern Education Foundation (SEF) have collaborated to provide such comprehensive learning assistance programs in a consortium of eleven colleges and universities in North Carolina. The SEF project focused on improving prospective teachers' performance on the multiple assessments used for admission to teacher education, retention, and certification. Project activities included, for example, test preparation sessions for students and faculty workshops aimed at incorporating testing objectives and test content into the teacher education curriculum.[*]

In the mid-1980s, the Southern Regional Education Board, with financial support from the Fund for the Improvement of Postsecondary Education, also initiated successful collaborative projects with several historically Black colleges and universities to improve their teacher education curricula. Developed as demonstration programs that could serve as models for other teacher education institutions, the projects focused on ways to strengthen the undergraduate curriculum as well as students' academic and test-taking skills so that graduates could meet new state standards for teacher education and certification (Brown and Moses, 1987).

The reporting of test results by testing companies and state education agencies should meet three criteria: 1) results should show the candidate's performance on the criteria measured by the test as well as in relation to other test-takers; 2) diagnostic information about the candidate's strengths and weaknesses should be provided; and 3) strategies for remediating weaknesses should be described. Follow-up sessions should be provided for those who fail

---

[*]For information about the North Carolina Consortium, contact the Southern Education Foundation, 135 Auburn Ave., Second Floor, Atlanta, GA 30303, (404) 523-0001.

teacher assessments to explain the type of assistance available to them to overcome their deficits. Both ETS and NES systematically provide teacher education institutions, test-takers, and sponsoring state education agencies detailed diagnostic and prescriptive reports that help test-takers improve their readiness for the classroom or prepare them to re-take the tests. Further, ETS, through its NTE programs, has sponsored numerous workshops for educators who work with minority students. The curriculum is designed to help college and university staff design remediation programs for students who are not successful on teacher assessments.**

CONCLUSION

Assessment in higher education can be an impediment to preparing minority teachers or it can be a valuable tool for increasing access without compromising academic standards—if the assessment system incorporates multiple sources of information and if it provides for diagnostic feedback, remediation, and peer support. Colleges of education are in key leadership positions to ensure that prospective minority teachers successfully complete their teacher education curricula by designing comprehensive teacher assessment systems coupled with comprehensive learning assistance programs.

REFERENCES

Anrig, G. R. 1986. Teacher education and teacher testing: The rush to mandate. *Phi Delta Kappan* 67: 447-51.

At risk: Pupils and their teachers. 1986. *Education Week* May 14: 28.

Brown, W. C., and D. Moses. 1987. *Strengthening minority students' test-taking skills: Progress report on an SREB project to improve the "pass rate" of students in historically Black colleges and universities on teacher certification and other standardized tests, progress report II.* Atlanta: Southern Regional Education Board.

Case, C. W., R. J. Shive., K. Ingebretson, and V. M. Spiegel. 1988. Minority teacher education: Recruitment and retention methods. *Journal of Teacher Education*, 54-57.

Childs, R. A., and L. M. Rudner. 1990. *State testing of teachers: The 1990 report.* (ERIC Digest No. EDO-TM-90-3. Washington, DC: Office of Educational Research and Improvement.

Cole, B. P. 1986. The Black educator: An endangered species. *Journal of Negro Education* 55, 3:326-34.

Educational Testing Service. 1988a. *Minority students in higher education.* Princeton,NJ: ETS.

**For information on the NTE Workshops, contact Educational Testing Service, Teacher Programs and Services, Princeton, NJ 08541-6051, (609) 921-9000.

Educational Testing Service. 1988b. *Special report on current trends in teacher assessment/ Update on NTE programs.* Research report Nos. CN00650 and 08650-9965. Trenton, NJ: ETS.

Fields, C. M. 1988. Close to 100 percent of Grambling U. students now pass teacher certification examination, up from 10 percent. *The Chronicle of Higher Education,* November 23: A23-A25.

Gifford, B. R. 1986. Excellence and equity in teacher competency testing: A policy perspective. *Journal of Negro Education* 55, 3:251-71.

Greer, R. D. 1986. Revitalizing education programs to meet the challenge of equity and excellence for minorities in teacher education. *Action in Teacher Education* 8, 1:27-30.

Haberman, M. 1988. Proposals for recruiting minority teachers: Promising practices and attractive detours. *Journal of Teacher Education* 39, 4:38-44.

Madaus, G. F., and D. Pullin. 1987. Teacher certification tests: Do they really measure what we need to know. *Phi Delta Kappan* 69, 1:31-37.

National Commission on Testing and Public Policy. 1990. *From gatekeeper to gateway:Transforming testing in America.* Chestnut Hill, MA.

National Evaluation Systems. 1988. *Improving education through certification testing.* Amherst, MA.

Orfield, G., and F. Paul. 1987-1988. Declines in minority access: A tale of five cities. *Educational Record* 68, 1:56-62.

Ramist, L., and S. Arbeiter. 1986. *Profiles, college bound seniors, 1985.* NY: College Entrance Examination Board.

Rendon, L. I. 1989. The lie and the hope: Making higher education a reality for at-risk students. *AAHE Bulletin* 41, 10:4-7.

Richardson, R. C. 1989. *Institutional climate and minority achievement.* Unpublished manuscript, National Center for Postsecondary Governance and Finance, Research Center at Arizona State University.

Shulman, L. S. 1989. The paradox of teacher assessment. In *New directions for teacher assessment, proceedings of the 1988 ETS invitational conference* edited by J. Pfleiderer, pp. 13-27. Princeton, NJ: Educational Testing Service.

Smith, G. P., M. C. Miller, and J. Joy. 1988. A case study of the impact of performance-based testing on the supply of minority teachers. *Journal of Teacher Education* 39, 4:45-53.

Spellman, S. O. 1988. Recruitment of minority teachers: Issues, problems, facts, possible solutions. *Journal of Teacher Education* 39, 4:58-63.

Texas Education Agency. 1990. *Annual report of performance on the examination for the certification of educators in Texas October 1988 through July 1989.* Austin, TX.

Thomas, G. E., and D. J. Hirsch. 1989. Blacks. In *Shaping higher education's future: Demographic realities and opportunities, 1990-2000* edited by A. Levine and Assoc. San Francisco: Jossey-Bass.

Zapata, J. T. 1988. Early identification and recruitment of Hispanic teacher candidates. *Journal of Teacher Education* 39, 1:19-23.

CHAPTER 16

Minorities in Graduate Education: A Need to Regain Lost Momentum

Mark Clark and Hector Garza

Why are increasing numbers of graduate professionals throwing up their hands in despair about minorities in graduate education? In the midst of successful student-recruitment models, increasing minority-student enrollment, and enhanced opportunities for graduate study, why the despair?

At a 1988 national meeting of the American Council on Education (ACE), Robert H. Atwell, ACE president, attributed this particular despair to "a lack of national leadership and a lack of recognition about the real progress that has been made within the last 25 years." He asserted that the federal administration "has not taken an active role in enforcing civil rights legislation, nor has it promoted equity by spending the necessary funds on education." He further suggested that our own inertia within the academy has led to the downturn of minority participation and graduation rates. In expressing the need for a new momentum, Atwell proposes that "a crucial first step in regaining the momentum is to take a careful look at what we have done, what has worked, and, most importantly, what obstacles still remain in our paths" (Atwell, 1988).

Following Atwell's suggestions for assessing the current status of minorities in graduate education, we begin this chapter by providing enrollment and degree attainment data. Using these data as a foundation, we proceed with a presentation about the impact of student- and institutional-related characteristics on minority graduate enrollment and degree attainment. Next, we call for more effective personal and institutional leadership by graduate deans to regain the momentum that has been lost during the last decade. Finally, we present exemplary programs and offer recommendations for improving current circumstances.

It is our opinion that the graduate dean and graduate education holds a unique position relative to improving the current situation of minorities in higher education. The graduate dean straddles both the student service and academic components of the university. Graduate education straddles educational preparation and entry into the professional workplace. It also holds the "key" to upward professional mobility. With this underlying tenant in mind we move into the remainder of this chapter.

SOME FACTS AND INTERPRETATION

From the outset it is important to note that national data of the sort present in this chapter are somewhat limited by their very nature. Nonreport of data, self-reported ethnicity, cross-sectional rather than longitudinal reporting, lack of consistent definition of "graduate" or "professional" degree, and different respondents in different reporting years are just a few of the "problems" that must be acknowledged when using this type of data. However, even with the noted limitations, trends reported here seem typically constant over time and "valid."

Mortenson (1991), in a recent report on the status of minorities in higher education, goes back as far as the 1940s to uncover trends. Based on several variables, he concludes:

> . . . the goal of equity of higher educational opportunity for all Americans that was partly achieved by the second half of the 1970s has been largely lost for blacks, Mexican-Americans, and those from low-income backgrounds during the 1980s.

Carter and Wilson (1991) found that although minority undergraduate-degree attainment increased between 1976 and 1989, this change was due primarily to increased Asian American participation (up 2.6 percent). During this time period, the percentage of degrees awarded to African Americans declined slightly (6.4 percent to 5.7 percent), Native American degrees remained constant (0.4 percent), and degrees awarded to Hispanics increased slightly (2.0 percent to 2.9 percent). (See Table 16-1.) They also reported that the percentage of minority-degree attainment decreases as students move higher in the educational hierarchy. Brown (1987) also notes a similar pattern of decreasing percentage of minority participation/enrollment (Asian American excepted) as students move higher into the educational hierarchy.

TABLE 16.1

PERCENTAGE OF DEGREE ATTAINMENT BY EDUCATIONAL LEVEL

	Associate's		Bachelor's		Master's		+Doctorate	
	1976	1989	1976	1989	1976	1989	1979	1989
African American		8.0	6.4	5.7	6.6	4.6	3.4	2.4
American Indian		0.8	0.4	0.4	0.3	0.4	0.3	0.3
Asian American		2.9	1.2	3.8	1.3	3.5	1.4	1.8
Hispanic		4.7	2.0	2.9	1.7	2.4	1.5	1.7
White		82.1	88.4	84.5	85.0	78.2	70.1	60.3
Non Resident		1.5	1.6	2.7	5.2	11.0	15.0	23.9
TOTAL		**100.0**	**100.0**	**100.0**	**100.0**	**100.0**	**92.4**	**90.4**

*Data NOT recorded for Associates Degree in 1976
+Data presented for 1979, non report of ethnicity and citizenship
accounts for subgroup percentages not equal to 100%
This table derived from data presented in Carter and Wilson (1991)

Why the high attrition rate as minorities pursue advanced education? Data on the percent of conferred bachelor's degrees by race/ethnic group in the United States, collected by the National Center for Educational Statistics (NCES) and reported by Brown (1987), indicate that U.S. minorities earned a considerably small portion of the total bachelor's degrees awarded in 1984: American Indian 0.43 percent; Asian American 2.7 percent; Hispanic 2.9 percent; African American 5.9 percent; and white 88.1 percent. Thus, the available pool of perspective minority graduate students remains small. Additionally, Brown (1987) noted that while non-Asian minorities continue to be concentrated in fields such as social/behavioral sciences and education, their undergraduate degree-attainment rates in these fields declined markedly between 1978-84. She too concludes that a dwindling minority degree attainment at the undergraduate level in part explains their declining enrollment at the graduate level. Brown further notes that while there has been a modest increase in minority GRE test-takers since 1975, their proportional representation remains relatively small; therefore, declines in the numbers of African American and Hispanic students in the GRE pool, particularly since 1981, should be of grave concern to the graduate education community.

According to Nettles (1987) and Brown (1987), the issue of minority underrepresentation in graduate education is more complex than low representation of minorities in the GRE pool. These researchers point to other factors that deter students of color from enrolling in graduate programs. These factors are the following: mean performance scores among minorities (especially African American and Hispanic) are substantially lower than others; minority students tend to earn lower grades at the undergraduate level; they have less interaction with undergraduate faculty; and admission standards to public colleges and universities are rising. All of these factors point to further erosion of the minority applicant pool for graduate study.

It should be noted, however, that a recent report by the Council of Graduate Schools (Syverson and Welch, 1991) indicates that enrollments at the graduate level are up for all minority groups. (See Table 16-2.) Similarly, Brown (1987) does noted a slight minority percentage enrollment increase at the master's and professional levels in the mid-1980s. These enrollment increases are not yet reflected in degree attainment. The reported CGS graduate enrollment increases include both master's and doctoral levels. These enrollment increases may indicate that percentage changes of degree attainment for minority groups may be on the rebound. A careful watch of these figures should be conducted over the next few years to ascertain if the current enrollment increases develop into granted degrees.

Assuming these enrollment increases do come to fruition as attained degrees, colleges and universities should not be too satisfied, since we still would have a long way to go to approximate graduate degree attainment with respective percentages of each ethnic group in the society as a whole. Graduate degrees are critical in professional and business advancement and the crucial link in developing faculty to work with future generations. If people of color are not represented in current enrollments and graduation rates at the graduate level, both advancement of the representative group is hindered and more general national development is slowed since the collective talents of these groups represent a growing percentage of American society (American Council on Education, 1988).

SOME OBSERVATIONS AND INTERPRETATION

Many minority students are often first-generation college-goers who tend to set and achieve educational and career goals in small increments. Lack of role models within their families provides no precedent for attaining advanced degrees.

Many students, in general, rely on faulty assumptions that impede their continuing education, like believing that one degree is all they need to be

TABLE 16-2

Trends in Graduate Enrollment by Ethnicity and Sex, 1986-1989 (U.S. Citizens Only)

Institution Type	1986	1987	1988	1989	% Change 1986-87	1987-88	1988-89	1986-89
Total U.S. Enrollment								
	572,899	570,533	583,169	591,508	-0%	2%	1%	3%
Men	236,620	233,435	238,950	240,658	-1%	2%	1%	2%
Women	262,856	261,300	268,482	275,630	-1%	3%	3%	5%
American Indian	2,577	2,329	2,547	2,613	-10%	9%	3%	1%
Men	942	897	971	942	-5%	8%	-3%	0%
Women	1,286	1,088	1,214	1,300	-15%	12%	7%	1%
Asian American	18,102	18,159	20,401	21,922	0%	12%	7%	21%
Men	9,350	8,951	10,614	11,503	-4%	19%	8%	23%
Women	6,249	6,074	6,955	7,726	-3%	15%	11%	24%
African American	26,556	26,718	28,907	30,065	1%	8%	4%	13%
Men	8,622	8,666	9,266	9,596	1%	7%	4%	11%
Women	14,172	14,236	15,808	16,759	0%	11%	6%	18%
Hispanic	18,665	18,847	20,111	21,294	1%	7%	6%	14%
Men	6,370	6,262	6,843	7,311	-2%	9%	7%	15%
Women	6,752	6,728	7,431	8,301	-0%	10%	12%	23%
White	506,999	504,480	511,203	515,614	-0%	1%	1%	2%
Men	211,336	208,659	211,256	211,306	-1%	1%	0%	-0%
Women	234,397	233,174	237,074	241,544	-1%	2%	2%	3%

NOTE: This table is based on the responses of institutions that provided ethnicity data for the years 1986 through 1989. Because not all insitutions responded to all items, detail variables may not sum to total.

Source: CGS/GRE Survey of Graduate Enrollment

successful in the labor market. Moreover, many undergraduate students, especially minorities, do not effectively use their university's career planning services and thus remain poorly informed about the credentials required for specific careers. Colleges and universities often compound the problem by not offering outreach services that explain to minority students the facts and benefits of graduate study.

For first-generation college-going students the bachelor's degree represents a milestone that surpasses any other in their family and thus temporarily satisfies their need for higher education. The reality of employment-market demands and infrequent on-the-job-promotions sets in only later.

Because minorities don't often aim for graduate study, they don't plan for it during their undergraduate experience. Research studies have found that the longer students postpone graduate study, the harder it is for them to return to school. In a 1987 study, Nettles found that Hispanic students average five years between undergraduate and graduate school as opposed to nine years for African Americans.

Our many years of experience in working with minority students have convinced us that they often operate with very limited information about graduate education. For example, many minority students believe that admission to graduate schools is next to impossible, as all graduate programs require the GRE as a primary admissions criteria.

Another misconception on the part of many minority students relates to financing graduate study: They believe that there is no financial assistance for them, and, therefore, they must find employment immediately after the bachelor's degree to earn enough money for graduate school. Many do not know that, in most cases, a graduate teaching or research assistantship pays for tuition and provides a modest stipend. They also do not know that other institutional, federal, and private financial aid can, in some instances, approximate the entry-level salary that they may received in a bachelor's-degree job. There are also students who think that *all* employers have a tuition-reimbursement program that will enable them to pursue graduate study and thus employment is necessary right after undergraduate school.

In some disciplines, such as a teacher education, many students believe that an advanced degree can actually serve as a disadvantage, in that school districts prefer to hire less-credentialed applicants at a lower salary.

In preparing outreach/intervention programs and student-recruitment strategies, graduate school professionals must understand these characteristics and misconceptions to improve the participation rates of U.S. minorities in graduate education. Similarly, Nettles (1990 and 1987) notes the necessity of understanding the complexities and paradoxes of socioeconomic and educational backgrounds of minority participants in the graduate experience.

THE DEAN'S ROLE

The role of graduate deans often provides excellent opportunities to interact, observe, and provide decanal leadership in virtually all areas of the academic enterprise. In an address to the Association of Graduate Schools, Dr. Gillian Lindt, former president of the Association of Graduate Schools and former dean of the Graduate School at Columbia University, noted that providing effective leadership in graduate school not only requires possessing the requisite management skills to "manage the store" but also includes the ability to creatively envision and articulate the specific mission of the graduate enterprise within the institution and to society at large. She further asserted that, beyond the managing role, graduate deans have the chance to be "movers and shakers" within their institutions, provided they maintain a "sense of purpose of creativity." Lindt (1990) defines the graduate dean as a "diplomat . . . furthering the goals of the graduate school" and as a "missionary" assuming an advocacy role, "whether it is advocacy in terms of rational and highly pragmatic assessments of means and ends, or whether it takes the form of a more emotional appeal and articulation of shared goals and aspirations of scholarship, research, and teaching that are at the heart of the institutions we represent." We agree that "mover and shaker," "advocate," "diplomat," and "missionary" are all required roles for providing effective leadership in minority affairs at the graduate level.

The increased national attention to diversity issues is undoubtedly placing increased demands on graduate schools and, as a result, effecting the role of the graduate dean. Because of the nature of graduate education and the power vested in their position, graduate deans can, and should, act as movers and shakers, especially regarding access and degree attainment for minorities. This type of decanal leadership helps to distinguish successful institutions from those with limited success in recruiting and graduating persons of color with advanced degrees.

What must graduate deans do to become a mover and shaker in the area of minority affairs? First the graduate deans should recognize the importance of their role in minority affairs; they should realize that while others (including assistant/associate deans and support staff) are critical to the success of minority affairs in graduate school, it is the deans who must demonstrate exemplary leadership since it is the deans who are most visible as committed or not to minority affairs.

Additionally, graduate deans should understand the centrality of their role in enhancing the minority presence in graduate education and the benefits of that presence to their institution and the country as a whole. Given current demographic trends, access and degree attainment for people of color can no longer be perceived or addressed as a "privilege" rather than a "right," nor can patronizing terms be used that portray institutions as social democratizers sacrificing quality for diversity. The reality is that our country's economic position is at stake and will increasingly require a populace educated beyond the bachelor's degree. Now, more than ever, institutions of higher learning must do their part to develop all our human resources as a means of solving complex domestic problems and maintaining our position within international markets.

Our experience in graduate-education administration, and many years of networking with graduate deans throughout the country, has exposed us to a wide range of discussions on providing decanal leadership in minority affairs. While graduate deans do admit that minority affairs are part of their role, relatively few seem to be demonstrating *personal* leadership in minority-specific endeavors. This fact is evidenced by the current downward trend in minority graduate-student enrollments and graduation rates. While decanal leadership alone cannot guarantee success in graduate minority affairs, stronger and more effective leadership *can* lessen regressive trends in minority enrollment and graduation.

There is no doubt that the role of the graduate dean has been changing and that the current role demands more time and energy than any one individual has. Thus, responsibilities are delegated, and minority concerns are frequently relegated to lower levels in the administrative structure—often to a minority professional at the assistant, associate, or director level. While some argue that minority graduate-school professionals are better prepared to administratively manage minority agendas, there are relatively few minorities serving as graduate-school professionals. Moreover, their rank is usually assistant or associate dean.

We agree that the active involvement of minority administrators in graduate school is key to the success of a minority affairs program. Yet we also believe that their contributions should be *complementary* to the work of all other graduate-school professionals, including full graduate deans. In other words, every graduate-school professional should be responsible and accountable for providing substantive leadership in minority affairs.

THE INSTITUTION'S ROLE

On university campuses, minority representation is usually discussed in terms of either the undergraduate student population or the faculty/staff ranks. Minority underrepresentation in graduate education gets attention typically when the limited supply of ethnic minorities for faculty positions is discussed. While this is a problem that some have characterized as a major crisis in American higher education, very few institutions go beyond acknowledging the problem. The academy must surely recognize that the crisis of minority faculty underrepresentation stems from and is perpetuated by low levels of minority graduate-student enrollments and completion rates. This concept is fairly simple to understand, and the benefits of rectifying the problem are clear, yet many institutions continue to de-emphasize issues related to minorities in graduate education.

Most of the literature that addresses minority affairs in higher education calls for a critical examination of the institutional culture/context of colleges and universities and their impact on minority students. Kuh and Whit (1988) in *The Invisible Tapestry: Culture in American Colleges and Universities* state that institutional culture is revealed through "an examination of espoused and enacted values and the core beliefs and assumptions shared by the institutional leadership, faculty and other constituents." They note that defining institutional context requires "an attempt to identify beliefs, guiding premises and assumptions, norms, rituals, customs and practices that influence the actions of individuals and groups."

With the recent increase in racial tensions on many university campuses, a number of institutions have begun to assess their institutional context as it relates to minority concerns. These assessments have tended to focus on quantifying special initiatives aimed at increasing minority undergraduate students, faculty and staff, and numbers of available minority-specific programs. While this is an important first step, it does not get to the root of the problem mentioned above— "an examination of the espoused and enacted values and the core beliefs, and assumptions of faculty and other institutional leaders" in relation to minority affairs (Kuh and Whit, 1988).

Some institutions attempt to deal with complex cultural-diversity issues by providing faculty-development programs and seminars focusing on the academic experience of minority students, pedagogical approaches, and differences in students' learning styles. While these seminars are no doubt useful, they also fall short of becoming open and candid discussions of the systemic values, core beliefs, and assumptions that operate, sometimes adversely, for people of color in graduate education. Thus, very little change in institutional practice is typically gained from these professional-development programs.

In his book, *Toward Black Undergraduate Student Equality in American Higher Education* (1988), and in another 1990 study focusing on doctoral students, Nettles asserts that the quality of life for minority students has virtually been ignored by many institutions. Nettles suggests that institutional researchers and administrators tend to concentrate on quantitative rather than qualitative factors in higher education, noting increases in the number of students but ignoring their experiences on campus.

Admissions Policies and Departmental Admission Practices

In graduate education, the faculty assume the key decision-making and gatekeeping role. It is the faculty that determine who gets accepted into their graduate programs and what financial and research opportunities will be made available to students. Thus, the academic and social integration of graduate students is, in large part, controlled by the faculty through the allocation of research and teaching assistantships; invitations to serve as presenters at national conferences; and opportunities to co-author manuscripts and scholarly works. It is therefore the faculty that graduate deans must first reach.

On many campuses, institutional admission policies and departmental admission-committee practices (controlled by the faculty) continue to hinder minority-student participation in graduate study. Many graduate programs, especially at the doctoral level, continue to rely heavily on standardized test scores in making admission decisions, despite clear warning from testing agencies about the appropriate use of test scores in admission processing. The Educational Testing Service (ETS) and the Graduate Record Examination (GRE) Program have conducted several studies that examine the relationship between GRE test scores and performance in graduate study. These studies have found that mean-score differences exist by race, ethnic group, and gender; they also found that the GRE General Test does not "assess every discipline-related skill necessary for academic work or all subjective factors important to academic and career success, such as motivation, creativity, and interpersonal skills" (ETS, 1991).

Uncovering these facts has prompted ETS to issue guidelines for the appropriate use of GRE scores and to call for the use of multiple criteria in the graduate-admission process. The ETS *Guidelines for the Use of GRE Scores* not only points to the limitations of the test scores but also emphatically warns against rejecting an applicant solely on the basis of these scores. Yet despite the research finding, repeated warnings, and established guidelines, many graduate-admissions committees continue to operate as they have done in the past.

Outreach Services and Recruitment Strategies

While some progress has been made in providing outreach to minority-student populations, these efforts have tended to be "special initiatives" often dependent upon the commitment of a few select individuals within the organization. These efforts have not, for the most part, been internalized as institutional practice and thus the majority of minority students continue to operate with limited and sometimes false information about graduate study. Overall, very few institutions have implemented formal and ongoing early-identification programs and other graduate-school preparation programs for their undergraduate minority students. Given the special characteristics of most minority students, these types of programs can be extremely beneficial in encouraging and preparing minorities to make the transition from undergraduate to graduate study.

Much can be learned from campuses that have made the recruitment, retention, and graduation of U.S. minorities an institutional priority. This type of commitment empowers the graduate dean with increased authority and financial support to establish the programs and services required to outreach and promote graduate study within minority communities. With this power the graduate dean can exercise leadership at the department level, working with graduate faculty in restructuring admission policies and practices to ensure equal access for minorities.

One example is the University of Alabama at Birmingham which, through institutional support of a Minority Faculty Development Program, was able to dramatically increase the number of African American students entering doctoral programs in science and engineering. To demonstrate the graduate school's support, the graduate dean committed his discretionary funds "to bring the most qualified prospective graduate students to campus and then *personally* acquaint them with the University and its graduate programs." According to Hickey and Roozen (1990), "these visits also provide the faculty with an opportunity to evaluate the 'whole' student and thus not base their admission recommendations solely on the students' grades and standardized test scores."

The ingredient for success in minority-student recruitment at the University of Alabama at Birmingham is clearly the student perception that there is a high degree of commitment from the institution, the graduate dean, and the academic departments. Prospective minority graduate students, especially those with strong academic backgrounds, are increasingly assessing the institutional climates and environments of support at the departmental level before applying for admission to graduate programs.

Other institutions (University of Kentucky, Ohio State University, Duke University) and consortia (CIC Alliance for Success, COFE) have set up similar early-identification and grad-prep programs. For example, the Graduate School at Michigan State University (MSU), with a grant from the Detroit Edison Foundation, has for the past four years hosted a Graduate School Information Conference for prospective minority graduate students. The purpose of this conference is to provide in-state and out-of-state minority undergraduates with the planning and decision-making skills necessary to get into graduate schools. The conference involves graduate faculty sharing pertinent information with undergraduate students. While MSU is hopeful that a large number will decide to apply to their university, the goal is to motivate students to consider graduate study in general, and to refer them to a Michigan institution that best fits their academic needs. The grant provides approximately 150 in- and out-of-state students with an all-expense-paid trip to participate in the conference. The conference program includes information about selecting a graduate program; the graduate admission process; test-taking strategies; writing personal statements; and financial-aid opportunities. While participants are chosen on the basis of an admissions pre-screening, the program does accept marginal candidates who demonstrate academic potential through a written personal statement. This consideration is important for less-qualified students as it allows them to meet with graduate faculty to discuss their individual strengths and academic portfolio. The interaction also allows the faculty to more broadly assess these students' potential for success in graduate study and to assume an advocacy role on the students' behalf.

Mentoring

Faculty/student relationships have long been recognized as an integral aspect of graduate study. In recent years, the increase in graduate-student attrition and in the time it takes to complete a degree (especially among minorities) has prompted the graduate-education community to pay closer attention to the faculty's role in student mentoring. Cusanovich and Gilliland (1991) distinguish mentoring from advising in the sense that mentoring is a personal relationship:

> It involves professors acting as close, trusted and experienced colleagues and guides. . . . It is recognized that part of what is learned in graduate school is not cognitive; it is socialization to the values, norms, practices, and attitudes of a discipline and university; it transforms the student into a colleague.

The research literature on minorities in graduate education and student retention notes that the mentoring process is especially problematic for minority students (Nettles, 1988; Clewell, 1987; Blackwell, 1981). Clewell (1987) indicates that frequently minority students find it more difficult to establish relationships with professors who are key to conducting their research, publishing in scholarly journals, and attending professional meetings. In addition, the climate of graduate departments are often more important than the institutions. If departments believe that minority students are accepted only on the basis of affirmative action, they will be viewed as a threat to established academic standards. This hostile environment may have a devastating effect on minority students pursuing graduate degrees.

To facilitate minority graduate-student/faculty relationships, research assistantships directly allocated to individual professors and/or teaching assistantships linked directly to the department may be directed to minority students, as opposed to fellowships not directly tied to departmental research and/or teaching.

On the importance of faculty advising and mentoring in graduate school, the graduate deans of the Association of American Universities (AAU) and the Association of Graduate Schools (AGS) issued the following statement:

Faculty advising—Advice and support from mentors are among the most important factors in determining the success of students' doctoral education. Faculty advisors must assist students in choosing coursework that meets their needs and interests without unnecessarily extending their programs. They should also encourage students to move on to seminars and laboratory work that will lead to dissertation topics, and define dissertation topics that are realistic in scope. Good advisors already do these things; to make sure that they happened more routinely, departments should establish explicit requirements for all faculty advising.

The graduate deans at the University of Arizona serve as a good example of the decanal leadership advocated in this chapter. Responding to the AAU-AGS recommendation, they, in concert with their graduate council, developed a position paper on the faculty/graduate-student relationship and incorporated official policies and procedures pertinent to student mentoring at the graduate level. Building upon Zelditch's (1990) definition of mentors as advisors, supporters, tutors, masters, sponsors, and models, this graduate council endorsed a new graduate-school policy that encouraged (in essence, required) academic departments to assign, or let the students select, mentors upon their arrival to the University of Arizona campus. The council noted that students may have multiple mentors and that the role of the mentors may change over time. They also noted the special significance of the mentoring process for underrepresented students. The graduate council summarized their expectations by stating

> that all departments have in place definable mentoring programs and that they have developed the appropriate infrastructure (courses, practices, procedures, etc.) to integrate students into the discipline fully. The depth and breadth of the mentoring program in any given department or program certainly will have an impact on [students'] ability to compete for resources within the Graduate College and the University (Cusanovich and Gilliland, 1991).

Conclusion

Numerous activities over the past 25 years have improved the participation and graduation rates of U.S. minorities. The problem, however, has been inconsistency. As institutional priorities have changed and available fiscal resources decreased, levels of institutional commitment to minority affairs decreased accordingly. It is this lack of consistent progress that has led graduate professionals to question the sincerity of institutions and faculty in their pursuit of minority participation in the graduate enterprise.

The examples of decanal leadership provided in this chapter, along with those referenced in other publications, lead us to believe that graduate deans do have the authority and responsibility to promote institutional change in support of minority affairs at the graduate level. While it is clear that this challenge requires internal and external financial support, as well as coopera-tion from the faculty, the crisis state of minority representation in graduate education leaves graduate deans no choice: They must seek the financial resources and personal commitments to get the job done.

THE FEDERAL ROLE

That minority enrollment and graduate declines are not only detrimental to our educational system but threatening to our national security appears to be the driving force behind increased national attention. In recommending strategies for action, articles and reports call for a renewed sense of commit-ment, leadership, and coordination among federal and state agencies, profes-sional education associations, accrediting agencies, and individual colleges and universities.

Constitutionally, the authority and responsibility for delivering higher education in America has been delegated to individual states and their postsecondary education institutions. Still, the federal government has played a critical role in our higher-education system by providing grants, fellowships, research/teaching assistantships to individual students for graduate study and research opportunities. Additionally, several agencies award federal dollars for students to conduct research and/or participate in international programs. Federal dollars have also strengthened institutions, research, programs, and services in graduate education.

The federal government's responsibility for enhancing the participation of ethnic minorities in graduate education has long been discussed within many minority academic circles, conferences, and professional association meet-ings. Despite the academic stance that the federal government should not mandate or dictate education policies and institutional practices, some mi-nority scholars are calling for a greater federal role in support of minorities in higher education. This increased federal role is advocated especially by those who have lost faith in states and institutions to reverse the negative participa-tion rate of minorities in higher education. The lack of centralized control over educational policies and institutional practices within some states has been cited as a reason for increasing the federal regulatory role. An increased federal role is envisioned as centralized authority, informed by government-sponsored research, that can improve educational equity for ethnic minori-ties.

Recommended Federal Action

In November of 1987, and again in July of 1988, the State University of New York at Stony Brook convened a group of minority faculty and administrators to assess the critical role of faculty in meeting the national need for African American, Native American, and Hispanic scholars. In their published policy document, *Meeting the National Need for Minority Scholars and Scholarship: Policies and Practices*, they made the following federal policy and action recommendations:

1. Provide or increase grants and funding to institutions that demonstrate or develop programs of outreach and identification, retention, and graduation of minority students at the graduate and professional level.
2. Fund a national research center for the study of higher education, with a major focus on the examination of factors affecting minorities in higher education. This center should be mandated to collect, compile, synthesize, and disseminate research.
3. Sustain and strengthen traditional ethnically based institutions of higher education, such as tribally controlled colleges, historically Black institutions, and comparable Latino institutions.
4. Increase the opportunities for returning minority graduate students through financial support and grant support.
5. For efficiency and cost-effectiveness, require that all federally funded programs aimed at improving education for minority students demonstrate that they are operating under a coordinated system with common procedures.
6. An overreliance on standardized examinations for identification of talent is negatively affecting African Americans, Native Americans, and Hispanics at the time they seek entrance to graduate education and when they exit the academy to move on to careers. Federal leadership and support are needed for research on a development of alternative measures of identifying potential and ability.
7. Encourage and foster the creation of industry-government sponsored activities and programs to identify and fund potential minority scholars. The field of engineering has demonstrated effective models in this regard over the last fifteen years.
8. More than a decade has passed since the National Board on Graduate Education produced a report with recommendations entitled *Minority Group Participation in Graduate Education*. The federal government should fund a comprehensive update of that report.

We concur with these recommendations. Interested readers may want to review this document in depth. Many additional recommendations specific to financial aid, redefining and reshaping research policy and practice, place-ment and employment, and accurate data reporting were presented.

CONCLUSION

We have tried to answer the rhetorical questions presented in the Introduc-tion of this chapter. Numerous activities have taken place over the past 25 years. However, "inconsistency" seems the "consistent" pattern. Initiatives have started and stopped as priorities have changed. Results have responded accordingly. It is the lack of consistent progress that has led graduate profes-sionals to question institutional and faculty intent in the pursuit of minority participation in the graduate enterprise.

As can be noted, the above recommendations advocate an increased and stronger federal role in higher education. While this position may be unpopu-lar with many traditional academics, the minority community has long recognized weaknesses in the present system and the need to improve it to help meet the human resource needs of our nation and the well-being of our communities. The implementation of even a fraction of these recommenda-tions will ensure that progress is made toward equalizing opportunities for U.S. minorities in graduate and professional education. The components required to improve current federal policy are for the most part in place.

The examples of decanal leadership provided in this chapter, along with examples referenced in other publications, lead us to believe that graduate deans do have the authority and responsibility to promote institutional change relative to minority affairs at the graduate level. While it is clear that this challenge requires internal and external financial support and coopera-tion with the faculty, we believe that quality leadership can overcome the present obstacles and current state of minority underrepresentation in gradu-ate education. By strengthening existing graduate student financial aid pro-grams, providing institutional incentives/rewards, and maintaining a closer federal/state partnership, the enrollment and graduation rates of minority graduate students should certainly improve.

REFERENCES

Adams, M. 1989. *Meeting the national need for minority scholars and scholarship: Policies and action.* Stony Brook, NY: State University of New York at Stony Brook.

American Council on Education/Education Commission of the States 1988. *One-third of a nation: A report of the Commission on Minority Participation in Education and American Life.* Washington, DC.

Association of American Universities (AAU) and the Association of Graduate Schools (AGS). 1990. Institutional policies to improve doctoral education: A policy statement of the Association of American Universities and the Association of Graduate Schools. Washington, DC: Author.

Atwell, R. 1988. *Minority participation in higher education: We need a new momentum*. Washington DC: American Council on Education.

Blackwell, J. G. 1981. *Mainstreaming outsiders: The production of Black professionals*. Bayside, NY: General Hall.

Brown, S. V. 1987. *Minorities in the graduate education pipeline*. Princeton, NJ: Educational Testing Service.

Carter, D. J., and R. Wilson. 1991. *Minorities in higher education*. Washington, DC: American Council on Education.

Clewell, B. C. 1987. *Retention of Black and Hispanic doctoral students*. Princeton, NJ: Educational Testing Service.

Cusanovich, M., and M. Gilliland. 1991. *CGS Communicator*. Washington, DC: Council of Graduate Schools.

Educational Testing Service. 1991. *Sex, race, ethnicity and performance on the GRE General Test*, Princeton, NJ.

Hickey T. L., and K. J. Roozen. 1990. The changing role of the graduate dean in minority student recruitment. *CGS Communicator*, March.

Kuh, G. D., and J. Whit. 1988. *The invisible tapestry: Culture in American colleges and universities*. Washington, DC: Association for Study of Higher Education.

Lindt, G. 1990. Managers, movers and missionaries: Who leads the graduate school? *CGS Communicator*, November.

Mortenson, T. G. 1991. *Equity of higher educational opportunity for women, Black, Hispanic and low income students*. Iowa City, IA: American College Testing.

Nettles, M. 1990. *Black, Hispanic, and White doctoral students: Before, during and after enrolling in graduate school*. Princeton, NJ: Educational Testing Service.

———. 1988. *Toward Black undergraduate student equality in American higher education*. New York: Greenwood Press.

———. 1987. *Financial aid and minority participation in graduate education*. Princeton, NJ: Educational Testing Service.

Syverson, P. D., and S. R. Welch. 1991. *Graduate enrollment and degrees: 1986-1989*. Washington, DC: Council of Graduate Schools.

Zelditch, M. 1990. *Mentor roles*. Tempe, AZ: Western Association of Graduate Schools.

CHAPTER 17

The Impasse on Faculty Diversity in Higher Education: A National Agenda

Shirley Vining Brown

A major national effort to attract minorities to academic careers should be launched in the near future and generously supported. Unless this is done, we believe affirmative action policies, even if carried out in good faith by campuses, will be inadequate to prevent serious erosion in the number and quality of minorities in the academic profession.

—*Bowen and Schuster (1986)*

The faculties in American higher education number over 824,000 individuals who, in 1990, served almost 14 million students on 3,501 campuses. Following World War II, these faculties grew at unprecedented rates of expansion, through sweeping changes in the student population, the curriculum, and educational technologies. But, after considerable progress during the 1960s and 1970s, the growth of minorities in higher education has tapered off. The shortage of minority faculty has been the subject of much public discussion. This chapter examines the benefits of faculty diversity in higher education, why the process of diversification has not been expedited, and the role of faculty members, administrators, and policy makers in the diversification process. The chapter begins with the history of racial and ethnic barriers in higher education, then describes the current status of minority doctorates and faculty, as well as the conceptual and substantive issues related to past and present inequities, and in the final section, recommends initiatives to alleviate the problem.

ANTECEDENTS OF THE MINORITY FACULTY SHORTAGE

Citadels of Segregation

Before looking at the barriers to faculty diversification, it is worthwhile to put the issue of employment equity into a historical context. From the beginning, the exclusion of Black Americans from higher education was sanctioned by law, custom, and tradition. Exclusionary employment and student admissions practices were so complete that Olivas (1988) describes these practices and learning environments as "segregated citadel(s)."

Thurow (1974) also stressed the significance of institutions that protected an unequal system of public education when he describes education as "one of the factors determining the economy's distribution of earned incomes." As a gatekeeper of social and economic progress, exclusionary educational policies systematically perpetuated the unequal stratification of race/ethnic groups in American society (Cross, 1986). Consequently, education became the prime battleground in the struggle for full equality and civil rights. Dismantling segregated institutions was key to the struggle that launched the desegregation movement.

Efforts to Desegregate Higher Education Faculty

Nineteenth-Century Efforts. Although separate and unequal education was practiced as public policy throughout the educational system, the first form of desegregation in higher education was the token admission of Black students and, in rare and isolated instances, the appointment of Black professors to White faculties in the late nineteenth century. In 1873, for example, two Blacks were appointed to faculty positions at Georgetown University and the University of South Carolina (Bond, 1972). But, except for the appointment of an assistant librarian, no other Black academic appointments were made in White institutions for the rest of the nineteenth century (Fleming, Gill, and Swinton, 1978). The policy of separatism that emerged out of Reconstruction was so firmly entrenched that White institutions closed off excellent opportunities to hire exceptional scholars such as W. E. B. DuBois, who had studied in Europe and earned his master's and doctorate degrees at Harvard.*

Sanctioned by custom and law, strict exclusionary hiring practices continued well into the mid-twentieth century. As an educational alternative,

---

*DuBois accepted the position of assistant professor of sociology at the University of Pennsylvania during the 1896–97 academic year where he had no contact with students and was given no official recognition. He was hired to study the living conditions of Philadelphia's Black population, which he describes in *The Philadelphia Negro*. For a further account of his experience, see DuBois (12).

religious and philanthropic organizations established several well-known traditionally Black institutions (TBIs) such as Fisk, Shaw, Hampton, and Morehouse Universities that provided learning and teaching opportunities for Black students and faculty.

World War II Efforts.   An important event that gave rise to the desegregation movement in higher education was the urgent demand for faculty during World War II. The shortage of White faculty led to what Fleming and his colleagues (Fleming, Gill, and Swinton, 1978) describe as a transition from "policies of exclusion" to "policies of experimentation" by hiring Blacks as faculty replacements for Whites who were serving in the war effort. The experimental period produced 26 Black faculty appointments in White institutions between 1940 and 1946. Underwritten by philanthropic organizations (e.g., the Julius Rosenwald Fund), these temporary faculty opportunities produced a brief period of optimism. Some Blacks foresaw the walls of segregation crumbling in the academy just as they had in other sectors such as the federal government. But, by the end of the 1940s, less than 7 percent of White institutions employed Black faculty (Fleming, Gill, and Swinton, 1978). Eventually the period of expectancy gave way to the realization that policies of exclusion were unyielding to change and would be an enduring reality for Black scholars nationwide.

Civil Rights Efforts.   The next important event giving rise to the desegregation movement in higher education occurred during the second half of the twentieth century and came out of the litigation strategies used in the 1940s and 1950s by the National Association for the Advancement of Colored People (NAACP) to open graduate and professional education to Black students in the South. These strategies led to two U.S. Supreme Court decisions that affected public policy on education.

In *Brown v. Board of Education*, segregated public education was declared unequal and unconstitutional. But it was the "Adams" (*Adams v. Richardson*, 1973) decision that spoke most directly to discriminatory practices in higher education. This decision ordered the desegregation of students, faculty, and administration in all public colleges and universities in 10 southern states. Within several years the number rose to 19 states, including several higher education systems in northern states (e.g., Ohio, Pennsylvania). The degree of state compliance to this order is still a point of contention, as the gap between minority and majority students narrowed and then widened again. (See chapter 11 for more details on the Adams case.)

Other Minority Groups.   Although the historical exclusion of Black Americans from public and private education was ubiquitous and longstanding, other minority groups were disadvantaged by similar exclusionary practices. Native Americans have a long history of systematic discrimination in education. Earlier failed policies severely limited the number of Native American students in higher education, and, consequently, Native American faculty are almost nonexistent in U.S. institutions. And even though 24 tribal colleges sprang up across the nation two decades ago, most faculty at these institutions are not Native Americans (Boyer, 1989). (See chapter 13 for a more detailed discussion.)

Hispanics also face structural barriers in education. According to Garza (1988), the most underrepresented minority group in higher education relative to their representation in the population are Hispanics. Before World War II, there were few Hispanic faculty in higher education. Today nearly half of all identifiable Mexican American faculty are employed in two-year institutions. Hispanic faculty at predominantly White institutions are often hired solely to teach in specialties such as race relations or Latino-related studies. Like most minorities, they are not afforded the opportunity to teach across the breadth and range of their disciplines.

Asian American students are not underrepresented in degree attainment at any level, and they earn graduate degrees in science and engineering fields at rates that rival those of White students. But Hsia (1988) argues that their success in higher education is backfiring because selective institutions are now practicing "reverse" discrimination against Asian American students by limiting the numbers admitted to their programs. Except in engineering departments, their sparse participation on faculties all but disguises their exceptional educational achievements in the sciences and mathematics. Of all new Ph.D. graduates, Asian Americans are least likely to pursue an academic career (Brown, 1988). Those who do, lag behind White and other minority faculty in tenure and academic rank. (See chapter 14 for a more detailed discussion.)

Prejudice and discrimination against Asian Americans is rooted in turbulent periods of anti-Asian sentiment in U.S. history. In the early twentieth century, California passed a law that allowed (but did not require) separate educational facilities for Japanese students (Feagin, 1978). After making educational strides in the 1930s, World War II rekindled anti-Japanese sentiments that led to their evacuation and confinement in relocation camps. Although the relocation period halted the educational achievement of Japanese during the war years, some Nisei (native-born Japanese citizens) were released from camps to attend selected colleges. Feagin (1978) believes that the selective release of a few Japanese youth for continued study is the basis for their postwar educational success. But he also stresses that the vestiges of past discrimination are ingrained and probably account for the chronic shortage of Asian Americans on faculties in states with large concentrations of Japanese and other Asian Americans.

Racial and ethnic chauvinism is not only the basis for current minority faculty shortfalls but is also the basis for the intractable dual system of academic employment. White faculty make up 89 percent of all full-time regular faculty in public institutions, over 90 percent in private institutions, and at traditionally Black institutions, they represent about one-third of the faculty. Most minority faculty are employed in institutions that primarily serve minority students (e.g., TBIs), that are low in prestige, and that are under public rather than private control (Wilson and Justiz, 1987/1988).

WHY THE IMPASSE?

Controversy over Definitions and Solutions

There is confusion and discord over the operational definition of employment equity, and as a consequence, how to achieve it. These issues are major obstacles to faculty diversity in higher education and, in Crossland's (1971) words, are "more talked about than understood."

The disagreement over the methods of redistributing social and economic advantages to minorities in the workforce mainly involves two hiring policies that reflect a bifurcation of group interests: affirmative action and meritocracy. At the heart of the controversy is the question of how to settle past and present inequities— "what is fair in the allocation of education and employment opportunities?" (Hartigan and Wigdor, 1989). The literature has duly noted sharp distinctions between the positions of affirmative action and merit advocates along with their respective perceptions about the causes of minority faculty shortfalls (Bowen and Schuster, 1986; Washington and Harvey, 1989). This section briefly reviews the most representative positions of both sides, although the line of public discourse on this issue is far more complex.

Meritocracy and the Supply-Side Argument

Generally, those who support meritocratic principles of hiring believe that faculty positions should be awarded to individuals on the basis of merit and justified by such academic qualifications as an earned doctorate, research and publication records, teaching ability, and experience. They believe in a system of open competition, where "everyone has an equal opportunity to compete for positions and is rewarded" accordingly (Hartigan and Wigdor, 1989).

Simply put, they argue that, regardless of race or sex, the opportunity to compete for faculty positions should be the same for all applicants. They also contend that access is already available to all groups under the merit system and by giving preferential treatment to minorities and women, affirmative action amounts to "reverse discrimination" for White males.

Based on this view, advocates of the merit principle believe that the crux of the minority faculty problem lies solely in the shortage of minority scholars who are qualified for faculty openings (Bowen and Schuster, 1986). Because they favor a supply-side theory of minority faculty shortfalls, they can point to well-known trend data showing that, over the years, American graduate education has routinely produced a small fraction of minority doctorates. In part, this situation is a problem. The year-to-year changes in Table 17-1 show that there is virtually no change in the number and percentage of minorities earning doctorate degrees.

Compared with their share of Ph.D.'s in 1977, the margin of growth of minority Ph.D.'s amounted to less than 2 percent by 1988. The initial small base of Native American (65 Ph.D.'s) and Hispanic (423 Ph.D.'s) doctorates underscores their incremental gains.

Asian Americans, who made the most progress, roughly doubled their number of Ph.D.'s after years of sustained growth. But, the total minority share is offset by the loss of Black doctorates, who dropped from a high of 1,116 Ph.D.'s in 1977 to 805 Ph.D.'s in 1988. By 1990, the number of Black Ph.D.'s rallied slightly to 828.

A closer look at these trends (Figure 17-1) reveals that, within each minority group, women made considerably more headway. With the exception of Black women, whose gains are smaller, minority women substantially raised their share.

But the more recent past presents a bleaker picture. Figure 17-2 shows a slowdown in the gains of minority women. The surge of doctorates earned by minority women hit a plateau during the 1980s and, for Black women, dropped by 3 percent during this period. Native American women are the only women that sustained a moderate rate of growth.

The stationary growth rate of minorities is most affected by the doctoral degree trends of minority men in the last half of the 1980s. Asian American men maintained their growth rate. Hispanic and Native American men made minimal progress. Black men, who lost rather than gained doctorates, were hit hardest. They dropped by 373 Ph.D.'s (55 points) below their 1977 level; in 1990, only 320 Black men earned Ph.D.'s.

While the relative growth rate of Hispanic men increased, the increase is somewhat misleading because, in absolute numbers, Hispanic men earned fewer doctorates in 1983 than they earned in 1977.

A better measure of progress is to compare the relative growth of minority Ph.D.'s in a shrinking doctoral pool. As an example, even though the

---

TABLE 17-1

Race/Ethnic Status of Ph.D.'s: U.S. Citizen,* 1977-1990

Numbers of Ph.D.s					
Year of Doctorate	**American Indian**	**Black**	**Hispanic**	**Asian American**	**White**
1977	65	1,116	423	339	23,065
1978	61	1,033	473	390	21,811
1979	84	1,056	462	428	21,920
1980	75	1,032	412	458	21,993
1981	85	1,013	464	465	21,979
1982	77	1,047	535	452	21,674
1983	82	921	538	492	21,673
1984	74	953	535	512	21,321
1985	95	909	559	515	20,641
1986	100	820	567	527	20,538
1987	116	767	619	542	22,991
1988	93	805	594	612	23,172
1989	94	821	582	625	23,014
1990	93	828	698	617	21,650
Percent of Ph.D.s					
1977	0.3	4.5	1.7	1.4	92.2
1978	0.3	4.3	2.0	1.6	91.8
1979	0.4	4.4	1.9	1.8	91.5
1980	0.3	4.3	1.7	1.9	91.8
1981	0.4	4.2	1.9	1.9	91.6
1982	0.4	4.4	2.2	1.9	91.1
1983	0.3	3.9	2.3	2.1	91.4
1984	0.3	4.1	2.3	2.2	91.1
1985	0.3	4.0	2.5	2.3	90.9
1986	0.4	3.6	2.5	2.3	89.4
1987	0.5	3.4	2.8	2.4	90.9
1988	0.4	3.5	2.6	2.7	90.8
1989	0.4	3.6	2.5	2.7	90.8
1990	0.4	3.5	2.9	2.6	90.6

*Excludes other races and no-report cases of doctorate recipients reporting race/ethnic status.

Source: National Research Council, Office of Scientific and Engineering Personnel, Survey of Earned Doctorates, 1977–1990.

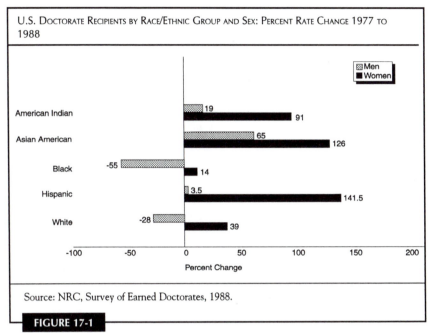

U.S. Doctorate Recipients by Race/Ethnic Group and Sex: Percent Rate Change 1977 to 1988

Source: NRC, Survey of Earned Doctorates, 1988.

FIGURE 17-1

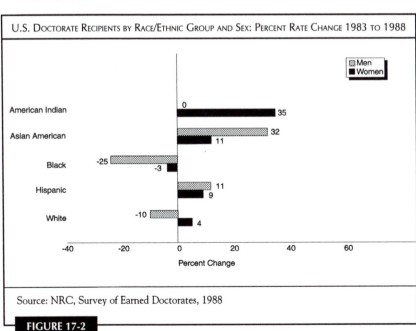

U.S. Doctorate Recipients by Race/Ethnic Group and Sex: Percent Rate Change 1983 to 1988

Source: NRC, Survey of Earned Doctorates, 1988

FIGURE 17-2

doctoral pool declined by 1,415 Ph.D.'s, the non-Asian American minority share of the pool grew less than 2 percent between 1977 and 1990. More recent statistics for 1991 indicate the possible beginnings of a rebound from past trends, particularly for Native Americans (N=123). The trend is also rising for Black Ph.D.'s (N=933) although the numbers for both men and women are below their numbers in the mid-1980s. Hispanics (N=763) are also increasing in number for both men and women except for Puerto Rican men and "other" Hispanic men and women who earned about as many doctorates as they did in 1990. However, so far, the general upturn has not been large enough to offset the sharp declines in the last half of the 1980s or to raise the relative share of Black Ph.D.'s in the pool to their 1977 level. Thus, those who favor the merit principle of faculty hiring still believe that the solution to minority faculty shortfalls is to increase the number of qualified minority candidates.

Affirmative Action and the Demand-side Argument

Proponents of affirmative action policies agree, in part, with the merit principle, the supply-side analysis of minority shortfalls, and even the equal opportunity hiring solution (Roder, 1974; Washington and Harvey, 1989). But they define the problem and the solution quite differently. Because of historical inequality in education and faculty employment, advocates of affirmative action believe that "inequality of opportunity" overrides the intent of the principle of "equality of employment opportunities." For them, group membership should be part of the range of criteria used to settle past and present inequities. The criterion of group membership is not new. It was group membership that afforded White faculty substantial benefits and, thus, argue the affirmative action proponents, structural changes in faculty hiring are needed to speed the process of full employment for minority and women faculty applicants.

Preferential treatment as a remedial tool is not particularly unique in American history. As Hartigan and Wigdor (1989) observe:

> We are all beneficiaries of overt preferential treatment, as a few examples will show. There is very wide social acceptance of the income tax write-off of mortgage interest. Very powerful forces support preferential treatment for veterans, including hiring preference in civil service and referral priority by the U.S. Employment Service. There are many other less obvious examples, such as water rights and agricultural subsidies. Preference is not novel; only the intended recipient is.

The most recent evidence of preference is exemplified in the 1991 Immigration Law that was passed into law by Congress. This bill establishes 140,000 employment-based visas, of which 55,000 are "diversity" visas that would increase the inflow of skilled and professional workers from Europe. In effect, the law creates a "preference system" for immigrants who are seen as desirable contributors to the economic, cultural, and educational interests of the United States. The tone and substance of the law is seen as diverting the nation away from developing a balanced human resource policy that bridges the training needs of minority citizens with immigration reform (Immigration Act of 1989).

How do proponents of affirmative action view the shortage of minority faculty? Some (Boyer, 1989; Fleming, Gill, and Swinton, 1978; Washington and Harvey, 1989; Wilson and Justiz, 1988) believe that in spite of the small number of minority Ph.D.'s, the minority supply still exceeds demand. They do not believe merit hiring will expand the number of minority faculty and has, in fact, resulted in trends like those shown in Figure 17-3. From the early to mid-1980s, these has been no substantial change in the participation of minorities on faculties in higher education.

Even in the degree fields where minorities are concentrated (e.g., education, social sciences, social work), the number of minority faculty is far below the expected level (Silver, Dennis, and Spikes, 1989; Washington and Harvey, 1989).

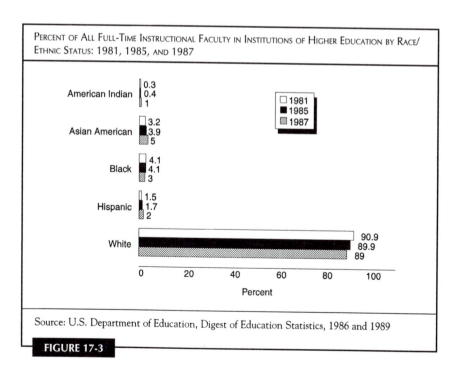

PERCENT OF ALL FULL-TIME INSTRUCTIONAL FACULTY IN INSTITUTIONS OF HIGHER EDUCATION BY RACE/ETHNIC STATUS: 1981, 1985, AND 1987

American Indian
- 0.3
- 0.4
- 1

Asian American
- 3.2
- 3.9
- 5

Black
- 4.1
- 4.1
- 3

Hispanic
- 1.5
- 1.7
- 2

White
- 90.9
- 89.9
- 89

Legend:
- 1981
- 1985
- 1987

Percent

Source: U.S. Department of Education, Digest of Education Statistics, 1986 and 1989

FIGURE 17-3

Although 38 percent of all minorities earn their Ph.D.'s in education, Figure 17-4 shows that only 19 percent have confirmed career plans to take jobs in higher education. Black Ph.D.'s, who earn over half of their Ph.D.'s in education, are perhaps the most underrepresented. One faculty survey (National Center for Education Statistics, 1990a) shows that out of 7 percent of the full-time Black faculty in departments of education, most are concentrated in traditionally Black institutions. The discrepancy is similar in the social sciences, where minorities are also concentrated.

To increase the number of minority faculty, affirmative action proponents contend that merit must be defined differently. Although the prestige of the recommending source, selectivity of the institution, number of publications, and years of postdoctoral research experience are valuable assets, they do not always predict or guarantee teaching ability, creativity, or the full range of knowledge and scholarship that are essential to the mission of undergraduate education. Nor do they provide for research interests and expertise that push the frontier of our knowledge beyond narrow perspectives in conventional research.

The controversy over affirmative action and merit-hiring has influenced recruitment and hiring practices in two ways. For one thing, it has revealed considerable ambiguity over how equity should be defined. For another, it has uncovered chauvinistic attitudes among rank-and-file faculty.

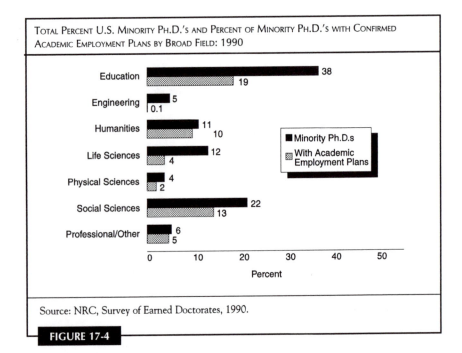

TOTAL PERCENT U.S. MINORITY PH.D.'S AND PERCENT OF MINORITY PH.D.'S WITH CONFIRMED ACADEMIC EMPLOYMENT PLANS BY BROAD FIELD: 1990

Source: NRC, Survey of Earned Doctorates, 1990.

FIGURE 17-4

Faculty Attitudes.   Until recently there was no hard evidence about faculty attitudes and opinions on affirmative action. The Carnegie (1989) opinion survey asked 5,450 college and university professors about their institution's affirmative action efforts. Almost two-thirds (71 percent) said they were either satisfied (50 percent) or had no opinion (21 percent) about the pace of affirmative action on their campus. Older faculty, faculty in two-year institutions, and faculty in engineering departments said they were most satisfied. Moreover, most faculty believe their institutions are doing a reasonable job of achieving staff diversity.

For instance, the large number of faculty in two-year institutions said they were satisfied or had no opinion (75 percent) about affirmative action. An even larger percentage of engineering faculty (81 percent) said they were satisfied or had no opinion. Yet, nationally, engineering departments have the lowest percentage of Black and Hispanic faculty (2 percent) on staff and have almost no Native American faculty.

A survey, conducted by the National Center for Educational Statistics (1990b), suggests that the commitment to affirmative action is also waning among academic administrators. When department chairs were asked what they consider to be the most important hiring criteria for new full-time faculty, among the top three factors was faculty "fit" with the department or institution (61 percent). Only one-third of the department chairs considered affirmative action to be very important in initial faculty hires for entry-level, tenure-track positions.

Optimism appears to be giving way to discouragement among some minority faculty, who see affirmative action as a vision that did not materialize (Fleming, Gill, and Swinton, 1978; Washington and Harvey, 1989). Key among Black faculty complaints is the lack of aggressive recruitment and retention of qualified minority faculty (Carnegie Foundation for the Advancement of Teaching, 1989).

Promotion, Tenure, and Attitudes.   Recruiting minority applicants opens the door of opportunity, but it does not guarantee career success. Minorities lag behind White faculty in favorable promotion and tenure decisions. Brown (1988) found that Black faculty are least likely to secure the rank of full professor and both Black and Hispanic faculty lag behind White faculty in obtaining tenure.

Silver and his associates (Silver and Spikes, 1989) shed some light on factors that act as signal-bearers for institutional climate. Promotion and tenure are key among factors that lower the morale and progression of Black faculty on White campuses. Even more, tenured Black faculty are more dissatisfied with tenure procedures than untenured Black faculty. Tenure procedures are described as poorly defined with tenure awards based on how candidates "fit in" with others in the department. Another concern dealt with their work. Two-thirds of Black faculty believed their skills were underutilized by their institutions. In the face of faculty retrenchment, Black men were least secure about retaining their jobs.

Credentialism, Job Competition, and Equity

Dissention over hiring policies and a sagging job market has increased the competition for jobs. Fueled by an excess of new doctorates produced in the 1970s and 1980s, faculty selectivity has also increased and adversely affected the job market for new faculty entrants. To the extent that job requirements are raised and the number of faculty openings are reduced, minority applicants are disadvantaged by credentialism (Bowen and Schuster, 1986; Freeman, 1974).

Hiring criteria based primarily on credentials (which may be differentially defined by institutions) falls more heavily on non-Asian minorities than other groups. First, applicants must have in hand an earned doctorate (or the promise of one) at the time of appointment. Second, some administrators no longer require minorities to be simply qualified, but competitive with the best qualified. Moreover, credentialism, when used as a screening device rather than a job requirement, is far from trivial in the literature and is used to consolidate economic and social privilege rather than to level differences between groups (Burke, 1987; Cross, 1986; Davis, 1963; Exum, 1983; Thurow, 1974).

LOOKING FORWARD TO THE FUTURE: THE ROLE OF POLICY MAKERS AND ACADEMICIANS

While American higher education is immobilized over how to achieve employment equity, a more unsettling prediction may be well underway: There may be more slippage and decline in minority talent during the last decade of the twentieth century (Bowen and Schuster, 1986). This section discusses several initiatives that could head off this prospect and bridge the redistribution of employment opportunities.

Faculty Diversity Implications: *Cui Bono*—For Whose Benefit?

Bowen and Sosa (1989) conclude that "the most important questions of policy pertain to graduate education." This statement is particularly relevant for minority graduate students. At issue is, for whose benefit should faculty diversity be attained?

The National Interest and Federal Involvement

The most compelling case for making personnel adjustments in faculty staffing patterns is that the nation cannot afford to squander its human resources, particularly in a changing labor market. Depending on the assumptions about employment trends, Bowen and Sosa (1989) estimate the total demand (e.g., net new positions and faculty replacements) for new faculty positions will range between 131,826 and 153,243 between 1992 and the second decade of the twenty-first century. To offset predicted faculty imbalances, minorities and women will be important sources of talent.

Faculty shortfalls will be greatest in the humanities and social sciences (Bowen and Sosa, 1989). Although minorities are somewhat better represented in these degree fields than in other disciplines, minority faculty shortages exist in all fields.

The federal government has an enormous stake in advancing minority graduate education and faculty diversity. Graduate education does "transcend state boundaries" (Bowen and Sousa, 1989). While this used to mean state and local boundaries, it now means national boundaries. Thus, the talent needed to revitalize America's technical and intellectual base will have to come from all groups in society.

What Can Be Done?

The most critical short-term remedy is for the federal government to invest in education and training programs and restore support for minority graduate education. This can be done in two ways.

National Leadership. Principled leadership from the president, the secretary of the Department of Education, and the Congress is needed to avoid the "wastage" of domestic talent. The United States is not producing enough American Ph.D.'s in critical fields such as science and engineering. Roughly 60 percent of all engineering doctorate degrees are awarded to foreign-born students and two-thirds of all postdoctoral appointments go to foreign-born citizens. Since most foreign-born Ph.D.'s return to their home countries, financial aid policies that provide more support for foreign students than U.S. citizens should be revised. This is not to say that funding for foreign students should be discontinued. But in light of drastic cutbacks during the 1980s, priority allocation of government funds should be targeted to U.S. citizens who strengthen the U.S. workforce.

Foreign-born Ph.D.'s also receive 60-70 percent of the university funds for graduate support. By contrast, in 1988, Native American (83 percent), Black (83 percent), and Mexican American (81 percent) Ph.D.'s supported their education with funds from family and self-support. The disparity in funding patterns is significant because indebtedness is a major deterrent to minority persistence in graduate education (Hauptman, 1986).

The Office of Technology Assessment (1988) found that the number of stipends awarded in science and engineering were positively correlated with the number of Ph.D.'s produced in these fields. Therefore, an increase in the level of support and the number of stipends for minorities is needed in all degree fields. Substantial increases in stipends should be provided to minorities who enter degree fields (e.g.,mathematics, science, engineering) where minorities are least represented. Portable stipends are needed that last throughout the normal duration of graduate study.

The government should realize a substantial return on investment in stipends and forgivable loans (e.g., loans that become grants based on the fulfillment of work requirements). In addition to occupying an important role in contemporary higher education, highly trained minorities are taxpayers and contributors who will benefit the nation's economy. For these reasons, stipends and forgivable loans are a financial investment, not a government handout.

Higher Education's Interest and Institutional Involvement

Higher education also has a vested interest in a diversified faculty. First, the production of U.S. minority doctorates can and must be increased to help meet future faculty and workforce needs. Second, the changing face of the U.S. population will include more minorities. Institutions will have to respond to the needs of a growing number of minority students who will be headed for college in the year 2000. Third, although there is resistance, institutions may be held accountable for their failure to recruit and retain minority students and faculty. In sum, an institution's best route to improving institutional quality is defined by its ability to produce desired student and faculty outcomes.

WHAT CAN BE CHANGED?

Short-term Solutions

Approximately 49 percent of minorities with Ph.D.'s in the sciences, engineering, and humanities are employed outside of academe. Because of the long training lag in producing more Ph.D.'s, short-term efforts might draw on the sizable cushion of experienced minority Ph.D.'s already in the workforce, working in nonacademic fields.

In education, for example, there are unique opportunities to recruit new faculty from among the elementary and high school administrators who are looking for midcareer job changes. In addition to expanding the pool, these individuals bring experience, a current level of expertise, and a confidence to their teaching that is uncommon for new faculty members.

Another short-term alternative is to hire minority Ph.D.'s employed in nonacademic jobs as part-time faculty. Many well-paid minority doctorates who work in business and industry may be reluctant to give up salaries that can range from $10,962 to $19,574 higher than the academic salaries they would be offered for comparable years of work experience (Brown, 1988). But, many might be attracted to part-time teaching positions. Similar to minority Ph.D.'s who are willing to make midcareer changes, the integration and teaching of practice and theory should come with more ease to experienced professionals in engineering, physics, law, or medicine. The benefits of providing minority students with role models and mentors (Blackwell, 1981) are substantial, particularly in technical fields, where there are virtually no minority faculty.

Long-term Solutions

What long-term solutions do institutions have at their disposal? Projected faculty supply-demand imbalances must involve a process that some call "planned-diversity." Anticipating and planning for future faculty supplies is essential and several issues of importance must be considered.

Financial Aid For Minority Graduate Students. The initiative for providing financial support to minority graduate students will, in part, depend on funding made available through government agencies and the priorities set by institutional decision makers (Bowan and Sousa, 1989). Without commitment to this first step, the relative impact of other solutions will be considerably weakened. Because university funds come primarily from state public funds, these funds should be used to train U.S. citizens, particularly in technical fields. Vigorous efforts should be made to provide adequate and long-term funding to attract and retain minorities, particularly minority women and Black men in graduate education. These groups are grossly underrepresented in science and engineering. The shift away from grants to loans and the stagnant growth of minority graduate students indicate, clearly, that these groups may not be willing or able to borrow against their future for prolonged study.

Institutional Response to Degree Distributions. A redistribution of Asian American and non-Asian minorities is critical to faculty diversification. The concentration of Asian Americans in the fields of engineering, mathematics, and science and their shortage in education, the humanities, and social sciences must be changed if true diversification is to take place. Similar degree field rearrangements are needed for non-Asian minorities to more evenly distribute them in curriculum areas other than the social sciences and education.

To encourage minorities to shift to new fields of interest, students must be made aware of alternative careers before they enter college and early in their undergraduate careers. To encourage and attract minority students into nontraditional graduate fields, financial assistance should be provided for students who choose to study in curriculum areas where there is a dearth of minority faculty. Designated grant funds should be awarded with the stipulation that recipients teach (full- or part-time) for a specified period after completing the doctorate.

Another concern among minority students is the narrow focus in the curricula and research in many graduate degree programs (Garza, 1988). The recognition of minority interests and concerns will require a willingness by institutions and faculty to make adjustments that include traditional and nontraditional learning and research perspectives.

Time to Degree. A major barrier to graduate study is the time it takes to complete the doctorate (Bowen and Sousa, 1989; Tuckman, Coyle, and Bae, 1989). Because of field choices, family, and financial obligations, Black, Hispanic, and Native American Ph.D.'s take even longer than other groups to complete their degrees.

The hardships associated with the lengthening time that it now takes to complete a Ph.D. are the following: Minorities are older when they earn their degrees (Brown, 1988; Thurgood, 1989), they are spending some of their most productive years earning the doctorate; and the loss of these prime work years is tied to a huge loss in overall earnings (Tuckman, Coyle, and Bae, 1989).

Institutions should consider a variety of responses to these problems, including:

- **Work-free fellowships.** Although work as a teaching assistant for one or two years may be desirable, institutions that have shortened the time to degree have provided work-free fellowships for a majority of their doctoral candidates. Work-free fellowships are most valuable during the dissertation stage when fellowships run out or work obligations compete with and often delay the process of completing the dissertation requirement.
- **Financial support for part-time students.** As a temporary measure, institutions should consider providing financial support for part-time students as a means of reducing the time to degree. At present, few

institutions support part-time students even though part-time study is the only viable option for many minority students (O'Brien, 1990).
- **Reexamine the doctoral process.** This is an appropriate time for institutions to reexamine the doctoral process for reforms. Closer monitoring of students during the dissertation stage should be a standard procedure to place boundaries around the time it takes to complete the dissertation. Frequent contacts between advisor and advisee are indicated because many potential Ph.D.'s are lost during the dissertation stage.

Improved Minority Faculty Development Programs. Recruiting and retaining minority faculty are not synonymous. To prevent the voluntary outflow of Native American, Black, and Hispanic faculty, institutions can offer programs and salary incentives that are competitive with business and industry.

Institutions should also provide minority faculty with incentives for professional and scholarly development. In some fields, postdoctoral appointments are crucial and should be encouraged, supported, and if necessary, supplemented with institutional funds. Finally, the criteria for promotion and tenure should be in writing and measurable so that faculty members are aware of the performance expectations in advance of the promotion and tenure process.

CONCLUSION

This chapter has discussed several public policy options aimed at increasing minority doctorates and faculty by the turn of the century. Past efforts have been ineffective. Competition and strife over limited faculty positions have resulted in a continuing impasse in revitalizing the faculty base in American higher education. Thus, the task set before higher education is monumental.

The future is more promising than it has been for several decades. Based on projections, for the first time in recent history—regardless of how equity is defined—institutions can and should develop an academic workforce that realistically reflects the diversity of the nation's citizenry.

REFERENCES

Adams v. Richardson. 1973. D.C. Circuit Court. *Federal Register.*

Blackwell, J. E. 1981. *Mainstreaming outsiders: The production of Black professionals.* Bayside, NY: General Hall.

Bond, H. M. 1972. *Black scholars: A study of their beginnings.* Detroit: Belamp.

Bowen, H. R., and J. H. Schuster. 1986. *American professors.* New York: Oxford University Press.

Bowen, W. G., and J. A. Sosa. 1989. *Prospects for faculty in the arts and sciences.* Princeton, NJ: Princeton University Press.

Boyer, E. L. 1989. Foreword *Tribal colleges: Shaping the future of Native America.* Princeton, NJ: The Carnegie Foundation for Teaching.

Brown, S. V. 1988. *Increasing minority faculty: An elusive goal.* Princeton, NJ: Educational Testing Service.

Burke, D. C. 1987. The academic marketplace in the 1980s: Appointment and termination of assistant professors. *The Review of Higher Education* 10, 3.

Cross, T. 1986. *The Black power imperative.* New York: Faulkner Books.

Crossland, F. E. 1971. *Minority access to college.* New York: Schocken Books.

Davis, J. A. 1963. Higher education: Selection and opportunity. *The School Review* 71:249-65.

DuBois, W. E. B. 1944. My evolving program for Negro freedom. In *What the Negro wants* edited by R. W. Logan. Chapel Hill: University of North Carolina Press.

Exum, W. 1983. Climbing the crystal stair: Values, affirmative action, and minority faculty. *Social Problems* 30:383-99.

Feagin, J. R. 1978. *Racial and ethnic relations.* Englewood Cliffs, NJ: Prentice-Hall.

Fleming, J. E., G. R. Gill, G. R., and D. H. Swinton. 1978. *The case for affirmative action for Blacks in higher education.* Washington, DC: Howard University Press.

Freeman, R. 1974. The implications of the changing labor market for members of minority groups. In *Higher education and the labor market* edited by M. S. Gordon. New York: McGraw-Hill.

Garza, H. 1988. The "barriorization" of Hispanic faculty. *Educational Record* 68:122-24.

Hartigan, J. A., and A. K. Wigdor. eds. 1989. *Fairness in employment testing.* Washington, DC: National Academy Press.

Hauptman, A. M. 1986. *Students in graduate and professional education: What we know and need to know.* Washington, DC: The Association of American Universities.

Hsia, J. 1988. Asian Americans fight the myth of the super student. *Educational Record* 68:94-97

Immigration Act of 1989. S.358, Report No. 101-55. Washington, DC. 101st Cong., 1st sess.

Lozier, G. G., and M. Dooris. 1987. *Is higher education confronting faculty shortages?* Paper presented at the Annual Meeting of the Association for the Study of Higher Education, November, Baltimore.

National Center for Educational Statistics. January 1990a. *A descriptive report of academic departments in higher education institutions.* Washington, DC: U.S. Government Printing Office.

National Center for Educational Statistics. January 1990b. *Institutional policies and practices regarding faculty in higher education.* Washington, DC: Government Printing Office.

National Research Council. 1989. *Fairness in employment testing.* Washington, DC: National Academy Press.

O'Brien, E. M. 1990. Longer road to Ph.D. completion filled with hardships and detours. *Black Issues in Higher Education,* 6, 22 (February).

Office of Technology Assessment. *Education scientists and engineers: Grade school to grad school, 1988.* Washington, DC: Government Printing Office.

Olivas, M. A. 1988. Latino faculty at the border. *Change*, (May/June): 6-9.

Reder, M. W. 1974. Elitism and opportunity in U.S. higher education. In *Higher education and the labor market* edited by M. S. Gordon. New York: McGraw-Hill.

Silver, J., R. Dennis, and C. Spikes. 1989. *Employment sequences of Blacks teaching in predominantly White institutions*. Atlanta, GA: Southern Education Foundation.

The Carnegie Foundation for the Advancement of Teaching. 1989. *Tribal colleges: Shaping the future of Native America*. A special report with a foreword by E. L. Boyer. Princeton, NJ.

Thurgood, D. 1989. *Doctorate recipients from United States universities*. Summary Reports, 1988. Washington, DC: National Academy Press.

Thurow, L. C. 1974. Measuring the economic benefits of education. In *Higher education and the labor market* edited by M. S. Gordon. New York: McGraw-Hill.

Tuckman, H., S. Coyle, and Y. Bae. 1989. *On time to the doctorate*. Washington, DC: National Academy Press.

Washington, V., and W. Harvey. 1989. *Affirmative rhetoric, negative action*. ASHE-ERIC Higher Education Report 2. Washington, DC: The George Washington University.

Wilson, R., and M. J. Justiz. 1987/1988. Minorities in higher education: Confronting a time bomb. *Educational Record, 68/69*:8-14.

CHAPTER

• • • • • • • • •

Equity in Higher Education: The State Role

Patrick M. Callan

The 1980s was a decade of policy innovation and leadership in state governments. In the absence of federal initiatives, it fell to the states during these years to formulate public policy responses to intensified international economic competition, the technological revolution, and demographic changes. Double digit unemployment rates and the recession of the early 1980s brought many states to the brink of unconstitutional deficits in the early and mid years of the decade. These crises brought the realities of change home to the statehouses and to their leaders. The result was a "new state activism," focusing initially on economic development initiatives (R.S. Fosler, 1988).

This shift of initiative in domestic policy in the 1980s toward the states was welcomed by some and lamented by others. Whatever one's philosophical

A version of this paper was presented at the Eleventh Annual University of Wisconsin System Colloquium on Ethnicity and Public Policy at the University of Wisconsin-Milwaukee on June 10-12, 1990. I have also drawn upon three earlier papers: P. M. Callan, "Minority Degree Achievement and the State Policy Environment," *The Review of Higher Education* 11 no. 4 (Summer 1988): 355-364; P. M. Callan and D. Kyker Yavorsky, "Sending the Right Signals: Using State Influence to Increase Minority Degree Achievement," in Morgan Odell and Jere F. Mock, *A Crucial Agenda: Making Colleges and Universities Work Better for Minority Students* (Boulder, CO: Western Interstate Commission for Higher Education, 1989), 61-70; and P. M. Callan and J. E. Finney, "State Policies and Minority Participation in Higher Education," *Peabody Journal of Education* 66 (Fall 1988) 6-19.

view on the appropriate role of the state and federal governments in the American system, there is little doubt that the shift did occur and that it put governors and legislators in a more central role, creating new expectations and evoking new responses. As then-Governor Bill Clinton of Arkansas put it, "Basically, since Mr. Reagan has been president, whether the Democrats or even the Republicans agree with everything he's done, he's made (all governors) more powerful" (A. H. Newharth, 1988). The intense economic competition and the pressures for state response resulted in a renewed emphasis on the improvement of education.

Stimulated by numerous national and state reports that identified deficiencies of schools and colleges, the strengthening of education took on a new urgency. Education reform became a centerpiece of the state policy agenda and the foundation of many new state initiatives to develop a competitive work force, attractive quality of life, and even to reform public assistance programs. In August of 1986, the governors of the 50 states adopted a set of recommendations for improvement of education at all levels (National Governors' Association, 1988). In 1989, the first education summit in the nation's history brought all the governors together with the president of the United States; early in 1990 the governors and the president formulated a set of national education goals. These events reflected the leadership role of states and of the governors as well as the growing sense of national interest in education.

In elementary and secondary education, most of the state initiatives of the 1980s emphasized minimum standards and greater accountability for students and teachers, along with increased financial support. In higher education, the primary emphasis was on research and development thought to stimulate economic growth, and on undergraduate education, particularly on the assessment of undergraduate student learning (Fosler, 1988; Neuharth, 1988; Chance, 1986; Doyle and Hartle, 1985; Osborne, 1988; Keane, 1988; Alexander, 1986; Clinton, 1988; Firestone, Fuhrman, and Kirst, 1989; Newman, 1987; Hines, 1988; Lenth, 1990). As the decade wore on, it became apparent to many leaders in state government that few of the initiatives affecting public schools or higher education were addressing the educational problems of America's minority populations, particularly African American, Hispanic, and Native American youth. These students represent a growing portion of the nation's young people, yet they are the populations which by any standard—progression through levels of schooling, graduation rates, measures of achievements on test scores, college-going rates, college graduation rates, enrollment in graduate and professional schools—the education system is least successful helping. Without improvement in the education of minorities, few states could hope to achieve their economic or educational goals. As the 1990s approached, the issue had moved closer to the top of the states' educational policy agenda, and there were calls for a larger federal role in minority education as well. In the elementary and secondary arena, states began aggressive assaults on the issues of urban education, often focused initially on governance. Proposals for declaring academic bankruptcy (New Jersey), and for urban school district reorganization (Illinois), reflected the increased importance attached to the education of minorities. Of course, many questions remain about the efficacy of these strategies (Pipho, 1988a; Pipho, 1988b; Wirt and Kirst, 1989; Chance, 1988; Kerr, 1990).

In higher education there were also signs that the state agenda was shifting towards emphasis on minority participation and achievement. Governors began to give the issue increased attention. A report by the State Higher Education Executive Officers calling upon its own membership to make the education of minorities "a predominant concern of the higher education community" received widespread attention. Several states, including California, Ohio, and Arizona, issued major policy reports, giving the issue public visibility and suggesting state strategies. These efforts, complemented by a report jointly sponsored by the American Council on Education and the Education Commission of the States, called for renewed efforts and received national attention. As with the elementary-secondary issues, the questions at the beginning of the new decade were whether the states would be able to develop effective strategies to engage colleges and universities in greater and more successful efforts to educate minorities, whether they would support those efforts, and whether minority education could be sustained as a high priority by the states and colleges and universities in the 1990s (Education Commission of the States, 1987; State Higher Education Executive Officers Task Force, 1987; Commission on Minority Participation in Education, 1988).

Thus, while it is not yet clear whether state strategies in elementary, secondary, and higher education to provide leadership for minority education will be successful, it is clear that the issue is receiving greater attention. It is the states that have become the major public policy actors in the education arena. Their effectiveness in providing leadership for improvement of minority education is a necessary condition for national progress. In the past, the nation has looked almost exclusively to the federal government for public policy leadership on matters of equity. Historically, the states have often been perceived as the problem, and discussions of the state role still evoke the image of the governor blocking the schoolhouse door. There is growing recognition, however, that the state leadership role is essential to a sustained and effective national and institutional policy (Kerr, 1990).

The state policy environment can be a powerful variable in determining the degree in which minorities successfully participate in higher education. Mounting frustration over the slow pace of change at the institutional level has highlighted the need—and intensified the pressure—for states to take on a forceful leadership role. While innovative programming emanating from a few venturesome states seems to be yielding some positive results, exercising state influence constructively is by no means a simple matter (Richardson, 1990).

The relationship between public policy and institutional responses is not always clear, especially in states with complex systems for the governance of higher education. Institutions in Texas and California, for example, may ultimately face similar pressures even though, in the former, attention to issues of minority participation has been largely driven by the federal courts and, in the latter, by deliberate state level policy action. Regardless of the impetus, state leaders need to shape policy that is as clear, as sensible, as politically sophisticated, and as productive as possible.

At their best, state-level policy initiatives work in synergy to clearly articulate and fulfill a state's commitment to serving all its population equitably. In doing so, they focus the energy and resources of all involved parties to effect meaningful change where it counts the most, on the campus. At their worst, state policy makers simply sidestep the issues entirely or, sensitive to charges of state intrusion into campus autonomy, they publicly exhort institutions in the state to do better and then withdraw from the playing field.

Between these two poles lie innumerable potential pitfalls. Where the determination to correct inequities is strong, policy makers may be tempted to be so prescriptive that they inhibit institutional risk taking and innovation and generate a compliance mentality that ultimately serves no one, least of all the minority student. More commonly, indecision, uncertainty, and political concerns can lead state officials to send conflicting signals or, even more regrettably, to deflect attention from the issue through cosmetic half measures.

Creating a sound state-level strategy for eliminating educational disparities requires sustained commitment, adequate resources, and a willingness to take risks and experiment. It also requires avoiding fruitless debates over categorical versus generic initiatives. Not every state will—or should—address the problem of disparities and achievement in like manner, but all are likely to find that an effective solution demands a combination of special programs targeted to assist minorities, along with a range of initiatives designed to strengthen educational opportunities and outcomes for all students. The consistency and comprehensiveness of a state's approach are more important than its specific programmatic elements. One or two high profile "minority-oriented" programs—no matter what their individual merits—cannot in and of themselves produce meaningful or lasting change. The need to ensure minority educational advancement must be woven through all major initiatives and included in the consideration of all state policy and funding issues so that those on campus are regularly reminded of its importance in a multitude of forms and contexts.

STATE AND INSTITUTIONAL COMMITMENT

Issues of equity and diversity do not easily find their way to the top priorities of colleges and universities or their leaders. Institutions tend to be internally focused and their leaders are often preoccupied with meeting the needs of constituents who are already present in the institution, particularly faculty. State leaders represent an external constituency whose support and goodwill is essential to most colleges and universities. When an issue becomes important to state leaders, it usually becomes important to presidents and institutional governing boards as well. One of the most important roles of governors, legislators, and state boards and commissions is that of helping to set the agenda and to assure that matters of high priority to society are reflected in the priorities of colleges and universities.*

The first responsibility of the states, then, is to set the agenda, an agenda for sustained progress in the enrollment and achievement of underrepresented minorities. It is important that goals be established and that they are clear, so that progress can be measured for each institution and for the state. Every institution, as the Education Commission of the State Task Force on Minority Achievement and Higher Education recently recommended, has responsibilities for improved access and achievement for underrepresented minorities. The goals that are set must include both enrollment and achievement, that is, the successful completion of programs and degrees. In the past, states have placed excessive emphasis, both in their goals and in the financial incentives inherent in their budgeting and funding systems, on enrollment and insufficient emphasis on achievement. Once goals have been established, monitor-

---

*The difficulties colleges and universities have in maintaining diversity as a high priority were reflected in two recent surveys. The American Council on Education, drawing on its *Campus Trends 1989* survey, reported that "although most administrators perceive more commitment to minority participation now—compared to 10 years ago—only one-third rated this level of commitment as high." The Carnegie Foundation for the Advancement of Teaching's 1989 survey of over 5,000 faculty in all types of American colleges and universities found 49 percent of those polled agreed with the statement, "I Am Satisfied with the Results of Affirmative Action at This Institution." D. J. Carter and R. Wilson, *Eighth Annual Status Report, Minorities in Higher Education* (Washington, DC: American Council on Education, December, 1989), 17; Carnegie Foundation for the Advancement of Teaching, *The Condition of the Professoriate, Attitudes and Trends, 1989* (Princeton: CFAT, 1989), 105.

ing systems should be put in place so that the institutions, the state, and the public all receive at least annual progress reports on each institution's progress. The results of this monitoring should be the subject, at least once a year, of a discussion convened by the governor—including the president and members of the governing board, the governor, legislative leaders, and state higher education boards and commissions. This meeting will help to focus account-ability at the level of the governing board and the president. While it is important that categorical and specially funded programs be regularly evalu-ated, this evaluation is not a substitute for the responsibility of the entire institution for contributing to improved enrollment and graduation rates (National Task Force for Minority Achievement, 1990; Richardson, 1990).

The agenda-setting role is one of the powerful levers of state leadership. It directs the energies of institutional leaders to issues of key critical public policy concern. State leaders should envision their role as stimulators of new effort, supporters of institutions and programs that produce results, and as evaluators of institutional progress. They should set challenging goals and insist upon accountability, leaving the tailoring and management of specific programs to colleges and universities. It is a delicate balance. If the states are not consistently tough-minded and results oriented on the issue of minority achievement, they will fail to engage the attention of institutions and their leaders. If they are too heavyhanded, they will only stimulate the mechanistic response to overregulation that so often characterizes institutional responses to public policy initiatives that are clumsy in their formulation or implemen-tation.

Finance

If states' identification of minority achievement in higher education is to be taken seriously, the states must be willing to support their commitments with dollars. This does not mean that every effort to improve minority participa-tion and achievement will require additional financial resources. In fact, a case could be made that most of the money for the education of these students is in the system already. However, some new efforts will require new re-sources, and, in other cases, state finance systems must be realigned so that incentives are properly aligned with priorities. Enrollment-driven formula funding, for instance, has often sent a message to institutions that the number of students enrolled was more important than the achievement of educa-tional objectives. If states wish institutions to place more importance on the retention and graduation of students, they should build the appropriate incentives into their systems of higher education finance (Jones, 1984).

Many states play a limited, but important, role in student financial assistance. In addition, during the last few years, about 35 states have tried to
develop schemes for helping middle-class families save for college, for guaranteeing tuition levels, or in some way reducing middle-class anxiety about how
students will pay for higher education. As attractive as these programs are,
and as important as it is to encourage those families who have the discretionary resources to save for their children's education, savings plans are unlikely
to address the financial problems of those whose needs are least well served by
American higher education. For many students on the low end of the
economic ladder, financing college through family savings is not an option
and the prospect of incurring debt to attend college is a major barrier. Most
states have passively drifted into policies that encourage excessive indebtedness of all students to the particular detriment of minority students. On a
more encouraging note, a number of states have moved to provide automatic
tuition waivers for low-income students or guarantees of student financial
assistance to students qualifying for colleges and universities ("Trends in
Student Aid"; Mortenson, 1990; McGinness and Paulson, 1989).

As large numbers of faculty retire and enrollments grow in many states, the
next 15 years will provide unprecedented opportunities to reshape the professorate and to significantly increase its ethnic diversity. This window of
opportunity, however, occurs at a time when African American doctoral
recipients have decreased by almost a quarter over the last decade and
progress in increasing the number of doctorates awarded to Hispanics and
Native Americans has been small. It was recently reported that minority
graduates students are less likely than White graduate students to have
research or teaching assistantships. States, even those with large student
financial assistance programs, have not generally placed a great emphasis on
financial support of graduate students. Yet the public interest and educational
policy arguments for diversity in the professorate are so compelling that states
should consider developing and enlarging programs of generous financial
support to minority graduate students and experimenting with incentives for
institutions and faculty who recruit and successfully educate and train such
students. A few states, including New Jersey, New Mexico, and California,
have programs that support minority graduate students in return for commitments to teach for a specified period of time after receipt of the doctorate
("Doctorate Recipients," 1990; Blumenstyk, 1990; Blackwell, 1990).

Student aid policies are by no means the only financial issues that affect
minorities. As each state decides where to assign its resources for higher
education, it makes trade-offs, sometimes without recognizing the implications. It is an important and significant decision, for instance, whether a state
puts new dollars into urban institutions that serve large underrepresented

minority populations or into institutions that serve the convenience of the suburban middle class. A real need exists for investment in institutions that serve underrepresented minorities, particularly urban institutions, and for funding mechanisms that provide enriched support for institutions, public or private, that enroll large numbers of minority students and do so in a manner that ensures that these students are well served.

The essential point is that when the time comes to allocate resources, states make sure their dollars flow in a manner that is consistent with their stated priorities. Ideally, this flow of funds should be structured to include a generous quotient of incentives and rewards, ranging from competitive grant programs (for example, to improve minority retention efforts or to provide special services for ethnolinguistic minority students or to develop multicultural curricula, as in New Jersey) to capitation awards based on minority enrollment transfer, graduation, and faculty hiring rates (as in Connecticut). While less preferable than positive inducements, states must also be willing to use the power of the purse to penalize institutions that consistently fail to demonstrate good faith efforts or to produce minimally acceptable results. Former Governor Thomas Keane of New Jersey, speaking before the College Board in 1986, gave his stamp of approval to such a strategy in his own state, testifying to its power to capture the attention of institutions:

> Boards of higher education should press public institutions to define plans to bring minorities on campus. They shouldn't be afraid of putting some teeth into those requirements. In New Jersey we stopped funding the programs of colleges that hadn't made progress. Believe me, that is one *sine qua non* that gets results (1986).

RETENTION, ACHIEVEMENT, GRADUATION

One of the most frequently overlooked avenues for progress, and the best prospect for short-term progress, is identifying minority students who enroll in higher education with the intention of pursuing a baccalaureate degree who tend not to complete programs or degrees. To some extent, the focus on improving public high schools—an absolutely essential task for American society—has detracted attention from the gains that could be made if colleges and universities were more successful in educating the minority students they currently enroll. Most college and university administrative and faculty leaders appear to be more comfortable in emphasizing the problems of the public schools than in confronting higher education's own pipeline problem (Richardson and Skinner, 1991; Porter, 1989).

In many states, the entry point to higher education for most minority students is the two-year community college. In these states, increasing the number of minority students, particularly in urban areas, who transfer from two- to four-year colleges and then complete the baccalaureate degree is an essential avenue of progress. States must assure that the courses needed for transfer are regularly available at urban community colleges. They should require institutions to establish clear and effective transfer policies and agreements, and they should consider establishing contracts with individual students that would set forth the conditions under which they would be able to automatically transfer. Financial aid should follow the student from a two- to four-year institution without complicated bureaucratic procedures and the uncertainty that goes with them (Richardson and Bender, 1987; State Higher Education Executive Officers, 1987).

COLLABORATION WITH SCHOOLS

There are encouraging programs all over the country in which institutions of higher education seek out students in the elementary/secondary years and provide motivation and preparation for higher education. These programs should be encouraged by state leaders who can provide financial support as well as assistance to colleges and universities in developing sources of financial support in the private sector. A relatively recent and promising dimension to such programs are the activities modeled after the "I Have a Dream" project established by Eugene Lang in New York, which guarantees financial support for college and provides mentoring support through the elementary and secondary years; this approach appears to have the potential to positively influence aspiration and preparation for college.

Many colleges and universities have been willing to undertake "missionary work" with public schools and with students. It should be recognized that much of this effort, as commendable as it is, is designed to identify students and save them from a poor educational environment rather than to participate in the systemic reform of basic education in America. Higher education should be a more significant actor in the efforts to systematically improve schools. Colleges and universities monopolize many of the resources needed for curricular improvement, research on improved teaching and learning, and teacher education. One of the disappointments of the 1980s was that these resources were generally not put to the service of reforming public schools, particularly schools that serve the most educationally and economically disadvantaged. State leaders should create both the expectation and the incentives for higher education, including arts and sciences as well as education faculties, to become a greater contributor to the efforts of every state to improve public schooling. Despite an array of reports calling for reform of teacher education, the preparation of future teachers for the schools remains a low priority on most campuses. In short, higher education has not yet responded effectively to the most pressing domestic policy concern of this era: the reform of the public school, particularly the improvement of schooling for those underrepresented populations who are least well served by our public schools (Goodlad, 1990; AACTE Presidential Address, 1990).

EDUCATIONAL MISSIONS

Many of the state and institutional policies that are most likely to increase participation and achievement of minority students, such as greater emphasis on retention, persistence, and transfer, would benefit students generally in American colleges and universities. Among these policies, none are more important than the reaffirmation of the centrality of the teaching mission of colleges and universities, and the preservation of diversity of institutional mission within state higher educational systems. One need not denigrate the other functions of higher education to assert that teaching and learning are the central business of colleges and universities. Yet there are a number of indications that in the face of the most challenging and diverse student population in the history of American education, commitment to the teaching missions of baccalaureate-granting institutions has eroded. President Donald Kennedy of Stanford University recently called upon his own institution to "reaffirm that education—that is, teaching in all its forms—is the primary task and that our society will judge us in the long run on how well we do it." The recent Carnegie Foundation for the Advancement of Teaching survey of faculty in American colleges and universities reported that more than half the faculty in research and doctorate-granting universities and over 40 percent of faculty in comprehensive universities agreed with the statement that "the pressure to publish reduces the quality of teaching at my University." It appears that the emphasis upon publication has intensified not only in institutions with research as a central part of their mission, but in institutions with teaching as their central mission, where faculty teaching loads are high and where resources to support research are scarce or nonexistent. All this sets up the prospect of an enormous mismatch between the needs of American society and the academy's willingness and ability to respond. Now is a time for increased commitment to teaching, for recognition of teaching as a scholarly activity, and for reassertion of the collective responsibility of faculty for the content, process, and quality of the teaching/learning mission (Carnegie Foundation for the Advancement of Teaching, 1989; Kennedy, 1990; "Business of Business," 1989; Boyer, 1990).

In addition to reaffirming the teaching mission of institutions and curtailing "mission creep," the states should work with colleges and universities to structure and support incentive and reward systems based on peer review to assure the vitality of teaching and learning for all students. The allocation and support of institutional mission responsibilities within state systems is a traditional responsibility of the states and at the heart of statewide higher education planning. All of the special programs, accountability, and other policies directed at minority student achievement in higher education will come to naught if they are put into place in policy and institutional environments where teaching and learning are denigrated.

I conclude from the above that the states have a major role to play if the American academy is to make strides toward fulfilling its responsibilities toward the realization of pluralism in the 1990s. The capacity of the states to exercise constructional educational policy leadership has been significantly enhanced in the 1980s. The policy tools available to the states for this work are the traditional levers of public policy leadership: mandates, planning and priorities, inducements, capacity building, and accountability. The key will be to use these tools in a consistent and tough-minded way that cuts across the major programmatic and fiscal areas where states and institutions interact. The objective is to stimulate institutional leadership that will change the culture of institutions in the 1990s and into the next century. The goal of the states must be proportional enrollment and comparable graduation rates for all populations served. I believe that state leadership will be a necessary condition for achieving this goal.

Finally, as noted above, much of the rationale and energy for educational improvement in the 1980s flowed out of concerns over economic productivity and international economic competition. The case for national and state self-interest in better education of all Americans, particularly of those least well served in the past and present, has been made and must continue to be made. However, the stakes in the realization of pluralism in American education are even higher. Our larger societal self-interest lies in preserving and enhancing values of equality, fairness, and justice and in the carrying forward of democratic values and institutions into the twenty-first century. I believe we have wrung as much progress from economic anxiety alone as we are likely to get. The energy for progress in the 1990s will come from leadership at the national, state, and institutional levels which taps the moral as well as the economic urgency of educational improvement.

REFERENCES

AACTE. 1990. 1990 AACTE presidential address, February 21, Chicago.
Alexander, L. 1986. *Steps along the way.* Nashville: Thomas Nelson Publishers.
American Council on Education. 1989. *Campus trends 1989.*
ckwell, J. 1990. Operationalizing faculty diversity in American colleges and universities. Address to American Association for Higher Education, April 2, San Francisco.

Blumenstyk, G. 1990. Spending by states on student aid will increase by 12 pct. this year, passing $2-billion mark. *Chronicle of Higher Education* (February 21).

Boyer, E. L. 1990. *Scholarship reconsidered*. Princeton: The Carnegie Foundation for the Advancement of Teaching.

The business of the business. 1989. *Policy Perspectives* 1 (May).

Callan, P. M. 1988. Minority degree achievement and the state policy environment. *The Review of Higher Education* 11, 4 (Summer).

Callan, P.M., and J. E. Finney. 1988. State policies and minority participation in higher education. *Peabody Journal of Education* 66 (Fall).

Callan, P.M., and D. K. Yavorsky. 1989. Sending the right signals: Using state influence to increase minority degree achievement. In *A crucial agenda: Making colleges and universities work better for minority students*, ed. M. Odell and J. F. Mock. Boulder, CO: Western Interstate Commission for Higher Education.

Carnegie Foundation for the Advancement of Teaching. 1989. *The condition of the professoriate, attitudes and trends, 1989*. Princeton: CFAT.

Carter, D. J., and R. Wilson. December 1989. *Eighth annual states' report, minorities in education*. Washington, DC: American Council on Education.

Chance, W. 1986. *The best of education*. Chicago: John D. and Catherine T. MacArthur Foundation.

————. 1988. Changing the terms of discourse: Restructuring education in America. In *In 10 states*. Denver.

Clinton, W. 1988. Teaching to rebuild a nation. *AAHE Bulletin* (May).

Commission on Minority Participation in Education and American Life. 1988. *One-third of a nation*. Washington, DC: American Council on Education.

Doctorate recipients: U.S. citizens by ethnic group. 1990. *Chronicle of Higher Education* (April 25).

Doyle, D. P., and T. W. Hartle. 1985. *Excellence in education, the states take charge*. Washington, DC: American Enterprise Institute for Public Policy.

Education Commission of the States and State Higher Education Executive Officers Association. 1987. *Focus on minorities: Synopsis of state higher education initiatives*.

Firestone, W. A., J. H. Furhman, and M. W. Kirst. 1989. *The progress of reform: An appraisal of state education initiatives*. New Brunswick: Center for Policy Research in Education.

Fosler, S. 1988. *The new economic role of American studies*. New York: Oxford University Press.

Goodlad, J. I. 1990. Teacher education: Loose couplings. Address to the American Association for Higher Education, April 2, San Francisco.

Hines, E. R. 1988. *Higher education and state governments*. ASHE-ERK Higher Education Report, no. 5.

Jones, D. 1984. *Higher education budgeting at the state level: Comments and principles*. Boulder: National Center for Higher Education Management Systems.

Keane, T. H. 1986. Address to the College Bound National Forum, October, New York.

————. 1988. *The politics of inclusion*. New York: The Free Press.

Kennedy, D. 1990. Kennedy shares vision of Stanford in 2010 with community. *The Stanford University Campus Report* (April 11).

Kerr, C. 1985. The states and higher education: Changes ahead. *State Government* 58, 2.

Kerr, P. 1990. New Jersey to shift school focus to the poor and to less testing. *New York Times*, May 14.

Lenth, C. S. February 1990. *Issues and priorities in higher education, state perspectives.* Denver: State Higher Education Executive Officers Association.

McGuiness, Jr., A. G., and C. Paulson. September 1989. *1989 survey of college savings and guaranteed tuition programs.* Denver: Education Commission of the States.

Mortenson, T. G. 1990. *The impact of increased loan utilization among low family income groups.* Iowa City: American College Testing Program.

National Governors' Association. 1986. *Time for results: The governors' 1986 report on education.* Washington, DC.

National Task Force for Minority Achievement in Higher Education. 1990. *Achieving campus diversity, policies for change.* Denver: Education Commission of the States.

Neuharth, A. H. 1988. *Profiles of power: How the governors run our 50 states.* Washington, DC: Gaunet Co., Inc.

Newman, F. 1987. *Choosing quality.* Denver: Education Commission of the States.

Osborne, D. 1988. *Laboratories of democracy.* Boston: Harvard Business School Press.

Pincus, F. L., and E. Archer. 1989. *Bridges to opportunity.* New York: Academy for Educational Development and College Entrance Examination Board.

Pipho, C. 1988a. Academic bankruptcy—an accountability tool. *Education Week* (February).

———. 1988b. Urban school districts and state politics. *Phi Delta Kappan* (February).

Porter, O. F. 1989. *Undergraduate completion and persistence at four-year colleges and universities.* Washington, DC: National Institution of Independent Colleges and Universities.

Richardson, Jr., R. C. 1990. *The state role in promoting equity.* Denver: Education Commission of the States.

Richardson, Jr., R. C., and L. W. Bender. 1987. *Fostering minority access and achievement.* San Francisco: Jossey-Bass.

Richardson, Jr., R. C., and E. F. Skinner. 1991. *Achieving quality and diversity.* New York: Macmillan Publishing.

Stalled. 1990. *Policy Perspectives* 2 (April).

State Higher Education Executive Officers Task Force on Minority Student Achievement. 1987. *A difference of degrees: State initiatives to improve minority student achievement.*

Goodlad, J. I. 1990. *Teachers for our nation's schools.* San Francisco: Jossey-Bass.

Trends in student aid. 1989. New York: The College Entrance Examination Board.

Watkins, B. T. 1990. 2-year institutions under pressure to ease transfer. *Chronicle of Higher Education* (February 7).

Wirt, F. M., and M. W. Kirst. 1989. *The politics of education: Schools in conflict.* Berkeley: McCutchan Publishing Co.

CHAPTER 19

An Optimistic Sense of Possibility

Frank Newman

I am not going to make the case that full participation of minorities in higher education and the professional life of the nation should be an urgent priority for the nation and for all of us involved in higher education, though I strongly believe that it should.

Instead, I am going to assume that full participation cannot fail to become an urgent priority. The evidence is compelling that careers *must be* open to talent if our political life, our culture, and our economy are to prosper, and so is the evidence that careers *are not*, yet, equally open to all.

In making that assumption, I may be accused of optimism. Certainly, other pressing issues compete for national attention and finite resources. Certainly, the problems of equalizing opportunities for minorities are less simple than we had, perhaps naively, hoped. Certainly, the problems confronting minorities can be found (and need to be addressed) not simply in higher education but at other levels of education and throughout society. Certainly, solving those problems now is a task not for the federal government alone but for states as well and for institutions of higher education and families and students.

But I am convinced that the best and most appropriate federal responses to the underrepresentation of minorities in higher education will be based on an optimistic sense of possibility.

- The federal government can, and should, draw on the best of its tradition of support for equal opportunity, though it must recognize that tradition alone is inadequate for solving problems that have changed with changing times.

- It can, and should, adapt that tradition to the challenge of making higher education not merely accessible to minorities in a narrow legal sense but feasible, desirable, and comfortable.
- It can, and should, augment tradition, seeking out new ideas and supporting ingenuity.

The issue of opportunity for minorities is evolving. The federal government needs to create new approaches that build on the successes of the past. Such approaches will require a great deal more subtlety than past approaches. But such approaches can be created.

I base my optimism on the lessons of history. Whenever "We, the people," set out to form a more perfect union, acting in concert on matters of deep conviction, we have proved a potent force. When we, acting through the federal government, created the G.I. bill after World War II and immensely expanded student aid by means of work/study, Pell Grants, and loan programs, to cite only the most obvious examples, we greatly affected the size and shape and power of higher education in America. Our American belief that higher education should be a pathway to social mobility led to the founding of the land-grant universities, the hundreds of state colleges, and, more recently, the widespread development of community colleges. Our efforts to improve higher education for minorities can, and should, be at least as determined.

DRAWING ON TRADITION

In retrospect, the actions by various branches of the federal government in the 1950s, 1960s, and early 1970s to end discrimination in education and other areas of national life appear to have a coherence that has seemed in short supply more recently.

The accomplishments of those years, seen in broadest outline, were to ensure that neither the lack of adequate laws nor the lack of money would bar access to higher education in America. Even as we begin dealing with the substantial problems that remain, we would do well to remind ourselves of those accomplishments. Otherwise, we are in some danger of subscribing to a myth that is dangerously inaccurate and could confuse thinking about current problems. The myth is that federal efforts to end discrimination did not work, and so further federal action would be pointless. But history simply does not bear out this view.

Inexorably, though more slowly and incrementally than many would have wished, federal courts declared segregated schools "inherently unequal," to use the term that became the law of the land with the Supreme Court's 1954 decision in *Brown v. Board of Education*. Federal courts have since spent more than three decades defining the consequences of that declaration. The Civil Rights Act of 1964 was landmark legislation that set up vital mechanisms for enforcing desegregation and supplied the momentum for a series of legislative initiatives that redrew the map of equal opportunity in America.

As the law opened doors that had been closed to minorities, the federal government undertook to supply the money many students needed to walk through those doors. I will come back to the shape and style of federal aid to students and its impact on minority enrollments. But the basic fact is that ever since the G.I. bill helped massive numbers of veterans get a college education, billions of federal dollars have made it possible for a far broader share of students to attend college. The existence of student aid sponsored by the federal government has also encouraged students to believe that they should attend, that they should aspire to a college education.

In 1953, a African American man like James Meredith was not permitted to enroll at a place like the University of Mississippi. In 1988, 35 years later, equal opportunity is the law of the land; the University of Mississippi—and every other public university and college—is open to all qualified students. In 1953, federal aid to students came to about $10 million; by 1987, the figure had risen to over $13 *billion*.

The fact is that in matters of civil rights and financial aid to students the federal government has been the agent of tremendous social change. That is the fact that refutes the myth of federal ineffectiveness. The critical issue is not what has already happened, but what should happen next. Reminding ourselves that the federal government has played a singularly significant role in opening up higher education to minorities is important for at least three reasons.

- We can give credit where credit is due.
- We can begin to understand why federal approaches that made a vital difference then may be insufficient now.
- We can move ahead with confidence that major problems yield to national resolve.

Allocating credit is useful to the extent that assessments of the past shape assessments of the present. We should look back at least long enough to realize that the equal education of minorities was then a far more daunting proposition than it is today. Though statistic after disappointing statistic shows that African Americans, Hispanics, and Native Americans are not availing themselves of higher education at the rates of other groups in the population, the reasons are different in important ways from the reasons that prevailed in the early 1950s.

We must now discover why thousands of young people do not desire to walk through those doors or do not feel it is possible; we must do whatever we can to make higher education attractive to minorities and workable for them.

As problems become more subtle, so must solutions. Although the deep involvement of the federal courts in the education system, omnibus social legislation, and generally rising aid for students have made progress possible, these approaches seem unlikely to suffice for the future. A person's *desire* to get a college education can be inspired, cultivated, aided, encouraged, but it cannot be legislated, and it cannot be adjudicated.

That present circumstances call for new and more imaginative approaches is demonstrated by the results of the Adams Case. In 1970, the NAACP Legal Defence and Education Fund filed a suit that charged HEW with the failure to obtain compliance with federal desegregation laws in 10 Southern states. Over a period of two decades the judge in the case, John Pratt, exercised tight judicial control over the higher education systems in those states. The results have been mixed with clear gains and yet stubborn unresolved issues.

There is no question that integration of higher education has moved forward in these states with both historically White and historically Black institutions becoming far more mixed in their student bodies. African American enrollment has increased sharply, and African American students have improved their education attainment narrowing the gap with White students. But for all this progress, there is still a considerable African American/White gap in both enrollment and performance. This is particularly true of the most prestigious institutions and the graduate and professional programs that lead to professional careers. While the Adams Case is in theory complete, there continue to be court challenges to many of the state settlements. In a number of states the debate has spawned state-specific law suits, which continue. In short, judicial action has brought substantial gains, but its limits in dealing with important but subtle problems are evident.

The time has come for this country to devote itself to finding new means of ending the underrepresentation of minorities in higher education—means that are, I hope, less litigious, less cumbersome, more workable, and more productive.

We can move ahead with some confidence that suitable means can be found, given a strong enough sense of purpose. This may be the most valuable lesson to learn from past federal successes, however incomplete we may now consider them. The federal actions in Congress, the courts, and the executive branch that have removed financial and legal barriers to equal opportunity were, in fact, far from inevitable. Progress has been possible in the past when diverse interests coalesced in a sense of national purpose. Progress will be possible now to the extent that we commit ourselves to the proposition that higher education must serve minorities fully as well as it serves other students.

ADAPTING A TRADITION: NEXT STEPS IN STUDENT AID

I alluded earlier to the role the federal government has played in removing financial barriers to higher education. Perhaps it would help to look more closely at federal aid to students now, to see how a federal policy that has already done measurable good can do better. The task will be to adapt current policies to our improved understanding of what works, particularly for minority students.

There is a good reason for taking a close look at this single aspect of federal involvement in higher education. If we can demonstrate how adapting a tradition could work in this one instance, the demonstration might well encourage the evolution of federal policy in other areas that affect the higher education minorities.

There are, of course, a great many other such areas. As Larry Gladieux and Gwendolyn Lewis remind us (1987):

> The federal government's activities in higher education are so decentralized and so intermixed with other policy objectives that simply trying to enumerate the programs and tally the total investment can be an accounting and definitional headache.

The many programs and substantial sums that were not consolidated into the U.S. Department of Education are:

> still scattered across the federal scene, from the Department of Defense and the Veterans Administration to the Department of Agriculture, the National Aeronautics and Space Administration, and the Smithsonian Institution. Fragmentary decision making about higher education within the executive branch is mirrored in Congress, where committee responsibilities tend to follow agency structures.

A comprehensive examination of the federal role in higher education should address not only these many decentralized and intermixed activities but also the varied functions of the federal government. The government clearly does much more than support programs and supply funds. Its tax policies affect higher education. It regulates higher education, supports research at institutions of higher education, and collects data about higher education.

The only common agent of change across such a broad spectrum is commitment. No single law or policy directive or executive order or court decision—and no finite combination of laws, directives, orders, or decisions—can adequately redirect that elaborate mechanism, "the federal government," toward the full participation of minorities in higher education. Only widespread, deep commitments to the idea of full participation can engender the interlocking and lasting changes that will make full participation possible.

With that broader objective in mind, it is easy to see how a commitment to full participation could, and should, change federal aid to students. In fact, I believe that we already know what we need to do, though we have not yet done it. We need to reverse direction—de-emphasizing loan, re-emphasizing grants, reigniting enthusiasm for work-study arrangements, and reaping the multiple benefits of linking financial aid to community service. The result will be a system of financial aid that more fully and appropriately meets the needs of minority students and all students.

The history of federal aid to students is a story told often enough that most of us are familiar with its general outlines. For many generations, a college education was, with very few exceptions, for the privileged few whose parents could pay for it. Access expanded slowly and steadily, but by 1940, only 10 percent of each age cohort entered college. Only since World War II has ability to pay been replaced by the quite different notion that no student should be denied access to college for lack of money. Following the phenomenal success of the federal G.I. bills that sent millions of World War II and Korean War veterans back to school, federal aid to students grew steadily and substantially in the 1960s and 1970s. In 1986-87, the federal government supplied more than $13 billion, or about three-fourths of all aid available to graduate and undergraduate students (Gladieux, 1987). Although the states invest about $1 billion each year and institutions of higher education and private sources supply several billion dollars more, most aid for students remains federal aid.

Amounts of federal aid are not constant, not in terms of dollars allocated, nor of "real" dollars adjusted for inflation, nor of aid dollars as a percentage of ever-rising college costs. Understandably, we have therefore seen a growing debate in the 1980s and early 1990s between people who consider the amount of federal aid to be too little or too great.

Since that debate is already joined, I would prefer to look at the *nature* of federal aid. For the fact is that most federal aid now comes in the form of loan, and that produces some unfortunate consequences.

The change in the nature of federal aid has been both rapid and radical. As Figure 19-1 shows, loans made up only one-fifth of federal aid to students in 1975 but accounted for more than two-thirds of that aid only nine years later. Grants meanwhile shrank from 27 percent of federal aid to only 21.9 percent.

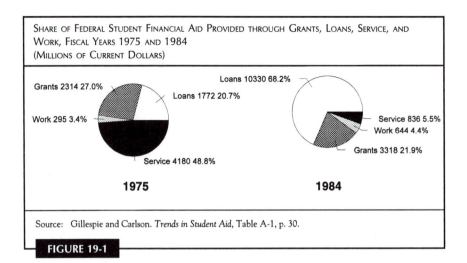

SHARE OF FEDERAL STUDENT FINANCIAL AID PROVIDED THROUGH GRANTS, LOANS, SERVICE, AND WORK, FISCAL YEARS 1975 AND 1984
(MILLIONS OF CURRENT DOLLARS)

Grants 2314 27.0%
Loans 1772 20.7%
Work 295 3.4%
Service 4180 48.8%
1975

Loans 10330 68.2%
Service 836 5.5%
Work 644 4.4%
Grants 3318 21.9%
1984

Source: Gillespie and Carlson. *Trends in Student Aid,* Table A-1, p. 30.

FIGURE 19-1

As was pointed out in a Carnegie Foundation report several years ago:

> As student aid has fallen and costs to the student have continued to rise, the growth in loans has accelerated. In 1983, over 3.5 million students borrowed an average of $2,525 per year under the guaranteed loan program. Students attending professional schools in particular have become dependent on loans . . . . Nearly one-third of 1984 medical graduates left school with more than $30,000 in debt (Newman, 1985).

Since then, the problem has deepened. In that report, I argued that encouraging too much student indebtedness is poor public policy. It is worth recapitulating the argument here. It is also important to emphasize, where appropriate, the particular hardships loans inflict on minority students and the particular promise of other forms of student aid.

As a supplement to other forms of aid, loans are useful, so I certainly do not advise eliminating them altogether. But it is important to use them as they were originally intended, as a supplement to other forms of aid and not as the primary way to support students. The problem is not loans as such, but loans as the dominant form of aid and the high levels of student indebtedness that this dominance has produced.

One promising idea is to offer students grants when they begin college, at the time when they are most tentative about higher education and supply loans primarily for students who are further along in their college careers and have a better sense of direction. Grants in the first two years of college should not be paid for with heavier-than-usual loans in the second two years, however, since this produces the same effect as shouldering loans throughout. Another idea is to link loans to service by, for example, arranging special loans for students who agree to repay them by teaching in inner-city schools or serving society in other ways.

When loans dominate either public policy or students lives, the consequences are variously undesirable.

- Perhaps most important, there has been a broad understanding that Americans, whether from rich families or poor, are on an even footing when they graduate from college. If students who come from poor families, particularly poor minority families, have heavy debts, that is hardly starting even.

- A large debt affects students choices of careers. The results can be unfortunate not only for students but also for the rest of us. The medical student who graduates $30,000 in debt is unlikely to become a rural doctor, for example, whatever his personal inclinations or society's need. His debt constrains his decisions. So, eventually, does the idea that the purpose of higher education is to increase the earning power of the individual.

- The students who borrow most heavily seem the least likely to complete their educations. The evidence of this sometimes gets as mixed as the forms of aid combined into "aid packages." Still, it is generally accepted that grants, work-study arrangements, and other forms of aid do a far better job than loans of generating the intense involvement in college life that seems to be the strongest indicator of persistence.

- The poorer the family, the greater its reluctance to borrow large sums of money for education. Given that the current cost of a year at an expensive private college now exceeds the annual income of many a poor family, that reluctance seems entirely understandable. Because minority students come disproportionately from poor families, they are disproportionately affected by this aspect of loan programs.

- From the government's point of view, the "buy now, pay later" way that loans work means that its ability to make loans to the next decade's students may be limited by its need to continue subsidizing loans already made. By 1986, subsidies to students who had already graduated accounted for two-thirds of the yearly cost of the Guaranteed Student Loan Program, and that cost is still growing. Anything that mortgages the government's future ability to help students disproportionately mortgages the futures of the minority students who are now underrepresented in higher education.

- Although loans initially cost the federal government less than other forms of aid, the overall costs to society are ultimately higher. In that sense, loans are socially inefficient.

- An excessive dependence on loans cuts students off from the benefits—often nonmonetary, perhaps, but substantial—of saving up for college and working their way through. The students who work their way through add self-confidence and a strong sense of worth to their academic knowledge.

Grants, on the other hand, do not burden students with debts that may affect their choice of careers. Grants seem not to aid persistence, but they do not hinder it. They do not daunt students from poor families. They are socially efficient, an investment in the future rather than an encumbrance on it. Students who have received grants begin their careers even with students fortunate enough to come from families who can afford to pay for a college education. For all these reasons, I consider grants a far more satisfactory type of aid than loans. I think it is vital that the federal government continue and strengthen the Pell Grants program.

There is an additional reason we should not allow loans to overbalance the student aid equation; one I first formulated in *Higher Education and the American Resurgence* (1985): "The design of student aid programs should reflect the values society seeks." The form of student aid is a message to students, one that has a powerful effect on their educational experience and personal development. So we would do well to send fewer of the messages that loans convey. We would also do well to send more of the messages conveyed not only by grants but, perhaps more important, by work-study programs and programs that link financial aid to various forms of community service.

Though the College Work-Study program (CWS), which was established by the Economic Opportunity Act of 1964, has been helping students for many years, it has more promise than it has fulfilled. It has remained only a small part of overall student assistance and in recent years the trend has been downward. According to the College Board (1984), CWS accounted for 5.1 percent of all student aid in 1970 but only for 3.7 percent in 1984. That work-study jobs should, to the "maximum extent practicable, complement and reinforce the educational program or vocational goals of each student receiving assistance," an idea reaffirmed in the statutory language of the reauthorized Higher Education Act (1976), has been more preached than practiced. In reality, the jobs are too often determined by administrative convenience.

One of the best descriptions of the potential of work-study comes from Patricia McDonough and Marc Ventresca (1986):

> The concept of organized work-study blends long American traditions of self-help and service to the community with experiential learning opportunities. By virtue of its relatively small share of student assistance, work-study cannot provide an answer to the broader individual and institutional challenges of financing post-secondary education, especially the loan burden issue. Rather, work-study is an aid source singularly amenable to innovative programmatic efforts, particularly those that would emphasize public and community service commitments.

Work-study is a concept broad enough to accommodate innovation, and the federal program is loosely enough structured to accommodate flexibility. Therein lies some of the considerable promise work-study holds for helping minorities in particular as well as all students generally. For if one thing has become clear, it is that we need considerable flexibility if we are to tailor programs that are effective in improving the college experience of minorities.

That work-study can dovetail so neatly with community service is a second major advantage. The possibility of earning while they go to school, through work that benefits their community, supports students in ways that are far more than financial. It gives them valuable experience, develops their competence and confidence, exercises their idealism, gives them a sense of significance that extends beyond themselves. That sort of experience can make a real difference for any student. For a minority student, it could make *the* difference—the difference between staying in school and dropping out, the difference between a productive, contented sense of connection to higher education and a discontented existence on the fringe.

One of the objections that has been raised to work-study is that students who work 20 hours a week simply cannot earn enough money. Well, why not subsidize their work? The federal government now subsidizes loans. If that is appropriate, why not subsidize work, which achieves so many more of society's objectives?

Here are a few of the ways that work-study and community service have been integrated.

- At Berea College in Kentucky, where every student is given a "labor assignment" each year and money earned applies against tuition, students work not only on campus but in nursing homes, hospitals, in the city park department, and at city hall. Some students even helped teach high school dropouts to read.
- At UCLA, students with high financial need can receive a fellowship that commits them to working 20 hours a week for a public

service organization in the Los Angeles area. UCLA students supply the funds for fellowships by making a $4 donation when they register.

■ Princeton, the University of Southern California, and 16 other colleges and universities participate in the "National College Work-Study Literacy Pilot Project," which gives work-study students the opportunity to tutor in mathematics, reading, and writing.

Many other options are only now being thought up, organized, and piloted. One university is exploring ways to tie the experience gained through work-study to courses in which students learn to evaluate the significance of their work. Another university seeks to link its efforts to recruit minority students to jobs for these students during the school year and summer breaks. Adaptions abound, and I suspect there are more to come.

I also suspect that strengthening community service as an aspect of student aid, productively combining community service with work-study, increasing grants and decreasing loans will help minority students most of all. Adapting the federal tradition of financial aid in the ways I am suggesting would bring more than financial benefits. We already do quite a lot to support students financially. We can do a lot more to support their aspirations and abilities.

AUGMENTING A TRADITION

Clearly, we are still in the early stages of inventing workable solutions to the problems that have kept minorities underrepresented in higher education. Though the problems themselves are not new, our recognition of how seriously they challenge our national well-being is relatively recent.

Now that we have begun to recognize the challenge—thanks, in significant part, to the efforts of people like the other contributors to this book—I anticipate that we will rise to meet it. As good solutions multiply, the federal government must develop its capacity to encourage and promote ingenuity.

Signs of Progress

Even as the statisticians, demographers, economists, and policy analysts continue to amass data on the extent of minority underrepresentation in higher education, progress is already apparent in some quarters.

■ I am impressed by the great strides the military has taken in attracting minorities into the all-volunteer armed services, thereby setting an example for higher education and not incidentally preparing young people to enter higher education after they leave the service.

financial aid. They also seek out ways to assist students and their parents to take maximum advantage of state and federal programs, offer . . . strong inducements to attract well qualified minority applicants, and work with community groups to attract new sources of scholarship support for their students.

These are only a few of many examples that could be cited. As the work of this group and others progress, I would expect to see consternation about the underrepresentation of minorities in higher education supplanted, slowly perhaps but surely, by wider application of such good practices.

Why more minority students at community colleges (where the majority of minority students enroll) do not transfer to four-year institutions is the focus of another interesting project. In *Fostering Minority Access and Achievement in Higher Education* (1987), Richard C. Richardson, Jr., and Louis W. Bender take a close look at a particular set of interlocking problems. "The inner cities of America, their minority student populations, and their public community colleges and public universities are the focus of this book," the authors announce. Then they narrow their focus further: "Although urban community colleges enroll disproportionate numbers of minority students, most pursue programs of study intended for job entry at the subprofessional and technical levels. The central question addressed in this book is why more of these students do not transfer and successfully complete baccalaureate programs." In the end, Richardson and Bender are able to offer well-grounded and very specific suggestions to community colleges, urban universities, and state coordinating boards.

The value of works like this lies not only in their suggestions but also in the divide-and-conquer strategy that made the suggestions possible. We are beginning to understand how to subdivide the very large issue of underrepresentation into some of its major components. That is certainly progress.

Creative solutions of other sorts are coming from the people who put together "bridge" programs, the ones who strengthen contacts with junior high schools or parents, the ones who search out potential new members of their professions. In a salute to ingenuity, I would like to list a few examples of the way in which people like these are trying to improve the college experience of minority students. The examples come from a recent report by the Western Interstate Commission on Higher Education, *From Minority to Majority: Education and the Future of the Southwest* (1987).

- Project YOU (Youth Opportunities Unlimited), administered by the Texas Coordinating Board . . . , provides an on-campus residential experience for at-risk 14- and 15-year-old students (mostly minorities) for 8 weeks each summer. From 270 students at four campuses four years ago, the program has expanded to 1,500 students on campuses in 1987. Experience with the first class shows a 90 percent graduation rate and a 50 percent college enrollment rate for a group that normally graduates at a rate of less than 50 percent.

- The Hispanic Mother-Daughter Program at Arizona State University gives 8th-grade Hispanic girls an opportunity to learn about the university, meet college faculty and staff, and learn how to prepare for college.

- The Baylor College of Medicine and the Houston Independent School District work together to encourage students to choose bio-medical careers. The High School for the Health Professions project, begun in 1973, combines a comprehensive academic program in senior high school with health-related courses. Fully 80 percent of the participants are minority . . . 85 percent of its graduates go on to college.

- The Texas State Scholarship Program for Ethnic Recruitment, established in 1983, provides $500,000 per year in student grants, one-half appropriated by the state and one-half matched by institutions. . . . In 1986-87, more than 600 grants were provided, mainly to Hispanic and African American students.

Programs like these are turning up all across the country, wherever people are trying to resolve the difficulties that have so far inhibited the full participation of minorities in higher education.

Encouraging Further Progress

Given these many signs of progress, the task of the federal government becomes one of aiding and abetting further progress. At such times of ferment, when many of the solutions that seem to work are still new and many other solutions are still being invented, the best way to further progress is not to require it or to mandate it but to encourage it.

I think an incentive strategy is the appropriate strategy for the federal government to follow now, not only because incentives seem especially well suited to the circumstances we now face in higher education but also because the strategy has proved powerful whenever it has been used well.

An example of the power of incentives comes from the tradition of federal support for basic research in the sciences. Originating in World War II and given great impetus by the publication of Vanevar Bush's *Science: The Endless Frontier* in 1945, the government-university partnership has produced remarkable results. To cite only a couple of the most striking results: From the

education work for minorities. If a couple of years of talk about the federal role is followed by not much action and the whole issue of educating minorities promptly returns to obscurity, too little will change for the minority student who is now in first grade or for his younger sister. The consequences of *not* educating students without regard to race or ethnicity are very real and very long term indeed. So should be our commitment to minority students.

Among its many other functions, federal policy serves to express what matters most to us as a nation. Federal policy therefore must not be mute on the many issues discussed here and elsewhere in this book. For certainly nothing matters to us more now, or to our future, than the full participation of minorities in higher education.

REFERENCES

Arbeiter, S. October 1987. Enrollment of Blacks in college: Is the supply of Black high school graduates adequate? Is the demand for college by Blacks weakening? *Research and Development Update*. New York: The College Board.

Crosson, P. 1987. Four year college and university environments for minority degree achievement. Unpublished paper submitted to "From Access to Achievement: Strategies for Urban Institutions, an invitational working conference held November 15-27, in Los Angeles, CA.

Department of Defense. November 1987. *Education programs in the Department of Defense*. Pensacola, FL: Defense Activity for Non-Traditional Education Support.

Fund for the Improvement of Postsecondary Education. 1987. *Comprehensive program information and application procedures fiscal year 1988*. Washington, DC: U.S. Department of Education.

Gladieux, L. E. 1983. The issue of equity in college finance, *The crisis in higher education*, vol. 35, no. 2 pp. 72-83. New York: Proceeds of the Academy of Political Science,.

———. November 1987. *Trends in Student Aid, 1980-87*. Washington, DC. College Board.

Gladieux, L. E., and G. L. Lewis. 1987. *The federal government and higher education: Traditions, trends, stakes and issues*. New York: The College Board.

Hodgkinson, H. L. 1985. *All one system: Demographics of education, kindergarten through graduate school*. Washington, DC: Institute for Educational Leadership.

McDonough, P., and M. Ventresca. 1986. *College and work-study programs: Opportunities for public and community service*. Briefing paper available from The Campus Compact, Providence, RI.

Newman, F. 1985. *Higher education and the American resurgence*. Princeton, NJ: The Carnegie Foundation for the Advancement of Teaching.

Ostar, A. W. 1987. What works: The military-higher education connection, *Higher Education and National Affairs* December 12. Washington, DC: American Council on Education.

Richardson, Jr., R. C., and L. W. Bender. 1987. *Fostering minority access and achievement in higher education*. San Francisco: Jossey-Bass.

WICHE Regional Policy Committee on Minorities in Higher Education. 1987. *From minority to majority: Education and the future of the Southwest*. Boulder, CO: Western Interstate Commission on Higher Education.

I N D E X

. . . .

by David Heiret